DICTIONARY OF

PC HARDWARE
AND
DATA COMMUNICATIONS
TERMS

DICTIONARY OF

PC HARDWARE
AND
DATA COMMUNICATIONS
TERMS

MITCHELL SHNIER

O'REILLY & ASSOCIATES, INC.
BONN • CAMBRIDGE • PARIS • SEBASTOPOL • TOKYO

Dictionary of PC Hardware and Data Communications Terms
by Mitchell Shnier

Published by O'Reilly & Associates, Inc., 103 Morris Street, Suite A, Sebastopol, CA 95472

Editor: Frank Willison

Production Editor: Jane Ellin

Printing History:

April 1996: First Edition

This book is printed on acid-free paper with 85% recycled content, 15% post-consumer waste. O'Reilly & Associates is committed to using paper with the highest recycled content available consistent with high quality.

ISBN: 1-56592-158-5   [9/96]

Dedicated to
my Margot, Grayson, and Diane
and to all the other people
who have been so nice to me

PREFACE

History

It happens to me all the time: I hear a new acronym. I worry that everyone knows something important that I should know. (Where do they learn these things? Why don't I have time to read as much as they must?) I don't know who to ask for an explanation, or I never get an explanation I understand. I don't even know what it stands for, or where to look it up.

I never intended to write a book. I am a data communications consultant, and I read magazines constantly. Realizing that I was not remembering most of what I carefully read, I began by writing down expansions of acronyms. Then I started recording juicy factoids and descriptions. Then things sort of got out of control.

Here is the result. Over several years it has grown to critical mass (and maintaining it is a big part of what I do every day). I hope you find it a fast and convenient way to get a basic or updated grasp of that newest acronym.

This book is not intended to be the definitive or authoritative work on any of the topics inside. It is a fast and condensed way to get up-to-speed on topics that you have heard mentioned by colleagues or seen in magazines and in advertisements but have not had the time to track.

Also, this is not intended to be your very first introduction to computer terms. For example, you need to already know what a PC is, what a bit and byte are, and the difference between a floppy and a hard disk drive.

Contents

Although there are over 900 entries here, they generally have one of the following themes:

- *Data Communication APIs (Application Program Interfaces)*: One of the reasons I find data communications so interesting is that it is a combination of hardware, application software, and operating system, each of which typically comes from a different company. The links between these components must therefore be well defined and, ideally, standardized. These software links are typically function calls, subroutines, software interrupts, and libraries, and are called APIs.

- *Wireless Communication*: For certain niche requirements, wireless communication (voice and data) is a big deal and becoming more so every day. There are many competing, complementary, and developing technologies.

- *The Internet and TCP/IP*: Of course, these are very trendy and important topics. Many related issues, such as network management and security, are also covered.

- *PC hardware*: The standard Intel-architecture personal computer is everywhere. Important PC issues, such as processor and bus types, interrupts, and disk drives are covered.

- *LANs (Local Area Networks)*: Networking within buildings is always getting faster and more heavily loaded. No longer is it simply that IBM shops use Token Ring and everyone else uses 10-Mbits/s Ethernet. The various types of LANs being deployed, developed, and standardized, as well as cabling and connectors, are presented.

- *WANs (Wide Area Networks)*: Data communication between buildings (and over any distance) has many limitations (costs, speeds, delays) that drive design and therefore business decisions. The types of WANs, interfaces, and modems and data sets are all part of the knowledge base required to use WANs effectively.

- *Multimedia*: There is a merging of computers, video, audio, data, and voice. You can no longer be a specialist in just one area. Many topics are presented, such as video standards, music concepts, and the networking requirements to carry this type of traffic.

Using This Book

Within these areas the coverage is quite broad. Of course, finding the right entry may be a task (at least for paper versions of this book). Some finding tips follow.

Unlike many glossaries, this one mixes acronyms with phrases, since it is not always clear when something is an acronym or not. For example:

- BISYNC is more like an abbreviation
- PING, TWAIN, and YAHOO are acronyms (some would say) but are not usually written that way

The sort order is:

1.   Numbers first
2.   Then spaces and special characters (such as /, *, and .—these are all considered as spaces for the purposes of sorting)
3.   Letters next

So *Frame Relay* comes before *FT1*, which comes before *FTAM*, and *X.25* comes several entries before *X/Open*, which is before *X-stone*, which is before *X Terminal*, which is before *XAPIA*.

If you can't find a topic, try only part of the phrase:

- Instead of *Trumpet WinSock*, try *WinSock*
- Instead of *IEEE 1284* try *1284*

If you can't find a topic, try something related. For example, instead of *Floppy Diskette Drive*, try *Disk Drive*.

Conventions

- A goal of this book is to explain acronyms, so the priority is always on putting the information in the entry for a term's acronym. Continuing with the example above, the entry for FTAM will begin with its expansion (File Transfer, Access, and Management), and then the explanation. In the alphabetical place for "File Transfer, Access, and Management," the entry says simply "See FTAM." If a term has no acronym (such as Frame Relay), then the explanation is in the entry for Frame Relay.
- Hexadecimal numbers are subscripted, for example, $D000_{16}$.
- The prefixes "k" and "M" are binary (2^{10} and 2^{20}, respectively), when referring to data storage. For example, 1 kbyte is 1×2^{10}, which is $1,024_{10}$ (base 10) bytes; 1 Mbyte of memory is $1,024 \times 1,024 = 1,048,576_{10}$ bytes.
  "k" and "M" are decimal (10^3 and 10^6, respectively) when referring to frequencies or data transfer rates. For example, 8 kHz is 8,000 cycles per second; 9.6 kbits/s is 9,600 bits/s; 1.544 Mbits/s is 1,544,000 bits/s.
- The `courier` font is used for things computers read and say, such as, file names and computer commands and output.
- *Italic* is used for emphasis and to keep a group of words or a phrase together (for example, *zero bit stuffing* or *Adobe Type Manager*). Typically, these are important key words that are related to the technology being discussed. The words may be more fully described elsewhere in the book, in which case they (or their acronym) will be mentioned at the end of that entry (for example, *See ATM and PostScript Page Description Language*).
- SMALL CAPITAL letters are used for acronyms, such as PC and ISDN.
- For additional or updated information, the Uniform Resource Locator (URL) for relevant World Wide Web (WWW) servers are often referenced. These references will always start with "http" (HyperText Transfer Protocol) and will be in *sans serif italic*. For example, *http://www.ieee.org*.
- References to directories and files on ftp sites are given in Web Browser format. For example, *ftp://rtfm.mit.edu/pub/usenet-by-group/* means that on the ftp site `rtfm.mit.edu`, there is a subdirectory `/pub/usenet-by-group`.

- When a table breaks across pages, there is a *table continued* line at the bottom of the first part and the table heads repeat at the top of the second part.

Where to Go from Here

We are trying an experiment with this book—the entire book (including the tables and graphics) is Internet-accessible (for free) at *http://www.ora.com/ reference/dictionary/*. All the book's cross-references (to other entries) and URL references (for additional information) are hypertext hot links. For your browsing pleasure, the home page is a form into which you enter the term or acronym. Click away, and watch this book come alive!

We hope that you find this helpful not only for your own reference, but also for online technical documents you may be writing—you don't need to write your own glossary of technical terms, just reference the appropriate entries from this book.

While I certainly hope that this book (and its online version) remains an important reference for you, new technologies, standards (and acronyms!) are being developed every day. It is important to have a wide variety of information sources to keep up. Here are some ways I track what is going on.

Magazines

Magazines are amazing. Of all the sources of information available to me, magazines are the most important. Pick two technical ones, and subscribe to them. Read every issue. Flip through every page, reading only articles and advertisements that are important to you and your job. My favorite two magazines are:

- *PC Magazine*. Unfortunately, it's huge (400 pages, twice a month), but it usually does a professional job of evaluating products and has good coverage of PC Hardware and some data communications coverage as well. It is at *http://www.ziff.com/~pcmag* and on almost every magazine stand. Fill out the subscription card or phone to request the magazine's network edition (it has additional articles and advertising concerning networking). The article index is searchable through what the magazine calls Ziffnet, which is reachable from CompuServe, for an additional monthly charge.
- *Data Communications Magazine*. It used to be a great, somewhat expensive magazine; now it is a great free magazine (for qualifying subscribers). It has first-class coverage of data communications issues. Phone 1-800-525-5003 or 609-426-7070 and ask them to mail or fax you a subscription request form.

You need to flip through every page because you never know when there will be one of those fantastic tutorial articles that fully explains a technology or mentions some new acronym or feature that you don't need today but will need to know about tomorrow.

Vendor World Wide Web (WWW) Pages

The progression from having a salesman visit to discussing a product with a knowledgeable inside sales person to asking for a brochure to be mailed out to using a faxback service has now gone to checking a vendor's WWW server for product information. I have included many references for relevant WWW servers, but the WWW search tools such as:

- Lycos at *http://www.lycos.com*
- WebCrawler at *http://www.webcrawler.com*
- Yahoo at *http://www.yahoo.com*

are essential (if not overloaded).

Also, there are some great pointer pages, such as the following:

- The Lawrence Livermore National Laboratory's *Telecommunications Page* at *http://www-atp.llnl.gov/atp/telecom.html* and their all–encompassing pointer page to everything about data communications at *http://www-atp.llnl.gov/atp/standards.html*
- The University of Michigan's *Telecom Information Resources* page at the site *http://ippsweb.ipps.lsa.umich.edu/telecom/telecom-info.html*
- The University of Texas' *Access to Network Information* page at the site *http://mojo.ots.utexas.edu/netinfo*
- The *Data Communications and Networking Links* page at *http://www.racal.com/networking.html*
- A pointer to almost every standards–setting organization is at the site *http://hsdwww.res.utc.com/std/gateway/orgindex.html*

The many FAQs online are excellent and are loaded with expert information. See the entry in this dictionary for FAQ.

Vendors can be a useful source of information:

- Stelcom Inc., an Internet service provider, has a home page of *Electronics Manufacturers on the Net* at *http://www.webscope.com/elx/*.
- The entry for Carriers has links to telephone companies' home pages, most of which have some information on their telecommunications offerings.

Finally, there is an acronym server at *http://curia.ucc.ie/cgi-bin/acronym*.

Usenet Newsgroups

With over 10,000 newsgroups, Usenet has a newsgroup for almost any topic. Use your news reader's newsgroup search function (which searches the text of each newsgroup's one-line description). Many newsgroups have FAQs that are constantly updated, and periodically posted in the newsgroup. Often, posted news items will refer to the site that has the most-recent FAQ for that newsgroup. It is becoming popular for FAQs to be in HTML, and therefore easily viewed and retrieved using your WWW browser.

Standards

Many technologies are completely described by their standards or RFCs (*request for comments*). I have included references to these when possible, and the entries for Standards and RFCs describe how to obtain these documents.

Also in the entry for Standards are several references to "Master" WWW pages of extensive references to other specialty sites of communications-oriented information.

Books

Although books are expensive and usually best as a detailed reference, they can be a great source of information. I am astonished (and overwhelmed) by the excellent technical quality and range of topics available in everyday bookstores. This kind of information never used to be available at all, let alone at your local bookstore.

If your local bookstore does not have what you need, a university or college bookstore, or a bookstore specializing in computer books, is a good place to go. Nothing can beat looking through an expensive book before purchasing it.

Many publishers and bookstores have Internet-accessible direct sales systems, such as O'Reilly & Associates at *http://www.ora.com*, as well as several on CompuServe (try `find book`).

Computer Literacy Bookshops are very good bookstores to know about. They put out an excellent newsletter with meaningful reviews (and interesting interviews), have very knowledgeable staff, and accept credit card orders by phone and over the Internet. Using their WWW server, you can search for books by title, author, and subject, and check the book's review, price, and whether it is in stock. Contact them at:

email	*info@clbooks.com*
fax	408-435-1823
ftp	*ftp.netcom.com/pub/cl/clbooks/README*
phone	408-435-0744 or 703-734-7771
WWW	*http://www.clbooks.com*

CompuServe

Everyone doing anything technical with computers should have access to one of the following:

- CompuServe (WWW at *http://www.compuserve.com*, phone 1-800-848-8990 or 614-529-1340 for further access information)
- The Internet (see the entry for ISP). Although CompuServe provides access to the Internet, depending on your location and monthly usage you may find a separate Internet service provider more economical.

For technical support (especially for people who are primarily PC-oriented), I find CompuServe indispensable (and as you can see from my email address, it is also my Internet access provider).

For people who are more UNIX-oriented, it would probably be best to have an account with a dedicated Internet service provider instead of, or in addition to, CompuServe.

Monthly Reports and Newsletters

Many very specialized monthly reports and newsletters are available. These typically cost $200 to $400 per year, and are a bargain if they target your area of interest.

For example, to keep up to date on the wide variety of Canadian telecommunications issues (regulatory, competition, wireless, costs, and management), Angus Telemanagement is superb (phone: 905-686-5050, WWW: *http://www.angustel.ca*).

Courses

Some people learn technology best from a real, live person. Taking a course may then be a good idea. I happen to teach courses for Learning Tree International (*http://www.learningtree.com*), and my honest opinion is that their courses and instructors are first-rate (of course, you could argue that I may be biased, but I wouldn't be teaching for them if they did not have a high-quality product).

Input

Finally—everyone is an expert in something. What we want to know is some of what everyone else knows. I hope this book helps you with that goal. Although thousands of hours have gone into this effort, there are going to be oversights, omissions, and outright mistakes. Also, technology is a frustratingly moving target to put into print. I welcome your comments and input.

Acknowledgments

There are many people who have been of great assistance in the development and production of this book.

First, I want to thank the technical reviewers: Ian Angus, Don Beattie, Mark Notten, Nuno Romao, and Ellen Vliet. Their expert insiders' input was excellent and needed.

Second, I'm here to learn, and the book production experience has been an education. I would like to thank the many O'Reilly & Associates people involved: Tim O'Reilly and Frank Willison for immediately being interested in publishing this book; Norm Walsh, Erik Ray, and Ellen Siever for converting the book to Microsoft Word format, then to Rich Text Format, and finally to SGML format, and then cleaning up the problems; Nancy Priest for the book design (check out those quality fonts and the paragraph spacing); Edie Freedman for the distinctive and appropriate cover design; Lenny Muellner for transforming the book design into an SGML DTD; Barbara Willette, the freelance copyeditor, for catching many typing and grammatical mistakes and correcting my non-conventional conventions; Jane Ellin, the production editor, for juggling inputs from all over the place and producing the final SGML source; Kismet McDonough and Cory Willing for copyediting and quality control; Seth Maislin "the indexer" for working on the cross-references and the alphabetization of the entries; Clairemarie Fisher O'Leary for the work on the biography and quality control; Chris Reilley for doing the figures; Sheryl Avruch, the production manager, for keeping morale and momentum high while the book was being produced; Sue Willing, the print coordinator; and Malloy Lithographing, the printing company, for transforming these millions of binary bits into paper and ink—a portable information appliance.

Next, I would like to thank my 25 MHz ALR PC, the Cyrix upgrade CPU in it, OS/2 2.1 and 3.0, WordPerfect for DOS 5.1 and 6.0b, and my trusty Hewlett-Packard LaserJet 4. Without them, this book would never have happened, nor have been so much fun.

Finally, I would like to thank the amazing magazines, well-written RFCs, detailed standards, vendor literature, occasional book, and the Internet that have made this book possible, and also necessary (sort of recursive, self-justifying proliferation).

Mitchell Shnier, P. Eng.
Toronto, Canada
Email: *72567.3304@CompuServe.com*

10BASE-F

A local area network that transmits data at 10 Mbits/s over fiber-optic cable.

An 802.3 media option that supports 10 Mbits/s Ethernet over optical fiber. The following table summarizes the characteristics of the three options, along with the 802.3 FOIRL option.

Media Option	Name	Intended Use	Characteristics
10Base-FB	Fiber backbone	Repeater-to-repeater links only	2-km maximum segment length, 15 repeater maximum cascade, must be built into repeater (no external transceivers)
10Base-FL	Fiber link	Workstation-to-repeater and repeater-to-repeater links	2-km maximum segment length, 5 repeater maximum cascade, can connect to FOIRL transceivers (with FOIRL limits)
10Base-FP	Fiber passive	Workstation-to-repeater and repeater-to-repeater links	Passive hubs, 500-m maximum segment length, no limit on number of hub ports but 33 ports currently available
FOIRL	Fiber-optic inter-repeater link	Repeater-to-repeater links	1-km maximum segment length, 4 repeater maximum cascade

All use 62.5/125 μm fiber-optic cable with ST connectors and a 800-nm to 910-nm (infrared) light source.

The 10BASE-FB option has a feature to detect jabbering transmitters and can automatically enable a backup link.

See *10BASE-T*, *802.3*, and *Ethernet*.

10BASE-T

A local area network that transmits data at 10 Mbits/s over copper cabling.

An 802.3 media option that supports 10 Mbits/s Ethernet over UTP. A nonstandardized full-duplex version (sometimes called full duplex switched Ethernet, FDSE) was developed by Kalpana and is supported by Compaq and a few other vendors.

See *100BASE-T*, *802.3*, *Cable*, *Connector*, and *Ethernet*.

100BASE-FX

A local area network that transmits data at 100 Mbits/s over fiber-optic cable.

A full- or half-duplex version of 100BASE-T *Fast Ethernet* that uses two strands of multimode optical fiber. Configuration rules are as follows:

- If only one repeater (concentrator): 225 m from repeater to switch, bridge, or router (making a 100 + 225 = 325 m network diameter)
- If no repeaters (workstation to switch or switch to switch): 450 m (if half-duplex 100BASE-FX) or 2 km (if full-duplex 100BASE-FX)

See the accompanying figure for a visual representation of these configurations.

See *100BASE-T*.

100BASE-T
100 Mbits/s Baseband Modulation on Twisted Pair

A local area network that transmits data at 100 Mbits/s.

Also called *Fast Ethernet* and briefly called IEEE 802.14. Will officially be 802.3u. An implementation of 802.3 "Ethernet" that uses 100 Mbits/s transmission and different bit encoding but otherwise is identical to 10BASE-T (same frame and message lengths, same collision detect scheme, same Ethernet drivers).

Four media options are defined: 100BASE-T2, 100BASE-T4 (not very popular), 100BASE-TX, and 100BASE-FX.

Will not have the reliability of FDDI (no secondary channel) nor the isochronous capability of ATM.

Does not support prioritization or multimedia (though 3Com's PACE technology is supposed to provide this capability), but Ethernet users should find it easier to

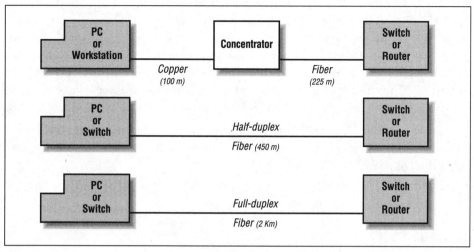

100BASE-FX−1

migrate to (and interconnect to) 100BASE-T than to 100VG-AnyLAN, since 100BASE-T should use the same drivers and MAC layer.

Promoted by the *Fast Ethernet Alliance*, whose main members are 3Com, Intel, Standard Microsystems (SMC), Sun Microsystems, Bay Networks (which is the name of the company created by the merging of SynOptics Communications and Wellfleet Communications), and Cabletron Systems. Also supported by Cisco Systems.

The following table summarizes the characteristics of 100BASE-T, 100VG-AnyLAN, and FDDI.

Technology	Speed (Mbits/s)	Suited to	Comments
100BASE-T	100	Desktop	Low-cost, easiest to upgrade from Ethernet
100VG-AnyLAN	100	Desktop	Low-cost, deterministic
FDDI	100	Desktop or backbone	Uses fiber, STP or UTP, dual ring architecture adds reliability, available now, strong management capabilities
ATM	25 to 622	LAN and WAN	Only solution with isochronous channel for voice and video, highest speed and cost

Designed for to-the-desktop rather than the backbone (though 100BASE-TX's and 100BASE-FX's support for full-duplex operation may result in backbone use).

An autonegotiation (NWay) function built into adapters permits dual–speed (10BASE-T and 100BASE-T) adapters to automatically sense and use the highest speed that is supported by both ends. On power–up, the adapter sends *fast link pulses* (in contrast, 10BASE-T devices' link pulses are 100 ns wide—which is one bit-time—sent every 16 to 24 ms). If the concentrator or switch also supports 100BASE-T, it will respond with fast link pulses, and the adapter will then use its 100BASE-T mode of operation. Otherwise, operation will be at 10 Mbits/s.

The NWay feature (see *100BASE-TX*) is also used for the negotiation of full- or half-duplex operation and for determining which media (for adapters that support more than one type of cable) are active.

See *100BASE-T2, 100BASE-T4, 100BASE-TX, 100BASEFX, 100VG-AnyLAN, FDDI, Isochronous, LAN, Multimedia, PACE,* and *UTP.*

100BASE-T2

A local area network that transmits data at 100 Mbits/s over copper cabling.

A half-duplex version of 100BASE-T that uses two pairs of Category 3, 4, or 5 UTP cable.

Officially called 802.3y.

See *100BASE-T.*

100BASE-T4

A local area network that transmits data at 100 Mbits/s over copper cabling.

A half-duplex version of 100BASE-T that uses four pairs of Category 3, 4, or 5 UTP cable. Transmission uses three pairs simultaneously (to reduce the bit rate on each), and the fourth pair is used for collision detect (see the accompanying table). Bit encoding is 8B/6T (8 bits represented by six ternary (three-state) symbols).

Pair	Pair Function When Workstation Is ...	
	Transmitting	**Receiving**
1	Transmits data to hub	Receives data from hub
2	Receives collision detect indication from hub	Receives data from hub
3	Transmits data to hub	Transmits collision detect indication to hub
4	Transmits data to hub	Receives data from hub

See *100BASE-T* and *Encoding.*

100BASE-TX

A local area network that transmits data at 100 Mbits/s over copper cabling.

A full- or half-duplex version of 100BASE-T that uses two pairs of STP or Category 5 UTP cable. The bit-encoding scheme (called MLT-3) is the same as that used for FDDI's TP-PMD.

The maximum Category 5 cable length (either station-to-station or hub-to-station) is 100 m. The maximum distance (in meters) between two stations (including the distance between the hubs between the stations) is

  total cable length = [400 - (repeaters × 95)] m

Usually, there will be two repeaters (hubs), and the two hub-to-station cables will be up to 100 m, so there can be up to 10 m between the repeaters. The maximum network diameter is therefore 210 m.

The intent is that it should be easy to install 100BASE-TX because many sites have Category 5 UTP already installed for 10BASE-T networks. The problem is that many installations have components that are not Category 5 (such as patch panels), so installation may be a substantial problem.

See *100BASE-T*, *Encoding*, *FDDI*, *LAN*, and *UTP*.

100VG-AnyLAN
100 Mbits/s on Voice-Grade Unshielded Twisted Pair Cable for Any (Ethernet or Token Ring) Local Area Network

A local area network that transmits data at 100 Mbits/s over copper cabling.

A 100 Mbits/s half-duplex LAN standard promoted by AT&T, Hewlett-Packard, and IBM, intended to be the successor to both Ethernet and (later) Token Ring. Hubs must be configured for *either* Ethernet *or* Token Ring frames. A 100VG-AnyLAN Hub (and therefore LAN segment) cannot carry both types simultaneously; a router is needed to connect two 100VG-AnyLANs that have different frame types.

A new *media access control* scheme (and therefore frame type) called *demand priority* provides two priority levels:

• *Isochronous* and therefore high-priority traffic (typically constant-bit-rate traffic from digitized voice or video) gets priority over regular traffic, making transmission more deterministic than 100BASE-T and suitable for multimedia
• *Asynchronous* (normal-priority) traffic is carried only if there is capacity left over for it

Hubs provide controlled LAN access for their directly connected stations, which request LAN access by using a round-robin (within priority levels) scheme that gives stations (one at a time) permission to send one frame. Stations with lower-priority messages will receive a priority boost if their messages have been waiting 250 μs or more (because of the high-priority traffic hogging all the bandwidth).

The normal polling for low-priority messages is interrupted (after any current frame is handled) as soon as any station has a high-priority frame ready to transmit.

Initially, each hub port will be manually designated as having low- or high-priority traffic. As applications and drivers provide support, the priority of frames will be specified by software on a per-frame basis (by the application software).

Hubs are cascaded below a *root hub*. When the root hub gives permission to a lower-level hub to transmit, the lower-level hub can send *one* frame received from *each* of the lower-level hub's ports.

The maximum link lengths (either station-to-hub or hub-to-hub) are as follows:

- 100 m, using four pairs of Category 3, 4, or 5 UTP cable (using *quartet signaling*, which splits the data among four pairs of cable)
- 150 m, using two pairs of STP or Category 5 UTP cable (still in development)
- 2,000 m, using single-mode or multimode fiber-optic cable (still in development)

The maximum network diameter is as follows:

- 500 m over Category 3 UTP (up to four hubs can be between any two stations)
- 1,200 m over Category 5 UTP
- 4,000 m over multimode fiber-optic cable (a maximum of one hub between stations)

Products usually support both standard 10 Mbits/s 10BASE-T Ethernet and 100 Mbits/s 100VG-AnyLAN (either manually configured or automatically switching between the two).

Also called 802.12 and demand priority. Competes with 100BASE-T (which cannot carry Token Ring frames but can use existing 10BASE-T drivers).

In addition to Hewlett-Packard and IBM, also supported by Cisco, Compaq, Newbridge, Proteon, and Texas Instruments.

See *100BASE-T*, *Isochronous*, *LAN*, *Multimedia*, and *UTP*.

1284

A standard documenting the existing operation of PC parallel ports and, most important, several additional capabilities.

IEEE Standard 1284 defines several enhancements and modes for a PC's parallel port (also called the *centronics port*), including support for bidirectional communications. The following tables describe these modes.

Mode	Capabilities	Transfer Rate (kbytes/s)	Suited to
Compatibility	8-bit output to printer Limited printer status monitoring Programmed and interrupt-based I/O Handshaking with printer for flow control	100 to 200 output only	Original PC and centronics use (see *Parallel Port*).
4-bit or nibble	4-bit input (two sequential transfers to transfer a byte from printer) *Compatibility Mode* used for Output Programmed and interrupt-based I/O	40 to 60 input	Printers or other applications in which the 4 input status bits can be used to input data to the PC.
8-bit or byte	8-bit input from printer Compatibility mode used for output Programmed and interrupt-based I/O	80 to 300 input	Printers but also other types of peripherals (such as disk or LAN interfaces) that require faster input to the PC. Implemented in most PCs manufactured after 1991 to 1993. A direction bit in the printer port registers controls the port's direction.
ECP	8-bit output and 8-bit input Programmed, interrupt-based, and DMA-based I/O 16-byte (or more) FIFO	More than 2,000	Highest-speed block transfers; for example, to printers or from scanners. Includes support for RLE data compression (2 bytes can represent up to 128 repeated bytes).
EPP	8-bit output and 8-bit input Programmed and interrupt-based I/O	Up to 2,000	Interactive communications. For example, to LAN adapters or to CD-ROM, disk, and tape drives. This is the most powerful and flexible mode.

ECP (*Extended Capabilities Port*) mode provides the fastest data transfer but is best-suited to simpler transfers. EPP (*Enhanced Parallel Port*) provides more complex control features.

The standard's emphasis is on the signaling format, pin assignments, and error detection and correction procedures (that is, what goes on outside of the PC). The BIOS functions, software interface, and control of the ports are not specified, so vendor-specific utilities and software will be required to configure the ports.

Three types of connectors are defined, as shown in the following table.

Connector Type	Description	Distance (m)	Comments
A	A DB-25 *subminiature D-shell* connector (as is also used by the incompatible EIA-232 Serial COM ports on a PC)	2[a]	Standard PC parallel port, used at the PC end. Female connector on PC. (EIA-232 uses a male connector on the PC.)
B	Traditional 36-pin centronics connector (is 5 cm wide)	2[a]	Standard PC parallel port, used at the printer end.
C	36-pin miniature centronics connector (is about 3 cm wide)	10[b]	New connector (and pin assignment) and interface voltages defined for higher-speed and greater-distance printer connections. Both ends must use Type C connectors and voltages. With the appropriate cable, a Type C connector can be connected to Type A and B PC ports, providing only Type A and B cable distances.

[a] The standard gives this as an example distance that will work. Hewlett-Packard allows up to 3 m.

[b] The standard actually specifies the only maximum cable propagation delay (58 ns), which works out to a length of just over 10 m for the velocity of propagation for typical cables.

The standard defines two levels of *compliance*, as shown in the following table.

Compliance Level	Interface	Comments
I	Type A and B connectors and existing (*Level 1*) voltages	That is, existing PC parallel ports.

(table continued on next page)

Compliance Level	Interface	Comments
II	Type C connectors and new high-performance interfaces (which use *Level 2* voltages)	Expected to be implemented on new PCs. Level 2 voltages require Type C connectors and work over greater cable distances (when connected to other Level 2 devices) or over Level 1 distances (when connected to Level 1 devices).

A 1284 parallel port powers-on to *compatibility mode*. The 1284 standard defines the negotiation process between software in the PC and a peripheral attached to the parallel port to determine which of the five modes the port should be switched to (it will be left in compatibility mode if there is no response). The PC can request certain modes, and the peripheral replies with the mode it chooses. Each of the modes defines the new functionality of the interface signals. Modes can be switched quickly. For example, the interface will be switched between compatibility and nibble for each transfer for an interactive "half-duplex" exchange of data.

1284-compliant devices need to implement only compatibility and nibble modes (that is, byte, ECP, and EPP modes are optional). Therefore printers with a standard centronics port that also support nibble mode (so the printer can send information back to the PC, 4 bits at a time) are IEEE 1284 compliant.

For example, a Hewlett-Packard LaserJet 4 Printer is IEEE 1284 compliant. HP calls this *Bi-Tronics* support. Bi-Tronics:

- Basically means support for nibble mode
- Does not support EPP (HP will likely never support this, since ECP is more suited to printer communications)
- Does not support ECP either (though HP has stated that future printers will include ECP support as part of their IEEE 1284 compliance)

To summarize all of these modes, parallel ports will be used in up to four ways, as shown in the following table.

Port Support	IEEE 1284 Modes Used	Used For
Traditional PC parallel port	Compatibility	Sending data to (and only to) printers
HP Bi-Tronics	Compatibility and nibble	Sending data to printers and receiving printer status information from a printer

(table continued on next page)

Port Support	IEEE 1284 Modes Used	Used For
Extended capabilities port	ECP	Highest-speed data transfers to and from printers
Enhanced parallel port	Byte and EPP	Disk, tape, and CD–ROM drives

Another optional feature is *device ID*, in which the PC requests the peripheral to reply with an ASCII string (which is prefaced by the string's length count). The string is a series of ;-delimited key: and *value* sequences (there can be more than one *value* for each key; multiple *values* are separated by a ,). If device ID is supported, then the MANUFACTURER, MODEL and COMMAND SET (optionally abbreviated as MFG, MDL, and CMD) keys must be part of the reply (vendors can add any others they want). For example,

```
MFG:Hewlett-Packard; MDL:LaserJet 4; CMD:PCL, PostScript;
```

"IEEE Std 1284-1994 compliant" cables are required for use with all modes and compliance levels. The standard specifies (among other things) the cable:

- Be clearly and permanently labeled "IEEE Std 1284-1994 compliant"
- Be 18-pair cable, with a foil *and* braid shield that is bonded 360° around to metal connector shells (at both ends of the cable)
- Shield coverage, grounding, pair twists per meter, impedance, and maximum attenuation
- Pin-out, including which ground pin wires are to be twisted to which control and data signal pin wires

The IEEE 1284 cable provides reliable bidirectional communications and support for the highest-speed (that is, ECP mode) data transfer. The optional Type C ports provide extended distance.

See *Compatible, Compliant, DB-25, DMA, ECP, EPP, IRQ, Parallel Port, PIO*, and *RLE*.

1394

An effort promoted by Apple and IBM for a shared media (cable daisy-chains to each device) peripheral-sharing bus. Has speeds of 100 Mbits/s, 200 Mbits/s, and 400 Mbits/s (each device on the daisy-chain can be a different speed) and a maximum of 4.5 m between devices. Uses six-pair shielded twisted pair.

This would permit a single port on a computer to support many peripherals.

Intended for higher-end applications, such as digitized video and photography (and supports isochronous communications, so it can do this well). May be used to replace SCSI too.

Also called high-speed serial bus, FireWire (by Apple), and P1394 (during the standard development process).

Promoted by Apple and consumer electronics vendors. Will compete with (and cost and do more than) DDC (which is based on ACCESS.bus and promoted by monitor manufacturers) and USB (promoted by Intel, Microsoft, and major PC vendors).

See *Bus, DDC, Isochronous, SCSI, USB*, and *V.35*.

16550A

The current standard integrated circuit for handling the serial data communications for a PC's COM ports.

The National Semiconductor 16550AFN UART. Has a built-in 16-byte receive buffer so that multitasking operating systems (such as Microsoft Windows, which gives higher priority to foreground task disk accesses) and MS-DOS 6 (when its SMARTDRV disk caching program flushes its delayed writes to disk) can reliably receive data at speeds above 9,600 bits/s. That is, the data are buffered (temporarily stored) in the UART while characters are being received, but the operating system is not able to read them out of the UART.

For example, a V.32*bis* modem (14,400 bits/s) using V.42*bis* data compression (4:1) should use a serial port speed of 57,600 bits/s. At this speed, a character is received every 174 μs. If the CPU is busy doing something else for much longer than this (even the older 8250 UART can receive a second character while waiting for the first to be read), then characters will be overwritten in the UART and therefore lost.

Data communications software can be more efficient, since the 16550A is programmed by the communications software to interrupt only after 1, 4, 8, or 14 characters have been *received*, so fewer interrupts are necessary (and more characters are read per interrupt).

Also, a 16-byte *transmit* buffer ensures that the processor does not need to be interrupted as often to transmit data.

Communication software must support this UART (to enable the buffering), since 16550AFN powers up to act like the older 8250 or 16450 UARTs, which have only a 1-byte receive and transmit buffer.

See *ESP, EIA/TIA-232*, and *UART*.

3172

A communications device for IBM mainframe computers that provides TCP/IP capability.

A PS/2 PC that (with expensive IBM software and a $25,000 Bus-and-Tag or ESCON channel attachment card, for a total cost of about $28,000) provides Ethernet and TCP/IP connectivity for IBM mainframes (and does not require an FEP).

Does some TCP/IP processing to reduce the load on the mainframe.

See *Channel, ESCON, FEP, TCP/IP*, and *tn3270*.

3174 and 3274
3174 Establishment Controller and 3274

A communications device for IBM mainframe computers that provides connectivity for fixed-function computer terminals.

An IBM *cluster controller* (sometimes called a *communications controller*) that supports up to 32 (a BISYNC limitation) or 253 (an SNA limitation) 3270-series terminals and printers. It is connected to a mainframe (if *channel-attached*) or, more commonly, to an FEP (usually through a 9,600- to 56,000-bits/s SDLC link).

A 3299 can increase the number of terminals and sessions. The 3274 was introduced in 1977. The newer 3174 supports:

- Higher-speed SDLC or frame relay links (up to 256 kbits/s) and Token Ring connection to FEPs
- Optional channel attachment, so an FEP is not needed to connect to the mainframe (this provides faster response times for the 3174-connected users but results in additional mainframe CPU loading)

See *3299, Channel, CUT, DFT, FEP, PU 2, PU 4*, and *SDLC*.

3270

The type of fixed-function computer terminals used with IBM mainframe computers.

A family of IBM terminals and support equipment. The 3278 series was introduced in the late 1970s and supports various sizes of monochrome character displays, as shown in the following table.

3270 Model	Display Size (horizontal characters × vertical rows)
2	80 × 24
3	80 × 32
4	80 × 43
5	132 × 27

The 3279 series support color and graphics. The 3290's screen can be split into four quarters, and a separate session can be established on each. The 3178 is a more modern terminal. The 3287 is a printer.

Data communication is at 2.358 Mbits/s through up to 1,525 m of RG–62A/U coaxial cable.

See *347x*, *CUT*, *DFT*, *LU 2*, *LU 3*, *RJE*, and *tn3270*.

3299

A communications device for an IBM mainframe computer.

A multiplexer that uses one of the coax terminal connections supported by the 3*x*74, and provides up to eight five-session DFT connections (therefore up to 40 sessions per 3299) on the 3299. This does not enable the 3*x*74 to support any *more* connections, it simply provides them on the 3299.

See *3174 and 3274*.

347x

The type of fixed-function computer terminals used with IBM mainframe computers.

A series of newer 3270 terminals. For example, the 3471-1 model 2 is 80 columns, and the 3472-4 model 5 supports 132 columns of text.

See *3270*.

37x5   See **FEP.**

3Com
Computers, Compatibility, and Communications

A big company that makes Ethernet and other data communications hardware.

The company founded by Robert Metcalfe to commercialize Ethernet.

The company operates a WWW server at *http://www.3com.com/*.

See *Ethernet*.

486DX

Intel's PC central processing unit that was popular between about 1990 and 1994.

A standard 168-pinned 486 with a built-in math coprocessor. Includes an 8-kbyte unified Level 1 cache (instructions and data share the same cache). Since this relatively small cache results in a low *hit rate* (the percentage of times that the required instructions or data are in the cache), an external (Level 2) cache is usually included in motherboard designs. These will usually be 64 to 512 kbytes in size.

These processors can often be replaced by an OverDrive (clock–doubled DX2) or Pentium processor to provide faster CPU operations.

See *Cache*, *DX4*, *Intel*, *OverDrive*, and *PC*.

486DX2

Intel's PC central processing unit that was popular between about 1991 and 1995.

A clock–doubled 486 that runs internally at twice the speed at which it runs externally. For example, a 486DX2-66-based system would have a motherboard that runs at 33 MHz, and internal CPU operations (math and instructions running out of the internal 8 kbyte Level 1 cache) would run at 66 MHz.

A 238-pin upgrade socket usually built into these PCs will accept a 32-bit bus version of the Pentium CPU (called the P24T).

See *Intel*, *OverDrive*, *PC*, and *Pentium*.

486DX4   See **DX4.**

486SX

Intel's PC central processing unit that was popular between about 1990 and 1993.

For Intel 486 CPUs, the *SX* suffix means that it does not have a built-in math coprocessor (or that it is disabled, as it was found to be defective after manufacture). Computers based on the 486SX therefore can cost less, with little user impact, since most software seldom uses the floating-point math operations that math coprocessors handle.

Has a 32-bit internal and external data bus and an 8-kbyte cache, just as the 486DX does. These systems usually have a socket that can accept a 487SX math coprocessor to upgrade the system to hardware math capability (rather than having the main CPU perform the math in software, a process that is much slower).

An OverDrive chip can usually be installed into the 487SX socket to provide faster main CPU operations (this disables the original 486SX).

See *Intel* and *PC*.

486SX2

Intel's PC central processing unit that was popular between about 1991 and 1994.

A clock–doubled 486SX. For example, it runs at 25 MHz externally and 50 MHz internally.

See *Intel* and *PC*.

5250

The type of fixed-function computer terminal used with IBM's AS/400 minicomputers.

A polled, page-mode terminal. Up to seven terminals can be daisy-chained (or
connected by using a T-connector) on up to 1,500 m of twin-ax cable (which is
like coax, but has a 110 Ω twisted pair in the center). The terminals communicate
at 1 Mbits/s. The cable is directly connected to either an AS/400, or to a 5394
workstation controller, which is then connected to the AS/400 through a WAN
link at up to 64 kbits/s.

See *LU 7* and *PU 2.1*.

800

The dialing prefix that provides usually toll-free (that is, toll-free to the caller; the
callee pays the long-distance charge) long-distance service.

Approximately 40% of all U.S. long-distance calls are 800 calls, and the service has
become so popular that the 7.6 million available numbers have been virtually
exhausted. Beginning April 1996, the 888 code will begin to be assigned; it was
thought to have a marketing advantage over the other reserved codes (877, 866,
855, 844, 833, 822, and 880), which will be used (in that order) as required in the
future.

To search for an AT&T "1-800" number, try AT&T's WWW server at
http://www.tollfree.att.net/dir800/.

See *DN*, *DTMF*, and *POTS*.

802.1h

IEEE's standard for *translational bridging*, which is used to convert (for example)
Ethernet frames to FDDI frames. Among other things, the conversion requires
changing the packet headers and trailers.

See *Ethernet* and *FDDI*.

802.2

A format used for the frames of data sent on Ethernet, Token Ring, and other
types of local area networks.

The LAN frame format standardized by the IEEE and used for OSI, NetWare 4.0,
and LLC2. Other common frame formats are SNAP and Ethernet II.

See *802.3*.

802.3

More commonly called Ethernet. The most popular type of local area network. However, Ethernet is a misnomer, since Ethernet was the name of the predecessor, which has minor but important differences.

It uses *Carrier Sense* (before transmitting, stations ensure that no other stations are already transmitting) and *Multiple Access* (any station can transmit) with *Collision Detection* (by detecting collisions, stations detect when the LAN is getting heavily loaded and adjust their transmitting algorithm). Hence 802.3's access method is often abbreviated CSMA/CD.

Several frame formats are used, as shown in the following table.

Frame Format	Used by	Comments
802.2	IBM's LLC2 NetWare 4.x	DSAP field identifies the upper-layer protocol.
802.3	NetWare 3.x	Uses the checksum field of the IPX (network layer) header to identify the upper-layer protocol.
Ethernet II	DEC's DECnet DEC's LAT Older TCP/IP	Original frame format used on Ethernet. Type field identifies the upper-layer protocol.
SNAP	Newer TCP/IP Apple's EtherTalk	5-byte overhead used to identify the protocol

Although an Ethernet segment (concentrator) can carry any number of frame formats simultaneously, each pair of communicating stations must use the same frame format.

See *802.2*, *Ethernet*, *Ethernet II*, *LAN*, and *SNAP*.

802.5 See **Token Ring.**

802.6 See **MAN.**

802.9a

An enhancement to Ethernet to support multimedia data traffic.

An effort first proposed (in 1992) by Apple, IBM, and National Semiconductor for a 16.144-Mbits/s LAN that supports multimedia. 10 Mbits/s is reserved for standard Ethernet asynchronous data, and the remaining 6.144 Mbytes/s is divided into 96 64-kbits/s channels to be used for multimedia. The 64-kbits/s channels are intended to be connected to, and synchronized with, the clock speed of ISDN B-channels.

Since typical video conferencing systems require two to six 64-kbits/s channels per connection, 802.9a will support 16 to 48 simultaneous multimedia connections in addition to the 10 Mbits/s traditional Ethernet. Will use standard 10BASE-T category 3 cabling. The hub will use switching for the 96 64-kbits/s channels.

Also called *Isochronous Ethernet* or *isoEnet*.

Proponents include PBX vendors L.M. Ericsson and Siemens.

See *ISDN* and *Multimedia*.

802.10

An enhancement to Ethernet that addresses some security concerns.

Addresses *secure data exchange* on LANs as well as virtual LANs. End-stations negotiate encryption and authentication parameters at Layer 2 (the MAC layer).

Bridges and/or Ethernet adapters add and check a 16- to 20-byte header added to each frame (between the MAC header and the payload data) that identifies which virtual LAN is to receive the frame (this is also called *colorizing* the frame). A 32-bit *group identifier* (or VLAN ID) in the header ensures that frames are seen only by members of the same group.

The specification also describes segmentation and reassembly of frames (to facilitate carrying frames over networks that have different maximum frame sizes).

See *Authentication, Encryption,* and *VLAN*.

802.11

The IEEE standard for wireless LANs operating in the 2.400 to 2.483-GHz frequency range. Still under development. Will likely include both hub-based and peer-to-peer capability. The physical layer options will likely include direct-sequence spread-spectrum, frequency-hopping spread-spectrum, narrowband microwave, and infrared transmission.

The frequency-hopping option will support data rates of 1 to 2 Mbits/s and 22 channels (each of which can support a network of users).

Other options will include speeds up to 4 Mbits/s.

See *PCCA* and *SWATS*.

802.12   See **100VG-AnyLAN.**

802.14

A standard for cable TV–based data communications (which is sometimes called *broadband*).

80386DX

Intel's PC central processing unit that was popular from 1987 to 1993.

A standard 80386. Has a 32-bit data bus and a 32-bit address bus.

See *Intel* and *PC.*

80386SX

Intel's PC central processing unit that was popular from 1987 to 1992.

For Intel 80386 CPUs (which are 32-bit internally, allowing up to 4 Gbytes of virtual memory), the *SX* suffix means that it has a 16-bit data bus (which provides slower memory and peripheral access than a 32-bit bus would) and a 24-bit address bus (limiting physical memory to 16 Mbytes). Computers based on the 80386SX therefore can cost less while providing full 80386 software compatibility.

See *Intel* and *PC.*

80486DX4   See **DX4, Intel, and PC.**

80487SX

The math coprocessor that can be added to a 486SX-based system to provide hardware math capability (such as faster multiplication and division).

See *486SX, Intel,* and *PC.*

8514/a

IBM's high-resolution graphics (1,024 × 768, interlaced) standard for PCs. Faster than VGA but no longer used.

See *VGA* and *XGA.*

88open

A failed effort by Motorola to get its 88000 RISC processor accepted. Realizing that a single company could not compete with Intel in a getting a new processor designed and accepted, Motorola then worked with Apple and IBM on the PowerPC instead.

See *Motorola, PowerPC,* and *RISC.*

8B/10B

A data encoding and transmission scheme patented by IBM and used for its ESCON data links (which connect IBM's mainframe computers to frontend processors).

Eight data bits are sent in 10 bits to provide the following:

- Error detection (called *disparity control*)
- Frame delimiting with data transparency (that is, you can send any bit pattern and still have a way to mark the beginning and end of a frame)
- Clock recovery: signal transitions assist the receiver in finding the center of each bit, even if many contiguous ones (or zeros) are sent and the sender has a slightly different transmission rate
- D.C. voltage balance (on average, the signal spends an equal time positive and negative; this is required if the signal is to be coupled through a transformer), to eliminate transformer core saturation

Also used for fibre channel and some ATM implementations (manufacturers license the technology from IBM).

See *ATM (Asynchronous Transfer Mode)*, *Encoding*, *ESCON*, *FEP*, *Fibre Channel*, and *Mainframe*.

A/UX

Apple's UNIX-like operating system implementation.

Instead of this, most Apple Macintosh computers run Apple's Macintosh operating system (Mac OS), such as System 6.*x* or 7.*x*.

See *Apple* and *UNIX*.

Acceptable Use Policy   See **AUP**.

ACCESS.bus

A lower-speed (than a LAN) limited-distance data communications method. The intent is to replace the PC's limited number of ports and specialized nature of those ports with a general-purpose, single port that can support many peripherals simultaneously.

A daisy-chain method of connecting low-speed I/O devices (such as mice, track-balls, modems, bar-code readers, printers, and a keyboard) to a computer. Used by VESA's DDC standard.

Up to 125 devices (seven-bit device addresses, minus the host and broadcast address) over a total cable length of 8 m is supported. Uses two-pair (ground/+5 volt power on one pair and clock and data on the other pair), stranded, shielded cable and modular jack–like connectors (they have locking tabs on each side of the connector).

To support the daisy-chaining, devices may have two connectors or may use a T-connector.

Data rates of up to 100 kbits/s are supported, and each device can use a different data rate.

All communication is either to or from the host computer (and not directly between two peripherals). Messages are from zero to 127 bytes in length plus the:

- Leading destination address byte
- Source address byte
- Length byte (the most significant bit of the length byte is 1 to indicate *control* and 0 to indicate *data* messages)
- Trailing bitwise `exclusive-or` checksum byte

Hot plugging (new devices can be connected while the computer is operating) is supported, as well as *auto-addressing* (devices are automatically assigned unique addresses). A new adapter card would be required for existing PCs.

Six host-computer-to-device control messages have been defined:

- `Reset`: to device's power-on state and default ACCESS.bus address
- `Identification request`: query device for its identification string
- `Assign address`: assign device with specified identification string to specified ACCESS.bus address
- `Capabilities request`: query device for the section of its capabilities response string, starting at the specified offset
- `Enable application report`: Enable or disable device to send application reports to the host computer
- `Presence check`: check whether a device is present at the specified ACCESS.bus address

Three device-to-host-computer control messages have been defined:

- `Attention`: informs host computer that device has completed its power-on reset and needs to be configured
- `Identification reply`: contains the device's unique identification string (which has information such as keyboard character set or mouse resolution)
- `Capabilities reply`: contains the section of the device's capabilities response, starting at the specified offset

The capabilities string is ASCII information based on keywords that are part of either the *base protocol* (apply to all types of devices) or the *application protocol* (apply to devices only of that type, such as keyboard, locator, or text).

Software drivers are required to provide the interface between application programs and the ACCESS.bus communications hardware in a PC.

Based on the Inter-Integrated Circuit (I²C) serial bus developed by Philips Semiconductors and Signetics and supported by DEC.

Initially defined and developed by DEC. The ACCESS.bus Industry Group (ABIG) is currently promoting the effort. Would compete with Intel's USB (and likely lose).

See *1394*, *ASCII*, *Checksum*, *DDC*, *SMBus*, *USB*, and *VESA*.

ACE
Advanced Computing Environment

A proposed standard platform effort, initially intended to compete with Intel. The group fell apart when Compaq withdrew its support and other things such as the PowerPC happened. The platform was to support OSF's UNIX, SCO's ODT, and Microsoft's Windows NT.

Initially backed by a consortium including DEC, Compaq, Microsoft, Silicon Graphics, and SCO. Initially required either the MIPS RISC (initially the R3000) or later the Intel 80386SX (or later) processor. This loss of potential market resulted in significant financial difficulties for MIPS, so Silicon Graphics (which depends on the MIPS processors) had to buy MIPS.

See *CHRP*, *DEC*, *MIPS Computer Systems*, *OSF*, *PowerPC*, *PReP*, *SCO*, and *UNIX*.

Acrobat

A method of exchanging documents so that they still look nice; that is, they maintain their font sizes and character attributes, such as underlining, bolding, and spacing.

Adobe System Inc.'s technology to support transportable documents (called *portable document files*, which are 7-bit ASCII) that maintain their appearance and character spacing even if the destination machine does not have the required font built in.

The document (generated with Adobe's *Exchange* utility, which appears as a printer driver, or from any PostScript file, using Adobe's *Distiller* utility) includes descriptions of its fonts to enable Adobe's *Multiple Master* fonts to be used to approximate the required font.

Using Adobe's *Reader* (its file viewer program), provides display-only capability, though the text can be exported to a word processor (losing the font information).

Is a subset of PostScript.

Formerly called Carousel.

See *Adobe*, *ASCII*, *ATM* (*Adobe Type Manager*), *Multiple Master*, *PostScript Page Description Language*, *PostScript Type 1 Fonts*, and *PostScript Type 3 Fonts*.

Adaptation Layer

Software that provides and matches services between two communications protocol layers in a protocol suite.

An ATM communications protocol layer that provides services such as the following:

- Segmentation and reassembly (to map higher-layer variable-length packets into fixed-length cells)
- Timing control and detection
- Handling of lost and out-of-order cells

See *ATM (Asynchronous Transfer Mode)*.

Address Resolution Protocol   See **ARP.**

Adobe

A company that developed a very successful page description language and designs nice fonts.

The company is named after the Adobe River, which is near where the company was founded (in California, where else?).

Adobe has a WWW server at *http://www.adobe.com/*.

See *ATM (Adobe Type Manager)*, *PostScript Page Description Language*, *PostScript Type 1 Fonts*, and *PostScript Type 3 Fonts*.

Adobe Type Manager   See **ATM.**

ADPCM
Adaptive Differential Pulse Code Modulation

A method of digitizing speech; that is, turning the analog signal (which can have any amplitude and frequency, within a range) into a series of binary ones and zeros.

A voice digitization scheme that uses a lower bit rate than *Pulse Code Modulation* (PCM). The G.721 method uses only 32,000 bits/s per voice channel, as compared to standard telephony's 64,000 bits/s (which uses PCM). Although the use of ADPCM (rather than PCM) is imperceptible to humans, it can significantly reduce the throughput of higher-speed modems and fax transmissions.

See *Fax*, *Modem*, and *PCM*.

ADSL
Asymmetric Digital Subscriber Line

A method of sending high-speed data (fast enough to carry digitized movies, for example) over the existing pair of wires from a telephone company's central office to most residences.

A line-encoding scheme (that uses both *carrier amplitude* and *carrier phase* modulation) that provides the following:

- A high-speed, one-way data channel at up to 6 Mbits/s (enough for MPEG-compressed full-motion, full-color movies)
- A full-duplex data channel at up to 576 Mbits/s, which can be subdivided in many ways to provide several simultaneous services
- Support for the existing analog POTS (voice, Group 3 Fax, etc.) even if the ADSL part fails

Runs over a single twisted copper pair (ideally, the one that already exists between your home and the central office), up to 23,000 ft in length.

An important use is expected to be providing digital, compressed video (to replace cable TV) and standard two-way telephone service on the existing telephone drop to a house.

HDSL provides a similar capability.

The ADSL Forum has a WWW server at *http://www.sbexpos.com/sbexpos/associations/adsl/home.html.*

See *C.O.*, *E1*, *HDSL*, *MPEG*, *Multimedia*, *POTS*, *T1*, and *Video*.

Advanced Computing Environment   See **ACE.**

Advanced Interactive Executive   See **AIX.**

Advanced Mobile Phone Service   See **AMPS.**

Advanced Network Services, Inc.   See **ANS.**

Advanced Peer-to-Peer Internetworking   See **APPI.**

Advanced Peer-to-Peer Networking   See **APPN.**

Advanced Program to Program Communications   See **APPC.**

Advanced Research Projects Agency Network   See **ARPAnet.**

Advanced SCSI Programming Interface   See **ASPI.**

Advanced Technology   See **AT.**

Advantage Networks

The marketing name for DEC's protocol software.

DEC's newer name for what it used to call DECnet Phase V, since in addition to being DECnet and OSI, it supports DECnet Phase IV, Pathworks (DEC's customization of Microsoft's LAN Manager), TCP/IP, IPX, and SNA. Runs over FDDI in addition to Ethernet.

See *DEC* and *NAS.*

AFP
AppleTalk Filing Protocol

Apple Computer's AppleTalk LAN protocol for sharing files.

See *Apple.*

AIX
Advanced Interactive Executive

IBM's UNIX-like operating system, which runs on IBM's RISC System/6000 (RS/6000) workstations. The first version was based on UNIX System V Release 2 (current versions on SVR3.2).

AIX/ESA is a version for IBM's System/370 and System/390 mainframe computers and is based on OSF/1.

See *IBM, Mainframe, Operating System, OSF/1, PowerPC, RISC, SVR4,* and *UNIX.*

Alliance for Strategic Token Ring Advancement and Leadership   See **ASTRAL.**

Alpha AXP

DEC's new RISC-based central processing unit, which is to replace the CISC-based processor previously used in DEC's VAXes and workstations.

DEC's RISC architecture. Features include the following:

- Designed from the beginning to be 64-bit everything (buses, registers, etc.), unlike most other processors, which began as 16- or 32-bit and were redesigned to be 64-bit, usually with the requirement that they be compatible with the earlier 16- or 32-bit mode (which complicates the design and probably reduces 64-bit performance)
- Runs OpenVMS, OSF/1, and Microsoft's Windows NT, using *Physical Architecture Layer* (PAL) software code, which permits the processor to be configured for efficiently running different operating systems

- Has 1.68 million transistors and runs on 3.3 v
- Superscalar

The three types of Alpha processor families were designed for different markets:

- 21066: Lower-cost desktop PCs, since it includes a built-in cache, DRAM, and 32-bit PCI I/O controller and runs at 33 MHz externally. Cache and DRAM share the same 64-bit bus.
- 21064: The first Alpha AXP (150 MHz), higher-performance (nonmultiplexed address and data bus).
- 21164: Newest, and highest performance. Will have a 64-bit PCI interface.

The following table lists the features of the Alpha processors.

Processor	Clock Speed (MHz)	Transistors (millions)	Bus Width (bits)		L1 Cache (kbytes)	Pins
			Internal Register and Address Bus	External Cache and DRAM Bus		
21066	33/166	2.2		64	16	287
21066A	33/233	2.4			32	
21064	150	1.6	64	128	16	431
	166					
	200					
21064A	233	1.8			32	431
	275					
21164	266	9.6		256	16 [a]	499
	300					

[a] Also has 96 kbytes of secondary (L2) on-chip cache.

To promote acceptance of the processor, DEC will license the chip design (there are not many takers on this one) and sell chips to others (this is a bit more popular).

See *Cache, OpenVMS, Operating System, PA-RISC, PC, PCI, PowerPC, RISC, SPEC, Superscalar,* and *VMS.*

American National Standards Institute   See **ANSI.**

American Standard Code for Information Interchange   See **ASCII.**

American Telephone and Telegraph   See **AT&T.**

AMPS
Advanced Mobile Phone Service

Standard analog cellular telephone service. Used in Canada, the U.S., Mexico, and Central and South America.

First implemented in Chicago in 1976 for a two-year test period.

Uses a 3-kHz (same bandwidth as a standard land-line telephone line) voice channel modulated onto 30 kHz FM carriers (one frequency for transmit, another for receive).

The total of 50 MHz of bandwidth is divided between two operators, each of which uses half of its bandwidth for the forward channel (from base station to mobile) and half for the reverse channel. The B *band* (or *block*) is assigned to the local telephone company ("wire-line carrier"), and the A band is assigned to a non-wire-line carrier.

The following table lists the frequencies used by the A and B bands.

Band	Frequency Range (MHz)	Use
A	824 to 835 and 845 to 846.5	Transmit from mobile
	869 to 880 and 890 to 891.5	Receive at mobile
B	835 to 845 and 846.5 to 849	Transmit from mobile
	880 to 890 and 891.5 to 894	Receive at mobile

Included in the table is the additional 5 MHz of bandwidth assigned in 1986, which provided each operator with an additional 83 channel pairs, for a total of 416 RF channel pairs each. For each pair, the mobile's receive frequency is always 45 MHz higher than its transmit frequency. 7 to 21 of the 416 channel pairs are used for control purposes (at 10 kbits/s), leaving 395 to 409 available channel pairs for voice conversations, per operator (790 to 818 conversations total).

The entire "cellular" concept was created to solve the problem that there are not enough frequencies (a city needs more than 818 simultaneous conversations). By using lower-power transmitters (for the mobile telephone) and directional (often downward-pointing, to limit their distance) antennas, smaller cells of radio coverage are formed.

The radius of a cell is typically ½ km (for an urban area that needs very high capacity) to 20 km (for a rural area that does not need high capacity).

Using a base station radio transmitter with an omnidirectional antenna (which provides 360° of coverage), the adjacent cell radio base station sites would then (very roughly) form a pattern of hexagons, with a base station at the center of each.

The base station radio at the center would use frequency 1 and would use this to communicate reliably with any mobile within its coverage area (the hexagon around it). To ensure that the two conversations don't interfere, that same frequency cannot be reused for a conversation in any cell immediately adjacent to that one. This requires that the cells around the first cannot use the same frequency.

The accompanying figure shows a frequency reuse factor of 4. Adjacent cells never use the same frequency, and each cell can use ¼ of the available frequency channel pairs.

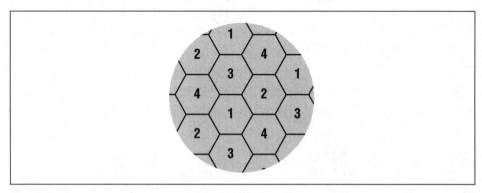

AMPS–1

By using antennas that cover less than 360° (usually 120° or 60° and possibly positioned at the corners of the hexagons and pointing inward), smaller cells can be constructed (this is often called *sectorizing*). This permits a given frequency to be reused more often in a given geographic area. This increases the number of simultaneous conversations that can be supported. For example, 120° antennas with a frequency reuse factor of seven could be as shown in the following figure.

The benefits of sectorizing and smaller cells are summarized in the following table.

Antenna Coverage	360°	120°	60°
Number of cells in frequency reuse pattern [a]	4	7	12
Frequency pairs (simultaneous conversations) per base station[b]	102	58	34
Relative capacity	1	22	140

[a] Number of adjacent cells that cannot use the same frequency.

[b] While sectorizing reduces the number of conversations per cell, the cells get smaller, so the total system capacity increases (as shown for the relative capacity).

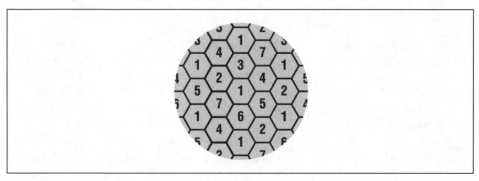

AMPS–2

As the cells get smaller, a lower transmit power must be used (so that the signal does not interfere with the same frequency being used in nearby cells). The mobile telephones have up to eight power levels (in 4-dB increments), from a minimum of 6.3 mW (which is the same as -22 dBW—decibels referenced to 1 mW) to a maximum of 0.6 W (-2 dBW) for handheld portables or 4.0 W (6 dBW) for car-mounted telephones.

Base stations sense the received signal strength from mobiles and send commands back to them to adjust the mobile's transmit power so that the lowest necessary transmit power is always used.

Remarkably, the lower maximum transmit power of hand-held portables is not due to battery power limitations, but to the concern that having a transmit antenna that close to your head is not good for you—think of a nice steamy cauliflower coming out of a microwave oven (these operate at 2,450 MHz).

Base stations typically have:

- A much higher transmit power (100 W) so that the mobiles only need small antennas)
- Large antennas to accommodate the mobile's low transmit power (which is necessary both for health concerns mentioned above and to extend the talk-time battery life) *100,000 as of 2000, according to Ed Davis*

There are approximately 11,500 cellular telephone base station cell sites in the U.S.

Cellular telephones need to be programmed (usually by the dealer) with many numbers before use (these are usually set from a telephone's diagnostic and configuration mode, which is often entered by first pressing the "0" key 13 times), as shown in the following table.

Number	Length (bits)	Use
Mobile identification number	34	The binary number corresponding to the telephone's 10-digit (decimal) directory number (DN). This sets the telephone's phone number. Binary is used because it is the most compact way to transmit the number).
Electronic serial number	32	Should be factory-set and unchangeable. Uniquely identifies the telephone.
First paging channel	11	Identifies the lowest of the radio channel numbers used to track and signal the telephone. Commands on this channel switch the telephone to another of the control channels (to reduce the loading on the first paging channel).
Last paging channel	11	Identifies the highest radio channel number used to track and signal the telephone.
Home system identification	15	Identifies the telephone's cellular service provider. *Roaming* agreements (in which operators exchange billing information and revenue) enable other cellular service providers to provide service when a phone is used out of its home geographic area.

While there has been a dramatic increase in capacity due to sectorizing, the popularity of cellular has increased even faster. This, combined with the need for encryption and data transmission, has resulted in other efforts. TDMA is the simplest expansion method and has been implemented in many areas, though many users complain that the voice quality is too low. Many operators are therefore considering CDMA and GSM (the European standard).

See *CDMA*, *DN*, *EMF*, *ESMR*, *GSM*, *SST*, and *TDMA*.

ANS
Advanced Network Services, Inc.

IBM and MCI together with Merit Inc. (a nonprofit consortium of Michigan schools) formed ANS, which now runs the Internet's U.S. backbone (which uses T3, and faster, circuits) and offers Internet access to commercial customers (such as Sprint Corp, Uunet Technologies, and Fonorola).

The U.S. National Science Foundation is a major ANS customer, and pays for a significant part of the backbone. The NSF specifies (through the AUP) what types of traffic can be carried on the part of the backbone it funds.

ANS has an interesting WWW server at *http:/www.ans.net* and is located in Elmsford, New York.

See *CIX*, *Internet*, *ISP*, and *T3*.

ANSI
American National Standards Institute

All U.S. national standards are created under ANSI's auspices. ANSI coordinates the U.S. voluntary standards system. ANSI recognizes several groups as *standards providers*, such as IEEE, EIA, and TIA.

ANSI also does standards development work, such as FDDI.

ANSI has a WWW server at *http://www.ansi.org/*.

See *ARCnet*, *ATA*, *FDDI*, and *Standards*.

API
Application Program Interface

The *calls*, *subroutines*, or *software interrupts* that comprise a documented interface so that a (usually) higher-level program such as an application program can make use of the (usually) lower-level services and functions of another application, operating system, network operating system, driver, or other lower-level software program.

The resulting library of functions provides a new capability, such as writing a file in an application program's proprietary format, communicating over a TCP/IP network, or accessing an SQL database. A very popular (and visible to the end user) API is the WinSock API, which gives your Microsoft Windows PC the capability to talk TCP/IP. This capability is required if you want to "surf the Internet."

The lower-level software may be integrated with the application program at compile/link time (using an `include` file or object library) or loaded (before the application program) as a driver, DOS TSR, Novell NLM, or Windows DLL (for example).

The accompanying figure shows an example API between an application program that needs the services of a protocol stack (such as a TCP/IP protocol stack) and the TCP/IP protocol stack (which itself has an interface to an Ethernet adapter).

APIs are very popular now that open systems are popular and customers insist that systems and products work with those of other vendors.

See *APPC*, *CDE*, *CMC*, *CPI-C*, *DDE*, *DMI*, *HLLAPI*, *MAPI*, *Messaging*, *MHS* (*Message Handling System*), *Middleware*, *Motif*, *OLE*, *OpenDoc*, *NAS*, *NDIS*, *NetBIOS*, *NLM*, *NSP*, *ODBC*, *ODI*, *PCMCIA*, *POSIX OSE*, *RPC*, *SAA*, *SDK*, *Sockets*, *SQL*, *TAPI*, *TSAPI*, *VIM*, *WABI*, *WinISDN*, *WinSock*, *Winx Windows APIs*, *WOSA*, and *XAPIA*.

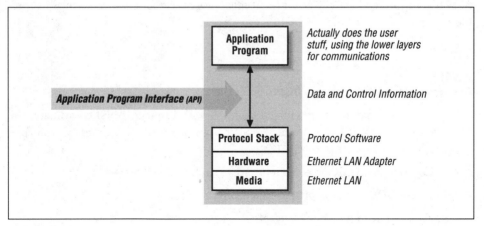

API−1

APPC
Advanced Program to Program Communications

IBM's method (and APIs) for interprocess communication (that is, SNA's support for *distributed processing*). The API has about 32 *verbs* (commands), also called *procedures*, such as ACTIVATE_DLC, ATTACH_LU, and SEND_DATA, and over 1,000 error conditions. APPC uses the LU 6.2 protocol (and PU 2.1), so the term "APPC" is often used interchangeably with "LU 6.2." The following table shows (as a gross simplification) the component of the "new SNA" for each layer of the OSI 7-layer reference model.

OSI Layer Function	"New SNA" Name
7	CPI−C
6	APPC
5	LU6.2
4	
3	APPN or TCP/IP
2	Token Ring
1	

Communications can be between applications either on two workstations or on a workstation and a mainframe.

IBM's AS/400 uses APPC to enable PCs to access AS/400 resources, such as disk drives and printers, as if the resources were local to the PC. A separate APPC session on an AS/400 is required for each session from a PC running IBM's PC Support/400.

See *APPN*, *CPI-C*, *LU 6.2*, *PU 2.1*, *SNA*, and *Token Ring*

APPI
Advanced Peer-to-Peer Internetworking

An SNA routing scheme proposed by Cisco that was to resolve some of APPN's weaknesses (an important one being IBM's multi-hundred-thousand-dollar licensing fee). It could also put SNA traffic over IP networks. The effort was abandoned when IBM became more open and reasonable about its APPN effort.

See *APPN* and *Cisco Systems*.

Apple
Apple Computer, Inc.

The company that makes Macintosh computers.

Usually, in the computer business, when you are first to market, you get the most market share. Also, there are two options in designing and introducing a new product: you can have all of a very small market or a small part of a very large market. (There are lots of bankrupt companies with a small part of a small market and extremely few Microsofts with a large part of a large market.) Although Apple's first product (the Apple II) was being sold more than a year before the IBM PC was announced, Apple blew it. The company decided to limit the interfacing and expansion information that was available so that it kept the entire (and therefore very small) market to itself.

In contrast, IBM did not actively prevent third-party products from being developed and marketed (also, IBM was not litigious and even published some valuable information), so it got a small part of a very large market. (IBM's subsequent attempt to capture back market share through licensing and restricting the information available for its MCA bus was a complete failure.)

Realizing that it may not be a stable thing to have just 10% of a market (and also to be incompatible with 90% of the market), Apple is now trying new ways to compete with the "Wintel" (Microsoft Windows and Intel architecture) market:

- Offering to license its operating system (though there are not many takers since Apple waited many years too long)
- Forming alliances with other companies (that used to be competitors) such as IBM and Motorola to try to compete

Apple has a WWW server at *http://www.apple.com/*. A company that is big on Apple communications products is Farallon Computing, Inc., at *http://www.farallon.com/*.

See *A/UX*, *AFP*, *Apple-IBM Alliance*, *AURP*, *CHRP*, *MCA*, *PC*, *PowerPC*, *QTC*, and *SMRP*.

Apple-IBM Alliance

An effort to make products to compete with Microsoft and Intel. *Kaleida*, *Somerset* (with Motorola), and *Taligent* are the joint ventures doing the work.

See *Apple*, *CHRP*, *Kaleida*, *Somerset*, and *Taligent*.

AppleTalk Filing Protocol   See **AFP.**

Apple Update-Based Routing Protocol   See **AURP.**

APPN
Advanced Peer-to-Peer Networking

IBM's peer-to-peer protocol developed to support computer-to-computer (that is, not to a 3270 terminal) communications. Derived from SNA. Runs over LANs and WANs (dedicated or switched links, load sharing supported).

A nonhierarchical (no FEPs required, either end can initiate a session), 1993 enhancement to PU 2.1 that supports SNA routing between two *end nodes* (where the applications are; they can be either clients or servers) through *network nodes* (which route data and find resources on the network by sending out broadcast messages).

A type of end node that supports a basic set of APPN functions is a *Low Entry Networking* (LEN) node.

Central directory servers are special VTAM hosts that can also be used to locate resources. The 3174 can run APPN network node software, which then queries a central directory server to find out where a CICS application resides and then communicates with that host using the most direct path.

The addressing scheme includes eight alphanumeric characters for LUs (nodes and resources) and eight alphanumeric characters for the subnet ID. Supports fair sharing of bandwidth among applications and congestion control by a prioritization based on *Class Of Service* (COS, which is something like ATM's QOS). Functions at the OSI network and transport layer.

Offers superior SNA integration, richer APIs, and better network management than TCP/IP (IBM would claim). Can (will be able to) carry NetBIOS and TCP/IP traffic by using IBM's MPTN.

The programmer interface is APPC or CPI-C.

APPN's very slow acceptance may result in it losing out to TCP/IP.

See *APPC, ATM (Asynchronous Transfer Mode), CPI-C, CICS, DLSw, DLUr and DLUs, FEP, LEN, LU 6.2, MPTN, PU 2.1, QOS, SNA,* and *VTAM.*

APPN+
APPN Plus

An enhancement to APPN (mainly to catch up to TCP/IP's features) that has better congestion control and dynamic rerouting around network problems (without dropping the session). Claimed to have 3 to 10 times the throughput of APPN through reducing the processing required by each intermediate network node.

Does not require hardware upgrades.

Also called APPN high performance routing.

See *APPN++* and *ATM (Asynchronous Transfer Mode).*

APPN++
APPN Plus Plus

A planned enhancement to APPN+ that will support ATM, Gbits/s line speeds, and multivendor protocols.

ARCnet
Attached Resource Computer Network

A LAN originally developed by the Datapoint Corporation. To promote its acceptance, Datapoint released technical specifications and supported development of complementary and competitive components (making it an industry standard).

Runs at 2.5 Mbits/s and is really low-cost. Was popular before Ethernet and while Ethernet was still expensive.

A newer development (ARCnetPlus) runs at 20 Mbits/s and can share cable (and communicate) with ARCnet stations.

Has recently been made an ANSI standard (878.1). Because of its late standardization and small size (maximum of 255 stations per LAN, maximum frame size of 516 bytes), it has limited WAN connectivity and trouble-shooting equipment support. Not a good choice for new installations. Ethernet would be better.

A low-cost proprietary enhancement called TCNS (Thomas-Conrad Network System) runs at 100 Mbits/s over STP, RG-62 coaxial cable, and fiber-optic cable but is unlikely to be selected for newer installations because of the many other 100-Mbits/s schemes that are now available.

See *100BASE-T, 100VG-AnyLAN, FDDI,* and *LAN.*

Ardis

A company that provides a cellular packet-switched radio data service in the U.S. Now completely owned by Motorola. (It used to be a joint venture with IBM.)

Initially (1984), the network was designed by Motorola for IBM field service technicians. The radio protocol is proprietary (designed by IBM and Motorola). Has about 34,000 subscribers, about 10 times the number that RAM Mobile has.

Data transmission is at 4,800 bits/s (using 240-byte packets, resulting in about 2,000 to 3,000 bits/s of user-data throughput) or 19,200 bits/s (in larger U.S. centers) using 512-byte packets, resulting in up to 8,000 bits/s of user-data throughput.

Usage charges are per kbyte of data transferred.

Sometimes called *Datatac*.

Competes with RAM Mobile Data's Mobitex system and CDPD.

Ardis has a WWW server at *http://www.ardis.com/*.

See *Bell Ardis*, *CDPD*, *ESMR*, *GSM*, *Mobitex*, *Motorola*, and *RAM Mobile Data*.

ARP
Address Resolution Protocol

A method of determining the 48-bit MAC (*Media Access Control*) address for a LAN-connected host running the TCP/IP protocol, as long as you already have the 32-bit IP address of the host (which you may have obtained by using the DNS).

The process is that you *multicast* (send to all LAN-connected hosts running the TCP/IP protocol) a message asking for the host having the specific MAC address of interest to reply. When it does, you typically store the results in an *ARP cache* so that you don't need to do this again.

Defined in RFC 826.

See *Cache*, *DNS* (*Domain Name System*), and *TCP/IP*.

ARPAnet
Advanced Research Projects Agency Network

The predecessor to the Internet, officially phased out in 1990. Began in 1969, linking four computer sites (Stanford Research Institute, the University of Utah, the University of California at Los Angeles, and the University of California at Santa Barbara) that were doing research for the U.S. Department of Defense.

Later called DARPAnet, for the *Defense Advanced Research Projects Agency* (which is an agency of the U.S. Department of Defense), which issued the request for a proposal for the network's development.

Initially a computer science experiment, then developed to provide communications between government agencies, military facilities, defense contractors, and universities, with the goal that the network should be operational even when important parts were unavailable (that is, not vulnerable to "nuclear decapitation"). The first network to use TCP/IP.

Using 56 kbits/s *leased lines* for the connections between sites, grew to about 50 sites in the early 1970s and to a few hundred in the early 1980s. By 1987 the number of sites was several thousand, and the National Science Foundation sponsored a T1 (1.544 Mbits/s) *backbone* (rather than just linking all sites directly to each other), and the network began to be called NSFNet. By 1991 the backbone was upgraded to T3 (44.736 Mbits/s).

See *ANS*, *Internet*, *T1*, *T3*, and *WAN*.

ASCII
American Standard Code for Information Interchange

A specification for the 7-bit patterns used to represent *control* (such as *carriage return*) and *printable* characters (the letters, numbers, and punctuation marks) in computers and for data communications between them.

Used by most of North America (except, for example, for IBM mainframes, which use EBCDIC).

The following table shows the hexadecimal for each ASCII character. For example, a *line feed* is represented as $0A_{16}$ and "$" is 24_{16}.

Least Significant Digit	Most Significant Hexadecimal Digit							
	0	**1**	**2**	**3**	**4**	**5**	**6**	**7**
0	Null	Data link escape	Space	0	@	P	'	p
1	Start of heading	Device control 1 (and X-on)	!	1	A	Q	a	q
2	Start of text	Device control 2	"	2	B	R	b	r
3	End of text	Device control 3 (and X-off)	#	3	C	S	c	s
4	End of transmission	Device control 4	$	4	D	T	d	t

(table continued on next page)

Least Significant Digit	Most Significant Hexadecimal Digit							
	0	**1**	**2**	**3**	**4**	**5**	**6**	**7**
5	Enquiry	Negative acknowl-edgment	%	5	E	U	e	u
6	Acknowl-edge	Synchro-nization character	&	6	F	V	f	v
7	Bell	End of transmission block	'	7	G	W	g	w
8	Backspace	Cancel	(	8	H	X	h	x
9	Horizon-tal tab	End of medium	)	9	I	Y	i	y
A	Line feed	Substitute	*	:	J	Z	j	z
B	Vertical tab	Escape	+	;	K	[	k	{
C	Form feed	Field separa-tor	,	<	L	'	l	|
D	Carriage return	Group sepa-rator	-	=	M	]	m	}
E	Shift out	Record sep-arator	.	>	N	^	n	~
F	Shift in	Unit separa-tor	/	?	O	_	o	Delete

With small changes (for example £ instead of $ or support for ¿ and é), used by most of the rest of the world, too.

Standardized as *International Alphabet 5*.

Since ASCII is a 7-bit code, it can represent only $2^7 = 128$ characters. Most computers support 8-bit bytes (which can represent $2^8 = 256$ characters), so many (unfortunately different) *extended character sets* have been defined (for example, by DEC, IBM, and Microsoft). These use the additional 128 codes for line-drawing characters (for example, ⌈ and ⌉) and other important things (☺).

256 characters are typically enough only for one country's characters (some countries need â, others need ä, and still others need å, for example), so *code pages* are usually defined (again, unfortunately, differently by each operating system). And each country gets its own code page.

This whole mess is supposed to be cleared up by everyone adopting Unicode.

See *Baud*, *EBCDIC*, *In-Band*, and *Unicode*.

ASPI
Advanced SCSI Programming Interface

Adaptec's interface to its SCSI disk controllers that permits multiple device drivers (for example, disk, tape, and CD-ROM) to share the disk controller. This is required when multiple devices are installed on a SCSI bus. Initially (in 1988, when it was first released) was called *Adaptec SCSI Programming Interface*, but Adaptec changed the name in the hope it would become an industry standard (and it has).

Competes with *Layered Device Driver Architecture* (LADDR, from Microsoft) and *Common Access Method* (CAM, from Future Domain and NCR), though ASPI is much more popular.

Adaptec has a WWW server at *http://www.adaptec.com/*.

See *ATASPI* and *SCSI*.

ASTRAL
Alliance for Strategic Token Ring Advancement and Leadership

A group of Token Ring equipment manufacturers (including 3Com, IBM, Madge Networks, and Olicom USA and UB Networks) that have noticed that more people always have and, increasingly, still seem to be installing Ethernet rather than Token Ring LANs.

They hope to educate potential customers about the benefits of Token Ring.

See *LAN* and *Token Ring*

Asymmetric Digital Subscriber Line   See **ADSL.**

Asynchronous

The type of serial data communications supported by a PC's COM port and usually the type used by PCs when using modems.

Literally, "not synchronous."

When used in low-speed data communications, it means that there is no predefined timing between the characters sent; typically, the characters are sent as they are typed by some human (and you know how unpredicatable humans are). The method was designed to handle the expected case that the sender's and receiver's bit rates will never be *exactly* the same and only one character will be ready to be sent at a time.

The following description, and figure below, are for the polarities used on EIA-232 circuits.

While there are no data to send (idle), the data circuit is at a negative voltage.

When a character of data is to be sent, the UART first sends a *start bit* (a one bit-time duration positive voltage), which is of the opposite polarity of what *was* happening.

The transition from negative to positive voltage occurs exactly at the boundary between two bit-times, so the receiver now knows where the bit boundaries are (that is, *bit synchronization* and *character synchronization* have been achieved).

The receiver senses this transition, waits ½-bit-time (the receiver must be preconfigured to nominally the sender's bit rate) to the center of the start bit, and *samples* (reads) the input again. If it is still a positive voltage, then the receiver can be somewhat sure that the initial edge was not just noise.

The receiver then begins assembling the first character of data (in this case, an ASCII d, by waiting a full bit-time, to the center of the first data bit (data are sent LSB first).

The input is then sampled, and the first data bit (a binary 0 in this case) is received. This is continued for (typically) 8 data bits total (the receiver must be preconfigured to the same number of data bits per character).

Then the receiver expects a stop bit. It is a one bit-time duration negative voltage, which is generated by the sender's UART. If one is not received (the line is still positive), then the receiving UART indicates a *framing error* (which may be interpreted as a *break signal*).

After the stop bit, either another character (beginning with a start bit) or an idle (a negative voltage of any duration) begins. Figure 1 illustrates this process.

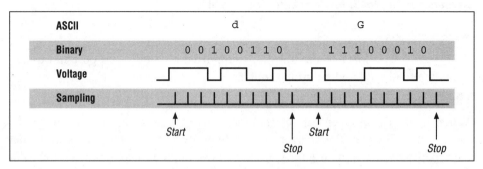

Asynchronous—1

Since the receiver samples at the center of each bit-time, it can be as much as ½ bit-time off (too soon or too late) and still read the bit correctly. Since both the sending and receiving clock may be wrong, each could be up to ¼ bit-time off (allowing for the worst case, in which one is ¼ bit-time too fast and the other is ¼ bit-time too slow). Since the clocks get resynchronized at the start of each character (by the transition to the start bit), the clocks have to be matched only so that they drift by less than ¼ bit-time in the (approximately) 10 bits per character. This requires an accuracy of ¼ bit-time in 10 bits, which is (¼/10 =) 2.5%, which is easily accomplished.

Because of asynchronous data communication's reliance on the addition of a start and stop bit to every character of data, it is usually less efficient than synchronous data communications (of every 10 bits sent, 2 are overhead). That is, 20% of the bandwidth is wasted on start and stop bits, so a 9,600-bits/s line provides only 7,680 bits/s of throughput. Some people call it *start/stop data communications* (IBM people say this in a derogatory way, as if the data lacked confidence and were prone to hesitation) in contrast to the *synchronous data communications* that are commonly used (for example) by IBM 3270-type equipment.

Asynchronous data communications equipment needs to be configured for the following:

- Bit rate (such as 9,600 bits/s)
- Number of data bits per character (such as 8)
- Parity type used (such as none)
- Number of stop bits (usually one, though stop bit durations of 1.5 and 2 bit-times are often settable, but these were needed only for ancient mechanical teletypewriters that needed more than one stop bit-time between characters)

Both ends of a link must have matching settings.

See *3270, Baud, EIA/TIA-232, LSB, Modem, Parity, Synchronous,* and *UART.*

Asynchronous Transfer Mode   See **ATM.**

AT
Advanced Technology

IBM's name for its (now ancient) 80286-based PC, the PC/AT, which was introduced in 1984.

The IDE hard disk drive interface was first implemented on the PC/AT. It used a disk drive controller developed by Western Digital.

See *Bus, Disk Drive, IDE, Intel, ISA,* and *PC.*

AT Command Set

The command language developed by Hayes Microcomputer Products, Inc. to control auto-dial modems from a (usually EIA-232 connected) dumb asynchronous terminal or a PC emulating such a terminal.

All commands (except for "A/" which repeats the previous command, and "+++" which escapes from online data mode back to command mode), begin with AT (or at). Most explanations are that these characters "get the modem's *ATtention*." While the letters AT do act as a command sequence delimiter, an important feature of those particular characters is that they have opposite parity. This enables the modem to automatically recognize and adjust to the terminal or PC's bit rate and parity.

The original core command set was implemented for Hayes's first product, the Hayes Smartmodem 300 (a Bell 103 type modem), which was introduced in 1981. It had only about 15 commands, such as ATDT 555-1234 to dial using touch-tone and ATH to hang up the phone.

Modern modems, such as one supporting V.34 modulation, can have more than 250 commands. Commands include configuring features such as data compression, diagnostics, and flow control. Many modems support new features such as security, distinctive ringing and caller identification, and manufacturers often make up their own commands for these features. These commands are then specific to each manufacturer, so modem set-up strings need to be customized to the modem used.

Remarkably, though Hayes developed the command set, which has become a de facto standard, it is not patented. Virtually all modems and data sets that support switched connections and asynchronous communications use some subset or extension of the AT command set with no benefit to Hayes. This is because Hayes determined that the command set was not patentable.

What Hayes did patent is its method of escaping from online data mode. Since, once connected to a remote modem, a modem simply modulates everything sent from the terminal and sends it over the modem link to the remote modem, the problem is how to get the modem to escape back to command mode.

Hayes's patented solution (*Improved Escape Sequence with Guard Time*, or the *Heatherington method*, or the *'302 Patent*, which refers to U.S. Patent 4,549,302) was developed by Dale Heatherington and has been used by Hayes modems since 1981. The modem escapes from on-line data mode to command mode if it detects the following sequence in the data sent from the terminal:

- At least one second of no data, then
- Three ASCII plus signs ("+++"), then
- At least one second of no data.

The idle time before and after the plus signs is called the *guard time* (the modem can be configured for a different escape character, and a different guard time duration). When the modem is in command mode, commands such as ATH (to hang up) or ATO (to go back online) can be sent.

Hayes licenses this method to other modem manufacturers (see *TIES*). Actually, the modem IC manufacturer is usually licensed; this is most often Rockwell International.

Hayes Microcomputer Products was founded by Dennis C. Hayes, but has recently run into tough times.

Hayes has a WWW server at *http://www.hayes.com/*.

EIA-602 standardizes some AT commands.

See *Asynchronous, Bell 103, de facto Standard, EIA, EIA/TIA-232, Fax, Modem, Parity, Patent, Rockwell International, SWATS, Switched 56, TIES,* and *V.25bis*.

ATA
AT Bus Attachment

Same as IDE.

When ANSI Standardized Western Digital's IDE disk interface, ANSI called it ATA.

See *ANSI* and *IDE*.

ATAPI
AT Attachment Packet Interface

ANSI's name for Western Digital's enhancement to the IDE (also called ATA) hard disk drive interface.

ATAPI:

- Provides support for CD-ROM, tape, and other drives in addition to hard disk drives
- Supports features such as *Plug and Play* (see *PnP*) and *Overlapped I/O*, in which one disk drive can be *seeking* (the read/write head moving to new data) while another is transferring data
- Is part of Western Digital's *Enhanced IDE* (E-IDE) specification (which was first released in 1994)

- Requires a software driver but otherwise simply requires that the CD-ROM drive (for example) be plugged into an available IDE connector in the PC
- Is a superset of IDE, so standard IDE disk drives can be plugged in to an E-IDE ATAPI connector

The term "packet interface" refers to the addition of transferring information between the adapter and peripheral using *packets* (some number of bytes of data with a defined format), rather than IDE's reading and writing to *registers* (specific memory or I/O addresses that have special functions). The packets specified were derived from SCSI (which is a proven technology for accomplishing a similar task).

E-IDE (and the ATAPI specification included in it) competes with (though is less powerful than) SCSI, and with the more common (but decreasingly so) proprietary interfaces otherwise required by CD-ROMs.

See *AT*, *CD-ROM*, *E-IDE*, *IDE*, *PnP*, and *SCSI*.

ATASPI
AT Attachment Software Programming Interface

A specification to provide a standard software interface to IDE (which is also called ATA) attached peripherals.

The goal is to support multiple devices and drivers on a single IDE interface.

Developed by Future Domain. ASPI is the similar specification for the SCSI interface.

See *ASPI*, *CD-ROM*, *E-IDE*, *IDE*, and *SCSI*.

ATM
Adobe Type Manager

A program that enables Adobe Type 1 fonts to be used on non-PostScript printers and video displays. This allows the printed output to match the displayed output. It *rasterizes* the *outline fonts* (turns them into bitmaps at the required resolution).

It is a separate program for Windows and Macintosh, but is integrated into the OS/2 Presentation Manager.

Adobe Type 1 fonts and the scalable fonts built in to Hewlett-Packard LaserJet III and LaserJet 4 printers are resolution-independent (unlike Windows TrueType fonts), so a change in printer resolution will not affect a document's pagination.

The font files include those shown in the following table.

Font Filename Extension	Function	Comments
*.AFM		Used at installation time to create the *.PFM files. Can be deleted after installation.
*.INF		
*.PFB	Font outlines	Required to show fonts on-screen and to rasterize them for printing.
*.PFM	Font metrics	
*.WFA		Created by WordPerfect from the *.PFM files to speed up screen redraws and printing times of PostScript fonts under DOS. Can be deleted, as WordPerfect will recreate them as needed.
*.WFO		

The c:windows\ATM.ini file shows the correlation between the DOS filename and the typeface name.

See *Adobe, Bitmap Font, Font, Multiple Master, Outline Font, PostScript Type 1 Fonts, PostScript Type 3 Fonts, Rasterize, SuperATM, TrueType,* and *Typeface Family.*

ATM
Asynchronous Transfer Mode

A very high-speed, connection-oriented (only PVC initially), fixed-length 48-byte (plus 5 bytes of overhead) cell-switching scheme that is suitable for data as well as digitized voice and video.

Was initially to be used with SONet to be the basis for B-ISDN but is now considered a separate technology. "Asynchronous" because each cell can be independently addressed to allocate bandwidth between many virtual channels as needed.

Could eliminate the distinction between LAN and WAN, since ATM can be used for both. WANs will probably first be implemented as private ATM networks, then become a public offering.

Data are formatted as fixed-length cells so that it is easier to handle them in hardware (which can juggle cells faster than software). Also fixed-length cells enable networks to have predictable response times (since you know when the current cell will finish because you know its length). This *isochronous* capability is required to handle multimedia traffic (such as digitized voice and video).

The cells are relatively small to provide short store-and-forward delays per switch (to reduce network delays, as required for interactive services such as video conferencing).

Will likely be used as the *switching fabric* to support frame relay (which currently uses access speeds up to T1) and possibly B-ISDN (which has accesses starting at OC-3).

The Network-to-Network Interface (NNI) specification describes how ATM networks connect to each other.

The *UNI* (User-to-Network Interface) specification defines the end user interface to an ATM network and includes the following transmission media:

- SONet; 155.52 Mbits/s OC-3 (single-mode and multi-mode fiber) and STS-3c (Category 5 UTP copper)
- DS-3 (also called T3)
- 100 Mbits/s FDDI
- 25.6 Mbits/s (strongly pushed by IBM as an enhancement to Token Ring)

Other interface specifications include *TAXI* and *DXI*.

Connectionless traffic is supported by the network quickly setting up and tearing down a virtual connection without any involvement of the user.

The ATM model has four layers, as defined in the following table:

Layer	Defines
User	User-to-Network interface (UNI)
Adaptation	How *Segmentation And Reassembly* (SAR) are handled for each of the ATM adaptation layers.
Cell	Defines the handling of the 53-byte cells
Physical	Cables and connectors for DS-3, Transparent Asynchronous Transmitter/receiver (TAXI) for 100-Mbits/s multimode fiber, fibre channel for 155 Mbits/s, and SONet.

The *ATM adaptation layer* (AAL) exists only in end-stations, not in switches, and is responsible for segmenting the information into 53-byte cells (and at the receiving end, reassembles it back into its original form). The following table describes the adaptation layers. AAL 5 and, to a lesser extent, AAL 1, are receiving the most interest from vendors and standards groups.

AAL	Use	Comments
0 or Null	When customer equipment does all AAL-related functions	Network AAL does not do anything in this case.
1	Isochronous, constant bit-rate services, such as digitized audio and video	Suitable for traffic that is sensitive to both cell loss and delay. Intended to replace fractional and full T1 and T3 services but has a far greater range of available speeds. Uses one payload data byte for sequence numbering (leaving only 47 per cell for the data).

(table continued on next page)

AAL	Use	Comments
2	Isochronous variable bit-rate services, such as compressed video	
3/4	Variable bit-rate data, such as LAN file transfers	Originally intended as two layers: one for connection-oriented services (such as frame relay) and the other for connectionless services (such as SMDS). It was later realized that only one layer was needed for both capabilities. Intended for traffic that can tolerate delay but not cell loss. Uses four payload data bytes for error detection. Supports multiplexing of ATM cells.
5	Variable bit-rate data, such as bursty LAN applications	Similar to AAL 3/4 but with fewer features (for example, no cell multiplexing), so it is easier to implement. There are no overhead bytes; all 48 cell bytes are available for payload. Sometimes called the simple and efficient adaptation layer (SEAL).

The accompanying figure illustrates the use of each bit of the 53-byte ATM cell.

Byte	Bit							
	8	7	6	5	4	3	2	1
1	Generic Flow Control				Virtual Path Identifier			
2	Virtual Path Identifier (continued)				Virtual Channel Identifier			
3	Virtual Channel Identifier (continued)							
4	Virtual Channel Identifier (continued)				Payload Type Identifier			Call Loss Priority
5	Header Error Contol							
6–53	Payload Data							

ATM−1

Two locations are connected by a *virtual path*, and there are 8 bits in the header to identify it, allowing connections to 256 locations.

Each virtual path can carry up to 65,536 *virtual channels* (simultaneous connections), each virtual circuit being identified by the 16-bit virtual circuit identifier (which uniquely identifies the connection, even through several cascaded virtual paths).

Any bits that are set in the *generic flow control* field identify that some form of priority for the traffic is being requested (both the ATM switch and the end-station must support this, which is confirmed by the end-station echoing back the priority bits).

The three bits of the *payload type identifier* specify the following:

- Which AAL was used to format the payload data
- *Explicit Forward Congestion Control Indication* (EFCI), which alerts the receiver that the cell (and others following it) may have been delayed by network congestion
- Whether the cell contains OAM: *Operations* (fault and performance management), *Administration* (addressing, data collection and usage monitoring), and *Maintenance* (analysis, diagnosis, and repair of network faults) information

The *Cell Loss Priority* (CLP) bit indicates that the cell can be discarded if necessary (for example, to reduce network congestion).

The *header error control* field is a check character for the other four header bytes. Cells with corrupted headers are discarded.

At least two methods are defined to carry LAN-type traffic:

- Classical IP over ATM provides direct support for IP (with a 9-kbyte maximum frame size).
- LAN Emulation (LANE) provides support for existing LAN protocols through the creation of *virtual LANs*. The goal is to use ATM's connection-oriented switching fabric to emulate the connectionless nature of a LAN.

Among other requirements, *LAN emulation* involves the development (and standardization) of a method to support broadcasts (ATM is connection-oriented, yet many LAN protocols depend on broadcasts for some important functions). Using LAN emulation enables NDIS and ODI devices to access each other and native ATM devices.

A LAN-to-ATM converter adds an ID header to the Layer 2 (Ethernet or Token Ring) frame header, strips off the CRC, and emits ATM AAL 5 PDUs (cells).

The requirements for LAN emulation are specified in the LAN emulation user-to-network interface (L-UNI, pronounced "loony").

LAN emulation requires LAN emulation client (LEC) software (either in the LAN-to-ATM converter or in the ATM device) and a LAN emulation service.

The LEC establishes a connection with the LES, for example to request the LES to map MAC addresses to ATM addresses (this is called *address resolution*).

The *LAN emulation service* (LES) provides these services:

- Supports unicast (point-to-point) data transfer
- Supports multicast (one-to-many) data transfer
- Responds to requests to resolve MAC addresses to ATM addresses

The LES requires three servers (which may all reside in an ATM switch or may be separate on other ATM-connected devices):

- *Configuration server* (provides configuration information about the ATM network, frame size allowed on LAN, and type of LAN and provides the address of the LES to the LEC)
- *LAN emulation server* (registers and resolves MAC addresses to ATM addresses)
- *Broadcast and unknown server* (BUS, supports multicasting, so the LEC has only to send a single message)

ATM's *service-specific convergence sublayer* maps different services to ATM (and back).

The *convergence sublayer* compensates for different physical interfaces (T1 to E1, for example) that can be used to access an ATM network. As long as users utilize the same service class, communication between them will be possible even if they each use different interfaces.

Specific SSCSs and CSs need to be standardized for each interface. Frame relay is the farthest along so far.

The accompanying figure shows the relationship of the convergence sublayers to the types of traffic handled by ATM.

20-byte addresses are used. These can be either Internet IP- or OSI NSAP-type addresses (for private use) or hierarchical telephone-type E.164 addresses (for public ATM network use).

Low-level addresses are determined by which port on the ATM switch you are connected to. User equipment does not have an address (just like telephone numbers; the telephone has no address—the central office switch determines what your telephone number will be).

To support ATM, a router uses the selected ATM adaptation layer to add the appropriate convergence header to the variable-length packet or frame of data. The convergence sublayer then adds a CRC to the end of the end of the message and adds pad characters so that the message is an integral multiple of 48 bytes. This message could now be sent on a DXI interface. Alternatively, the message is segmented into 48-byte cells by the SAR sublayer, and the router adds the five-byte cell header from the ATM sublayer and sends the cell out on whatever physical interface is being used (a SONet OC-3, for example).

The ATM Forum's User-to-Network Interface (UNI) 3.0 specification defines four *service classes*, which specify the *quality of service* (required bandwidth, allowable

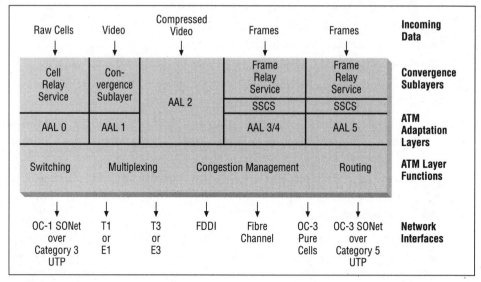

ATM—2

error rates, and other characteristics to meet the needs of voice, video, and data). At connection time, the end-station requests the required quality of service, and the network will establish the connection only if it (including all switches along the path) can supply the resources that are necessary.

The service classes are listed in order of decreasing data priority in the following table.

Service Class	Flow Control Method	Service Characteristics
CBR	*Single Leaky Bucket.* Network detects and discards traffic that exceeds the negotiated PCR.[a]	*Constant Bit Rate* (sometimes called *Class A*): At connection time, the user equipment specifies the *cell delay variation tolerance limit* (maximum allowed jitter) and the bandwidth required (PCR), which the network then reserves for the duration of the connection. Maximum cell loss rate is known. Intended for emulating T1 links and for data such as real–time digitized voice or video that need a guaranteed, fixed bandwidth—no more and no less.

(table continued on next page)

Service Class	Flow Control Method	Service Characteristics
VBR	*Dual Leaky Bucket.* Network checks for violations of both PCR and SCR,[b] and discards excess traffic (which the user equipment must then retransmit).	*Variable Bit Rate* (sometimes called *Class C*): At connection time, the user equipment specifies the jitter allowed and the PCR and SCR required. User equipment can exceed the SCR (up to the PCR) as long as, over the averaging period, the SCR is not exceeded. Also, if the equipment bursts at the PCR for longer than the *burst tolerance*, then the user equipment must send at a lower rate for a period of time so that the network can carry ABR and UBR traffic. Maximum cell loss rate is known. Intended for bursty LAN traffic (though in practice, it will probably not be possible to characterize traffic bursts as required to efficiently use this service class). Two subclasses are defined: *Real-Time* (VBR-RT), which guarantees low jitter and is suitable for compressed digitized video or voice. *Non-Real-Time* (VBR-NRT), which has higher network jitter and is suitable for short, bursty data messages, such as transaction processing and LAN interconnect.
ABR	Uses *closed-loop, rate-based* flow control, initiated by the network's ATM switches, to ensure that users do not send more data than the network can carry. The network guarantees to carry traffic at least the negotiated MCR.[c]	*Available Bit Rate*: At connection time, user equipment specifies the PCR (which defaults to the access line rate) and the minimum bandwidth needed (MCR, which defaults to zero cells per second). The switch does not specify the maximum jitter or a burst tolerance. Uses bandwidth available after CBR and VBR service classes have received the bandwidth they need (though this service class does provide a minimum bandwidth guarantee). Maximum cell loss rate is known. Best service class for non–real-time bursty traffic, since flow control handles situations of network congestion without requiring cells to be discarded if the burst is unexpectedly long.

(table continued on next page)

Service Class	Flow Control Method	Service Characteristics
UBR	No flow control. Applications keep on transmitting when network congestion occurs. Once switch buffers overflow, network discards cells.	*Unspecified Bit Rate*: At connection time, no maximum jitter or bit rate is specified. The network offers no guarantee of whether or when the data will arrive at the destination. (The user application does this if necessary.)

[a] *Peak Cell Rate*, the maximum legal burst rate in cells per second.

[b] *Sustained Cell Rate*, the average rate allowed for a specified period of time (3 seconds, for example).

[c] *Minimum Cell Rate*.

The *Available Bit Rate* (ABR) service class uses the *Enhanced Proportional Rate Control Algorithm* (EPRCA), which includes several flow control mechanisms: a basic method (EFCI) and optional enhancements to it. The following table summarizes these (each can build on the capabilities of the method above it).

ABR Flow Control Method	Description
EFCI	*Explicit Forward Congestion Indication*: Any ATM switch (along the path from source to destination) that detects network congestion sets the EFCI bit in the cell header. When the cell gets to the destination, the user equipment modifies the *Resource Management* (RM) cells (that it has been sending every n cells) it sends back to the source, requesting the source to reduce its data rate. This method requires that both the source and destination implement this form of flow control. The longer the path from source to destination, the greater the time until the source reduces its data rate (so the network will require more buffering).
	If a source notes that some of the RM cells it should be receiving back from its destination are missing (presumably discarded because of network congestion), then the source must reduce its data rate.
	The source decides how to allocate its allowed bandwidth among its virtual circuits.
	The source also transmits RM cells (every n cells), which indicate the sending station's current transmission rate and the higher rate it would like to use.
ERM	*Explicit Rate Marking*: Switches along the path from Destination to source can modify the RM cells (generated by the destination) to request the source to reduce its transmission rate even faster than originally requested by the destination.

(table continued on next page)

ABR Flow Control Method	Description
Segmented VS/VD	*Segmented Virtual Source/Virtual Destination*: Some of the network's ATM switches can generate the RM cells (as if they were a "virtual destination"), so there is no need to wait until the real Destination generates the cells (this is important for large networks). These switches can also respond to RM cells, thereby reducing the data rate they forward toward the congestion (and possibly discarding some of the traffic from the real source), therefore protecting the rest of the network from congestion.
Hop-by-hop VS/VD	*Hop-by-hop Virtual Source/Virtual Destination*: All of the network's ATM switches can generate and respond to the RM cells.

In addition to the WWW references given in the entry for standards, ATM information is available from ATM equipment vendors, such as those listed in the following table.

3Com Corporation	*http://www.3com.com/*
General Datacomm, Inc.	*http://www.gdc.com*
Cisco Systems, Inc.	*http://www.cisco.com*
Newbridge Networks Corporation	*http://www.newbridge.com*

See *Adaptation Layer, ATM Forum, B-ISDN, Carrier, Cell, DXI, E.164, Isochronous, Multimedia, NNI, SMDS, SONet, Standards, TAXI, UTP,* and *VLAN.*

ATM Forum
Asynchronous Transfer Mode Forum

"A world-wide organization, aimed at promoting ATM within the industry and the end-user community."

Most ATM work is being done by the *ATM Forum,* which "develops implementors' agreements" (it has no authority to develop international standards). Since there always appears to be more work, it is difficult to know when the technology is ready for commercial use.

There are three types of members:

- *Principal* members participate in committees and vote on specifications
- *Auditing* members do not participate in committees but do receive technical and marketing documents

- *User* members participate only in end–user roundtables, such as the *Enterprise Network Roundtable* (ENR), which consists of about 120 corporations and institutions

Formed in 1991 by Adaptive Corp., Cisco Systems, Northern Telecom, and Sprint Corp.

The ATM Forum has a WWW server at *http://www.atmforum.com/home.html/*.

See *ATM* (*Asynchronous Transfer Mode*).

AT&T
Previously American Telephone and Telegraph

They used to be called "the Bell System," "Ma Bell," or "the phone company." The first dramatic change came in 1968 when the FCC's *Carterfone* decision (which set out only to allow customers to attach a shoulder holder onto handsets to facilitate talking on the phone hands-free) forced phone companies to allow customers to buy their own telephone equipment. A second major event came in 1977, when the *Data Access Arrangement* (DAA) or coupler could be incorporated into products, since it did not have to come from the phone company.

As people became more concerned about AT&T being a monopoly and that AT&T might therefore be restricting competition or not providing new technology and fair prices, in 1982 a U.S. federal court ordered AT&T to answer charges of anticompetitive behavior. Rather than face a full trial, AT&T agreed to give up ownership of the local phone companies (and couldn't even use the bell-inside-circle logo). This breakup (which occurred in 1984) was called *divesture*.

AT&T was left with its long-distance business, manufacturing, and the research operations (Bell Laboratories).

As part of the divesture, competition in the form of multiple IXCs was allowed.

AT&T later bought NCR Corp. (previously National Cash Register) for $7 billion in 1991 and changed that group's name to Global Information Solutions (GIS).

AT&T has a WWW server at *http://www.att.com,* and GIS has a WWW server at *http://ncrinfo.attqis.com/*.

See *Bellcore, Carrier, FCC, IXC, LEC, RBOC,* and *Teradata*.

Attached Resource Computer Network   See **ARCnet.**

AUP
Acceptable Use Policy

The U.S. National Science Foundation's one-page policy on what types of traffic the federally funded part of the Internet can carry.

Initially interpreted to mean that the Internet can be used to carry only research- and educational-oriented traffic (for example, the only advertising allowed was for new products and services for research and education), it is now generally accepted that this applies only to the part of U.S. backbone that is funded by the NSF.

Commercial providers of Internet access therefore usually charge commercial traffic users more, since the providers cannot route the traffic over the free part of the backbone and must use their own facilities or pay ANS (which runs the entire backbone) for access.

See *ANS*, *CIX*, *Internet*, and *NSFnet*.

AURP
Apple Update-Based Routing Protocol

Apple's link-state replacement for its RTMP router-to-router protocol.

See *Apple*, *Link-state*, and *RTMP*.

Authentication

Generally, a method to verify the source of a document and that the document has not been changed since it was sent (*data authentication*), or that a user logging on to a network is really who he or she claims to be (*user authentication*).

Data authentication is handled by encryption schemes, such as PGP. An authentication check can produce three results. The data can be:

- *Authentic* (it really is from the person it claims it is from, and has not been altered)
- *Forged* (it is not authentic)
- *Unverifiable* (since we don't have the sender's public key, we can't check whether it is authentic or not)

User authentication usually uses passwords, but better methods are needed and are being implemented. Passwords are too easy to guess (especially with the help of computers) or steal (for example, by monitoring data communication lines or reading others' electronic mail).

Two improved methods of user authentication are becoming popular: time synchronous intelligent tokens and challenge-response intelligent tokens. An *intelligent token* is a credit card–sized device that has an on-board processor and memory, and possibly a numeric LCD display and a keypad as well.

With time-synchronous intelligent tokens, each user gets a token. Using a preprogrammed 64-bit unique, imbedded, secret key, the token generates a new (usually) six-digit random number (usually) every minute, which is shown on its LCD display. Software or hardware at the central site knows the token's secret key and can calculate which number each user's token will be displaying at any time. Users logging in at a terminal's keyboard are prompted to enter a (usually) four-digit number identifying themselves and the number currently displayed on their token.

The central system adjusts its number-tracking algorithm for tokens that are found to be running slightly too fast or too slow.

The advantage of this scheme is that nothing needs to be plugged in to the remote user's communication line (this simplifies things and may be necessary if the remote device is LAN-connected or is a fax machine or voice-mail system).

Problems are that users need to type in numbers (within a short period of time), the method does not provide encryption for the subsequent data exchange, and there is a chance that someone monitoring a user's communication line could get the user's current random number and quickly (before the minute elapses and the number changes) log in elsewhere on the network.

With challenge-response intelligent tokens, a security device at the central site (and connected between the incoming communication line and the host to which access is being protected) sends a randomly generated number to the remote token. The remote token (which is connected between the incoming communication line and the remote PC) encrypts this number, usually using DES and an encryption key that was preprogrammed into the token (by a security administrator) by plugging it into a programmer before it was issued to the user.

The remote-token-encrypted number is then sent back to the security device (at the central site), which has a database of all valid encryption keys. If the remote Token's encryption key is found to be valid (that is, the returned encrypted number matches one that is generated at central by using the same random number), then the central security device allows communication with the host.

The intelligent token may then perform encryption/decryption for the subsequent data exchange.

The advantages of this method are that the user does not need to type anything and the data exchange can be encrypted.

Both of these methods are suitable for dial-up or Internet access as well as LANs and dedicated circuits.

Dial-back modems, in which you dial in and identify yourself, and the modem dials back to where that user is (securely) registered to be, are no longer considered secure. The problem is that some data burglar could use call-forwarding on your telephone line to redirect the call-back to any other location.

See *DES, Encryption, Kerberos, PGP, RSA*, and *SESAME*.

AVI

The filename extension for compressed video usually used under Microsoft Windows. *Key frames* are compressed by eliminating redundant information. Subsequent *delta frames* are constructed by recording only the differences from the immediately preceding frame (a process called *differencing*). The decompression is usually handled entirely in software.

Competes with MPEG-1, though MPEG-1 produces higher-quality video and requires specialized hardware for decompression.

See *MPEG* and *Video*.

B8ZS
Bipolar, with 8-Zero Substitution

The method developed by AT&T to provide *clear channel* 64 kbits/s data communication service on a DS-0 (rather than the more common 56-kbits/s data communication service), while ensuring that T1's "1s density" rule is enforced. This rule requires that the average number of 1s in the data be at least 12.5% (one in eight) and that there be no more than 15 consecutive 0s in a T1 data stream (since 1s are required to keep the sender and the receiver in synchronization).

That is, the worst case allowed is as follows:

- Time slot 24 has 10000000
- Time slot 1 has 00000001
- The framing bit (between those two time slots) is a 0

In summary, every time slot must contain at least one 1.

To back up a little bit, bits on a T1 line are sent as follows:

- A pulse indicates a binary 1, and each time a pulse needs to be sent, it is opposite in polarity to the previous one
- The absence of a pulse (that is, nothing) indicates a binary 0

This is called *Alternate Mark Inversion* (AMI). The purpose of the alternating polarity is to ensure that the average D.C. voltage is zero (since the signal spends an equal amount of time at each polarity), which is important in coupling the signal through a transformer (which would otherwise saturate and would therefore distort the signal).

To allow a transmitter to send any bit pattern, including eight consecutive 0s in a time slot, several methods are available:

- B7ZCS (*Bipolar 7, with Zero Code Suppression*) or another scheme that sets one of the eight 0 bits to a 1. Digitized speech listeners cannot perceive this messing around with the bits, but you can bet that a computer using the channel for data would. The method requires the full-time use of the eighth bit in each time slot, for use by the carrier (this bit is sometimes also used for line supervision). This leaves only seven of the eight bits for user data, which provide a (7 bits × 8,000 frames per second =) 56,000-bits/s data channel. This method is widely installed (historically, T1 circuits have been used for digitized voice, so there was no impact), but because of its inefficiency for T1 circuits that are used for data (8,000 bits/s of user data throughput is wasted), it is being replaced by other methods that can offer clear channel (full 64,000 bits/s) service.

- ZBTSI (*Zero Byte Time Slot Interchange*) is an ANSI standard (based on a slightly different and proprietary method developed by Verilink) that buffers four frames, switches time slots to avoid 1s density violations, and indicates which slots were interchanged using 2 kbits/s of the ESF framing supervisory data channel.

  While ZBTSI can often be implemented more easily than B8ZS (which is described below), this method of providing clear channel service is not very popular, partially because of the expense (the electronics are expensive due to the buffering) and the requirement to use part of the supervisory data channel.

- B8ZS is becoming a very popular method of providing clear channel 64-kbits/s service for each T1 time slot. Time slots with all 0s are converted to a specific pair of *Bipolar Violations* (BPVs).

  This is shown in the diagram (which assumes that the last 1 in the previous time slot was a positive pulse—the opposite polarity pulses and bipolar violations would be used if the last 1 in the previous time slot were a negative pulse). Note that the average D.C. voltage is still zero.

  The conversion from the user's clear channel 64-kbits/s data to the B8ZS encoding is done by the CSUs. The CSUs at both ends of a link (typically one CSU at a customer site and the other in the nearest telephone company central office) must have B8ZS support. The B8ZS encoding is done for each point-to-point link and so may need to be done for each point-to-point link in a typical end-to-end connection. Usually, the CSUs will also support ESF.

B8ZS is used on T1 lines that provide primary rate ISDN (so all 24 time slots can carry a full 64 kbits/s of user data).

See *CSU, DS-0, Encoding, ESF, ISDN, PRI,* and *T1.*

B-ISDN
Broadband ISDN

A very high-speed data communications service.

ISDN at more than T1 or E1 speeds (such as OC-3). WAN-oriented. Will use ATM switching and support voice, video, and data. Usually simply called "ATM," since anything with "ISDN" in it doesn't sell well.

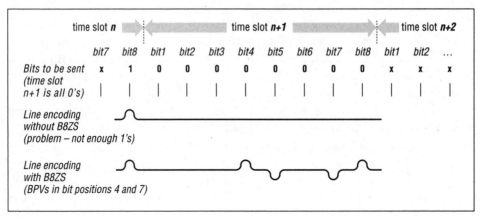

B8ZS—1

SMDS is a similar service and (in some places) is currently available, but not widely used.

See *ATM, E1, ISDN, Narrowband ISDN, OC-x, SMDS, SONet, T1,* and *Wideband ISDN.*

Baby Bell

An RBOC.

See *IXC, LEC,* and *RBOC.*

Bandwidth on Demand Interoperability Group   See **Bonding.**

Basic Input/Output System   See **BIOS.**

Basic-Rate Interface   See **BRI.**

Batteries

Correctly, a battery is two or more *cells* (a container with two *electrodes* in contact with an *electrolyte* that produces a voltage determined by the chemistry used) typically connected in *series* (to produce a higher voltage).

For example, a standard 12-volt automobile battery is six 2.2-volt cells connected in series (which produces a nominal 13.2 volts D.C.). However, people usually call a cell a battery (for example, a single "size D battery").

There are two main categories of batteries:

- Primary batteries (which are not rechargeable, since the chemical reaction that produces the electricity is not reversible)
- Rechargeable batteries (also called secondary batteries)

Batteries have a rated capacity, abbreviated as "C" and stated in amp-hours (Ah). It is usually measured at a discharge rate of C/10 at 20°C (the capacity is very dependent on the discharge rate and temperature).

For example, a battery with a capacity of 1 Ah can supply 100 mA for 10 hours before dropping to below its rated voltage.

There are many types of primary batteries, as shown in the following table.

Type	Features
Standard zinc-car-bon	Invented over 100 years ago (by someone named Leclanché). Advantages are mainly lowest cost. Problems include poor discharge characteristics (they become continuously weaker, rather than maintaining a high output and then quickly dropping) and unsuitability for high-current requirements (life shortens too much).
Heavy-duty zinc-carbon	Have only slightly better energy density (energy per unit volume) but are much better at high-current applications and wider-temperature operation than standard zinc-carbon batteries.
Alkaline	Widely used (for example, Duracell ®). Good for low-current, long-life applications (such as clocks). Advantages include better energy density and shelf-life than zinc-carbon. Problems include the same poor discharge characteristic as, and only slightly better temperature range than, zinc-carbon. Slightly more expensive than zinc-carbon.
Lithium	Several types (chemistries) available, but all have very high energy density, wide temperature range, very long shelf-life (more than 20 years at 70° C) and very good discharge characteristics. Problems include the potential fire hazard of the high energy density (high short-circuit current output) and the very toxic chemicals used. Commonly used to supply backup power to memory.
Silver oxide	Commonly used in watches and cameras. Very good discharge characteristics but shorter shelf-life than lithium.
Zinc-air	Extremely high energy density. Starting to be used as a replacement for mercury batteries in hearing aids and pagers.

Some primary battery characteristics are shown in the following table.

Characteristic		Zinc-Carbon		Alkaline	Mercury	Lithium
		Standard	Heavy-Duty			
Capacity (Ah)	D	1.5		17		0.6 to 5 (depends on size)
	C	1.0		7.8		
	AA	0.18		2.6		
	AAA	0.07		1.15		
	9V			0.57		
Energy density (Wh/in.^{3})		2	2.5	3.5	7	8
Temperature range (°C at 85% capacity)	Low	10	5	2	3	-30
	High	55	65	70	75	100
Cell voltage (volts)	Full	1.5	1.5	1.5	1.4	4
	Empty	0.45	0.7	1	1.3	3.8

Note: These numbers (especially the capacity-related ones) will change significantly with temperature (lower capacity at lower temperature) and discharge rate (lower capacity at higher discharge rate).

There are several types of rechargeable batteries as shown in the following table.

Type	Features
Nickel-cadmium (NiCd)	Can overheat if overcharged (charged at too high a rate after already charged).
	Short shelf-life (completely discharges in 3 months).
	Good discharge characteristics (output voltage stays constant until almost discharged, then drops rapidly).
	A trickle-charge rate of C/16 is often used to maintain a rechargeable battery in a fully charged state. With suitable batteries and temperature monitoring, fast-charging (C/3 to 4C) can be used. Normal battery charging is at C/10 or less.
	The battery should not be used after the output voltage drops below 1.1V.
	At least 60% of the time, the batteries should be fully discharged (to 1.1V) before charging (this erases the *memory effect* to which some say NiCd is still susceptible).
	Lasts about 500 recharges.
	A mature technology unlikely to have substantial improvements.

(table continued on next page)

Type	Features
Nickel-metal hydride (NiMH)	Similar to high-performance NiCd but has 30% higher energy density than high-performance NiCd and 100% to 150% more energy density than standard NiCd. Similar charging as NiCd but heats up more during normal charging. Usually requires a different charger or special settings. Can be damaged (more easily than NiCd) by excessive charge or discharge rates. Has less memory effect than NiCd. Self-discharges at about 25% per month. Lasts 300 to 500 recharges.
Lithium-ion	Characteristics similar to those of primary lithium. 3.6V per cell. About 50% more energy density than NiMH (by volume) and 80% more energy density than NiMH (by weight); that is, lithium-ion is lighter than NiMH. Self-discharges at about 10% per month (much better than NiCd and NiMH). Has no memory effect. Lasts 500 to 800 recharges.
Sealed lead-acid	Same chemistry as automobile lead-acid batteries. Advantages are high current output capability, low cost, long life (discharge/charge cycles), good shelf-life and discharge characteristics, and wide temperature range. Problems include low energy density (making for very heavy batteries). Usually charged at C/4 until the cell voltage reaches 2.4V. Trickle-charged at C/10 to maintain a cell voltage of 2.25 to 2.3V.
Silver-zinc	Used for military and aerospace applications. Manufactured without their electrolyte (so they have a 5-year shelf life), which is added only when they are about to be used. They then have a 2-year life of up to 200 discharge/charge cycles. Advantages include light weight, high energy density, excellent capacity retention, and excellent discharge characteristics. Problems include being expensive and high-maintenance and their short life. Unlikely to be used in consumer equipment but may be found in surplus equipment.

Some rechargeable battery characteristics are shown in the following table.

Characteristic			NiCd	NiMH	Sealed Lead-Acid
Capacity (Ah)[a]		D	1.2 to 5	[b]	1.2 to 120
		C	1.1 to 2.8		
		AA	0.5 to 0.9		
		AAA	0.18 to 0.22		
		9V	0.1		
Energy density (Wh/in.^{3})			1.2	1.8	1
Temperature range (°C at 85% capacity)	Low		-15	-20	-50
	High		40	45	50
Cell voltage (volts)	Full		1.35	1.4	2.4
	Empty		1	1.1	1.6
Self-discharge rate (%/month)			25	30	6
Number of charge/discharge cycles			800	500	200 to 2000

[a] The capacity of standard consumer NiCd batteries is at the lower end of the range. Specialty batteries (costing more and capable of faster charging or higher discharge rates) have higher capacity. That's why your camcorder battery pack costs so much more than the replacement cells you can buy at Radio Shack.

[b] The capacity of NiMH and sealed lead-acid batteries depends on their physical size.

Battery rechargers initially charge at a *bulk charging rate* until a trigger *overcharge voltage* is reached. They then switch to a *trickle-charge rate* to maintain a cell's *float voltage* (this can be continued indefinitely without damage to the battery to keep it in a fully charged state).

See *SBD* and *SMBus*.

Baud

The baud rate of a data communications system is the number of symbols per second transferred. A symbol may have more than two states, so it may represent more than one binary bit (a binary bit always represents exactly two states). Therefore the baud rate may not equal the bit rate, especially in the case of recent modems, which can have (for example) up to nine bits per symbol.

For example, a Bell 212A modem uses *Phase Shift Keying* (PSK) modulation, and each symbol has one of four phase shifts (of 0°, 90°, 180°, or 270°). Since it requires two bits to represent four states (00, 01, 10, and 11), the modem transmits 1,200 bits/s of information, using a symbol rate of 600 baud.

Usually the baud rate of a modem will not equal the bit rate and is of no interest to the end user—only the data rate, in bits per second, is.

Therefore in referring to the data rate of a modem, use bits/s (or kbits/s, etc.), not baud rate.

Named after J. M. Emile Baudot (1845–1903), who was a French telegraph operator who worked out a five-level code (five bits per character) for telegraphs. It was standardized as International Telegraph Alphabet Number 2, and is commonly called Baudot (and is a predecessor to ASCII). Since 2^5 is only 32 and the uppercase letters, numbers, and a few punctuation characters add to more than that, Baudot uses *Shift In* and *Shift Out* characters (analogous to how the Caps Lock key on a PC keyboard reduces the number of keys needed by enabling each letter key to represent two characters).

See *ASCII, Asynchronous, Bell 212A, EIA/TIA-232, Encoding, Modem, Synchronous,* and *V.34.*

Bayonet Neil Consulman   See **BNC.**

Bayonet Nut Connector   See **BNC.**

BBS
Bulletin Board System

Software (usually implemented on PCs) that supports multiple simultaneous callers (usually running terminal-emulation software on PCs) to send and receive files and email. Most now provide Internet access as well. Common software packages include Mustang Software's Wildcat! and Galacticomm's *The Major BBS* (Galacticomm has an ftp site at *gcomm.com*).

Often run by a company to provide software updates and technical support, though this function is often being replaced by the large service providers (such as CompuServe) and Internet access.

See *CompuServe, Internet, ISP, RIPscrip,* and *Usenet.*

Bell 103

An old, very low-speed modem modulation method used in North America.

A zero to 300 bits/s, full-duplex, two-wire *asynchronous* modem modulation standard for use on standard dial-up telephone lines. More than 20 years old but still widely used, for example, for retail store credit card authorization terminals.

Similar in technology to, but incompatible with, V.21 (which was popular in Europe, though it is also used by fax machines).

See *Asynchronous, Fax, Modem,* and *V.21.*

Bell 212A

An old, low-speed modem modulation method used in North America.

A 1,200-bits/s, full-duplex, two-wire *synchronous* (*asynchronous* data is supported by a built-in converter) modem modulation standard for use on standard dial-up telephone lines.

Similar in technology to, but sometimes incompatible with, V.22 (which was popular in Europe).

See *Asynchronous*, *Baud*, *Modem*, *Synchronous*, and *V.22*.

Bell Ardis

A joint venture of BCE Mobile (60%) and Motorola (40%) that offers wireless digital data communications service at up to 19,200 bits/s nationally in Canada.

See *Ardis*.

Bellcore
Bell Communications Research

The common research and development organization that was required to be supported for 10 years after the (1984) AT&T divesture, by the resulting seven U.S. Regional Bell Operating Companies (RBOCs).

Works on standards that are useful to all RBOCs (such as SMDS and T3), but as some RBOCs are now diverging in their research interests, many want to sell it.

Bellcore has a WWW Server at *http://www.bellcore.com/*.

See *AT&T*, *RBOC*, and *HDSL*.

Berkeley Software Distribution UNIX   See **BSD UNIX**.

BGP
Border Gateway Protocol

A router–to–router protocol.

A replacement for IP's *exterior gateway protocol* that provides *policy-based routing* (that is, including factors such as the traffic's importance in determining routing) between administrative domains.

See *RIP*.

Big Endian

A colorful way of describing the sequence in which multibyte numbers are stored in a computer's memory.

Storing the most significant byte in the lowest memory address, which is the address of the data. Since TCP defines the byte ordering for network data, end-nodes must call a processor-specific convert utility (which would do nothing if the machine's native byte-ordering is the same as TCP's) that acts on the TCP and IP header information only. In a TCP/IP packet, the first transmitted data is the most significant byte.

Most UNIXes (for example, all System V) and the Internet are Big Endian. Motorola 680*x*0 microprocessors (and therefore Macintoshes), Hewlett-Packard PA-RISC, and Sun SuperSPARC processors are Big Endian. The Silicon Graphics MIPS and IBM/Motorola PowerPC processors are both Little and Big Endian (bi-endian).

The term is used because of an analogy with the story *Gulliver's Travels*, in which Jonathan Swift imagined a never-ending fight between the kingdoms of the Big-Endians and the Little-Endians, whose only difference is in where they crack open a hard-boiled egg.

See *Little Endian*, *MS*, *Operating System*, and *UNIX*.

Binary Large Object   See **BLOB**.

Binary Synchronous Communications   See **BISYNC**.

BIOS
Basic Input/Output System

Low-level routines (programs) in a PC that provide standard program interfaces to perform hardware-oriented functions such as writing to the screen and accessing disk drives.

Code (that is, a small program) to read an operating system from diskette or disk into memory (which is what your PC does when you power it on) is also included. The BIOS software itself is stored in (usually 64 kbytes of) nonvolatile EPROM so that it is available even after the PC has been powered off and on (normal PC memory is erased when the power is turned off).

The method of accessing BIOS functions (a *jump table* starting at a predefined location in RAM) makes it easy for software to replace or augment the PC's built-in BIOS functions. This is often how drivers loaded from `config.sys` (DOS disk drivers, for example) provide their functionality.

A typical BIOS call first loads specific CPU registers with values defined for that BIOS call. For example, to send a character out of a PC's COM1 serial port, you would load register:

- AL with the character (for example, 31_{16} is an ASCII 1)
- DX with the port (0 for COM1, 1 for COM2, and so on)
- AH with 1 (this specifies that the interrupt 14_{16} *output character* service is to be used)

Then an Int 14_{16} (software interrupt 14_{16}) instruction would be issued (normally, this would be done from a program, but you could do it interactively from the DOS' debugger DEBUG as well), and the character would be output. On return from the interrupt, Register AH has status information, such as whether the call was successful. Previously, another BIOS function (Int 14_{16}, service 0) would have been used to initialize the port (to set the bit rate, the number of data and stop bits per character, and the parity).

The BIOS reserves the first (that is, the lowest, starting at address 0000:0000) $1,024_{10}$ bytes of memory (RAM) for the jump table. There is a possibility of 256 software interrupts (since the Int assembler instruction has a 1-byte field to specify the interrupt number). Each BIOS jump table entry is 4 bytes and specifies the *offset* and *segment* (a 20-bit linear address is formed by shifting the offset 4 bits to the left and adding it to the segment).

The BIOS jump table is therefore 256 4-byte entries, which requires 1,024 bytes total.

An Int 14_{16} (which is Int 20_{10}) looks in the 20th jump table entry, which is memory location 80_{10} (which is 50_{16}) for the address of the BIOS routine to be run to handle the Int 14_{16}. On my PC (and most others), location 50_{16} is storing the value F000:E739 (that is specified in the PC's segment:offset format, which is the same as $FE739_{16}$).

This BIOS routine is in the upper 64 kbytes (which is $F0000_{16}$ to $FFFFF_{16}$) of a PC's first 1 Mbyte of memory (which is 00000_{16} to $FFFFF_{16}$). This is as expected, since the entire BIOS is usually within this upper 64 kbytes. Note that running another operating system (such as OS/2) or loading COM drivers will likely change this *interrupt vector* to point to somewhere else in memory (wherever the entry point for that driver is).

The 256_{10} bytes of memory after the BIOS jump table (that is, from 0040:0000 to 0040:00FF, which is the same as 00400_{16} to $004FF_{16}$) is also reserved by the BIOS. It is used to store system information, such as disk drive and keyboard status. For example, to turn on your keyboard's Num Lock LED, run your debugger (for example, DEBUG from a C:> DOS prompt), and enter E 0040:0017 20. This writes ("enters") 00100000_2 into memory location 00417_{16} which is where (among other things) the keyboard's LED status is stored—and bit 5 is the Num Lock LED. `E 0040:0017 00` will turn off the Num Lock LED. The `Q` command quits out of DEBUG back to DOS.

Since this also writes other bits (such as whether `Insert` is active), you should be running DOS (not Windows) and reboot your PC afterward. Also, do be careful when playing in DEBUG. It is possible (though unlikely) to (for example) write over important parts of your disk drive.

See *ASCII*, *Bootstrap*, *FAT*, *IDE*, *NetBIOS*, *PC*, *PIO*, *RAM*, and *Shadowed BIOS*.

BISYNC
Binary Synchronous Communications

The type of data communications used from older IBM terminals to mainframe computers.

A *character-oriented* (since specific characters such as the STX and ETX control characters have special meanings), synchronous, link layer protocol that provides simple error correction and flow control. There is some disagreement about exactly what BISYNC stands for. Some people say that it gets its name because there are two sync characters before the message (to establish bit, byte, and message synchronization); some say there are two devices involved in the communication; and some say it is because the data are binary. If I knew, I'd tell you. (Say, why do they call a baseball pitcher's warm-up area the bull pen?)

The ASCII and EBCDIC sync characters are different (00010110_2 and 00110010_2, respectively). Which is used depends on the data being carried (IBM uses the EBCDIC sync, everyone else uses the ASCII sync). Both have the same important characteristic that they never look like a shifted copy of themselves (as 00100010 would, for example).

Uses *synchronous* (rather than *asynchronous*) data communications.

Also called BSC.

Weaknesses of BISYNC include the following:

- The difficulty of carrying certain control characters (such as ETX) as data, since they indicate the end of the message
- Support for a window size of only 1 (so higher-speed and longer time-delay links and would provide lower throughput than necessary, since a second block of data cannot be sent until the acknowledgment to the first is received)

HDLC (and its many variations) solves these problems and is a much more powerful and widely implemented *bit-oriented* successor.

See *3270*, *ASCII*, *Asynchronous*, *DLC*, *EBCDIC*, *HDLC*, *Mainframe*, *SDLC*, *Synchronous*, and *V.25bis*.

Bitmap Font

A method of describing the shape of characters.

Also called an *image* or *raster* (as in a television raster, which scans horizontally across, then down a line to scan again) *font*. A nonscalable font (though lousy scaling can be done by duplicating or deleting raster rows).

Video display fonts are bitmap and can be produced on the fly from *outline fonts* by the Adobe Type Manager or TrueType.

Printers usually use outline fonts to provide high-quality scaling. The printers convert the outline fonts to raster while they are printing.

Bitmap fonts are less flexible than outline fonts but often look better, since they can be hand-tuned to produce the best quality output for that specific *point* size. Bitmap fonts will usually display and print faster, since rasterizing is not required.

See *ATM* (*Adobe Type Manager*), *Font*, *Speedo*, *Outline Font*, *Point*, *PostScript Type 1 Fonts*, *PostScript Type 3 Fonts*, *TrueType*, and *Typeface Family*.

BITnet
Because It's There Network or Because It's Time Network

A UUCP-based, worldwide, store-and-forward, email-based, academic-use-oriented network that uses TCP/IP and has a limited connection to the Internet.

See *Internet*.

BLOB
Binary Large Object

A large linear data type, such as a graphical image or multimedia object. That is, it does not have separate components, such as records or fields.

Blue Lightning

IBM's clock-tripled 25-MHz and 33-MHz 486 CPUs. They have 16 kbytes of Level One (internal) cache, a 386 (that is, slower than 486) type bus interface, and no math coprocessor.

See *Intel* and *PC*.

BNC
Bayonet Nut Connector or Bayonet Neil Consulman

The type of connector that is often used for coaxial cables, such as those for Thin-Wire Ethernet or RGB video.

Some say that BNC stands for "Bayonet Nut Connector" (the push and turn action like that used for a Nikon camera lens is often referred to as a bayonet mount, probably because rifle bayonets are mounted that way).

Some say that it stands for "Bayonet Neil Consulman," for the people (person) who developed the Connector (Mr. Bayonet taking the lead, no doubt).

I have also heard that it stands for "Bayonet N Connector," since it is like a quick-connect N connector (an N connector is the large CATV-like connector used on ThickWire Ethernet).

Still others say that the BNC connector was invented by the *Bently Nevada Corporation* (which makes vibration-monitoring equipment for rotating machinery so that you know the ball bearings on your 5,000-horsepower electric motor need replacing before they turn red-hot and seize). Well, Bently Nevada didn't invent the connector and it is not named after them (though they do use the connectors).

In any case, while the mating side of BNC connectors have always had the same dimensions, the side that connects to the cable has different diameters according to the type of coax (RG–58, RG–59, etc.) for which the connector is designed, and whether that coax is to be made of PVC (polyvinyl chloride)—the soft, flammable, plastic type of insulation—or Teflon (which is Dupont's trademarked name for polytetrafluoroethylene, which they call fluorinated ethylene propylene—FEP). Coax cables made of Teflon are nonflammable and have a smaller diameter than PVC coax.

So make sure you order the right kind. (Nothing is more frustrating than a bag of the wrong-size coax connectors—and a job that has to get done by morning.)

See *Coax*, *Connector*, *Ethernet*, *LAN*, and *RGB*.

Bonding
Bandwidth on Demand Interoperability Group

A specification for combining 56,000 (or 64,000) bits/s DS-0 channels from different T1 circuits and resolving the timing differences between them. This provides faster data transmission than a single DS-0.

Because of its support for inverse multiplexing (and its descriptive name), the term "bonding" is also sometimes used to refer to combining the two B channels of a basic-rate ISDN line into a single 128-kbits/s channel.

Sometimes called "bundling."

See *BRI*, *DS-0*, *Inverse Multiplexer*, *ISDN*, and *T1*.

Bootp
Bootstrap Protocol

A TCP/IP protocol that enables (for example) a diskless workstation to learn its IP address from a centrally administered server. DHCP may replace it some day.

See *DHCP* and *IP Address*.

Bootstrap

The term often used for starting a computer, especially one that loads its operating software from disk.

A conundrum: How do you read the operating system (which is basically bits on a disk) from a disk drive when the programs that know how to control and read the disk drive are only on the disk (and not yet in the computer's memory). Sounds impossible, like pulling yourself up off the ground by your own *bootstraps* (those are the straps on the top sides of the boots that help you pull them on).

Somehow, this analogy led the process of starting a computer (especially one with the operating system on disk) to be called bootstrapping and now simply *booting* (not to be confused with what you feel like doing to your computer when it is, shall we say, not exactly enhancing your productivity).

Many solutions to this problem (that is, the one about reading the disk on power-up) have been implemented, but all generally do the following:

- The computer has some nonvolatile memory (that is, it is programmed at the factory, and it never forgets, even after being powered off or the computer going loony) in which is stored a simple disk-reading program. (It usually only looks at a specific location on the disk, such as the very beginning.)
- On power-up, the CPU has been designed to start reading and executing at the location in nonvolatile memory where the disk-reading program is stored (possibly first doing some basic hardware checks). If the disk is *bootable*, then stored at the beginning of the disk is a program (sometimes called a *loader*) that is smarter (and larger).
- This loader is read into memory and, when executed, reads enough of the operating system into memory that the operating system can take care of itself (without so much as a "thank you" to the loader—in fact, the operating system simply writes over the now memory-resident copy of the loader).

IBM calls this process *Initial Program Load* (IPL).

See *BIOS* and *Operating System*.

Border Gateway Protocol   See **BGP**.

Branch Prediction

A technique for increasing the processing speed of computers.

A capability of most new processors with multistage execution units to predict which branch of a conditional jump or loop the processor will take (so it knows which instructions to read ahead and start executing).

Intel's Pentium's *dynamic branch prediction* maintains a table of jump history and assumes that if the processor encounters a jump it has seen before, it will take the same path as before, since most jumps are either almost never taken (for example, they test for error conditions) or taken many times (for example, looping to process some data).

See *Intel* and *Pentium*.

BRI
Basic-Rate Interface

A digital, WAN-oriented data communications service.

An ISDN service that provides two B channels plus one D channel.

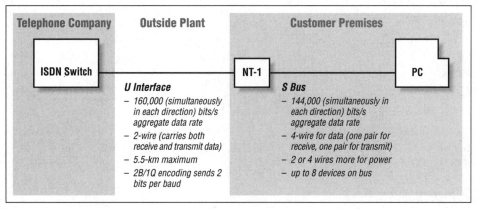

BRI—1

As shown in the accompanying figure, the *S bus* carries a total of 144 kbits/s (2 × 64,000 + 16,000 bits/s), and the U interface carries 160 kbits/s. The extra 16,000 bits/s is used by framing (12 kbits/s) and maintenance (4 kbits/s) overhead.

If the PC does not have an ISDN interface, then a *terminal adapter* can be connected to the S bus. The terminal adapter's EIA-232 (for example) interface could then be connected to a PC's standard COM port. Some terminal adapters have built-in NT-1s.

Some *ISDN adapters* (a card in a PC that provides an ISDN S bus interface from the PC to the outside world) and terminal adapters can split their data over the two B channels so that the data rate is effectively 128 kbits/s. Since this is two telephone calls, double the normal long-distance charges would apply (for long-distance calls). Typically, long-distance charges are the same (per call) as standard analog telephone calls. A compatible device must be used at the other end of the call, as there are no widely accepted standards for such "bonding."

See *Bonding, EIA/TIA-232, ISDN, NT-1, PRI*, and *WAN*.

Broadband ISDN   See **B-ISDN.**

BSD UNIX
Berkeley Software Distribution UNIX

A type (flavor) of UNIX.

University of California at Berkeley's UNIX, the main competitor to USL's SVR4. The most recent version is 4.3BSD. Originated features such as vi, C shell, memory paging, good job control, and networking (TCP/IP, Ethernet).

See *Operating System* and *UNIX.*

BTW
By the Way

A common email abbreviation.

Bugs

While most people are caught up with *software bugs* (things that don't work the way one would expect them to, probably because of a programming mistake), I was surprised to learn that current U.S. standards allow up to 75 insect fragments per 50-gram grain sample (really—check it out for yourself: *BusinessWeek*, September 5, 1994, page 83).

Bulletin Board System   See **BBS.**

Bundling   See **Bonding.**

Bus

A bus is a data communications connection between two or more communicating devices.

Serial buses (which send 1 bit at a time) are typically used for longer distances and (perhaps) lower cost and lower performance. Examples are 10BASE-2 Ethernet LANs, ACCESS.bus, and USB.

Parallel buses send some number of data bits (such as 8 or 16), plus control and address signals, at the same time. Parallel buses are typically more limited in length because of the high cost of the multiconductor cable and connectors and for electrical reasons—the signals don't travel at the exact same speed in all conductors (*signal skew*), so the data rate must be reduced for longer cable runs (making the bus less desirable).

Some parallel buses are implemented by using cables and connectors (for example, IEEE-488 and SCSI). However, the rest of this description will discuss parallel buses that are internal to a PC and implemented on the motherboard of the computers.

A parallel bus is the collection of electrical connections, connectors and voltages, timing, and functionality defined for plug-in printed circuit boards (sometimes called *adapters*) in a computer to communicate with each other.

Each computer platform usually has a unique bus. Some examples are given in the following table.

Manufacturer	Equipment	Bus Used
Apple	Macintosh	NuBus
Compaq and others	80386-based PCs	EISA
DEC	Alpha-based workstations	TurboChannel
IBM and compatible	PC and PC/XT	8-bit XT
IBM and compatible	PC/AT and later	16-bit ISA
IBM and compatible	486 PCs	VL-bus
IBM and compatible	Pentium	PCI
IBM	RS/6000 and PS/2 PCs	MCA
Sun	SPARC workstations	SBus

Some characteristics of PC buses are shown in the following table.

Bus	Released	Bus Speed (MHz)	Data Path Width (bits)	Peak Throughput (Mbytes/s)
XT	1982	4.77	8	2
ISA	1984	8.33	16	8
MCA	1987	10	16	20
			32	40
EISA	1988	8.33	32	33
VL-bus v1.0	1992	33	32	132[a]
		40		148
VL-bus v2.0	1994	50	64	267
PCI v1.0	1993	33	32	132
			64	264
PCI v2.0		66		

[a] 132 Mbytes/s for reads, 66 Mbytes/s for writes.

Some additional comparisons are listed in the following table.

Bus	Address Bus Width (bits)	Interrupts	DMA Channels	Pins
XT.	20[a]	6[b]	3[c]	62
ISA	24[d]	11	7	62 + 36[e]
EISA	32	15	7	100
MCA	32	11	0[f]	182
VL-bus v1.0	32	1	0[g]	116
VL-bus v2.0	64			
PCI v1.0	64[h]	4	0[g]	188[i]

[a] This bus's 20 address lines support only 1 Mbyte of memory.

[b] There are actually eight interrupts, but the highest-priority interrupts 0 and 1 are not brought out to the bus, as they are used for the timer and keyboard (which are implemented on the motherboard). The six remaining interrupts were required for the floppy and hard disk drive controllers, serial ports, and parallel printer port. This does not leave many spare for additional functions, such as LAN adapters and sound boards.

[c] There are actually four DMA channels, but one is permanently assigned to the memory refresh function. Of the three remaining, two of these are required for the floppy and hard disk drive controllers.

[d] This bus's 24 address lines support only 16 Mbytes of memory.

[e] There are two connectors: the original 8-bit bus 62-pin connector and an additional 36-pin connector that provides the extra address, DMA, and interrupt lines.

[f] Up to 16 busmasters are supported (each uses its own DMA controller).

[g] Busmaster DMA is supported, so every adapter can have as many DMA channels as is provided hardware for.

[h] Address and data bus lines are multiplexed together.

[i] Including keys to ensure that 3.3-V and 5-V cards cannot be plugged into the wrong voltage slots.

Finally, what they are typically used for is shown in the following table.

Bus	Suited to
XT	Obsolete, as XT (8088 and 80286) PCs are.
ISA	80386-based PCs (with either less than 16 Mbytes of memory or, more commonly, a proprietary bus for memory)
MCA	PS/2 PC and RS/6000 workstations.
EISA	High-end PCs, such as file servers.
VL-bus	The video adapters (and sometimes SCSI disk controllers or LAN adapters) in 486 PCs. ISA slots are used for other cards (such as serial ports and low-end disk and LAN adapters in these PCs)
PCI	Video adapters, disk controllers, and LAN adapters in Pentium PCs. ISA slots are used for low-end cards in these PCs.

See *ACCESS.bus*, *Bus Master DMA*, *DMA*, *EISA*, *IRQ*, *ISA*, *LAN*, *Local Bus*, *MCA*, *PCI*, *SCSI*, *USB*, and *VL-Bus*.

Bus and Tag Channel   See **Channel.**

Bus Master DMA
Bus Master Direct Memory Access

A method of transferring data between components of a computer system (such as a LAN adapter, the memory, and a disk controller).

A faster data transfer technique (at least for larger transfers) than standard CPU-based DMA, for the following reasons:

- The peripheral (a LAN adapter, for example) writes from its memory directly to the PC's memory in one bus cycle (reducing the load on the bus), rather than the two-step process of the CPU's DMA controller first reading the data (from the adapter) and then writing it to the PC's memory in a second bus cycle.
- Often, the adapter will do its transfer as the data are received from the LAN, so no, or little, on-board LAN adapter memory is required (this saves money).
- Uses much less CPU time than other methods. For example, programmed input-output (PIO) requires the CPU to first check for the availability of the data, then read the data, and then write the data. This requires bus and CPU time for both fetching the CPU's instructions and for reading and writing the data. Also, bus master DMA is faster than standard DMA, since the CPU does not even need to load the DMA registers (for example, with the source and destination addresses) to set up each transfer.

Ungermann-Bass LAN boards use this technique.

Since the peripheral writes directly to the PC's RAM, the peripheral does not get the benefit of the CPU's memory mapping (for example, an 80386 processor's mapping of extended memory into the upper memory space between 640 kbytes and 1 Mbyte). Therefore bus mastering DMA controllers must usually write into conventional (below 640 kbytes) memory, since it is not memory-mapped (and the drivers may not work when loaded into high memory).

Also, the AT bus supports only one bus mastering controller (since there is no provision for arbitrating between two simultaneously requesting bus master devices).

Burst mode allows more than one data transfer cycle to take place without releasing the bus back to the CPU (though with a maximum time per burst, such as 15 ms for the MCA bus).

Streaming mode allows a block of sequential data (which most blocks are) to be transferred (perhaps in burst mode), sending only the starting address of the block at the beginning of the transfer. (Having to put the address on the bus only once per block of data speeds up the transfer.)

Data multiplexing (during a streaming mode transfer) allows the data and address lines to carry data (since they are needed only to carry address information once, at the beginning of the block), allowing more data to be transferred per cycle (perhaps 64 bits rather than 32 bits).

For smaller transfers, the time taken to set up all the DMA controller registers may be longer than the time saved by using DMA, so using programmed I/O (in which the CPU handles each byte) may be faster than DMA.

See *Bus*, *DMA*, *PIO*, and *PC*.

Cable

A cable is typically two or more insulated *wires* (electrical conductors) held together and protected by an overall *jacket*.

Many types of cables are commonly used for data transmission, as summarized in the accompanying figure.

The use of cabling in buildings is covered by the following standards:

- EIA/TIA-568 *Commercial Building Telecommunications Wiring Standard*. Also EIA/TIA's TSB-36 Technical Service Bulletin *Additional Cable Specifications for Unshielded Twisted Pair Cables*. The similar Canadian standard is CAN/CSA-T529-M91 *Design Guidelines for Telecommunications Wiring Systems in Commercial Buildings*. These standards cover the technical requirements for cabling.

- EIA/TIA-569 *Commercial Building Standard for Telecommunications Pathways and Spaces*. The similar Canadian standard is CAN/CSA-T530-M90 *Building Facilities, Design Guidelines for Telecommunications*. These standards cover the building architectural requirements for cabling systems.

See *10BASE-T, 100BASE-TX, ARCnet, CATV, Coax, Connector, EIA/TIA-232, Ethernet, STP, Tip and Ring, Token Ring, TSB*, and *UTP*.

Cache

Faster-access memory used to temporarily store information to provide a faster response time. There are many types of caches.

Disk caches are used to store data recently read from or written to a disk, to speed up writes and subsequent reads. There are several implementations. They all use RAM (usually ¼ to 16 Mbytes) to speed up disk accesses. The disk cache memory may be on the disk controller, part of the disk drive, or the main processor memory (and the caching done by the disk driver software or a TSR).

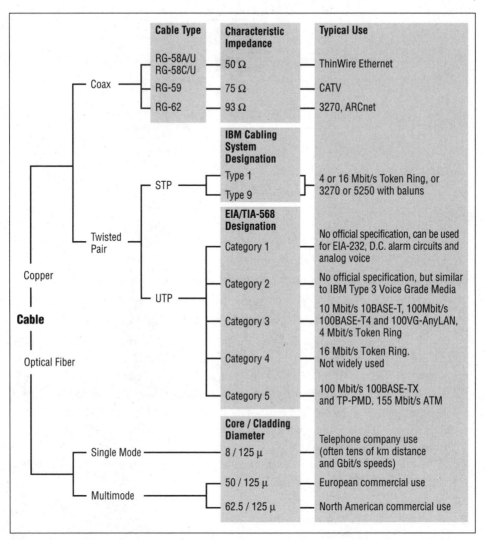

Cable Type	Characteristic Impedance	Typical Use
RG-58A/U RG-58C/U	50 Ω	ThinWire Ethernet
RG-59	75 Ω	CATV
RG-62	93 Ω	3270, ARCnet

Coax

IBM Cabling System Designation	Typical Use
Type 1	4 or 16 Mbit/s Token Ring, or 3270 or 5250 with baluns
Type 9	

STP

EIA/TIA-568 Designation	Typical Use
Category 1	No official specification, can be used for EIA-232, D.C. alarm circuits and analog voice
Category 2	No official specification, but similar to IBM Type 3 Voice Grade Media
Category 3	10 Mbit/s 10BASE-T, 100Mbit/s 100BASE-T4 and 100VG-AnyLAN, 4 Mbit/s Token Ring
Category 4	16 Mbit/s Token Ring. Not widely used
Category 5	100 Mbit/s 100BASE-TX and TP-PMD, 155 Mbit/s ATM

UTP — Twisted Pair — Copper — Cable — Optical Fiber

Core / Cladding Diameter	Typical Use
8 / 125 μ	Telephone company use (often tens of km distance and Gbit/s speeds)
50 / 125 μ	European commercial use
62.5 / 125 μ	North American commercial use

Single Mode / Multimode

Cable–1

Write-behind or *write-back* disk caching initially writes data to RAM (freeing the application to continue immediately, as if the data had been written to disk). The data are later automatically written to disk (usually within a few seconds) either timed, or when the cache holds a preset percentage of unwritten data. This reduces the possibility that a problem (such as a power failure) will prevent the data from being successfully written to disk.

Write-through caching always writes directly to disk, ensuring that the application is never tricked into believing that the data are on disk when they may not be. This results in the highest data integrity, though with slightly reduced performance.

In both cases, cached data are read directly from the RAM.

Look-ahead caching (or *buffering*) reads disk sectors ahead of those requested, on the assumption that those will soon be requested. *Segmented look-ahead* can store several such look-aheads. This is important for multitasking computers, which may interrupt a long sequential disk read to service another task.

A common measure of a cache's effectiveness is the *hit rate*—the percentage of disk accesses that are served by RAM.

CPU memory caches are a small amount (typically 1 to 512 kbytes) of very high-speed RAM that the CPU can typically access at its full clock speed. Current processors are usually much faster than the main RAM, so *wait states* (in which the processor waits a few clock cycles) must be added to leave time for the slower main RAM to respond.

A *look-aside cache* design puts a request to both the cache and main memory at the same time so that if the cache does not contain the required data, the request to main memory is already in progress. The lower performance *look-through* design does not begin the main RAM access until it has been determined that the cache does not have the required data.

Write-through caches cache only reads from memory. Writes must wait until data have been written to main memory (since the data are "written through" the cache to main memory). This is a bigger problem on multiprocessor systems because of memory bus contention.

Posted write-through or *write-back caches* cache data both read from and written to memory. Written (and therefore cached) data are written (also called "flushed") to main memory later (depending on the cache design, perhaps when another bus master device tries to read that main memory location or when the data have been in the cache for too long). This type is generally faster than write-through.

A *direct-mapped cache* design maps each location in main memory to a cache location. If two main memory locations compete for the same cache location, then only one main memory location gets cached.

A *two-way set-associative cache* has two locations in cache for each main memory location. If both main memory locations are to be cached, then one goes into the alternative cache location.

Four-way set-associative designs extend this to four possible cache locations for each main memory location, increasing the possibility that data will be available in the cache but increasing the time needed to search the cache.

Fully-associative cache lets any block of memory be cached anywhere in the cache.

A problem with all CPU memory caches and (especially preemptive) multitasking operating systems is that when the processor switches tasks, the entire cache becomes mostly useless, reducing the benefit of caching. Larger or switchable caches may solve this problem.

Recent CPUs typically have 1 to 32 kbytes of cache built in to the same integrated circuit chippy as the processor itself. This is called *Level 1 cache*.

Tests show that there is a substantial performance improvement if there is more cache, but it is too expensive to make Level 1 cache larger (increasing the chance of a bad memory cell, making the whole IC useless), so external but very fast memory is added. This *Level 2 cache* is usually 128 kbytes to 1 Mbyte in size.

Many other types of caching are done by application programs and protocol software, such as the following:

- An *ARP cache* remembers the mapping of IP addresses to MAC addresses, so the ARP process does not need to be repeated
- *Name caching* remembers which network names (such as NetBIOS names) are at which locations, so broadcasts need not be sent over WAN links every time a new station starts up and picks a name (to ensure the name is not already taken)
- *Route caching* remembers which path (through which bridges) Token Ring frames should be sent, so the route discovery process does not need to be repeated

See *Alpha AXP, ARP, DLSw, NetBIOS, PC, PowerPC, RAM,* and *Token Ring.*

Cairo

Microsoft's interim name for its major upgrade to Windows NT. Will be object-oriented. Will support symmetric multiprocessing, X.500 directory services, and Intel, MIPS, and PowerPC platforms.

May be released in 1997.

See *Intel, Operating System, PowerPC, SMP, Windows NT,* and *X.500.*

Canadian Intellectual Property Office   See **CIPO.**

Canadian Internet   See **CA*net.**

Canadian Open Systems Application Criteria   See **COSAC.**

Canadian Radio-Television and Telecommunications Commission   See **CRTC.**

CANARIE
Canadian Network for the Advancement of Research, Industry, and Education

An initiative first proposed in 1988 to link Canadian universities and research organizations. Now a private, federally incorporated nonprofit organization with the mandate to support the development of the information highway and to provide collaboration between the Canadian information technology industry and the federal government.

Established in March 1993 and run by a 15-person board, has more than 140 fee-paying members ($2,500 to $20,000, depending on the size and type of organization). Members include:

- Industry (carriers and information technology and content providers)
- Institutions (universities, nonprofit corporations, provincial and federal government departments)
- Nonvoting associate members (suppliers, consultants, etc.)

Will be merging with CA*net Inc.

Several phases of the upgrading of CA*net have been defined (and some have been completed), as shown in the following table.

Phase	Objectives
I	Upgraded CA*net's leased backbone network, which connects to 10 regional network nodes, to T1 (1.544 Mbits/s). This was completed in 1994. Funded partly by user fees paid by the regional networks, partly by federal government funding through CANARIE.
	Development of new user-friendly products, applications, and services for regional network users.
	Technology Development and Diffusion, a matching-funds program to support industry development of innovative high-speed networking products, such as advanced networking technologies, applications software, and services.
	Establishment of a high-speed experimental test bed network to act as laboratories in high-speed networking (such as ATM). Stentor and Unitel provided T3 circuits starting in 1994 to link OCRInet (in Ottawa) and Rnet (British Columbia). Other projects elsewhere in Canada may be connected later.
II	Upgrade CA*net's leased backbone network to T3.
	Stimulation of the development and use of new networking technologies, products, applications, software, and services that will either use or support a national communication network.
	Operation of the experimental test networks.
	Prepare detailed plans for Phase III.
III	Upgrade CA*net to Gbits/s speeds.
	Migrating technologies developed during earlier phases to commercial use.

The Phase I projects were funded by a $26 million contribution from the federal government plus anticipated contributions of $87 million from CANARIE members, clients, and project participants.

Phase II was funded by an $80 million contribution from the Department of Industry (announced in December 1994). Phase II ends in 1999.

CANARIE has the features shown in the following table.

An operational network	Interconnecting the 10 regional hubs and the Internet (with connections to the U.S. from Vancouver, Toronto, and Montréal).
A high-speed test network	A national and regional test network for the collaboration of public and private organizations in exploring new hardware and software.
A funding program	From both public and private sources.

CANARIE maintains a WWW site at *http://www.canarie.ca/*.

See *Internet*, *T1*, and *T3*.

CA*net
Canadian Internet

The part of the Internet backbone that is in Canada. Established in 1989. Managed by the University of Toronto Computing Services Department. Links Canadian universities and commercial institutions. Actual communication circuits are provided by the Canadian network reseller Integrated Network Services (INSINC) as a result of competitive bidding in 1990 and again in 1994.

Has 10 regional hubs for the regional networks shown in the following table.

NLnet	Newfoundland and Labrador Network
NSTN	Nova Scotia Technology Network
PEInet	Prince Edward Island Network
nb*net	New Brunswick Network
RISQ	Réseau Interordinateurs Scientifique
ONet	Ontario Network
MBnet	Manitoba Network
SASK#net	Saskatchewan Network
ARnet	Alberta Research Network
BCnet	British Columbia Network

Each regional network is responsible for establishing its own acceptable use policy (there are significant differences between the various AUPs) and provides access for local Schoolnets, Free-Nets, community networks, universities, and other organizations. Used to use 56-kbits/s leased lines, but upgraded to T1 lines by mid-1994 as part of the CANARIE initiative.

Growing at about 14% per month. Replaced NetNorth and CDNNet. Run by CA*net Networking Inc., which will be merging with CANARIE Inc.

They have a WWW Server at *http://www.canet.ca/*.

See *CANARIE, DNS)Domain Name System), ISP,* and *Internet.*

CardBus

The new name for the higher-speed PCMCIA (or PC Card) interface.

See *PCMCIA.*

Carrier

A public communications service provider, such as a telephone company. Many have WWW servers (some with excellent data communications information or pointers). Examples are listed in the following table.

Telephone Company	WWW Server URL
Ameritech	*http://www.aads.net*
AT&T	*http://www.att.com*
BCTel	*http://www.bctel.com*
Bell Atlantic	*http://www.bell-atl.com* and *http://www.ba.com*
Bell Canada	*http://www.bell.ca*
Bellcore	*http://www.bellcore.com*
BellSouth	*http://www.bst.bls.com*
McCaw Cellular	*http://www.airdata.com*
MCI	*http://www.mci.com*
Pacific Bell	*http://www.PacBell.com* and *http://www.pacbell.com/Products/fastrak.htm*
RBOCs	*http://www.bell.com/bells.html*
SaskTel	*http://www.sasknet.sk.ca*
Southwestern Bell	*http://www.sbc.com* and *http://www.tri.sbc.com*

(table continued on next page)

Telephone Company	WWW Server URL
Sprint	*http://www.sprintlink.net*
Stentor	*http://www.stentor.ca*
Teleglobe Canada	*http://www.teleglobe.ca*
US West	*http://usw.interact.net* and *http://www.service.com/cm/uswest/home.html*
WilTel	*http://www.wiltel.com*

See *AT&T, CPE, IXC, LEC, POP, POTS, RBOC, Stentor, Teleglobe, Inc., Telephone Companies*, and *Telesat Canada.*

CAS
Communicating Applications Specification

The software interface to a fax board.

An API specification developed by Intel and Digital Communications Associates to provide support for programs sending data to other devices and computers. The initial (and likely only) versions of the specification only describe functions for a program to interact with a fax modem board.

Supported by Intel's Satisfaxtion boards (cute name, not a very popular standard though).

Competes with Class 1, 2, and 2.0.

A copy of the specification is at *ftp://ftp.faximum.com/pub/documents/cas.txt.*

See *API* and *Fax*.

CATV
Community Antenna Television

Standard cable TV, which currently brings lots of entertainment (!) to your home television. Maybe someday it will bring Internet access and telephone service too.

In the beginning, it was just a big antenna shared by a community, with a coaxial cable bringing the signal to everyone's house. Now, with pressure to cram more channels into the cable, it gets more complicated (cable converters, pay-TV decoders).

It all starts with standard broadcast television, which has two main frequency bands:

- VHF (very high frequency), which provides Channels 2 through 13 in the frequency range 54 to 216 MHz

- UHF (ultra high frequency), which provides Channels 14 through 69, in the range 470 to 806 MHz. (It used to go up to Channel 83, 890 MHz, but the top 14 channels were reallocated in 1974 to make spectrum available for cellular telephone service, which is officially called AMPS.)

As is shown in the table below, the radio frequency spectrum assigned to broadcast channels 2 through 69 is not contiguous. There are several reasons for this:

- Frequencies are usually assigned lowest first (these are the most desirable, since electronic equipment is easier to design for lower frequencies and lower frequencies usually travel the farthest). By the time television needed more channels, other services (such as amateur radio and the police) had been assigned frequencies.
- Even the original television broadcast band had gaps to ensure that no television channels existed at the second harmonic (double the frequency) of other channels (this simplifies the design of television tuners—which reduces their cost).
- Some frequencies have physical significance for studies such as radio astronomy and so are not available for assignment.

Since cable TV providers want to provide as many television channels as possible (and each channel requires 6 MHz of bandwidth), and since it is expensive to provide a greater range of frequencies (the cable attenuates higher frequencies more, and higher-frequency amplifiers are more expensive), cable TV services move channels to different frequencies.

For example, on cable, channels 14 through 22 are shifted down into the space between channels 6 and 7. For televisions with a built-in cable TV converter, you must tell the television whether it is receiving its signal from cable TV or not so that it knows which frequency to tune to. For example, as is shown in the table, channel 14 uses 470 to 476 MHz when broadcast but is moved to 120 to 126 MHz when on cable. So if there is a power failure, your television or VCR forgets that you are on cable, and that's why you don't get what you expected (except for channels 2 through 13, which don't get moved).

CATV uses 75Ω impedance coaxial cable. For residential installations, RG-59 cable and Type F connectors are used (that's the official name for the coaxial cable connector on the back of your TV). Distribution systems (which bring the signal along the street, to your house) require amplifiers. These are mounted in aluminum enclosures that are ½-meter wide × 20 cm high × 10 cm thick and either hang from an aerial CATV cable or are placed in a (usually green cylindrical or brown rectangular) *pedestal* (the meter-high enclosures sprouting from people's lawns, near the street). They are typically powered by 60-V, 60-Hz power sent along the coaxial cable from battery backed-up power supplies (you often see these small-suitcase-sized enclosures mounted on hydro poles, where they get their power), with a 2-cm diameter coaxial cable running out (bringing the power to a three-port coupler that connects to the distribution cable).

Some CATV systems carry a *reverse channel* (often from 5 to 42 MHz), which brings signals back from customers to the CATV head-end (perhaps for interactive TV, or to support Internet access). This requires separate amplifiers, which are mounted in the same enclosures as the forward channel amplifiers. Therefore it costs money to provide this capability.

Some CATV people say that future systems will put 6 to 12 digitized, compressed television channels in the 6-MHz bandwidth that is currently occupied by a single television channel. This way, CATV systems could offer hundreds of channels, and compete with the 500-channel satellite dishes that threaten to put cable TV out of business.

The cost of such compression equipment (and especially of decompression, since every television would need it), development and deployment of HDTV, quality of picture required, and many other factors will all affect what eventually happens with compressed video CATV systems.

Cable Television Laboratories, Inc. ("CableLabs") was established in May 1988 as a research and development consortium of cable television system operators. It has a WWW server at *http://www.cablelabs.com/*.

Broadcast		Frequency (MHz)		CATV Channel	Comments
Use	TV Channel	From	To		
VHF TV	2	54	60	2	Channels 2 through 13 use the same frequencies and channel numbers for both broadcast and CATV use
	3	60	66	3	
	4	66	72	4	
Private radio	Not used for broad-cast TV	72	76	1	This 4-MHz chunk is too small for an entire CATV channel and so is not used
VHF TV	5	76	82	5	
	6	82	88	6	

(table continued on next page)

Broadcast		Frequency (MHz)		CATV Channel	Comments
Use	TV Channel	From	To		
FM radio	Not used for broadcast TV	88.1		FM Radio	Most CATV systems carry FM radio stations instead of CATV television channels 95, 96, and 97
		88.3			
		88.5			
		and so on, through to 107.7			
		107.9			
		90	96	95	Not usually used for CATV (see above)
		96	102	96	
		102	108	97	
Private radio		108	114	98	Not usually used for CATV
		114	120	99	
		120	126	14	With a cable TV converter (which can tune to these channels and convert them to one that a standard television tuner can receive, usually channel 3 or 4), these channels are also available. A 21-channel system therefore also requires a 216-MHz CATV system (see below).
		126	132	15	
		132	138	16	
		138	144	17	
		144	150	18	
		150	156	19	
		156	162	20	
		162	168	21	
		168	174	22	
VHF TV	7	174	180	7	12-channel CATV systems require a bandwidth of 216 MHz to carry channels 2 through 13
	8	180	186	8	
	9	186	192	9	
	10	192	198	10	
	11	198	204	11	
	12	204	210	12	
	13	210	216	13	

(table continued on next page)

Broadcast		Frequency (MHz)		CATV Channel	Comments
Use	TV Channel	From	To		
Private radio	Not used for broad- cast TV	216	222	23	A 35-channel system requires a bandwidth of 300 MHz
		222	228	24	
		228	234	25	
		and so on, up to			
		288	294	35	
		294	300	36	
		300	306	37	A 60-channel CATV system requires a bandwidth of 450 MHz
		and so on, up to			
		438	444	60	
		444	450	61	
		450	456	62	
UHF TV	14	470	476		The UHF broadcast channels start at 470 MHz
	15	476	480		
	16	480	486		
	and so on, up to channel 69				
		534	540	76	A 75-channel CATV system requires a bandwidth of 540 MHz
		618	624	90	A 90-channel CATV system requires a bandwidth of 625 MHz
		744	750	111	A 110-channel CATV system requires a bandwidth of 750 MHz
	68	794	800		
	69	800	806		Highest broadcast UHF channel. Since lower frequencies travel farther, most UHF stations choose low frequencies
Cellular tele- phone		824			
	82	878	884		
	83	884	890		UHF used to go up to channel 83, but cellular telephones were assigned those frequencies (824 to 894 MHz)

(table continued on next page)

Broadcast		Frequency (MHz)		CATV Channel	Comments
Use	TV Channel	From	To		
Private radio	Not used for TV	996	1,002	153	A 1–GHz CATV system can carry about 152 channels (numbering starts at 2)

See *AMPS*, *Coax*, *Connector*, *FCC*, *HDTV*, and *NTSC*.

CCIR
Comité Consultatif International Radio

The previous name for the ITU-R. Also called the *International Radio Consultative Committee*.

See *ITU*.

CCITT
Comité Consultatif International Télégraphique et Téléphonique

The previous name for the ITU-T.

Also called the *International Telegraphy and Telephony Consultative Committee*.

See *ITU* and *ITU-T*.

CCP
Compression Control Protocol

A method for negotiating data compression over PPP links so that multiple data compression algorithms (including open methods, such as V.42*bis*, and proprietary methods, such as Stac Electronics, both of which have a typical maximum compression ratio of 4:1) can be supported.

Both switched and dedicated (leased line) circuits are supported. Part of the negotiation process is that if one end of a link does not support data compression, then the connection will work, it just won't get any data compression.

For example, a router with built-in data compression could communicate over a WAN link with another router that has external data compression (by a V.42*bis* modem or a DSU with built-in LZS). Or two routers from different manufacturers could communicate over a WAN, while using their built-in data compression.

See *Data Compression*, *DSU*, *LZS*, *PPP*, *Stac*, *V.42bis*, and *WAN*.

CDE
Common Desktop Environment

A common UNIX graphical desktop environment approved by X/Open. The intent is to define a standard UNIX platform so that the UNIX industry can compete with Microsoft (especially Windows NT, which competes with UNIX most directly). The hope is that on the basis of CDE, *shrink-wrapped* (binary compatible) UNIX software will be possible, just like the PC industry has.

As it is, there are so many flavors of UNIX that shrink-wrapped software is not currently possible.

The effort includes the following:

- The X Window System functionality (the X11R5 version) and window management
- A single set of APIs (including messaging and drag-and-drop support)
- A visual-oriented scripting language
- A single graphical user interface (based on Motif version 1.2.3)
- A common look and feel (file management, online help, internationalization)

As of Fall 1995, no complete implementations were commercially available.

It is based on the following (these companies are the main proponents—I sure hope this stuff glues together cleanly):

- HP's *Visual User Environment*
- IBM's *Common User Access* model
- Novell's *UnixWare client tools*
- Sunsoft's (part of Sun Microsystems) *Deskset tools*

Some further information can be found at *http://www.austin.ibm.com/powerteam/tech/ aixpert/aug94/aixpert_aug94_CDE.html* and *http://www.lib.ox.ac.uk/internet/news/faq/archive/ cde-cose-faq.html/*.

The CDE effort is the main product of COSE.

See *API, COSE, DEC, Motif, Portability, UNIX, X/Open*, and *X*.

CDMA
Code Division Multiple Access

An improvement on AMPS and TDMA cellular telephone. Uses a technology called direct sequence *spread spectrum* to provide more conversations for a given amount of bandwidth and digital service.

Defines 64 channels (forward direction, transmitted from base station), which support a maximum of 63 simultaneous users, per 1.25-MHz frequency band taken from the standard AMPS allocation (this is 42 standard AMPS channels, which is 10% of an operator's 12.5-MHz bandwidth).

Mobiles simultaneously communicate with both base stations (the new one and the soon-to-be-previous one) before a handoff (constantly receiving whichever signal is stronger), providing a *soft handoff*, which eliminates the gap inherent in AMPS' break-before-make scheme.

Initial development indicated that each mobile had to have a carefully selected pseudo-random *spreading code* (to reduce interference with other users); hence the name (perhaps it should be called spread spectrum multiple access). Now uses a $2^{41}-1$ bit spreading code (which is the same for every user, but every user starts at a different place in the pattern), and every mobile is factory-assigned a worldwide unique starting point. System engineering (for example, limiting the number of active users and ensuring that all users have equal transmit power) ensures that interference is limited.

Voice is digitized at 8,000 bits/s. With overhead, this requires a raw data rate of 9,600 bits/s per mobile.

Requires that the base stations and mobiles be synchronized to within 0.8 μs. This is accomplished by reserving one of the forward channels to carry a synchronizing code (and transmitting it at six times the signal strength of the other channels so that it is easier to find).

Uses GPS to synchronize the time between base stations.

Can fit about 130 conversations (assuming that because the gaps in an individual conversation and their half-duplex nature, a conversation is active less than 40% of the time) into the 42 AMPS channels' bandwidth. In contrast, because of the typical 1 in 7 frequency reuse (to avoid interference with adjacent *sectors* or cells), an AMPS system could have only six conversations in these 42 channels.

CDMA therefore provides an improvement by a factor of almost 22 times (quick—buy some of that company's stock). In actual implementation (due to fading, etc.), the improvement may only be 10 (some say 15) times (oops, this technology stuff is so risky).

Developed and promoted by Qualcomm (which has a WWW server at *http://www.qualcomm.com/*).

Defined in IS-95. Data transmission capability has not yet been developed.

Competes with GSM.

See *AMPS*, *CDPD*, *ESMR*, *GPS*, *GSM*, and *TDMA*.

CDPD
Cellular Digital Packet Data

A method proposed (1993) and developed by IBM and McCaw Cellular Communications, Inc. (now owned by AT&T) to more efficiently carry data on existing analog (AMPS) cellular radio systems.

138-byte packets of data are sent at 19,200 bits/s during gaps in conversations or on unused (no voice conversation established at that time) channels, using the full 30-kHz bandwidth of the channel. Voice always has priority.

Actual air traffic consists of blocks of 63 (47 are information, 16 are *forward error correction* information) six-bit symbols, resulting in a user data rate of about 9,000 to 14,400 bits/s. The forward error correction can correct up to eight six-bit symbol errors.

Advantages over Ardis and Mobitex include the following:

- Use of the existing cellular radio infrastructure (CDPD overlays it), resulting in lower usage charges
- Built-in encryption and authentication
- The *land-line* interface is TCP/IP
- Security, since the data for a conversation are carried over many cellular radio channels (according to whichever has spare capacity), so it would be difficult to monitor the communication
- V.42*bis* data compression
- Multicasting (to subsets of users)
- A full-duplex option

Will be an open specification that will compete with the proprietary systems from Ardis and RAM. May be available in 1996. Is a packet-oriented service, so the call setup time is fast (much faster than circuit-switched), charging is by the kilobyte of traffic carried, and it is best-suited to smaller transactions (up to 5 kbytes of data— larger transfers are better handled by circuit-switched methods, such as analog cellular with modems).

Promoted by five of the seven U.S. RBOCs and Motorola, Microcom, and some cable TV companies.

See *AMPS, Ardis, Authentication, CDMA, Encryption, ESMR, GSM, Mobitex, RAM Mobile Data*, and *TDMA*.

CD-ROM
Compact Disc, Read-Only Memory

One of many formats based on the same technology that is used for standard audio compact discs.

A 120-mm (4.72") diameter, 1.2-mm-thick polycarbonate plastic disk coated with reflective aluminum (so that the *pits* and *lands* can be read by a *laser diode*). The table at the end of this definition shows the many formats.

A standard *Mode 1* CD-ROM stores up to 74 minutes of audio (depending on how close to the outer edge of the CD-ROM data are stored—manufacturing is more difficult if they are too close), which is the same as up to 333,000 2,048-byte *sectors* of data (681,984,000 bytes), which is 650 Mbytes (where 1 Mbyte is 1,024 × 1,024 bytes), plus a whole lot of error detection and correction, directory, and other bits.

Mode 2 CD-ROMs don't store error detection and correction bits and can therefore store more data (333,000 2,336-byte sectors, which is 741 Mbytes). This would be done only for audio or video, for which bit-errors would not be a problem, or when there is another error detection scheme.

Other than capacity, another significant specification for a CD-ROM drive is the *access time*, which is the sum of the *seek time* (time for the drive's read/write head to move from its current position to the track to be read next) plus the *rotational latency* (time for the disk to rotate to the starting position for the next data).

Higher *data transfer rates* are obtained by spinning the CD-ROM faster (this also improves the access time). The rotational latency is usually specified as half the time for a full rotation of the disk (since this is the average needed to access data located at a random location on a given track).

The seek time may be given as the time for:

- *Full-stroke*: the time to move the read/write head over the entire disk surface, for example, the most inside track to the very outside track
- *½-stroke* or *⅓-stroke*: the time to move the read/write head over one-half or one-third of the disk surface
- *Track-to-track*: the time to move a single track

The relevant specification depends on where the data are. For example:

- If large amounts of contiguous data are to be read, then track-to-track may be most relevant
- If data at a random location on the disk are to be read, then ½-stroke may be most relevant
- If the disk's directory information is located near the disk's middle track (a smart thing to do to minimize the average seek distances) and the directory needs to be read before almost every seek, then ⅓-stroke may be best

Most drive specifications in published product literature exclude the rotational latency when quoting "access times" (they should then be calling it the seek time but usually don't) and don't clearly state whether full-, ½-, or ⅓-stroke seek times are being provided.

So have fun comparing disk drive specifications, and good luck. For the record, a typical fast CD-ROM will have a full-stroke seek time of 250 ms and a ⅓-stroke seek time of 125 ms.

Data are stored on a CD–ROM starting at the center, and spiraling out (with only 1.6 μm between spirals—the spiral is over 5 km long). In contrast, a standard magnetic hard disk stores data in concentric rings, called *tracks*.

The bits on a CD–ROM are recorded as *pits*, which are each:

- 0.5 μm × 0.833 to 3.054 μm long (much smaller than an eensy-weensy spider)
- ¼-wavelength deep, so even if light does reflect off the bottom of the pit, the reflected light produces destructive interference (since it will differ in phase by ½-wavelength), so very little light will reflect back

These pits are read by using a 780-nm laser diode (this is infrared light and therefore invisible, as is the light from your TV remote control's infrared LED).

Also unlike standard magnetic hard disks, a CD–ROM drive uses *Constant Linear Velocity* (CLV), so the CD–ROM must spin faster (about 1,000 rpm) when reading near the center of the CD–ROM and slower (about 400 rpm) when reading near the outside of the CD–ROM (these values are for a double-speed drive). This provides the maximum possible capacity, but the requirement to change the speed of the disk rotation when seeking to different tracks increases a CD–ROM's seek time (this is not a problem for audio CD–ROMs, which usually play an entire song at a time—one long spiral, with no sudden track changes).

ISO's IS-9660 standard specifies the CD–ROM disk format, is based on the previous *High Sierra* format, and has two levels.

ISO IS-9660 *Level One* specifies the following:

- Directory names and filenames can use only uppercase letters, the numbers, and "_" (no special characters such as $, -, +, =, ~, !, @, #, or a space)
- Filenames are MS-DOS-style "8.3"—either the filename or the extension (but not both) can be empty (but usually neither is empty)
- Directory names are eight characters only (no extension)
- Filenames include a 15-bit *file version number* (from 1 to to 32,767), using the DEC-VAX-style of separating the filename and version with a semicolon—for example, `filename.txt;15` (most file systems do not support this feature)
- Up to seven levels of subdirectories plus the root- (or top-) level directory (to make eight levels total)

ISO IS-9660 Level Two supports:

- More than one period in a filename
- Up to 32 characters per filename

Level Two CD–ROMs are not supported by MS-DOS.

Microsoft's `mscdex` (*Microsoft CD-ROM extension*) provides CD–ROM support for MS-DOS.

Original CD-ROM drives read at 150 kbytes/s, but double-speed (300 kbytes/s), triple-speed, and faster drives are now common.

Multisession capability means that data can be added (as long as there is room) to the disk incrementally (for example, new pictures added to a Photo-CD that already has some pictures on it).

Audio CD-ROMs (developed in 1981) and the initial extensions for computer data storage were developed by Sony and Philips.

Some additional information is in *ftp://ftp.cdrom.com/README, ftp://ftp.cdrom.com/pub/cdrom/readme.txt, http://www.cd-info.com/cd-info/CDInfoCenter.html, ftp://cs.uwp.edu/pub/cdrom*, and *ftp://ftp.apple.com/cdrom/README*.

The CD-ROM FAQ is in *ftp://ftp.cdrom.com/pub/cdrom/faq/faq1* (or another file with a name similar to that, in that directory) or *http://saturn.uaamath.alaska.edu/~gibbsg/cdromlan_FAQ.html/*.

The following table lists CD formats and their uses.

Format	Use
3DO	A new game format that has better colors, resolution, and sound than Sega CD or CD-I.
CD Audio or CD-DA	Standard digital audio CDs (sometimes called *Red Book*), these usually have "Digital Audio" printed below the disk logo. Stores data in 2,352-byte sectors, as two channels (which provides stereo) of PCM-digitized audio, each channel at 44,100 16-bit samples per second. The playback rate is therefore (44,100 samples/s × 16 bits/s × 2 channels =) 176,400 bytes/s, which is 75 sectors/s. Developed by Sony and Philips and standardized in IEC 908, which is called *Compact Disc Digital Audio Standard*.
CD-E	Erasable and can then be rewritten.
CD+G	Provides low-resolution still images on a conventional audio CD useful for karaoke sing-alongs. Not widely used.
CD-I	CD-interactive (sometimes called *Green Book*) disks that store interleaved text, stereo sound and video (and software) and currently run only on Philips and Magnavox CD-I players. Intended for consumer multimedia and home entertainment systems. Uses MPEG-1 and requires an MPEG decoder IC to handle the decompression of the video. Standardized by the American CD-I Association, 213-444-6619. Philips has information at 800-845-7301. Further information is at *ftp://ftp.cdrom.com/pub/cdrom/cdi*.
CD+MIDI	Can play through MIDI synthesizers. Not widely used.

(table continued on next page)

Format	Use
CD-R, CD-MO, or CD-WO	CD-recordable (sometimes called *Orange Book*), which can be *magneto-optical* ("Part I," which are rewritable) or *write-once* ("Part II," or hybrid disk, which can be written once only). Kodak's Photo-CD uses the write-only CD-R format. A CD-ROM that is *recordable* using a $1,000 to $10,000 recorder attached to a standard PC. So that a low-powered laser diode can record on it, gold, rather than aluminum, is used as the reflective surface (making the disks gold- rather than silver-colored). Both types can have an area permanently written (using the Red, Yellow, or Green Book standards) when the disk is manufactured. The user-recordable area gets a TOC (table of contents) written for each recording session (requiring a CD-ROM drive with *multisession* capability to read recording sessions after the first). Two sizes are available: a 63-minute disk (550 Mbytes) and a 74-minute disk (650 Mbytes). Can be read by standard CD audio and CD-ROM drives. Kodak's Photo-CD is an example of CD-WO technology. Sometimes called WORM: "Write once, read mostly" (or "many"). Developed by Philips and Sony, with specifications available only to their licensees.
CD-ROM	Standard computer CD-ROMs (sometimes called *Yellow Book*). Can only have *Mode 1* data sectors (that is, they have error-detection and -correction information) and therefore store only 2,048 bytes per sector. For "single-speed" CD-ROM drives, the playback data rate is therefore (75 sectors/s × 2,048 bytes/sector =) 153,600 bytes/s, which is 150 kbytes/s (where a "k" is 1,024 bytes). Developed by Sony and Philips, and standardized in ISO 10149.
CD-ROM XA	CD-ROM extended architecture. A standard for interleaving audio and video while maintaining synchronization between them ("lip-sync"). Uses *Mode 2* sectors (sectors without error-detection and -correction), which can be *Form 1* (which are like *Mode 1* sectors, in that they have 2,048 bytes of data plus error-detection and -correction bytes)—Kodak's Photo-CD uses this format—or *Form 2* (which have 2,324 bytes of data—usually digitized audio or video). Interleaved, on the same CD-ROM. The CD-ROM drive usually plays the audio directly and passes the other information to the computer. Is a subset of CD-I and an extension to the Yellow Book standard. Requires support in the CD-ROM drive.
CD-V	Provides short music videos for a laser-disk player that can also play standard audio CDs. Not widely used.

(table continued on next page)

Format	Use
Photo–CD	Developed by Kodak. Uses CD-recordable (CD-R) technology. Can be played on CD-I or CD-XA drives. Can store about 100 very high-quality photographic images digitized from standard slides or prints. Pictures can be added incrementally (you don't need to record them all at the same time). Each picture is stored in five 24-bit color resolutions: 3,072 × 2,048 (16Base) 1,536 × 1,024 (4Base) 768 × 512 (Base) 384 × 256 (Base/4) 192 × 128 (Base/16) The three lower-resolution resolutions are stored as bitmaps (not compressed) for fast searching. The two higher-resolutions are stored as the *Huffman-encoded* difference (*lossless compression*) from the middle-resolution image. Typical images require 6 Mbytes of storage. Any CD-ROM XA player can read Photo-CD disks. More information is in *ftp://ftp.kodak.com/pub/photo-cd/*.
Sega CD	A new format for game software for Sega and JVC machines. Will offer better resolution and motion.
VideoCD	A DVD format, similar to CD-I, but will be able to store a full-length 135-minute movie (using MPEG encoding) on a new high-density CD-ROM. The CD-ROM uses a shorter-wavelength laser diode to store 3.7 Gbytes per disk. Developed by Philips Electronics NV and Sony (as is everything for CD-ROMs) and supported by Mitsumi Electric, Ricoh, and TEAC (these three make lots of diskette drives). A double-layer disk technology (developed by 3M) would enable a disk to store a total of 7.4 Gbytes. Also called *White Book*. Competes with SD.

See *ATAPI*, *ATASPI*, *Disk Drive*, *DVD*, *Lossy Data Compression*, *Mini-Disk*, *MPC*, *MPEG*, *PCM*, *SD*, and *WORM*.

Cell

Typically, the 53-byte unit of data carried by ATM switches.

A fixed-length, usually small unit of data. A user's (variable-length) packet of data would likely need to be split into many cells. Fixed-length has the advantages of more hardware-oriented switching (therefore higher speeds) and deterministic delays (so isochronous services for video can be handled).

48 bytes (plus a 5-byte header) is a common size (used in SMDS, B-ISDN, and ATM). It is a compromise between 32 bytes (best for voice—less store-and-forward delay) and 64 bytes (best for data—more efficient).

See *ATM (Asynchronous Transfer Mode)*, *Isochronous*, and *Multimedia*.

Cellular Digital Packet Data   See **CDPD.**

Cellular Telephone   See **AMPS.**

Central Office   See **C.O.**

Central Processing Unit   See **CPU.**

CERT
Computer Emergency Response Team

A group responsible for monitoring and advising about security on the Internet.

A U.S. government–funded organization with its *coordination center* located in Pittsburgh, at Carnegie-Mellon University. The *Incident Analysis Group* tracks and reports security problems on the Internet and recommends actions to be taken.

Founded a few weeks after November 3, 1988, which was when Robert Morris released a *worm* (a program that attempts to propagate itself to all machines on a network and can cause security or data integrity problems) into the Internet.

Information is available as shown in the following table.

email	*cert@cert.org*
Fax	412-268-6989
ftp	*info.cert.org*
List server	*cert-advisory-request@cert.org*
Phone	412-268-7090 (hotline for system administrators to report potential problems)
Usenet	*comp.security.announce* (announcements from CERT) *comp.security.misc* *alt.security* *comp.risks* *comp.virus*
WWW	*http://www.sci.cmu.edu/technology/cert.cc.html*

See *Internet.*

CGI
Common Gateway Interface

The method of sending information (such as a request or a response) to a WWW server.

A standard for interfacing (that is, providing a *gateway* to) an external application (such as a database server or an order-entry system) with a WWW server (a machine that runs an *HTTP daemon*). Can provide information to, and accept information from, people running WWW browsers (such as Netscape) elsewhere (anywhere) on the Internet.

Standard HTML documents retrieved from WWW servers are *static* (the exact same text is retrieved every time). In contrast, CGI enables a program (a *CGI program*, running on the WWW server) to communicate with another computer to generate "*dynamic*" HTML documents in response to user-entered information (entered through a form on the user's WWW browser).

CGI programs have the following features:

- Are executables, located in a /cgi-bin subdirectory on a WWW server (a security feature to limit which programs can be run)
- Have URLs and are run when a user executes them (by clicking on a reference to them)
- Can be a *compiled* program (for example, written in C or Fortran) or be *interpreted* (for example, a Perl, Tcl, or UNIX shell script)
- Receive input as the string of characters that appear after the first "?" in the URL (as constructed by the WWW browser)
- Output back to the user (in one of many formats, such as HTML, ASCII text, or another format, such as audio or video)

That is, CGI programs parse the input from the user, get the requested information, format a (usually HTML) response, and send the response back to the user.

See *HTML*, *HTTP*, *Tcl/Tk*, and *WWW*.

Channel

The 3.0- or 4.5-Mbytes/s, 400-foot maximum connection from an IBM mainframe to its front end processor and other communications-related devices. Uses a scheme called *bus and tag* to address peripherals.

See *ESCON*, *FEP*, and *Mainframe*.

Channel Service Unit   See **CSU.**

Checksum

A method of detecting errors in received data.

A type of *block check character* that is easier to compute in software than a CRC but provides less protection than a CRC. Is usually 8-bits, generated by the binary addition (or sometimes exclusive-ORing) of each of the bytes in the block of data.

The weakness is that if (for example) the same bit in two different bytes is corrupted, then the checksum will not detect the error.

Was popular when messages were small, error detection was done in software, and computers were slow. Not used in new protocols, as the messages are too long and there is specialized hardware available that can do a better job of detecting errors.

See *CRC*, *ECC*, *FCS*, *Parity*, and *XModem*.

Chicago

Microsoft's widely-publicized development code name for the successor to Windows 3.1. Initially it was expected to be called Windows 4.0, but Microsoft decided to call it Windows 95.

See *Operating System*.

CHRP
Common Hardware Reference Platform

A specification for a hardware platform to compete with Intel PCs.

A PowerPC-based hardware platform specified by Apple and IBM that can run any of the Apple Macintosh Mac OS, Microsoft Windows NT, Sun Solaris, IBM OS/2 Warp, and IBM AIX operating systems and applications (or so they hope).

The intent is to encourage other manufacturers to make this platform so that PCs have some competition and these vendors can sell operating systems and PowerPC CPUs.

Intended to compete with PCs. Uses PCI. Replaces the PReP effort (and perhaps the ACE effort before that).

Pronounced "chirp."

See *ACE*, *Operating System*, *PCI*, *PowerPC*, and *PReP*.

CICS
Customer Information Control System

An IBM mainframe user interface providing a transaction-oriented communications service (application driver) that supports hosts at several sites. Runs under

MVS. Well suited to systems with frequently run applications. An alternative is TSO.

See *MVS* and *TSO*.

CIDR
Classless Inter-Domain Routing

A method for dealing with the problem that there are no more worldwide unique Class A IP addresses and very few Class B addresses available for new networks.

A block of many Class C addresses is assigned to a single organization.

A problem with this method is that the InterNIC did not want to administer these addresses, so they assigned large blocks of them to the Internet service providers, which then charge per address and assign the addresses only in quantities that are powers of 2 (1,024, 2,048, etc.), so you will probably have to pay for many more addresses than you need.

Another method is described in RFC 1597.

See *InterNIC*, *IP Address*, and *RFC 1597*.

CIPO
Canadian Intellectual Property Office

The Canadian federal government organization that administers legislation on the following:

- *Copyrights* for literary, artistic, dramatic, and musical works and computer software
- *Patents* for inventions (new kinds of technology)
- *Industrial designs* for the shape, pattern, or ornamentation of an industrially produced useful object
- *Trademarks*: words, symbols, or designs (or combinations of these) that are used to distinguish the goods or services of one person (or entity) from those of another
- *Integrated circuit topographies*: the three-dimensional configurations of electronic circuits embodied in integrated circuit products

Part of Industry Canada.

CIPO has a WWW home page at *http://info.ic.gc.ca/opengov/cipo/*.

See *Copyright*, *Design Patent*, *Industry Canada*, *Intellectual Property Protection*, *Patent*, and *Trademark*.

Cisco Systems

A company based in California that makes multiprotocol routers and has over 60% (by units shipped) of that market. The next largest competitor (Bay Networks, which was called Wellfleet before merging with SynOptics) has under 10%.

The products communicate over LANs with DEC, Novell, UNIX (TCP/IP), and many other computers using those protocols' native routing methods. For IP routing information, the Cisco routers can also communicate among themselves, using their proprietary IGRP.

Has bought several other companies, such as:

- Kalpana (which means "imagination" in Hindi) for its Ethernet switching technology
- Cresendo, for its FDDI switching technology
- LightStream Corp., for its ATM technology

Cisco Systems has a WWW server at *http://www.cisco.com/*.

See *DLSw+*, *IGRP*, *Link-state*, *RIP*, and *Switched LAN*.

CIX
Commercial Information Exchange

The part of the Internet's U.S. backbone that is funded by the companies providing commercial access to the Internet, such as Performance Systems International (PSInet), BARRnet, CERFnet, NEARnet, Sprint Corporation, Uunet Technologies, and NYSERnet. These companies directly connect their networks either to each other or to a CIX router located in California.

It has no restrictions on the type of traffic it can carry (unlike the U.S. government–funded NSFNet, which can carry traffic only as permitted by the *Acceptable Use Policy*).

CIX has a WWW server at *http://www.cix.org/*.

See *AUP*, *Internet*, and *ISP*.

Classless Inter-Domain Routing   See **CIDR**.

Client/Server

The currently usually-desirable computer system architecture in which *clients* request a service and a *server* provides that service. Each machine can then be optimized for the task.

A common example would be a client using a database server. In this case the entry and display of users' data are separated (often on separate machines) from the storage and retrieval of the data. The client may have a large color display with a graphical user interface. The server may have dual power supplies (in case one fails), fast duplicated hard disks (in case one fails and to increase the number of disk requests that can be serviced per second), and a built-in tape drive for fast backup.

This provides a more flexible and open environment than the traditional "dumb-terminal and mini/mainframe computer" method, in which the program on the computer determines the user interface and the types of terminals that may be used.

Major client/server architectures are DEC's NAS, IBM's SAA, and OSF's DCE.

See *DCE* (*Distributed Computing Environment*), *OSF*, *SAA*, *SQL*, and *X*.

CLNP
Connectionless Network Protocol

An OSI network layer protocol. It may replace IP on the Internet someday (but you seem to hear less and less about OSI every day). The other OSI network layer protocol is CONP.

See *Connectionless*, *CONP*, and *OSI*.

CMC
Common Mail Calls

An API developed by the XAPIA for application program messaging. Used mostly for cross-platform messaging. Supported by Microsoft and Lotus.

See *MAPI*, *VIM*, and *XAPIA*.

CMIP
Common Management Information Protocol

The OSI method of doing what SNMP does but is *object-oriented* (another one of those trendy things, like user friendly, GUI, and client/server) and more powerful. Carriers and U.S. government agencies are the likely first adopters—and someday the federal deficit will be paid off :).

See *GUI* and *SNMP*.

CMS
Conversational Monitor System

An IBM mainframe editor and foreground driver for native application development under VM.

See *VM*.

C.O.
Central Office

The building at the other end of the telephone cable that comes to your house (the cable, not the building, comes to your house).

A usually nondescript, well-kept, one- or two-story, windowless building owned by the local phone company. Since analog voice signals from a telephone can travel about 5 km before they get too quiet or noisy, a C.O. will typically serve all the customers within a 5-km radius from the C.O.

Therefore C.O.s are located so that all customers will be within about 5 km of their serving C.O.

From a C.O., one pair of wires goes to each house, apartment, and business (and additional pairs for each additional phone line they may have). Higher-capacity lines (such as fiber-optic cables) go to adjacent C.O.s.

Inside a C.O. will be the switching equipment and power supplies to run the telephone system.

See *Carrier*, *DMS*, *LEC*, *PBX*, *RBOC*, and *Tip and Ring*.

Coax
Coaxial Cable

The type of cable that is used by cable TV and that used to be common for data communications (such as for Ethernet and 3270 terminals).

A round cross-section, two-conductor cable consisting of a single center solid wire (or stranded conductor) symmetrically surrounded by a braided or foil (or one or more of each) conductor (which is usually grounded).

Both conductors share the same axis (so they are *coaxial!*).

Coaxial cables have a *characteristic impedance* (expressed in ohms, just as D.C. resistance is—even though the two are not related), which is determined by the relative diameters of the two conductors and the material used for the insulator between the two conductors (which is officially called a *dielectric*).

The popular (in office and residential applications) types of coaxial cable are listed in the following table.

Cable Type	Characteristic Impedance (Ω)	Use
RG–58/U	53.5	Often used for Ethernet (is cheaper, and the connectors are easier to install) but should not be, as it is the wrong impedance and usually has a shield with too little coverage (too much space between the braiding)
RG–58A/U or RG–58C/U	50	10BASE2 CSMA/CD (ThinWire Ethernet)
RG–59/U	75	CATV (cable TV)
RG–62/U	93	IBM 3270 terminals, ARCnet

RG stands for "radio guide," as the cable is guiding *radio frequency* signals. The "/U" means "general utility."

Coaxial cables are generally falling out of favor for the following reasons:

- They are too single-purpose; you need a different type for each application, and you can't use any of them for Token Ring, FDDI, RS-232, telephone, or ISDN.
- For the same length of cable, coaxial cable can have 5 to 500 times more attenuation (depending on many factors, such as the type of coax and the frequencies used) than fiber-optic cable.
- Running coaxial cable between buildings creates problems of ground-potential difference (the building grounds will be at different voltages), so the coax shield must be insulated from building ground in at least one of the buildings.
- Outdoor runs need lightning protection.

For the last two points, fiber-optic cable is a better choice, as it is an insulator (sometimes called a dielectric), so it does not need lightning protection.

See *3270, BNC, Cable, CATV, Connector, Ethernet, STP,* and *UTP*.

Code Division Multiple Access   See **CDMA.**

CODEC
Coder/Decoder

The device that digitizes voice or video signals for transmission over digital data services and undigitizes it at the other end.

An analog-to-digital (A/D) converter optimized for audio signals.

See *ADPCM* and *PCM*.

Color

Computers and data communications handling color rather than monochrome information are becoming more popular. So here is some background information on color and the methods of representing it.

People perceive colors, which range from purple (about 380-nm wavelength) to red (about 780-nm), using retinal sensors called *rods* and *cones*.

Rods are located mostly at the periphery of the retina, are most sensitive to low light levels, are most sensitive to green light (about 500 nm), and are used mostly to detect overall brightness and fast light changes (presumably to see dangerous animals out of the "corner of your eye," now mostly where you see CRT flicker).

There are three kinds of cones (L, M, and H), which are sensitive to low, medium, and high frequencies, so called because they are most sensitive to the 570-, 550- and 440-nm wavelengths (near red, green, and blue light, respectively). Cones are mostly concentrated near the center of the retina.

Color is displayed or represented by using several different methods, as shown in the following figure.

See *Composite Video Signal, IrDA, NTSC, RAMDAC, RGB*, and *Video*.

Comité Consultatif International Radio   See **CCIR**.

Comité Consultatif International Télégraphique et Téléphonique   See **CCITT**.

Commercial Information Exchange   See **CIX**.

Common Desktop Environment   See **CDE**.

Common Gateway Interface   See **CGI**.

Common Hardware Reference Platform   See **CHRP**.

Common Mail Calls   See **CMC**.

Common Management Information Protocol   See **CMIP**.

Common Open Software Environment   See **COSE**.

Common Programming Interface for Communications   See **CPI-C**.

Communicating Applications Specification   See **CAS**.

Community Antenna Television   See **CATV**.

Method	Specifies	Comments
CMYK	Cyan, magenta, yellow, and black	These (with the exception of black) are often referred to as the *subtractive primary colors*, as subtracting these colors from white can produce any color. Black is added to provide a better black and to save money (it is less expensive than an equal amount of the other three). Used in the printing industry (sometimes called a four-color process), and by ink jet printers. Combinations of these color inks are used to create (almost) any color.
HSV or HSI or HSL	Hue, saturation, and value (or intensity or luminance)	• *Hue* specifies the color (not including white, grey, or black, which are specified by having equal portions of the three primary colors at different brightnesses). Picture specifying a color in a rainbow. • *Saturation* is how intense or washed-out a specific color is (that is, how much white light is added to "dilute" the color). • *Value* is how light or dark the color is (imagine adjusting the brightness of the room lights while viewing a page with a color of a specific hue and saturation). These methods are closest to how people think of color.
RGB	Red, green, blue	Specifies how much of these three *additive primary colors* to combine to create the desired color. This method of representing color can be envisioned as a three-dimensional orthogonal axis, with a primary color along each. Cyan — Green — White — Yellow — Blue — Magenta — Red Since this is similar to how electronic equipment usually works (for example, color monitors and televisions generate the three primary colors), it is most accurate and is often used by high-end video monitors (which therefore require three separate color signals).
YUV or Y/C	Luminance, Chrominance	• *Y-signal* — the luminance (or brightness) of a signal, which is the equivalent of a monochrome signal (as if the signal were shown on a black-and-white television). Contributes the fine details and brightness to a color television signal. Made up of 30% red, 59% green, and 11% blue (which matches human color perception). • *Chrominance* — the color of a signal, which has two components. The hue (also called tint) specifies what the color is. The saturation specifies how much white light is in the signal (making the color look washed out)—or conversely, how intense the color is. The chrominance is expressed as a two-dimensional value: • *Phase angle* (which determines the hue) • *Magnitude* (which determines the saturation) This two-dimensional polar-coordinate value can be resolved into rectangular components, and those (orthogonal) axis are called U and V. Used by color television broadcasting.

Compact Disc   See **CD-ROM.**

Compatible

A term that indicates that a product meets *some* parts (a subset, not all) of a specification. For example, only some modes of operation may be supported.

Two devices that are *compatible* with a specification may not be interoperable (that is, they may not work when connected to each other) because each implements a different (and incompatible) subset of features. It is therefore better to have *compliant* devices than *compatible* devices. Another choice is to define standard subsets of features.

See *Compliant* and *Standards.*

Compliant

A term that indicates that a product fully meets a specification or standard. For example, all modes of operation are supported.

Two devices that are compliant with a specification should be interoperable (that is, they should work when connected to each other).

See *Compatible* and *Standards.*

Composite Video Signal

The signal that specifies everything a television needs to display monochrome (called RS-170) or color (called NTSC) pictures. Called "composite" because the signal (which can be carried by a single coaxial cable) is a *composite* of the following:

- *Luminance* information: the brightness of the electron beam as it scans across the television screen assuming that you have a *Cathode-ray tube* (CRT) type of screen; produces a monochrome (black and white) picture
- *Blanking* information: turns off the electron beam that creates the picture while the raster scan returns to start the next line (*horizontal blanking*) or field (*vertical blanking*)
- *Synchronizing* information, so that the beam knows when to start the next horizontal (*horizontal sync*) or vertical scan (*vertical sync*)

These three signals are combined into one, in which the *amplitude* indicates the luminance, with zero brightness blanking the signal and pulses of less than zero brightness indicating the synchronization pulses (the pulse width determines whether it is a horizontal or vertical sync pulse).

A *color composite video signal* will also include the *chrominance* information, which is made up of the *hue* (which color) and *saturation* (how intense the color is—for example, red to pink toward white).

(In contrast, RGB is not a composite signal, since it does not combine all the information into a single signal.)

To carry this chrominance information, an NTSC composite video signal modulates the monochrome (luminance) signal with a *color burst* reference signal that has a frequency of 3.579545 MHz (therefore producing a *color subcarrier* 3.579545 MHz above the luminance signal). This is sent at the beginning of each raster scan line and is used so that the receiver can determine the *phase* of the frequency sent during the rest of the scan line. This phase (during the rest of the scan line) represents what color (hue) is being sent, and the *amplitude* of the color subcarrier represents the saturation.

This composite video signal (whether monochrome or color) is then used to *amplitude modulate* (AM) the video carrier's frequency for whichever channel is being used. This video carrier frequency is always 1.25 MHz above the lower boundary for the 6-MHz bandwidth. For example, channel 2 uses 54 to 60 MHz, so the video carrier is at 55.25 MHz, and the color subcarrier will be 3.579545 MHz above that (58.829545 MHz).

Video signals generally have an amplitude of 1 volt, measured peak to peak.

See *Color*, *NTSC*, *RGB*, and *Video*.

Compressed Slip   See **CSLIP**.

Compression Control Protocol   See **CCP**.

CompuServe

A company owned by H&R Block (the tax people) that operates a large (3 million subscribers, a total of 42,000 dial-in lines in hundreds of cities all over the world) information service and private data communications network. Provides Internet access too.

Competes with other major, general-purpose information services, such as America Online, Prodigy, and Genie.

CompuServe operates a WWW server at *http://www.compuserve.com/*.

See *BBS*, *GIF*, and *ISP*.

Computer Emergency Response Team   See **CERT**.

Computer Telephony Integration   See **CTI**.

Computers, Compatibility, and Communications   See **3Com**.

Connectionless

Data communications that does not require that a connection be established before data can be sent or exchanged. Analogous to mailing a letter (you may have addressed the letter incorrectly, but you don't find out about the problem until after the network has received the message). Usually requires that the higher-layer protocols provide more robust error detection and correction than connection-oriented protocols or networks.

Ethernet and the UDP protocol are connectionless.

See *CLNP*, *Connection-oriented*, *Ethernet*, and *UDP*.

Connectionless Network Protocol   See **CLNP**.

Connection-oriented

Data communications that requires that a connection first be established (*caller* calls and requests a connection, *callee* accepts the connection) before data can be exchanged. Analogous to a telephone call; you can't just pick up the phone and start talking (well you can, but you would be wasting your time talking to the dial tone).

Since it is known that the callee is "listening" (that is, you dialed the right number, the callee was available, and you have their attention), usually provides more reliable communication than connectionless protocols or networks.

X.25 networks and the TCP protocol are connection-oriented.

See *Connectionless*, *CONP*, *TCP*, *WAN*, and *X.25*.

Connection-Oriented Network Protocol   See **CONP**.

Connector

The devices on the ends of cables that permit them to be mated with, and disconnected from, other cables.

The type of cable used usually determines the type of connector used, as shown in the following table.

Cable	Connector	Comments
Coax (ThickNet)	Type N	Like a larger Type F, in which a threaded coupling nut on the plug keeps it mated with the receptacle.
Coax (RG-58, and RG-62)	BNC	While all BNC connectors mate, the cable end must be sized according to the type of coaxial cable.

(table continued on next page)

Cable	Connector	Comments
Coax (RG–59)	Type F	Used for standard cable TV (CATV) coaxial cable.
Fiber-optic cable	ST	Stands for "Straight Tip" (as opposed to a conical type that is seldom used now). Each connector pair (male and female) connects one strand, so two connector pairs are usually required (one strand for the transmit, the other for the receive data).
	SC	A newer, and push-on, pull-off type. Preferable to the ST type, as SCs can be spaced closer together (since room to grasp and twist the connector is not required). A *duplex* type (two connectors—one for the transmit, and one for the receive) is usually used for ATM.
STP	DB–9	The DB-9 is used to connect STP cable to LAN adapters in PCs (since the IBM universal data connector is too wide for the slot available at the back of a PC) and for non-IBM uses (such as FDDI over STP).
	IBM universal data connector	For IBM cabling system uses, such as Token Ring wall plates and *multistation access units*.
UTP	8-pin modular *plug* (male) and *jack* (female, socket or receptacle)	Some people call these RJ-45 connectors, which is a misnomer, since that refers to the use of an 8-pin modular connector *wired for use with an AT&T Definity PBX*.
EIA-232	DB–9	The 9-pin D-subminiature connector is often used for the EIA-232 COM port on PCs, since only *asynchronous data communication* is used, so 9 signal pins are enough. Also, the DB-9 requires less space than a DB-25 (especially important for laptop PCs) and costs less.
	DB–25	The 25-pin D-subminiature (because it is shaped like a letter "D") connector is used for modems (female connector) and most other EIA-232 applications.

AMP Incorporated is a major manufacturer of all types of connectors. AMP has a WWW server at *http://www.amp.com/*. Some other component suppliers with WWW servers include Hamilton Hallmark (*http://www.tsc.hh.avnet.com*) and Anixter (*http://www.anixter.com/*).

See *BNC*, *Cable*, *CATV*, *Coax*, *DB-25*, *EIA/TIA-232*, *LAN*, *RJ-45*, *Tip and Ring*, and *WAN*.

CONP
Connection-Oriented Network Protocol

An OSI network layer protocol, suitable for use over X.25, point-to-point WAN links and Ethernet, Token Ring, and FDDI LANs. The connectionless OSI network layer protocol is CLNP.

See *CLNP*, *Connection-oriented*, and *OSI*.

Control Unit Terminal   See **CUT.**

Conversational Monitor System   See **CMS.**

Copyright

Literally, "the right to copy," and everyone else not having the right to copy.

Protection against others copying and selling the *expression* of ideas "verbatim"—not the ideas, concepts, principles and discoveries, processes, methods of operation, procedures, or systems themselves. Copyrights therefore will not protect the techniques used in a program or anything about the content of the program itself.

Copyrights *do not* cover the following:

- Song titles (unless the title is original and distinctive, in which case it may be protected as part of the work to which it relates)
- Names (and other short-word combinations and catch-phrases, though some short-word combinations, such as "business reengineering" and "change management" may be trademarked)
- The idea for a story's plot (only the *expression* of that plot, for example, as a play or movie, can be copyrighted)
- Facts in an article
- Computer program names (though these could be trademarked)

Copyrights *do* cover the following:

- Literary works: books, magazine articles, pamphlets, poems, and other works consisting of text, including computer programs
- Dramatic works: films, movies, videos, plays, screenplays, and scripts

- Musical works: compositions that consist of both words and music or music only (lyrics only are considered literary works)
- Artistic works: paintings, drawings, maps, game board surfaces, photographs, sculptures, and architectural works

Copyrights also apply to all kinds of recordings, such as records, cassettes, and compact discs (which are called *mechanical contrivances*). These are copyrighted separately from the creative works themselves.

Without the copyright holder's permission, the copyright laws also prohibit others from copying substantial parts of the work, including translations.

A copyright owner has the exclusive right to:

- Do or authorize the publishing, reproduction, and distribution of copies of the work
- Prepare derivative works
- Perform, deliver, transmit, or display the work

Contravening any of these is called *infringement*, which can result in requiring that the copies be destroyed and other legal remedies (not to mention having to deal with lawyers).

Proving infringement requires showing that the infringer had (or must have had) access to and saw the material and that the material must have been copied (for example, it is just not likely that two people could write a word-for-word identical article for a magazine).

Fair use (also called *fair dealing*) allows brief passages to be quoted for purposes of (for example) article reviews or newspaper summaries, provided that the source and the author's name are included.

The Canadian Copyright Act provides that:

- The author normally owns the copyright
- If the work is done as an employee, then the employer owns the copyright
- The copyright for works done for commission is owned by the person paying, unless a written agreement says otherwise
- When doing work on a contract basis (that is, not as an employee), the author of the work owns the copyright, unless a written agreement states otherwise

I bet the lawyers had a good time arguing those last two. I would do an agreement to clarify the copyright issue regardless of which side I was on and whether I thought it was commission or contract work.

Owners of copyrights can *assign* their copyrights to others, but the author still retains *moral rights* (though the author can waive these). Moral rights require that the work cannot be changed (the *right of integrity*) or associated with a product or service that damages the author's reputation or honor and also that the author's name must still be associated with the work.

If the original author's moral rights are violated, remedies can be the same as if there was an infringement.

Assignments can be for all or only some rights, for a specific time period or until the copyright expires, and for everywhere or only specified geographic areas.

A *license* gives someone permission to use a work for certain purposes and under certain conditions, but does not assign the copyright; the owner still owns the copyright. Licensing agreements often require that royalties or fees be payable to a copyright owner each time a work is performed or played.

The *Universal Copyright Convention* provides that copyrighted works have a *mark* such as: "©Mitchell Shnier, 1996," but there is no requirement in Canada for copyrighted works to be marked in any way. They are automatically covered. However, the mark does serve to remind potential infringers that the work is copyrighted. Some countries that are members of the Universal Copyright Convention but not of the *Berne Copyright Convention* require such a mark.

Works can be *registered* as well (in which case you get a certificate which helps when asserting your ownership of the copyright). The mark can be used whether the work is registered or not.

Registration:

- Requires that you fill out a form and send in a fee (but not the work—the copyright office does not assess the work or want to store it, though the National Library requires two copies of every book published in Canada, as required under the *National Library Act*)
- Still requires that the owner of a copyright initiate legal action if necessary (the government won't do it)
- Does not prove that the work is original (if this is contested, only a court of law can confirm this)

Countries that are members of the Berne Copyright Convention or Universal Copyright Convention recognize each other's citizens' copyright claims (though these Conventions do not cover sound recordings).

A copyright lasts for the lifetime of the author plus 50 years (though there are exceptions, such as for photographs and sound recordings, for which the protection lasts 50 years after they were made).

To prove copyright infringement, it must be shown that the work was copied and not independently created.

The Canadian Copyright Office is part of the Canadian Intellectual Property Office.

There is some U.S. copyright information at *http://www.law.cornell.edu/usc/17/overview.html*

See *CIPO, Copyright, Intellectual Property Protection,* and *Trademark.*

Cordless Communications 2   See **CT2.**

COS
Corporation for Open Systems

An organization sponsored by OSI software vendors to provide conformance testing. Does not do interoperability testing. As with other OSI efforts, you don't hear much about this one any more.

See *OSI.*

COSAC
Canadian Open Systems Application Criteria

A Canadian government specification of which OSI standards to use and which options available in each standard to use to implement various computer communications functions.

The problem is that there are too many OSI standard ways of implementing systems, and the intent is to narrow these choices so that OSI-based systems will interoperate. GOSIP is the name of the U.S. and U.K. equivalent efforts (though all three specify different options).

See *GOSIP* and *OSI.*

COSE
Common Open Software Environment

OSF's "process" started in March 1993 by Hewlett-Packard (HP), IBM, Santa Cruz Operation (SCO), Sunsoft (Sun Microsystems), Univel (Novell), and USL (which was part of Novell) to standardize the UNIX desktop and application development environment (so that they can better compete with Microsoft). The main product of this work is CDE, which uses each vendors' technologies.

Other COSE work includes standards for graphics, multimedia, system management, objects, distributed computing, and a Windows-type interface that is compatible with Microsoft Windows.

Not very active lately (these coalitions all have enthusiastic announcements, but then everyone has other work to do, and you don't hear much from them).

Pronounced "cozy."

See *CDE, HP, IBM, OSF, SCO, Sun, Univel,* and *USL.*

CPE
Customer Premises Equipment

A term usually used by telephone companies (common carriers) for equipment located at a customer's site, which is needed (and sometimes provided by the carrier) to use the carrier's communications network.

Examples are leased telephones and data sets.

See *Carrier*.

CPI-C
Common Programming Interface for Communications

IBM's APIs, available for all of their platforms (and, they hope, third-party platforms as well), that facilitates cross-platform communications by providing a common programming interface.

Can run over MPTN, so can use APPN, TCP/IP, or other network layer protocols.

Pronounced "c-pick."

See *API, APPN, LU 6.2, MPTN,* and *TCP/IP*.

CPU
Central Processing Unit

The (usually) single integrated circuit (IC) that does the actual interpreting of program instructions and processing of data in a computer. Other parts of a computer are the memory, disk drive controller, and video adapter.

See *Alpha AXP, Intel, MPP, PA-RISC, PC, PIO, PowerPC, RISC,* and *SMP*.

CRC
Cyclic Redundancy Code

A key component in the error-detecting capabilities of many protocols.

A number of bits (usually 16 or 32) generated from, and appended to the end of, a block of data to provide error detection. The message receiver also generates a CRC from the block of data and compares it to the one appended to the received message. If the two match, then there is a high probability that the received message has not been corrupted.

There are two commonly used 16-bit CRC *generator polynomials*. The ITU-T (CCITT) standard 16-bit generator polynomial (used on X.25 networks, and by the Kermit, YModem, and ZModem file transfer protocols, for example) is represented by $x^{16} + x^{12} + x^5 + 1$. This is called CRC-CCITT and represents the binary number 1000100000100001 (note that there is a one in bit positions 16, 12, 5, and 0).

IBM protocols such as SDLC use CRC-16, which is represented by $x^{16} + x^{15} + x^2 + 1$.

In either case, the CRC is the remainder after binary division of the message (taken as a long string of ones and zeros, regardless of byte boundaries) by the generator polynomial.

$$\text{generated } CRC = \text{the remainder of } \frac{\text{message received}}{x^{16} + x^{12} + x^5 + 1}$$

CRC-CCITT CRCs detect:

- All single- and double-bit errors
- All errors of an odd number of bits
- All error bursts of 16 bits or less (the length of an error burst is the number of bits between and including the first errored bit and the last errored bit—any number of bits between may be errored)
- In summary, 99.998% of all errors (that is $1-\frac{1}{2^{16}}$)

Because of these error-detection capabilities, 16-bit CRCs are usually limited to use with message of less than 4 kbytes (there are enough ways to corrupt messages larger than 4 kbytes that catching "only" 99.998% of them is considered inadequate).

32-bit CRCs are used for messages up to 64 kbytes in length. Such CRCs detect 99.999999977% (that is, $1-\frac{1}{2^{32}}$) of all errors. The generator polynomial for the 32-bit CRCs used for both Ethernet and Token Ring is $x^{32} + x^{26} + x^{23} + x^{22} + x^{16} + x^{12} + x^{11} + x^{10} + x^8 + x^7 + x^5 + x^4 + x^2 + x + 1$.

See *Checksum, Parity, HDLC, Kermit, MNP, V.42*, and *XModem*.

CRTC
Canadian Radio-Television and Telecommunications Commission

The federal agency that regulates Canada's broadcasting and telecommunications industries.

The CRTC's WWW site is *http://www.crtc.gc.ca/*.

The equivalent U.S. organization would be a combination of the FCC and the *Public Utilities Commissions*.

See *FCC* and *PUC*.

CSLIP
Compressed SLIP

A more efficient version of SLIP, intended for use on dial-up connections.

See *PPP* and *SLIP*.

CSU
Channel Service Unit

A device usually required on a T1 (or FT1 or T3) line that performs several protective and diagnostic functions, such as the following:

- Lightning protection (protect the user's equipment from damage)
- "Ones density" enforcement (if the user equipment transmits more than 15 consecutive zeros, then the CSU either alarms and stuffs some ones in or implements some trick, such as B8ZS)
- Loopback (for diagnostic testing)

Both inputs and outputs to and from a CSU are raw T1:

- ±3-V signaling (±20%)
- *Alternate mark inversion* encoding (a binary zero is no pulse, a binary one is one +3V or -3V pulse), each pulse being the opposite of the previous
- Two twisted pairs (using a terminal strip or DB-15 connector for connection to the lines from the phone company)

For data applications, often integrated with the DSU.

See *B8ZS*, *DSU*, *FT1*, *T1*, *T3*, *V.25bis*, and *V.54*.

CT2
Cordless Communications 2

A digital wireless communications standard that supports digitized voice and data at up to 32,000 bits/s.

See *PCTS* and *PCS*.

CTI
Computer Telephony Integration

Providing a link between telephone systems and computers to facilitate incoming and outgoing call handling and control.

The two main APIs to control the telephone systems are TAPI and TSAPI.

See *ECTF*, *POTS*, *TAPI*, and *TSAPI*.

Customer Information Control System   See **CICS.**

Customer Premises Equipment   See **CPE.**

CUT
Control Unit Terminal

The mode of operation of 3270-series terminals in which the controller (3274 or 3174) has most of the intelligence and the 3270 terminal has little. The other mode of operation is the newer DFT.

See *3174 and 3274, 3270*, and *DFT*.

Cyclic Redundancy Code   See **CRC.**

DASD
Direct Access Storage Device

The disk drive subsystem of an IBM mainframe.

See *Disk Drive*, *IBM*, and *Mainframe*.

Data Circuit–Terminating Equipment   See **DCE.**

Data Encryption Standard   See **DES.**

Data Exchange Interface   See **DXI.**

Data Link Control Layer Protocol   See **DLC.**

Data Link Switching   See **DLSw.**

Data Service Unit   See **DSU.**

Data Terminal Equipment   See **DTE.**

Data Compression

A process of reducing the number of bits required to represent some information, usually to reduce the time or cost of storing or transmitting it.

Some methods can be reversed to reconstruct the original data exactly (*lossless data compression*); these are used for faxes, programs and most computer data.

Other methods (*lossy data compression*) do not exactly reproduce the original data, but this may be acceptable (for example, it is probably good enough for a video conference, and not having to travel is appreciated). In addition, the reduction in image quality may be imperceptible; many voice and video compression schemes eliminate parts of the signal (for example, the phase relationship between frequencies) that are not discernible to people.

See *CSLIP, CCP, Lossy Data Compression, Fax, LZS, LZW, MNP, RLE, Stac, V.42bis,* and *Video.*

Database Administrator   See **DBA.**

Dataroute

The Stentor (Canadian) name for a longer-distance (between cities, for example) digital *leased line* (also called a digital *dedicated circuit*). Available data rates are 1,200- to 56,000-bits/s, asynchronous or synchronous data communications.

The equivalent U.S. service is often called DDS.

See *Asynchronous, DCS, DDS, Stentor, Synchronous,* and *WAN.*

Daylight Savings Time

Setting clocks one hour ahead at 2:00 a.m. on the first Sunday in April to provide more sunlight in the evening (though many would argue that it provides more darkness in the morning so that the children don't get up at 5:00 a.m.).

When *Daylight Savings Time* is in effect, the time zone is, for example, *Eastern Daylight Time* (EDT) rather than Eastern Standard Time (EST).

The time is set back one hour at 2:00 a.m. on the last Sunday in October, so there is no net effect. (Wouldn't it be a hoot if we didn't do this?)

See *UTC.*

DB-25

The 25-pin connector. This is often used for EIA-232 (formerly RS-232-C).

For EIA-232 a female connector is used on the DCE (*Data Circuit-terminating Equipment,* such as modems), and a male connector is usually used on the DTE (*Data Terminal Equipment,* such as PC COM ports).

Also a female DB-25 is used on computers for parallel printer ports (on PCs) and Macintosh SCSI ports.

See *1284, Connector, DCE, DTE, EIA/TIA-232, Parallel Port,* and *SCSI.*

DBA
Database Administrator

A person who is responsible for maintaining, designing, and implementing changes to, tuning, and expanding a database.

See *SQL*.

DCE
Data Circuit–Terminating Equipment

Usually a modem, though it may be a data set, DSU, or other device that is used to connect a computer to a data communications service.

For example, the typical use of modems is to connect two DTEs (*Data Terminal Equipment*), such as a terminal and a computer, over a network (such as an analog leased line data circuit).

That is, the modems are *Data Circuit-terminating Equipment* (DCE), since they terminate the data circuit. In the RS-232-C standard, modems were referred to as data communications equipment, since that is what they did. (I suppose they still do that, but someone thought you could look at it another way.)

The accompanying diagram shows the classic setup. Starting at the left, we have a DTE, which is a terminal (or a PC emulating one, for example), to an EIA–232 connection from the terminal to a modem, to a switched telephone network or a leased line, to another modem, which is connected to a computer, using another EIA–232 connection.

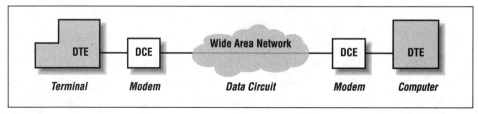

DCE–1

See *DSU, DTE, EIA/TIA-232, Modem, V.54*, and *WAN*.

DCE
Distributed Computing Environment

OSF's specification for the core services (sometimes called *middleware*) needed for cross-platform (that is, computers with different hardware and operating systems) *distributed computing* (which is more trendily called a *client/server* environment).

Since the function of, and communication between, these services is standardized, services can be provided by different suppliers and still be interoperable.

Includes specifications for the following:

- Threads, which are single processes that can have more than one section of code executing simultaneously
- *Remote Procedure Calls* (RPCs), which are used for communications between services
- Directory Services, which are used to locate services, are called *cell directories*, and use X.500
- Time service to have all computers' time-of-day clocks synchronized (with allowance for time-zone differences and Daylight Savings Time)
- Security, using *Kerberos*
- Distributed file and print services, similar to NetWare file servers or NFS mounts

Version 1.1 of the specification was released in September 1994.

The OSF has some DCE information at *http://www.osf.org/dce/index.html*.

See *Client/Server, Kerberos, Messaging, NFS, OSF, UTC, RPC,* and *X.500*.

DCI
Display Control Interface

Intel's specification (now supported by Microsoft) to offload some video processing to the PC's video adapter.

If the PC's CPU is not busy, then the processing is done by the Windows GDI (*Graphics Display Interface*) driver. The goal is to support faster display updates for *multimedia*.

The Windows DCI driver (and its associated *DCI registry*) will tell an application whether the PC's video adapter directly supports DCI, and if so, the application will communicate directly with the video adapter. If the video adapter is busy at the time, then the Windows GDI driver handles the display update.

Also supports features such as color-space conversion (analog YUV to digital RGB), interpolation, and image scaling.

Renamed *direct draw* because of its support for direct writes to the video adapter (which is sometimes called a *graphics accelerator*, since it does more than just display a bitmap given to it).

See *Color, Multimedia, NTSC, PC,* and *Video*.

DCS
Digital Channel Service

The Stentor Canada name for a digital *leased line* (which is also called a *dedicated data circuit*). The service supports speeds of 1,200 to 56,000 bits/s, asynchronous or synchronous. A DCS leased line has its ends within a *wire center* (an area served by a single *central office*) or a *rate center* (also called an *exchange*, which Stentor describes as a single metropolitan area—which may be served by many central offices).

Stentor's similar service for circuits to different cities is called Dataroute.

See *Dataroute, Stentor*, and *WAN*.

DDC
Display Data Channel

A VESA standard for bidirectional communication between PC monitors and video adapters. The monitor continuously sends its 128-bit *Extended Display Identification* (EDID) message to the video adapter. This specifies the following:

- Screen resolutions supported (and refresh rates for each)
- Screen dot-pitch and the monitor's bandwidth
- Power-conservation capabilities (that is, DPMS support)
- Product information, such as the model number (to help match the video driver software to the adapter and monitor) and MPR support

This enables the video adapter to automatically select the highest resolution supported by a monitor and prevent users from selecting unsupported modes.

The monitor can also be controlled (for example, setting the refresh rate, resolution, color temperatures, screen position, brightness, and contrast), through the use of easier-to-use standard PC utilities, rather than monitor-specific utilities or front-panel push-buttons.

Uses *ACCESS.bus*. Some monitors will have an ACCESS.bus port on them (for connection to additional peripherals), simplifying the cabling.

See *1394, ACCESS.bus, DPMS, MPR II, PnP, USB*, and *VESA*.

DDE
Dynamic Data Exchange

A method used by Microsoft's Windows products to exchange data between applications.

Data in one application (called the *container*—a spreadsheet or word processor, for example) are linked (sometimes called a *live-link*) to another (the *client*—a database, for example) so that if the original data are changed, the data in the container application are automatically changed.

See *OLE*.

DDS
Digital Dataphone Service

AT&T's name for a *leased line* digital circuit with speeds of 1,200 to 56,000 bits/s.

See *DCS*, *Dataroute*, and *WAN*.

de jure Standard

An official standard, usually produced by an international organization which has no specific (biased to any one company) commercial interests.

Latin for "according to law."

See *de facto Standard*.

de facto Standard

An informal standard, developed as most people (or manufacturers) gravitate to doing something the same way.

A standard that has been accepted by a significant part of the industry (and therefore sometimes called an *industry standard*) without going through an official standards-setting process.

For example, for the more than 20 years until the fourth version of RS-232 was released, everyone used a DB-25 connector for it, but the connector type was not written in the standard.

Latin for "existing in fact."

See *DB-25*, *de jure Standard*, and *EIA/TIA-232*.

DEC
Digital Equipment Corporation

A large company that popularized the idea of a minicomputer (something smaller, less expensive, and more fun than a mainframe) before there were PCs.

Their PDP (Personal Digital Processor) and VAX (Virtual Address Extension) minicomputers became the standard for real-time, scientific, and UNIX computing. Industry-wide benchmarks are still based on DEC's VAX-11/780, which was introduced in 1977.

Unfortunately, DEC's glory days ended in the late 1980s, as DEC was slow to adopt industry standards (such as UNIX and TCP/IP)—even though many were developed on DEC machines!

DEC also completely missed the personal computer revolution in the office (DEC's legendary founder, Ken Olsen, said, "There's nothing personal about business"). Even now, rather than promoting industry standards (such as CDE), DEC is working more with Microsoft on proprietary solutions.

DEC maintains a WWW server at *http://www.dec.com,* and the Digital Equipment Computer Users Society (DECUS, pronounced *dee*-kus) has a WWW server at *http://www.decus.org/*.

See *Advantage Networks, Alpha AXP, CDE, DECnet Phase IV, DECnet/OSI, DNS (Digital Naming Service), LAST, LASTport, LAT, MIPS, NAS, OpenVMS, Operating System, OSF, Pathworks, SPEC,* and *VMS.*

DECnet/OSI

An OSI-compliant version of DECnet originally called DECnet Phase V. Uses SPF (the Dykstra) routing algorithm. Now part of DEC's Advantage Networks.

See *Link-state.*

DECnet Phase IV

DECnet is the data communications protocol supported by all DEC operating systems and hardware platforms. (This used to be a bigger deal when DEC had several popular operating systems and computing platforms.)

DECnet Phase IV is a version of DECnet that uses Ethernet v2.0, rather than 802.3 and 802.2. It uses a distance-vector routing algorithm.

See *802.3, DEC, Ethernet, RIP,* and *VMS.*

Demand Protocol Architecture   See **DPA.**

DECT
Digital European Cordless Telecommunications

A European wireless LAN standard that supports handoff between base stations. The range is about 200 m, and the speed is up to 384 kbits/s.

See *GSM* and *PCS.*

Dependent LU Requester and Server   See **DLUr and DLUs.**

DES
Data Encryption Standard

A private-key-only (also called *single-key* or *symmetric*) encryption method that uses the same secret 56-bit key to encrypt and later decrypt the message. Being a single-key system, it requires that the secret keys be securely distributed to both ends of the connection.

It was initially designed with a 64-bit key (making it 256 times more secure—maybe even more; how many people actually understand this stuff?). But the U.S. government's *National Security Agency* (which gets to control these things) changed it to 56 bits, leading many to believe that it did this because that was (at least then) the limit of what it could decipher. Governments usually feel that, for security purposes (catching crooks, eavesdropping on interesting conversations), they must be able to know what people are saying to each other.

This perceived weakness plus these points have limited the popularity of DES:

- DES-based cryptography equipment that uses keys 56 bits in length or longer cannot be exported outside of Canada or the U.S. (this limits the potential market size).
- Low cost DES integrated circuits are available, and hundreds or thousands of them could be (or maybe already have been) built into machines which would be able to apply all the DES ICs in parallel—to more quickly decipher messages (this limits the perceived strength of the security).

Therefore, DES is not widely adopted outside of situations which are required to use it (such as transactions between financial institutions).

To help keep DES a secure method of data encryption, the algorithm it uses was designed to be difficult to implement in software (and it therefore runs slowly in software). This makes software-only methods of breaking DES codes undesirable. Also, the U.S. government restricts sales of DES hardware, so obtaining DES hardware for the purposes of breaking codes would also be difficult.

Triple DES (the plaintext is encrypted three times, each time with a different key) is often used to provide better security than standard DES.

Originally developed about 1975 and standardized in 1981 in ANSI X3.92.

See *Authentication*, *Encryption*, *PGP*, and *RSA*.

Design Patent

The type of *intellectual property protection* in the U.S. that is similar to a registered Canadian *industrial design*. Protection lasts for 14 years.

See *Industrial Design*, *Intellectual Property Protection*, and *Patent*.

Desktop Management Interface   See **DMI**.

Desktop Management Task Force   See **DTMF**.

DFT
Distributed Function Terminal

The newer mode of operation supported by 3174s and required by the 3290. Supports up to five logical sessions per physical connection, though the 3290 supports only four simultaneously.

See *3174 and 3274*, *3270*, and *CUT*.

DHCP
Dynamic Host Configuration Protocol

A TCP/IP protocol that enables hosts (for example, diskless workstations or mobile users) to obtain temporary IP addresses (out of a pool) from centrally-administered servers. The host runs the DHCP server, and the workstation runs the DHCP client.

Clients *broadcast* a message to locate a DHCP server, which responds with the:

- Assigned IP address, which is valid for an administrator-configured time period (hosts can request an extension to this time period)
- Subnet Bit Mask
- Duration for which the IP address assignment is valid

DHCP is flexible so that other information can also be stored and retrieved.

A shortcoming is that there is currently no way to update *Domain Name Servers* with the new IP address for a user's DNS name (DNS names remain permanently assigned to hosts). Since important destination machines (such as servers) would use permanently assigned IP addresses, this should not be a big problem (until a solution is standardized).

May replace bootp.

See *Bootp*, *DNS (Domain Name System)*, *IP Address*, and *Subnet Bit Mask*.

DID
Direct Inward Dialing

A service offered by telephone companies in which the last few (typically three or four) digits dialed by the caller are forwarded to the callee on a special *DID trunk*, usually by *dial pulse* (just as if the caller had a rotary phone) or by *Multifrequency Tones* (MF—these are different from the DTMF tones and are usually used only within telephone networks). Some telephone networks can also use DTMF tones.

For example, all the phone numbers from 555-1000 to 555-1999 could be assigned to a customer with 20 DID trunks. When a caller dials any number in this range, the call is forwarded on any available trunk of the 20 (that is, the trunks are *equivalent*, which is also called being in a *hunt group* or a *rotary*). If the caller dialed 555-1234, then the digits 2, 3, and 4 (assuming three-digit outpulsing was used) will be forwarded. These DID trunks could be *terminated* on (for example):

- A *Private Branch Exchange* (PBX), so it knows which number was called and rings that phone extension. This makes it look as though 555-1234 and the other 999 lines all have direct outside lines, while only requiring 20 trunks to service the 1,000 telephone extensions.

- A *fax server*, so it can provide routing for inbound faxes. Each fax user is assigned a unique telephone number. When the fax server gets the number dialed (from the DID trunk), it forwards the subsequent fax to the specified (according to the phone number dialed) person's PC (where it can be viewed, printed, or stored).

See *DN*, *DTMF*, *Fax*, and *POTS*.

Digital Channel Service   See **DCS.**

Digital Dataphone Service   See **DDS.**

Digital 800

A digital, toll-free, circuit-switched dial-up WAN connection. Any number of DS-0 channels (providing any speed from 64 kbits/s to a full T1) can be used.

Standard "1-800-" type telephone numbers are used. The same number can often be used for both standard voice 1-800 calls, and digital 1-800 calls (the network knows whether the call is analog or digital (from where it originated) and routes the call accordingly.

At the calling-end, access to the service is typically through a switched 56 or ISDN service. An *inverse multiplexer* can be used to provide this high-speed switched service—it makes as many simultaneous 56 (or 64) kbits/s calls as needed to supply the speed of service requested. At the receiving (that is, the called) end, a switched 56, or ISDN BRI or PRI, service is used (depending on the maximum aggregate speed of the calls which must be accepted).

AT&T calls its service *Worldworx 800* and MCI's is called *800 Digital Service*.

See *BRI*, *DS-0*, *Inverse Multiplexer*, *ISDN*, *Switched 56*, *PRI*, *T1*, and *WAN*.

Digital Equipment Corporation   See **DEC.**

Digital European Cordless Telecommunications   See **DECT.**

Digital Multiplex System   See **DMS.**

Digital Naming Service   See **DNS.**

Digital Signals   See **DS-0, DS-1, and DS-3.**

Digital Transmission Rate   See **T1, T2, T3, and T4.**

Digital Video Disk   See **DVD.**

Direct Access Storage Device   See **DASD.**

Direct Draw   See **DCI.**

Direct Inward Dialing   See **DID.**

Direct Memory Access   See **DMA.**

Directory Number   See **DN.**

Disk Drive

The electromechanical device that still has the best combination of lowest access time and cost of storage and the highest storage capacity for read/write digital storage. It is therefore the main method of storing data on computers.

The speed of many (if not most) file servers and user applications is limited by the number of disk drive operations (reads and writes) that can be performed per second.

The following table shows the times required for a typical disk operation (based on estimates by Western Digital).

Operation	Percentage of time spent	Comments
Head seek to required cylinder	35	Typical high-performance disk drives can move the read/write head over half the disk surface (an average seek) in 8 to 12 ms. Newer (and therefore higher capacity) disks are typically closer to 8 ms.
Rotational latency (wait for disk to spin to correct location)	25	At 5,400 revolutions per minute (a typical high-performance value), the disk does a half-revolution in 5.55 ms. Older disks (usually those less than 540 Mbytes) spin at 3,600 RPM. Drives larger than 1 Gbyte are often 7,200 RPM.
Data transfer from disk to controller	25	While an IDE interface transfers data at a burst rate of about 2 Mbytes/s and SCSI typically transfers data at 10 Mbytes/s, the data is read from the actual disk drive at 5 Mbits/s to 48 Mbits/s. A 4,096 byte transfer (a typical cluster size) would transfer in 0.5 to 2 ms.

(table continued on next page)

Operation	Percentage of time spent	Comments
Disk driver soft-ware handling	10	Depends on the speed of the PC's CPU.
Data transfer from controller to memory	5	Depends on the type of bus used in the PC. ISA transfers at about 2 Mbytes/s, and PCI transfers at up to 132 Mbytes/s.

Some technical information on disk drives is available at the major disk drive manufacturer sites, as shown in the following table.

Maxtor Corporation	*ftp://ftp.maxtor.com/pub/*
Seagate Technology Inc	*http://www.seagate.com*
Western Digital Inc	*http://www.wdc.com*

See *ATA, ATAPI, ATASPI, Bus, Cache, CD-ROM, DASD, Disk Formatting, E-IDE, Fast ATA, FAT, IDE, RAID, SCSI, SLED, Small Form Factor Committee,* and *Winchester.*

Disk Formatting

Under DOS a hard disk is formatted to combine 2^n 512-byte *sectors* (where n is some integer) into *clusters* (the smallest unit of disk space that can be allocated to a file).

See *Disk Drive* and *FAT.*

Display Control Interface   See **DCI.**

Display Data Channel   See **DDC.**

Display Power Management Signaling   See **DPMS.**

Distributed Computing Environment   See **DCE.**

Distributed Function Terminal   See **DFT.**

Distributed Management Environment   See **DME.**

Distributed Queue Dual Bus   See **DQDB.**

DLC
Data Link Control Layer Protocol

The link layer protocols used by IBM's SNA. The most common protocols are the following:

- LLC2 (*Logical Link Control*, Level 2), which is used on Token Ring LANs
- SDLC (*Synchronous Data Link Control*), which is used on recent EIA-232 and WAN links
- BISYNC (Binary Synchronous Communications), which is used on old EIA-232 and WAN links

Functions performed by these link layer protocols include error detection (through the use of a check character), error correction (through time-outs and retransmissions), flow control (through delayed acknowledgments and *receiver not ready* response frames), and multiple devices on the same media (through polling and acknowledgments).

See *BISYNC*, *Checksum*, *CRC*, *DLSw*, *EIA/TIA-232*, *FCS*, *LLC2*, *SDLC*, *Spoofing*, *QLLC*, and *WAN*.

DLL
Dynamic Link Library

Software (executable code or data, such as icons or fonts) used by Microsoft's Windows and IBM's OS/2 to provide services (such as a LAN driver or a distributed filing system) to applications.

One memory-resident copy of the DLL can be simultaneously shared by all applications.

DLLs with only data are called resource-only DLLs.

DLLs may have (for example) a `.exe`, `.dll`, `.drv`, or `.fon` extension. They may have no extension. Some DLLs can be automatically loaded when needed by a program, and others (usually drivers) must be loaded at system startup.

See *WinSock*.

DLSw
Data Link Switching

IBM's recently announced and widely accepted method for integrating SNA SDLC traffic and standard LAN traffic on a single internet (WAN link).

For example, it handles SNA (from SDLC links) and NetBIOS (which are both nonroutable) and APPN traffic (on Token Ring links) over (at least initially) TCP/IP networks.

Uses *encapsulation* (the packets and frames are carried in TCP/IP packets) so that *routing* can be used instead of *bridging*, therefore providing all the advantages of routed networks, such as more efficient WAN utilization.

Also intended to replace Token Ring's *source route bridging*, which has problems such as the following:

- The maximum hop count is seven (only seven bridge-to-bridge hops are allowed between any two communicating stations)
- There is substantial broadcast traffic (from *source route discovery* frames and *Net-BIOS name queries*) which wastes WAN capacity
- *Keep-alive* and *acknowledgment* frames are sent end-to-end, which also wastes WAN capacity
- There is a lack of flow control and prioritization

DLSw supports *name caching* (to reduce broadcasts) and specifies how to convert SDLC (from low-speed synchronous links) to LLC2 frames (which are used on Token Ring LANs).

DLSw supports both LLC2 and SDLC sessions. These are IBM's most popular DLC (Data Link Control) protocols. To provide more efficient WAN utilization, DLSw supports local termination (which is an example of spoofing), as shown in the examples below:

- For SDLC (on EIA-232 links), DLSw responds locally with a fake acknowledgment (so polls and their acknowledgments do not travel over the WAN). At the remote end of the link, DLSw generates the necessary polls.
- For LLC2 (on Token Ring LANs), DSLw responds locally to keep-alive messages (so these periodically-generated messages do not load the WAN).

DLSw encapsulates WAN traffic into TCP/IP packets, so the WAN link will be error-free (due to TCP/IP's error detection and correction), and routers will be easier to configure (since most sites already use TCP/IP).

Local termination both reduces WAN bandwidth requirements (no polls or acknowledgments on the WAN) and ensures that WAN time delays don't cause DLC protocol time-outs. (Polling doesn't wait long for a response, so putting the polling on a WAN link that occasionally gets congested with other traffic would be a problem.)

A significant benefit of DLSw should be multivendor interoperability of SNA traffic encapsulated in TCP/IP. (Each vendor has developed its own proprietary methods in the absence of a standard.)

First used in IBM's 6611 multi-protocol router, and later released as an open standard, with further work being done by the *DLSw Working Group* of the *APPN*

Implementor's Workshop. IBM defined the first version in RFC 1434, but this had significant shortcomings such as lack of support for:

- Flow control (currently, overloads are handled by discarding frames)
- SNMP
- Prioritization
- Standard subsets of features (therefore interoperability could not be guaranteed—a significant problem)

IBM, Cisco, and other router vendors have since defined a new draft standard that includes flow control and an optional SNMP MIB, as shown in the following table.

Category	Feature	RFC 1434	DLSw	DLSw+
Transport	TCP	✓	✓	✓
	Direct connection			✓
Media Conversion	SDLC → LLC2	✓	✓	✓
	LLC2 → SDLC			✓
	QLLC → LLC2			✓
	QLLC ↔ SDLC			✓
Performance	Flow control		✓	✓
	Custom queueing			✓
	Prioritization		✓	✓
	Load balancing			✓
Scalability	Caching			✓
	RIF reduction	✓	✓	✓
	Peer groups			✓
	On-demand peers			✓
Availability	Backup peers			✓
Management	Standard MIB		✓	✓
Interoperability	Standard-based		✓	✓

Token Ring frames have a *Route Information Field* (RIF), which has room for a maximum of eight ring number/bridge number entries. Since these entries (which are read by Token Ring bridges so that they can determine whether to pass a frame) specify the exact end-to-end path, this limit restricts the size and configuration of Token Ring bridged networks.

DLSw solves this by *terminating* the link. That is, the RIF need only describe how to get the frame from its source to a DLSw router (and not all the way to the destination). At the remote end, the DLSw router nearest the destination builds the

RIF with only the entries to get the frame from that remote DLSw router to the final destination.

See *APPN, Compatible, Cache, DLC, DLUr and DLUs, Encapsulation, LAN, LLC2, Prioritization, RFC, SDLC, SNMP, Spoofing, Token Ring,* and *WAN.*

DLSw+
Data Link Switching Plus

An enhancement to DLSw, developed by Cisco. Addresses issues such as the following:

- Availability (by storing alternative paths to destination so that if a link is lost, an alternative path can be used immediately without dropping the user's session)
- Any-to-any connectivity in very large networks (using name caching and other methods to reduce the need for broadcasting discovery frames)
- Simplified configuration (reducing the number of routers that need to be configured)
- Load balancing (by using all available paths)
- Supporting other transport methods, such as using only HDLC between directly connected DLSw+ routers (which avoids the extra overhead of TCP/IP)

Can also automatically detect and interoperate with other Routers that support:

- Cisco's previous Token Ring support—*Remote Source Route Bridging* and *SDLC-to-LLC2 conversion* (SDLLC)
- DLSw
- DLSw+

Another feature is that it can automatically learn which destinations are on a local LAN before (needlessly) broadcasting over the WAN to find them.

See *DLSw.*

DLUr and DLUs
Dependent LU Requester and Server

One of IBM's methods (another is DLSw) of enabling APPN to carry and route 3270 traffic (that is, poll/response SDLC stuff).

3174s can be configured to support DLUr, and VTAM hosts can be configured to support DLUs.

Since this method works at the LU level, traffic does not need to be routed through mainframes along the path (which would needlessly waste their CPU time and slow the response time).

See *3174 and 3274, APPC, APPN, DLSw, SDLC, SNA,* and *VTAM.*

DMA
Direct Memory Access

A fast way of transferring data within (and sometimes between) computers.

For example, DMA is often used to read data from a LAN adapter board and write it into a PC's memory (and vice versa). A DMA controller (often on a PC's motherboard) seizes the bus periodically (for example, once for every 16-bit transfer) to read data from the adapter, then seizes it again to write it to memory (therefore requiring two bus cycles per transfer).

A DMA channel is the combination of bus signals (to request use of the channel and to receive acknowledgment that use of the channel has been granted) and the counters that provide the addresses for the source and destination of the transfers. 16-bit ISA Bus PCs have eight DMA channels, though not all are available for use by add-on peripherals.

Most devices require a dedicated DMA channel (so the number of DMA channels that are available may limit the number of peripherals that can be installed).

A limitation of DMA is that the DMA writes must be to conventional PC memory since extended memory that is mapped to upper memory blocks is mapped only for CPU accesses (since the 80386 memory mapping is on-chip, not on the motherboard). Therefore device drivers that use DMA usually cannot be loaded into upper memory (unless the data buffers are in conventional memory or there is hardware support for *scatter/gather* to provide the memory mapping for the DMA controller). The following table summarizes the DMA channel assignments in an ISA bus PC.

ISA DMA Channel	Use	Comments
0	Was used for memory refresh on early PCs and is therefore not on the 8-bit ISA bus. Current PC dynamic memory (DRAM) is refreshed by a refresh circuit that does not use a DMA channel, and DMA channel 0 is on the 16-bit ISA bus.	Performs 8-bit transfers only. Maximum 64 kbytes per transfer. Only these four channels were supported by the original PC and PC/XT.
1	Available	
2	Floppy and hard drive controller.	
3	Hard disk controller in (now-ancient) XTs only. Usually available in current PCs.	

(table continued on next page)

ISA DMA Channel	Use	Comments
4	Cascade line to link controller for DMA channels 4 through 7 to controller for DMA channels 0 through 3. Not available for use.	Can perform 16-bit transfers. Maximum of 128 kbytes per transfer. These four channels were added when the 16-bit PC/AT bus was introduced.
5	Hard disk controller (in PS/2s only). Usually available on other current PCs.	
6	Available	
7	Available	

DMA channels 2 and 4 are not available for add-on peripherals (such as LAN adapters or sound boards), and the first four DMA channels are capable of transferring only 8 bits at a time (since these channels are compatible with the original PC's 8-bit bus). Therefore the best DMA channels to choose for add-on peripherals are 5, 6, or 7.

See *Bus*, *Bus Master DMA*, *PIO*, *PC*, and *Shared Memory*.

DME
Distributed Management Environment

OSF's multivendor distributed database support. Includes management of hubs, bridges, and routers.

See *OSF*.

DMI
Desktop Management Interface

The API defined by the *Desktop Management Task Force* to provide a common interface to let users (and management software) gather information and manage all the components of a desktop computer, such as application software, add-in boards, and peripherals.

Platform-independent (PC, Macintosh, etc.), operating system–independent (DOS, NetWare, OS/2, UNIX, Windows, etc.), and protocol-independent (TCP/IP, IPX, etc.).

The *agent* is implemented as a DLL (Windows), separate program (OS/2), or TSR (DOS).

It gathers information from the following:

- The system (memory and CPU type, for example)
- ASCII *management information files* (for peripherals, such as hard disks, CD-ROMs, and fax boards), which must be supplied by manufacturers with their products (a potentially big problem).

  In their MIF, vendors could include any information, such as the following:
  - Model number, serial number, warranty information, and the installation date
  - Firmware version number and speed
  - User-settable characteristics such as I/O addresses and screen resolutions available

When each peripheral is installed, its MIF is stored in a database on the PC's hard disk.

Requires management software vendors to use the DMI agent's APIs in their software (in addition to the agents already developed by the vendors).

Does not specify a transport protocol but could be used to report information to an SNMP agent.

Supported by Microsoft and Intel.

See *DTMF* (*Desktop Management Task Force*), *PnP*, and *SNMP*.

DMS
Digital Multiplex System

Northern Telecom's line of usually huge, and central office–oriented, voice and high-speed data switches. A DMS switch typically provides telephone service for 10,000 or more customers—with less than two hours of down-time in 40 years.

See *C.O.* and *PBX*.

DN
Directory Number

A standard telephone number, in the form 555-1234 (plus an optional area code). Standardized in ITU-T E.163.

As a side point, the 555 exchange is used for most sample telephone numbers (especially on television) since it is not assigned to anyone (other than 555-1212, which is for long-distance directory assistance).

The *international* format for a telephone number is as follows:

- A plus sign ("+"), which indicates that the caller is supposed to first dial whatever local prefix is required for international long-distance calls (for example, from North America, 011 is usually first dialed for a direct-dialed "overseas" call and 01 for a calling-card "overseas" call)

- The *country code* (for example, 1 for Canada or the U.S., 44 for the U.K.)
- The *routing code* (also called the *area code*)
- The *local number* (which is seven digits for North America)

For example, +1-416-555-1430.

See *800*, *AMPS*, *DTMF*, *E.163*, *E.164*, *Fax*, and *POTS*.

DNS
Digital Naming Service

DEC's network name service, soon to be X.500 based.

See *DEC* and *X.500*.

DNS
Domain Name System

The Internet's standard for host names and a hierarchical system of *domain name servers* to resolve them into IP addresses (such as 199.12.1.1). Other information, such as type of hardware, services supported, and how long to cache the entry can also be stored.

Replaces the hosts.txt file on individual machines that used to perform this function (and becomes difficult to administer when there are more than a few stations on a network).

Each name server has the IP address of a name server higher in the hierarchy to which it sends queries that it cannot resolve itself.

A full DNS name (for example) is *gateway.noodle.ajax.com*. *gateway* is the name of our host in the subdomain, *noodle*. *ajax* is the name of our network, all in the *commercial* "top-level domain."

Absolute names are complete. *Relative names* contain a smaller subset of the name (such as *gateway*). A specific user (with *username* on machine *gateway*) is often addressed as *username@gateway* (to send that user email from within the same network).

Some top-level domain names are listed in the following table.

Domain Name	User
arpa	ARPAnet
com	Commercial organizations

(table continued on next page)

Domain Name	User
edu	Educational institutions
gov	Government organizations
mil	U.S.-based military
net	Internet access providers
org	Nonprofit organizations
other	Countries outside the U.S., such as *uk* for the United Kingdom and *on.ca* for Ontario, Canada

A recent change is shown in the last row: top-level domain names are now often geographically related. ISO 3166 specifies the two-letter country codes to be used.

Limitations are as follows:

- DNS limits each name (*noodle*) to a maximum of 63 characters, and the entire name (*gateway.noodle.ajax.com*) cannot exceed 256 characters
- The InterNIC requires that for the Internet, the entire name be a maximum of 24 characters (plus the top-level domain name).

DNS is distributed in that name servers keep track of hosts that are below them in the hierarchy. Usually, each site has a name server for its local machines. The most popular implementation of DNS is the *Berkeley Internet Name Daemon* (`bind`), it is usually just another process on a UNIX host.

Name servers can be:

- *Primary Master* (has the actual files)
- *Secondary Master* (periodically checks the primary to see whether anything has changed and requests an update if so, also backs up the primary)
- *Caching* (temporarily stores responses and responds on behalf of a master when it can)

Name servers usually have IP addresses only for names up to two levels below them. Resolving longer names therefore may involve a higher-level name server querying a lower-level name server to respond to a request.

End-user stations have a *name resolver* that caches frequent DNS queries. Their name resolver configuration file has IP addresses of a few nearby name servers.

The process for *registering* for a (guaranteed worldwide unique and known) domain name (and IP address) involves filling out a form. Usually, your Internet service provider will do this for you, but you can do it yourself as well (though you need to know the address of your name server). Where the form comes from (and to whom you return it) depends on the type of name desired.

- Names in the (for example) *.com* and *.net* top-level domains are administered by the InterNIC, which can be contacted at *http://internic.net/*.
- Names in the *.ca* top-level domain are administered by the CA domain registrar, which can be contacted under *http://www.canet.ca/*.

Determining the registered DNS name for an organization can be done by telnet-ting to the InterNIC (to *rs.internic.net* and running the whois command or to *ds.internic.net* and select the White Pages menu item) or, using WWW, use URL *http://www.csi.nb.ca/domain* (for the *.ca* domain).

DNS is specified in RFCs 1034 and 1035.

See *Cache*, *CA*net*, *DHCP*, *Internet*, *InterNIC*, *IP Address*, *ISP*, and *TCP/IP*.

DPA
Demand Protocol Architecture

3Com's capability of swapping protocol stacks in and out of a PC's RAM (to reduce the memory requirements).

See *3Com*.

DPMS
Display Power Management Signaling

A specification from the Video Electronics Standards Association defining how a PC's video adapter can request the monitor to go to one of several power-saving modes (so that the monitor can be *Energy Star* compliant).

- *Standby Mode* saves about 30% of the power required for normal running mode and allows for instant-on as soon as needed.
- *Suspend Mode* saves more power (by powering-off the CRT's main heater) but requires up to 5 seconds to turn back on.
- *Off Mode* saves more power by turning power off to everything except the monitor's microprocessor.

Typically, the display is fully powered-on when any keyboard key is pressed.

See *DDC*, *Energy Star*, and *VESA*.

DQDB
Distributed Queue Dual Bus

The *access mechanism* (method to obtain permission to transmit) for a metropolitan area network that never became popular.

A protocol defined in the IEEE's 802.6 MAN specification that provides an access mechanism to a network. Two one-directional buses are used: a station with data to transmit puts a request to transmit on one bus and later transmits on the other bus.

See *MAN* and *SMDS*.

DRAM
Dynamic Random Access Memory

The type of memory usually used in PCs (and most other computers too) for the main memory (such as your "8 Mbytes of RAM"), since it is lower-cost (albeit slower) than other types (such as *Static Random Access Memory*—SRAM).

"*Dynamic*" refers to the memory's method of storage—basically storing the charge on a capacitor. Like all capacitors, the memory cells of a DRAM integrated circuit self-discharge over time (in this case, within about a millisecond) and need to be *refreshed*. This is done by circuitry (which cycles through memory addresses) that is part of the computer's memory subsystem.

Standard DRAM does not have a fast-enough *access time* (the fastest is currently about 70 ns) to permit recent processors to work at full speed. Specialized types of DRAM (such as EDO RAM and VRAM) have therefore been developed.

See *EDO RAM*, *RAM*, and *VRAM*.

DS-0
Digital Signal Level 0

One of the 24 64,000-bits/s channels in a T1 data communications link.

Users likely have access only to 56,000 bits/s of this 64,000 bits/s (unless B8ZS is used).

See *B8ZS*, *FT1*, *PCM*, *Subrate*, and *T1*.

DS-1
Digital Signal Level 1

The bit format used for transmission on a T1 data communications link. A T1 provides 1.544 Mbits/s transmission over copper, fiber, or radio links (for example).

The term "DS-1" is usually used interchangeably with "T1."

See *T1*.

DS-3
Digital Signal Level 3

The bit format used for transmission on a T3 data communications link. A T3 provides 44.736 Mbits/s transmission over copper, fiber, or radio links (for example).

The term "DS-3" is usually used interchangeably with "T3."

See *T3*.

DSU
Data Service Unit

The device required to convert the digital data from a (for example) router to T1 voltages and encoding. Usually uses a V.35 interface to the router.

Because of proprietary extra features, such as multiplexing and diagnostics, units from the same manufacturer must usually be used at both ends of a link. Often integrated with the CSU, so the unit is then called a CSU/DSU.

Some CSU/DSUs have built-in *data compression*.

A manufacturer of CSU/DSUs is Digital Link Corporation, which has a WWW server at *http://www.dl.com/*.

See *B8ZS*, *CCP*, *CSU*, *Encoding*, *T1*, and *V.35*.

DTE
Data Terminal Equipment

Usually a computer terminal or a PC emulating one. Or a computer.

That is, equipment that sources or sinks data, as shown in the accompanying figure (so it is the *terminus*).

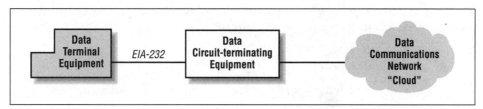

DTE−1

See *DCE* (Data Circuit-Terminating Equipment), *EIA/TIA-232*, *Modem*, *V.54*, and *WAN*.

DTMF
Desktop Management Task Force

A group of hardware vendors establishing a standardized way to report the software and hardware in a (currently, DOS- and Windows-based) workstation. This won't result in an *SNMP agent* but would make developing an SNMP agent easier (since there would be a standardized way for it to gather the information it needs).

See *DMI* and *SNMP*.

DTMF
Dual Tone Multi-Frequency

The *in-band* signaling method used by touch-tone telephones. Pairs of frequencies are assigned to each of 16 buttons (though most telephones only have 12). The following table shows the frequencies that are used.

		High Group Frequencies (Hz)			
		1,209	1,336	1,477	1,633
Low Group Frequencies (Hz)	697	1	2	3	A
	770	4	5	6	B
	852	7	8	9	C
	941	*	0	#[a]	D

[a] AT&T calls this an *octothorpe*.

The frequencies were chosen so that none were integral multiples of others. This simplifies the design of the filters required for the DTMF receivers.

See *DID*, *DN*, *In-Band*, *POTS*, and *SIT*.

DVD
Digital Video Disk

A technology to put video (such as movies) on things that look like CD-ROMs.

There were initially two competing technologies (but industry associations forced them to work together on a single standard):

- Toshiba and Time-Warner's SD
- Sony and Philips' video–CD

Both systems were to have supported at least 270 minutes of audio and video on a disk.

See *CD-ROM* (*Video CD*) and *SD*.

DX4

Intel's central processing unit, which was popular from about 1993 to 1995.

A 3.3-volt 486DX (earlier 486s were 5-volt) with a built-in math coprocessor. They are usually clock-tripled, but can also run at 2, 2.5, or 3 times their external speed, as shown in the accompanying table. For example, a 100-MHz DX4 runs at 33 MHz externally and 100 MHz internally.

Has a 16-kbyte (which is double that of earlier 486s and the same size as a Pentium) internal (also called *Level 1*) RAM *unified* (not divided into separate sections for code and data) cache.

In contrast, the Pentium processor has separate sections for code and data. DX4-based PCs will typically have at least 256 kbytes of external (also called *Level 2*) cache.

The "4" in DX4 is supposed to remind you of 486. Intel is dropping the "486" part of the name, since it cannot be copyrighted.

DX4 Internal Speed (MHz)	External Speed (MHz)	Clock Multiple	Comments
75	25	3	Intended for laptop PCs
83	33	2.5	
100	33	3	

See *486DX*, *Cache*, *Copyright*, *Intel*, and *PC*.

DXI
Data Exchange Interface

An interface between routers and CSU/DSUs that enables existing routers (that don't have the hardware capability to support ATM's cells) to support ATM—with only a software upgrade (but only at sub-SONet access speeds).

The trick is to have the CSU/DSU provide the *Segmentation and Reassembly* (SAR) functions (splitting the router's frames to ATM cells) at T1 or fractional T1 speeds. The router sends variable-length frames to the CSU/DSU, making it look (to the router) as though the ATM network accepts variable-length frames.

The router outputs CSPDUs (*Convergence Sublayer Protocol Data Units*) from ATM *adaptation layers* 3/4 and 5 (up to 4,090 bytes per frame).

Specifications include how LAN packets are segmented into ATM cells, the electrical interface (V.35, or HSSI at up to 45 Mbits/s), and the exchange of *local management information*.

Two modes of operation are defined:

- *Mode 1* handles up to 1,024 virtual circuits, supports AAL 5, uses a 16-bit CRC, and has a maximum packet size of 8 kbytes (limited by the CRC)
- *Mode 2* devices handle up to 16 million virtual circuits, support AAL 3/4 and 5, use 32-bit CRCs, and have a maximum packet size of 64 kbytes (again, limited by the CRC)

Based on the SMDS DXI. Frames use a 2-byte header with a 10-bit address (as does frame relay). *Quality of Service* (QOS) for each virtual circuit (including minimum throughput rate and maximum delay) can be specified.

Carriers may offer this service, making the link from the customer site to the C.O. switch more efficient—ATM's 53-byte cells are at least (5/53 =) 9.4% overhead. At this "low speed," competes with frame relay.

Now called DX-UNI.

An extension is the *Frame User to Network Interface* (FUNI), which supports all of the *User Network Interface* (UNI) functionality, including end-to-end signaling, traffic management, and network management, but does the SAR functions at the carrier's site, not the customer's. (The expectation is that it will be more cost-effective to do the SAR at a centralized location, for many customers.)

See *ATM* (*Asynchronous Transfer Mode*), *CRC*, *CSU*, *DSU*, *HSSI*, *SMDS*, *T1*, and *V.35*.

Dynamic Data Exchange   See **DDE**.

Dynamic Host Configuration Protocol   See **DHCP**.

Dynamic Link Library   See **DLL**.

Dynamic Random Access Memory   See **DRAM**.

E.163

The ITU-T standard that specifies the format for standard international telephone numbers. They are formally called *directory numbers* and are 12 digits (maximum).

See *DN* and *E.164*.

E.164

The ITU-T standard that specifies the telephone number–type address format used for ISDN.

Addresses are a maximum of 15 digits and are a geographically hierarchical structure (which is well-suited to worldwide routing). Addresses are assigned by carriers.

In contrast, other addressing schemes (such as for the IP addresses for the Internet) are organizationally oriented.

ITU-T standard E.164 (*Numbering Plan for the ISDN Era*) is the same as ITU-T standard I.331.

See *ATM*, *Carrier*, *DN*, *DNS Digital Naming Service*, *DNS IP Address*, and *SMDS*.

E1

The European equivalent of North America's T1. A point-to-point, dedicated, 2.048-Mbits/s digital communications circuit that carries 32 64,000-bits/s channels:

- 30 user–data 64,000-bits/s channels
- A 64,000-bits/s control channel
- A 64,000-bits/s synchronization channel

Because of the higher speed (than T1), repeaters on copper links are required more often than every 6,000 feet.

Also used in Australia.

Also called CEPT-1 (*Conférence Européenne des Administrations des Postes et des Télécommunications–1*).

A *framing* standard specified by the CCITT is G.703, which is similar (in function, not format) to T1's ESF.

See *DS-1*, *E3*, *ESF*, *PCM*, *T1*, and *WAN*.

E2

A communications circuit that supports four E1s. The actual bit rate is 8.848 Mbits/s.

Rarely implemented.

See *E1* and *E3*.

E3

The European equivalent of North America's T3. Carries 16 E1 circuits on a 34.368-Mbits/s channel. This is 480 conversations (and each conversation is the same as a 64,000 bits/s circuit).

Also called CEPT-3.

See *E1*, *SDH*, *SONet*, *T1*, and *WAN*.

E4

The European point-to-point digital circuit with a speed greater than E3: 139.264 Mbits/s. Carries four E3 circuits, which are 64 E1 circuits. This is 1,920 conversations (and a conversation requires the same bit rate as a 64,000-bits/s circuit).

See *E3*, *SDH*, *SONet*, *T3*, and *WAN*.

E5

A communications circuit that supports four E4s (a total of 7,680 conversations).

The actual bit rate is 565.148 Mbits/s.

See *E3* and *E4*.

EBCDIC
Extended Binary Coded Decimal Interchange Code

The 8-bit character coding scheme used by IBM mainframes and minicomputers (such as the AS/400—*Application Server 400*). Alphabetic characters are not represented by consecutive codes, because of EBCDIC's origin as the coding used for IBM Hollerith punch cards. The rest of the world (even the PC, which was designed by IBM) uses ASCII and maybe someday, Unicode.

The following tables show the hexadecimal for each EBCDIC character. For example, a *line feed* is represented as 25_{16}, and "$" is $5B_{16}$.

Least Signifi-cant Digit	Most Significant Hexadecimal Digit							
	0	**1**	**2**	**3**	**4**	**5**	**6**	**7**
0	Null	Data link escape	Digit select		Space	&	–	
1	Start of heading	Device control 1	Start of signif-icance				/	
2	Start of text	Device control 2	Field separator	Synchro-nization character				
3	End of text	Tape mark						
4	Punch off	Restore	Bypass	PN				
5	Hori-zontal tab	New line	Line feed	Record separator				
6	Lower-case	Backspace	End of trans-mission block	Uppercase				
7	Delete	Idle	Escape	End of transmis-sion				
8		Cancel						
9	RLF	End of medium						\
A	Start of manual message	Cursor control	Set mode		¢	!	¦	:
B	Vertical tab	Customer use 1	Cus-tomer use 2	Customer use 3	.	$	,	#
C	Form feed	Inter-change file sepa-rator		Device control 4	<	*	%	@
D	Carriage return	Inter-change group separator	Enquiry	Negative acknowl-edgment	(	)	_	'

(table continued on next page)

Least Significant Digit	Most Significant Hexadecimal Digit							
	0	1	2	3	4	5	6	7
E	Shift out	Inter-change record separator	Acknow-ledge		+	;	>	=
F	Shift in	Inter-change unit sepa-rator	Bell	Start of special sequence	¦ or [	¬ or]	?	"

Least Significant Digit	Most Significant Hexadecimal Digit							
	8	9	A	B	C	D	E	F
0					{	}	'	0
1	a	j			A	J		1
2	b	k	s		B	K	S	2
3	c	l	t		C	L	T	3
4	d	m	u		D	M	U	4
5	e	n	v		E	N	V	5
6	f	o	w		F	O	W	6
7	g	p	x		G	P	X	7
8	h	q	y		H	Q	Y	8
9	i	r	z		I	R	Z	9
A								
B								
C								
D								
E								
F								

Pronounced "*eb*-sa-dik."

See *ASCII*, *Baud*, *Mainframe*, and *Unicode*.

ECC
Error-Correcting Code

A memory system that has extra (usually called "redundant" or "check") bits per word so that most memory errors can be detected and corrected.

To calculate the fewest number of redundant (r) bits necessary to detect and correct single-bit errors in a message of length m use the following equation:

$$(m + r + 1) \leq 2^r$$

Therefore, for a 32-bit word, at least 6 ECC bits must be added, since $(32 + 6 + 1) \leq 2^6$. Each memory location would then need to store 38 bits. Errors in the check bits are handled in the same way as errors in the data bits.

A typical actual implementation requires seven check bits for every 32 data bits stored. This ensures that all single-bit errors are detected and corrected, all occurrences of 2 bits in error (per 32-bit word) are detected, and some occurrences of 3 and more bits in error are detected.

In 1950, a smart guy named Richard W. Hamming figured out a method of implementing ECC memory using the theoretical minimum number of redundant bits (this is called the *Hamming Code*).

Sometimes called *Error Detection and Correction* (EDAC).

See *FCS*, *Parity*, and *RAM*.

ECP
Extended Capabilities Port

An enhancement to the original parallel port on a PC, which provides the following:

- Data transfer rates of more than 2 Mbytes/s
- Bidirectional 8-bit operation (a standard parallel port only has 4 input bits)
- Ability to specify bytes sent between the PC and peripheral (by the sender raising a signal line) to be either data or commands
- Support for CD-ROM and scanner connections to PCs
- Hardware strobe generation (the PC software does not need to raise and drop the strobe line to the printer for each byte transferred)
- 16-byte (or more) FIFO buffer to speed data transmission
- Support for *run length encoding* data compression, in which rather than sending many repetitive bytes (which, for example, is common from scanners), a single byte and a count of the number of times that the receiving driver should repeat it, are sent
- DMA support to increase transfer speed and reduce processor overhead

Developed by Hewlett-Packard and Microsoft (which have a big interest in faster and better communications to printers). Current development work is being done within the IEEE 1284 group.

See *1284*, *EPP*, *HP*, *Microsoft*, *Parallel Port*, *PC*, and *RLE*.

ECTF
Enterprise Computer Telephony Forum

Formed by Dialogic, DEC, Ericsson, Hewlett-Packard, and Northern Telecom to encourage industry-wide consensus and interoperability in standards implementations for *computer telephony integration*.

ECTF is now the owner of the following:

- The widely-supported *Signal Computing System Architecture* (SCSA)—developed by Dialogic Corporation as an open hardware/software architecture to incorporate CTI products from many vendors
- T*map* software, developed by Northern Telecom, which provides interworking between Microsoft's TAPI and Novell's TSAPI

Dialogic and Northern Telecom have WWW servers at *http://www.dialogic.com/* and *http://www.nt.com/*, respectively.

See *CTI*, *TAPI*, and *TSAPI*.

EDAC
Error Detection and Correction

See *ECC*.

EDI
Electronic Data Interchange

There are estimates that 80% of what is printed by one computer is manually entered into another. In the process of doing business, companies will send and receive price lists, product orders, waybills, invoices, statements, and many more standard (for their industry) documents. The retyping of this information into other computer systems introduces unnecessary expense, delays, and errors.

EDI enables computers of different types to send and receive information directly.

Even once protocols and standards are worked out so that two computers could directly communicate, there are several potential problems. What if:

- The receiver's computer was down because of communication line problems, scheduled maintenance, or a hardware problem when the sender wanted to send the file?
- The receiver accidentally deleted the received file before processing it?
- The sender claims to have sent a file that the receiver has no record of receiving?

To avoid these problems, an EDI sender and receiver usually do not communicate directly. Instead, a trusted third-party service provider acts as a store-and-forward mailbox. Many companies offer this service, such as General Electric Information

Services (GEIS), IBM Information Exchange, and Stentor TradeRoute. The third party:

- Guarantees to be up all the time
- Retains all transferred files for a few days, in case the receiver wants to re-receive it
- Keeps a log of all activities

In addition, the third party can do edit-checks on the data to ensure that the files are in a valid format.

Typically, the third party charges per line item transferred and uses the X.25 protocol to establish connections to the companies.

GEIS has a relevant WWW home page at *http://www.ge.com/geis/overview/ecsoverv.html*.

See *PGP* and *X.25*

EDO RAM
Extended Data Out Random Access Memory

A faster (than standard DRAM) type of *Dynamic Random Access Memory*.

It uses latches so it can continue to output the accessed memory location's contents (so the computer has time to read it) even after the computer starts specifying the address of the next location to be read. This enables the memory cycle time to be faster, as is required for faster CPUs such as the 120-MHz Pentium.

Burst EDO RAM automatically supplies data for the next few sequential memory locations (memory accesses are largely to sequential memory locations), speeding up the cycle time even more.

See *DRAM*, *Pentium*, and *RAM*.

EIA
Electronic Industries Association

A group that produces many electrical and electronics-oriented standards. Perhaps the most famous one (and certainly my personal favorite) is EIA/TIA-232 (which used to be called RS-232).

See *EIA/TIA-232*, *Standards*, *TIA* (*Telecommunications Industry Association*), and *TSB*.

EIA/TIA-232
Electronic Industries Association/Telecommunications Industry Association
Recommended Standard 232

A standard specifying the interface between (for example) a modem and a computer so that they can exchange data. The computer can then send data to the modem (which somehow sends them over a telephone line), and the data that the modem receives from the telephone line can then be sent to the computer.

Officially called *Interface Between Data Terminal Equipment and Data Circuit-Terminating Equipment Employing Serial Binary Data Interchange*. It specifies the connector, pin functions, and voltages used to connect two devices together so that they can send data to each other.

One device is the *data terminal equipment* (such as the COM1 serial port of a PC), and the other is the *data circuit-terminating equipment*, previously called *data communications equipment* (such as a modem).

PCs use a male DE-9 (standardized in EIA/TIA-574) or DB-25 (standardized in EIA/TIA-232) connector.

A "binary" interface is used, with the following two states:

- A "high" signal is a positive voltage (anywhere between +3 and +25 volts D.C.). It has the following characteristics:
  - It is considered on ("RTS is *high*"—or *on* or *true* or *asserted*)
  - It is a space (the line is in a "spacing condition," or the bit is a "space parity" bit)
  - It represents a binary 0 (the datum is a zero bit)
- A "low" signal is a negative voltage (anywhere between −3 and −25 volts D.C.). It has the following characteristics:
  - It is considered off ("CTS is *low*"—or *off* or *false* or *deasserted*)
  - It is a mark (the line is in a "marking condition," or the bit is a "mark parity" bit)
  - It represents a binary 1 (the datum is a one bit)

The following table shows the interface signals (or *pin-out*) for 9-pin and 25-pin connectors (when used for *asynchronous* data). Signal names are relative to the DTE (the transmit data signal is data from the DTE).

DB-25 Pin Number	DB-9 Pin Number	Pin Name	Direction DTE | DCE	Pin Function
2	3	TxD	→	Data transmitted from DTE to DCE (for example, from PC to modem)
3	2	RxD	←	Data received from DCE to DTE (from modem to PC)
4	7	RTS	→	DTE requests permission to send data to modem
5	8	CTS	←	DCE grants permission to send

(table continued on next page)

DB-25 Pin Number	DB-9 Pin Number	Pin Name	Direction DTE	DCE	Pin Function
6	6	DSR		←	DCE indicates that it is operational (the modem is powered on)
7	5	Signal ground		↔	Common ground reference
8	1[a]	DCD		←	DCE indicates that it is receiving carrier from remote modem
20	4	DTR		→	DTE indicates that it is operational (powered on)
22	9[a]	RI		←	DCE indicates that the phone is ringing

[a] Some DB-9 to DB-25 adapters do not connect these signals, thus providing hours of rewarding troubleshooting practice for lucky people.

For *synchronous* communications, *clock* signals are also required. A clock is a square-wave signal, at the same rate as the data. The falling edge of the clock (positive to negative voltage transition) indicates the center of the data bit.

Usually, *external clock* is used—the modem (which is "external" to the DTE) generates the signal (either internally or derived from the data received from the remote modem). The *transmit clock* signal (which is on pin 15) determines the rate at which the DTE transmits data. The receive clock (on pin 17) specifies the rate at which the modem is sending data to the DTE.

Sometimes, the *internal clock* is used (for example, when there is no modem). The DTE then generates the clock signal (on pin 24), and this specifies the data rate at which the DTE is transmitting data.

There are no standard abbreviations for the signals, but some commonly used ones are shown in the following table.

DB-25 Pin Number	Abbreviation	Meaning (when on)
2	SD or TD or TxD	The PC is sending (transmitting) data to the modem
3	RD or RxD	The PC is receiving data from the modem
4	RTS[a]	The PC will accept data from the modem
5	CTS[a]	The modem will accept data from the PC
6	MR or DSR	Data Set (or Modem) Ready—the modem is powered on

(table continued on next page)

DB-25 Pin Number	Abbreviation	Meaning (when on)
8	CD, DCD, RLSD, or CS	(Data) Carrier Detect, or Received Line Signal Detect or Carrier Sense
20	TR or DTR	Data Terminal Ready—the PC is powered on and ready to accept an incoming call
22	RI or AA	Ring Indicator or Auto-Answer—the phone is ringing (when flashing), or the modem is set to automatically answer incoming calls (when on constantly)
b	HS	High Speed—the modem is communicating with another modem and has negotiated a modulation with a data rate (for example) of: 2,400 bits/s or less (flashing), 4,800 to 14,400 bits/s (OFF), or 16,600 bits/s or faster (ON)
b	OH	The modem has the telephone line Off-Hook (a phone call has been or is being, made or answered)
b	TM	The modem is in a Test Mode

[a] As described in the table, these signals are now usually used for *hardware flow control* (rather than their original intent for controlling half-duplex modems). For example, the modem puts a negative voltage on pin 5 while it cannot accept more data from the PC (because the PC has been sending data faster than the modem can transmit it to the remote modem). The modem will put a positive voltage on pin 5 when it has transmitted most of its buffered data to the remote modem and is ready to receive more from the PC.

[b] These are not EIA-232 signals but are usually shown on modem status displays along with the other EIA-232 signals.

The combination of ITU-T's V.24 and V.28 (which is basically what EIA/TIA-232 is called outside of North America) are equivalent to EIA/TIA-232. So why does it take ITU-T two standards to say what EIA/TIA says in one? Well, it's because ITU-T is being more modular, and separately specifies signal names, and their functions in V.24 and electrical characteristics (voltage and current limits) and the pin assignments in V.28.

A previous version of the standard was RS-232-C (it was commonly called "RS-232"). It was released in 1969 and was the current version when most existing computer equipment was designed. At that time, the EIA referred to all of its standards as *recommended standards* and prefaced the number with "RS".

In 1987, EIA-232-D was released with the following changes:

- The EIA decided that it could raise its profile by getting rid of the somewhat meaningless "RS" and putting its own name there instead, so EIA-232-D is simply the successor to RS-232-C.

- The connector is defined (the DB-25, which was already being used).
- A *local loopback* function is defined, in which the DTE can put a positive voltage on pin 18 (which was previously unassigned) and the DCE will perform a local analog loopback (V.54 loop 3) until the signal on pin 18 is deasserted.
- A *remote loopback* function is defined, in which the DTE can put a positive voltage on pin 21 (which was previously used as a signal quality indicator from the DCE but seldom used) and the DCE will signal the remote DCE that it should go into *remote digital loopback* (V.54 loop 2) until the signal on pin 21 is deasserted.
- An indicator that the DCE is in either of these *test modes* is defined. Pin 25 is asserted (pin 25 was previously unassigned).

In 1991, EIA/TIA-232-E was released, with the following changes:

- The EIA began to work with the TIA on standards that concern telecommunications, so TIA gets its name in the standard too.
- Rather than the modem's *ringing indicator* (pin 22) always being asserted at about the same time as the phone rings, the DCE can be sensitive to telephone company *distinctive ringing* and assert pin 22 only if certain distinctive ring cadences occur.
- To support hardware flow control, pin 4 (previously *request to send*) can instead be used as *ready for receiving*, to indicate that the DTE can accept data. The use of request to send is necessary only for half-duplex operation, which is seldom used now, since modems are typically full-duplex. (Request to send is considered constantly asserted when pin 4 is used for flow control.)
- Also to support hardware flow control, the DCE can deassert pin 5 (*clear to send*) to signal to the DTE that the DTE should temporarily stop transmitting data to the DCE (for example, because the DCE is performing a retrain/entrain or error correction or is not able to compress the DTE's data enough to send it over the communications channel as fast as the DTE is sending it). Previously, pin 5 was used only for half-duplex operation.
- An alternative 26-pin (though the 26th pin is left unconnected) connector "Alt A" is defined. It is smaller than a DB-25 (about 20 mm wide, versus 40 mm) and uses square pins. The female of this connector is used on both DTE and DCE, and cables with male connectors on both ends are then used (unlike the DB-25, in which the DCE has a female connector and the DTE usually has a male connector).

- Pin 1 is redefined to be *shield* (for shielded cables) rather than *protective ground*. If the shield connection is used, then the cable's shield can be connected at the DTE only. If frame ground bonding of the DTE and DCE is required, then a separate conductor should be used (meeting local electrical codes).

See *16550A, Asynchronous, DB-25, DCE, DTE, Encoding, ESP, Full-duplex, Half-Duplex, In-Band, Modem, Out-of-band, Standards, Synchronous, UART, V.34, V.35, V.42bis,* and *V.54.*

EIA/TIA TSB-37a

The interim name for a standard specifying types of analog communication line impairments (such as time delays, noise, and frequency, nonlinear and phase distortions) that are useful for simulating, to test modem performance.

Twenty-four types of C.O. trunks and seven types of lines are defined.

See *Modem, PCM,* and *V.56bis.*

E-IDE
Enhanced IDE

An popular interface that is used to connect a computer to its hard disk drive (and other peripherals).

Also called Fast IDE and ATA-2. Enhancements include support for ATAPI tape and CD-ROM drives.

The specification was developed by Western Digital and is shown in the following table.

	IDE	E-IDE
Disk drive capacity (Mbytes)	504	8,033
Data transfer rate (Mbytes/s)	1 to 3	Up to 16.6
Drives per adapter[a]	2	4
Types of drives supported	Hard disk	Hard disk, tape, CD-ROM, and more

[a] Assuming two controllers (primary and secondary) per E-IDE adapter.

IDE's cable limitation of 18 inches still applies, so drives remain restricted to being internal to the PC.

The following table shows a PC's disk drive capacity limitations.

		BIOS Maximum	IDE Maximum
Cylinders		1,024	65,536
Heads per drive		255	16
Sectors per track[a]		63	255
Maximum drive capacity (assuming DOS's 512 bytes per Sector)	bytes	8,422,686,720	136,902,082,560
	Gbytes	7.8	127.5

[a] A track is a cylinder's data on one disk surface (that is, all the data that a single read/write head can see without *seeking*.)

The storage capacity of a PC's IDE drive is limited by the smaller of either the BIOS or IDE limitations. The storage capacity can be calculated as follows:

- 1,024 cylinders (BIOS maximum)
- 16 read/write heads (disk surfaces) per drive (IDE maximum)
- 63 sectors (DOS uses 512-byte sectors) per track (BIOS maximum)

So the maximum IDE disk drive capacity is $(1,024 \times 16 \times 63 \times 512 =)$ 504 Mbytes, where 1 Mbyte is $(1,024 \times 1,024$ bytes $=)$ 1,048,576 bytes.

Enhanced IDE can remap blocks of data so that the BIOS sees more heads (but the enhanced IDE drive sees more cylinders) so that the BIOS maximum of 7.8 Gbytes becomes the maximum capacity of an enhanced IDE drive. (The remapping converts all requests to a 28-bit *Logical Block Address*—LBA.)

Standard IDE controllers typically use *Programmed I/O* (PIO) to transfer data to and from the processor (and do not require disk driver software—since the PC's BIOS handles IDE disk controllers). However, Enhanced IDE can use PIO—which is slower but simpler (since a PC's BIOS will typically already support PIO, so no drivers need to be loaded), and DMA (which provides faster data transfers, but additional disk driver software or an enhanced BIOS is required).

Using programmed I/O, maximum transfer rates are as follows:

- 2 to 3 Mbytes/s (on ISA bus systems)
- 11.1 Mbytes/s (when using *Mode 3 PIO*)
- 16.6 Mbytes/s (when using *Mode 4 PIO*)

Using DMA, maximum transfer rates are as follows:

- 4 Mbytes/s transfers (when using Type B DMA, which is used for EISA bus adapters)
- 6.67 Mbytes/s or 8.33 Mbytes/s—both are defined, and either speed can be implemented by a manufacturer, depending on which PCI/ISA chip set is used (when using Type F DMA, which is used on a local bus, which will usually be PCI)

- 13.3 Mbytes/s, which is double the 6.67–Mbytes/s speed above, since multiple words are transferred during each DMA (when using *Mode 1 Multiword DMA*)
- 16.6 Mbytes/s, which is double the 8.33–Mbytes/s rate above, since multiple words are transferred during each DMA (when using *Mode 2 Multiword DMA*)

These transfer rates and timings are specified by the *Small Form Factor Committee.*

Products can support any subset of these transfer modes and still be called Enhanced IDE. (Makes it a bit difficult to compare products, doesn't it?)

IDE PIO data transfers are sometimes called *blind PIO*, since the PC reads data with no feedback about whether it is reading faster than the disk drive can supply the data. (This concern was never a problem when PCs were slow.) The IDE interface was designed to be slow enough to prevent a fast PC from reading too fast. Unfortunately, this needlessly reduces the performance of fast disk drives, such as those with high disk rotation speeds or built-in caches.

E-IDE supports feedback (that is, *flow control*). The PC tries to transfer data as fast as it can. The disk drive can slow the transfer if it cannot provide the data as fast as the PC is requesting it, by using the PC bus's *I/O channel ready* signal.

To ensure that both PC and disk drive support flow control, the PC sends a command to the disk drive to enable the feature.

Support for four IDE devices is provided by putting two controllers (each controller can support two devices) on the same printed circuit board (PCs have reserved addresses for this second IDE controller). Each of the two controllers has its own 40-conductor flat ribbon cable (and each cable has two connectors, one for each device). Usually, one controller (the *primary* "channel" or "connector") is PCI bus-based, and the other controller (the *secondary*) uses only the ISA bus signals (even though this controller is on a PCI card). This reduces the cost, as the secondary channel is intended for slower devices (such as CD-ROM drives).

Since MS-DOS 3.0, DOS has had support for up to seven disk drives, so only a BIOS change is needed for E-IDE support under DOS or Windows. The disk drivers for other operating systems, such as OS/2, NetWare, and Windows NT have support for both the primary and secondary IDE controllers.

IDE support for CD-ROMs (and soon, tape drives, CD-R, and other types of drives) has been defined by Western Digital using the *AT Attachment Packet Interface* (ATAPI), which specifies the new commands (which are based on the SCSI-2 commands) and controller registers required. BIOS support will be required for ATAPI. This will substantially lower the cost of CD-ROM drives, since a SCSI or additional (proprietary) interface will not be required (since most PCs already have an IDE interface for the hard disk drive).

Mixing fast and slow devices (for example, hard disk and CD-ROM drives) on the primary controller may cause slower data transfer for the hard disk (all transfers may go at the speed of the slower device). Put only hard disks on the primary controller.

Competes with *Fast ATA*.

Western Digital has a WWW site at *http://www.wdc.com/*.

See *ATA, ATAPI, ATASPI, BIOS, Cache, CD-ROM, Disk Drive, DMA, Fast ATA, IDE, ISA, PC, PCI, PIO, SCSI*, and *Small Form Factor Committee*.

EISA
Extended Industry Standard Architecture

A 32-bit bus used in some (but not many) higher performance PCs. The newer PCI bus is better.

Supports many more features than ISA (for example, more than two bus masters and *switchless configuration*). A burst mode provides double the transfer rate (the address is supplied only at the start of the burst, and all subsequent data are assumed to go to sequential memory locations).

Runs at 8.33 MHz. The theoretical maximum transfer speed is 33 Mbytes/s. Competed with MCA. A main advantage over MCA is that ISA boards can be plugged into the EISA bus (though with no additional benefits or capabilities) but not into the MCA bus.

MCA was never widely accepted. (IBM was the main source of MCA PCs.) EISA is (was) used mainly in servers. PCI is the current high-performance PC (and other platform) bus.

Developed by the "Gang of Nine" (nine non-IBM manufacturers of IBM-compatible PCs, led by Compaq) when a 32-bit PC bus standard was needed and IBM wanted high royalties for its MCA bus.

See *Bus, ISA, MCA*, and *PCI*.

Electronic Data Interchange   See **EDI.**

Electronic Industries Association   See **EIA.**

Electronic Mail Broadcast to a Roaming Computer   See **EMBARC.**

Electromagnetic Field   See **EMF.**

ELF
Extremely Low Frequency

Frequencies of 300 Hz and less. For *electromagnetic fields* (and the MPR II standard), frequencies of 60 Hz (which are generated by power lines) and multiples of this are usually of most interest.

See *EMF*, *MPR II*, and *VLF*.

EMBARC
Electronic Mail Broadcast to a Roaming Computer

A pager-oriented broadcast (one-way only) data service for sending and receiving wireless electronic mail. Small devices receive the messages (for example, PCMCIA cards plugged into PCs that have their own RAM to store messages when the PC is powered off).

See *PCMCIA*.

EMF
Electromagnetic Field

The *electric* (and its related *magnetic*) *field* radiated by an electrical conductor in which a current is flowing.

EMFs are increasingly prevalent (and proximate), as they are generated by computers, cellular telephones, and other electronic devices. The EMFs generated have different frequencies (measured in hertz) and field strengths (measured in *teslas*, and very dependent on the distance to, and configuration of, the source of the EMF). A hot topic these days, since there are some studies that almost link some of these emissions with harmful health effects.

Since the electromagnetic field may interfere with the operation of other equipment (one person's music is another's noise), the EMF is often referred to as *Electromagnetic Interference* (EMI).

There are no North American standards, but compliance with the Swedish MPR II standard is widespread (those monitor manufacturers will do anything to sell more monitors).

A WWW server with lots of EMF-related information is at the site *http://www.infoventures.microserve.com/*.

See *AMPS*, *ELF*, *Encoding*, *MPR II*, *T*, *TCO*, and *VLF*.

Encapsulated PostScript   See **EPS**.

Encapsulation

Carrying frames of one protocol as the data in another, usually for one of the following reasons:

- The first protocol is not routable (such as LAT, NetBIOS, SDLC)—and many networks will not carry nonroutable protocols (since these networks are built using routers). Even for networks that can carry nonroutable protocols (using the bridging capability built in to most routers), it is usually not desirable since bridged networks do not scale well (bridging usually makes inefficient use of WAN links, and service interruptions often occur when network connectivity changes).
- So that only one protocol needs to be carried by the network—hopefully simplifying the WAN administration and router configuration.

Usually, the encapsulating protocol will be TCP/IP (it's so popular these days).

Unfortunately, encapsulation is usually undesirable, since it is inefficient. Each protocol (the encapsulator and the encapsulatee) has its own error detection and acknowledgments (wasting CPU time and WAN and router capacity), and the packets get needlessly larger (wasting more WAN capacity).

Also, handling broadcasts is difficult (the simplest option is to establish links to every possible broadcast destination and send the encapsulated broadcasts along each of them), so the number of broadcast destinations is usually limited—for example, to 10. Not a very scalable solution.

However, there *are* benefits, such as providing rerouting around network failures (this is part of what TCP/IP routing does) without dropping sessions. Without this rerouting, SNA traffic and users of Token Ring *source route bridging* get unceremoniously disconnected if the part of the network they are using goes down—even if other parts of the network that provide the connectivity they need are still up.

Also called *Tunneling*.

See *DLSw, MPTN, Scalable Architecture*, and *Spoofing*.

Encoding

Encoding can mean many things, but a common use of the term in *synchronous data communications* combines the clock and data into a single signal. This is necessary since LAN and WAN links are typically only a single signal (in each direction), and both clock and data are needed to send synchronous data. The receiver uses the clock so that it can "lock on" to the exact data rate of the received data (by using a *digital phase locked loop circuit*, which adjusts its frequency according to the transitions received).

Encoding schemes are designed for specific features, such as the following:

- Self-clocking (at least one transition will occur during each bit-time, regardless of the data)
- No D.C. voltage (that is, the average voltage is zero—important for transformer-coupled circuits to prevent the transformers from saturating or over-heating)
- Lowest possible bandwidth (reducing the number of transitions to reduce radiated *Electromagnetic Interference*—EMI)

Since there are often conflicting requirements (most commonly self-clocking with low bandwidth), there are many encoding schemes, each optimized differently.

Some common encoding methods used are described in the following table and illustrated in the accompanying figure.

Encoding Method	Commonly used for	Description
Alternate Mark Inversion	T1	A pulse indicates a 1. No pulse indicates a 0. Each pulse is the opposite polarity of the previous.
NRZ (Non Return to Zero)	Some IBM BISYNC environments	Actually, is not encoded. Just a confusing way of saying the binary data are sent as is.
NRZI (Non Return to Zero Inverted)	Most IBM BISYNC environments	A transition at the start of each bit-time indicates a 0. No transition at the start of a bit-time indicates a 1. The data must have enough 0s to keep synchronization (for example, HDLC's *zero-bit stuffing* ensures this).
Manchester	Ethernet, IBM 3270 and AS/400 5250 terminals	The complement of the data is sent during the first half of each bit-time, followed by a transition to the opposite polarity (un-complemented data) at the center of each bit-time. This transition is used for the clock. Another way of saying this is that the direction of the transition at the center of the bit-time indicates the data (a rising edge is a 1, a falling edge is a 0). Another transition will be needed at the start of each bit-time if two consecutive bits are the same.

(table continued on next page)

Encoding Method	Commonly used for	Description
Differential Manchester	Token Ring LANs	A transition at the start of each bit-time indicates a 0. No transition at the start of a bit-time indicates a 1. A transition at the center of each bit-time is used for the clock.

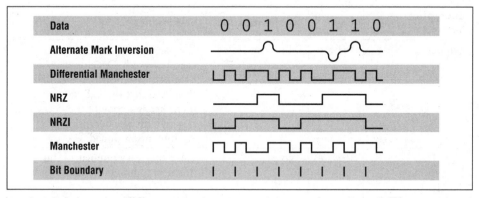

Encoding—1

See *100BASE-T4, 100BASE-TX, 8B/10B, B8ZS, Baud, BISYNC, EMF, Ethernet, FDDI, HDSL, Synchronous, T1*, and *Token Ring*.

Encryption

The process of changing a digital message (from *plaintext* to *ciphertext*) so that it can be read only by intended parties (also called *enciphering*), or to verify the identity of the sender (*authentication*), or to be assured that the sender really did send that message (*nonrepudiation*).

Some encryption schemes are described in the table below.

A *private key* (also called *secret key*, or *symmetric*) method has one key that is used to both encrypt and decrypt the message. Therefore the key must be kept secret. This makes the system more difficult to use, since the keys must be regularly changed, which requires secure distribution.

Public key (or *asymmetric*) systems use two keys. One of the keys (the public or nonsecret key) is used to encrypt messages, which can be decrypted only by using the secret corresponding decryption key (which only the intended recipient has). Or the secret key can be used to encrypt the message, and if it can be decrypted by using the public key, then the identity of the sender is assured. This brilliant concept was invented by Whitfield Diffie.

Some schemes provide authentication, to ensure that the message has not been modified without the sender's knowledge. Authentication can be added with a separate algorithm, such as the proposed digital signature standard.

Some schemes provide nonrepudiation, which provides the receiver with proof of who the sender is, so the sender cannot later deny sending the message ("*Hey, I'd never subscribe to a magazine like that!*").

Encryption Method	Key	Authentication	Comments
Clipper	Private	No	Uses an encryption algorithm called *Skipjack*. Developed by the U.S. National Security Agency. Proposed that the U.S. government keeps a copy of the decryption key for all encryption equipment produced.
DES (Data Encryption Standard)	Private	No	Currently very popular in the financial industry.
RSA (Rivest, Shamir, Adleman)	Public	Yes	The basis for the security in Netscape.

Many types of encryption developed in Canada and the U.S. (all of the good ones) are restricted from being exported (the idea is that the U.S. should not be helping other countries to keep secrets from the U.S.) by the Offices of Defense Trade Controls and Munitions Control, U.S. Department of State.

For a good FAQ, call *http://www.rsa.com/pub/faq/faq.asc.*

The Electronic Frontier Foundation has a great deal to say about the social impact of encryption. The Foundation has a WWW Server at *http://www.eff.org/.* Also, there is a good pointer page at *http://draco.centerline.com:8080/~franl/crypto.html.*

See *Authentication, DES, FAQ, IDEA, Kerberos, PGP, RSA,* and *WWW.*

End System   See **ES.**

Energy Star

A program of the Global Change Division of the U.S. Environmental Protection Agency to reduce the power requirements of PCs and their peripherals.

To receive certification (and be allowed to put the logo on the product), PCs, monitors, and most printers must draw less than 30 watts each when in idle (or stand-by) mode. Larger printers can draw 60 watts. Typical non–Energy Star PCs draw 150 watts (including the monitor).

In idle mode, Energy Star PCs shut off power to add-in boards (such as Ethernet cards). Therefore network connections (for example, to a file server) will be lost unless the board has been specifically designed for Energy Star PCs.

A list of Energy Star–compliant products is available by phoning 202-775-6650. Information is also available at the sites *http://www.epa.gov* and *http://www.epa.gov/ docs/energy_star.*

See *PC.*

Enhanced IDE   See **E-IDE.**

Enhanced Serial Port   See **ESP.**

Enhanced Specialized Mobile Radio   See **ESMR.**

Enterprise Computer Telephony Forum   See **ECTF.**

Enterprise Systems Connection   See **ESCON.**

EPP
Enhanced Parallel Port

An effort by Intel, Xircom, and Zenith Data Systems to define faster and bidirectional data transfer through a PC's parallel port.

Features include the following:

- Data transfer at up to 2 Mbytes/s
- Bidirectional 8-bit operation (a standard parallel port only has 4 input bits)
- Addressing to support multiple (daisy-chained) peripherals on a single PC parallel port
- Hardware strobe generation, so the PC software does not need to raise and drop the strobe line to the printer for each byte transferred; the PC's CPU can therefore use the very fast `rep outsb` instruction (repeat output string of bytes in sequential memory locations to the I/O port)

DMA is not supported (programmed or interrupt-based I/O is used).

Originally defined by its implementation by the Intel 360SL I/O integrated circuit (and called EPP v1.7). When the EPP group was merged into the IEEE 1284 multimodal port effort, the resulting IEEE 1284 EPP mode differed from EPP v1.7 enough that original EPP v1.7 peripherals are incompatible with the IEEE 1284 EPP parallel port. Newer EPP peripherals can be designed to be compatible with both the original EPP v1.7 and the IEEE 1284 EPP mode.

See *1284, ECP, Parallel Port,* and *PIO.*

EPS
Encapsulated PostScript

A PostScript file intended to be embedded in another document rather than printed directly (the "unencapsulated Postscript" format is used to print directly).

To elaborate, Adobe's *PostScript Page Description Language* is used for two purposes:

- As PostScript commands to be sent to a printer to print text, an image, or a combination of these. In this case these commands can be directly sent to a PostScript printer or stored on disk in a file (usually to be later sent to a printer). These files are called *PostScript* (PS) files.
- As PostScript commands (usually a file of commands that describe a graphic image) that are (or are to be) embedded in another document—for example, placing clip art (an image from a collection or created by using a different drawing program) into a word processing document. These files of commands are called *Encapsulated PostScript* (EPS) files.

That is, from your drawing program, you save your work in PostScript format if you will be printing the file. Save your work in encapsulated PostScript format if you will be embedding that file into another one.

EPS files consist of two parts:

- A preview image (often in TIFF or Macintosh PICT format) so that the image can be displayed and positioned when editing the document
- The actual PostScript commands that are required to generate the image (and that typically omit the PostScript showpage command which actually causes the image to be printed—since the entire document will be printed by using the document's word processing program)

Some notes on EPS files:

- EPS files are usually created by saving to that format; the original file (in Corel Draw or Adobe Illustrator format, for example) is usually the only one that can be subsequently edited.
- At the beginning of the file, it will usually have EPSF 3.0, to identify the file's format to the document into which the file will be embedded.
- EPS files must produce an image that prints on a single page.
- EPS files usually cannot be edited from the word processing program.
- Usually, EPS files will not print if sent to a PostScript printer.

See *Adobe*, *PostScript Type 1 Fonts*, *PostScript Type 3 Fonts*, and *TIFF*.

Error-Correcting Code   See **ECC.**

Error Detection and Correction   See **ECC**.

ES
End System

A host computer on an OSI network.

See *Host*, *IS*, and *OSI*.

ESCON
Enterprise Systems Connection

A 10-Mbytes/s (originally) or 17-Mbytes/s (introduced in 1991), fiber-optic LAN for linking IBM mainframes to disk drives (DASD) or other mainframes. Links up to 3 km (and up to 15 miles with repeaters) are supported. Intended to replace the traditional IBM mainframe *Bus-and-Tag* channel, and compete with DEC's VAX-cluster technology.

May support 27 Mbytes/s in the future.

Never as popular as (IBM) hoped, especially with smaller- and medium-sized shops.

See *Channel*, *DASD*, *FEP*, and *Mainframe*.

ESF
Extended Superframe

A framing standard for T1 that provides many useful benefits.

T1 uses a 193-bit frame (which is sent 8,000 times per second, which is every 125 μs). In each frame there are 24 channels, each carrying 8 bits of information, plus a framing bit.

In *Basic Superframe* (SF, also called D4 framing), 12 consecutive frames comprise a *superframe*. The 12 framing bits in this superframe (one framing bit per frame) goes through the 12-bit pattern 100011011100. That is, the framing bit is a 1 in the first frame, then 0 for each of the next three frames, then a 1 for the next two frames, and so on. By looking for this specific pattern in every 193rd bit, the receiver can establish *frame synchronization*—and then identify which 8 bits are for which of the 24 channels.

Extended Superframe extends this to not only provide frame synchronization, but also error detection and a data channel, all using the framing bit. In this case, 24 consecutive 193-bit frames make up an *Extended Superframe*, and the framing bit goes through a 24-bit cycle:

- Every fourth bit of this 24-bit cycle (that is, the framing bits for frames 4, 8, 12, 16, 20, and 24) goes through the pattern 001011 (note that this pattern never looks like a shifted copy of itself). This provides the frame synchronization.

- The framing bits for frames 2, 6, 10, etc. are used to send a 6-bit CRC, generated from the data in the previous 24 frames. This provides error detection. The receiving CSU can then track the error rate and generate an alarm if it gets too high. (This error checking is done constantly while the link is in service and for any type of data—neat, huh?)
- The remaining framing bits (for frames 1, 3, 5, 7, etc.) provide a 4,000-bits/s supervisory data channel that is used for other functions such as remote configuration and monitoring of CSUs.

See *B8ZS*, *CRC*, *CSU*, *E1*, *PCM*, and *T1*.

ESMR
Enhanced Specialized Mobile Radio

A two-way radio technology developed by Motorola and implemented in its *Motorola Integrated Radio System* (MIRS, announced in 1991). First implemented in Los Angeles in 1994.

Uses TDMA technology to put six simultaneous conversations into one traditional 25-kHz UHF radio channel (in the 806- to 821-MHz band).

Is overlapping-cell-based (like traditional AMPS cellular telephone), but cells are larger. Can do seamless hand-off (also like traditional cellular telephone) but is more complex.

In one handset, provides simultaneous:

- Cellular Telephone (to compete with traditional AMPS service and PCS)
- Mobile Dispatch (the traditional use for the SMR service but with a wider range)
- Radio Paging (to compete with traditional alphanumeric pagers)
- Mobile data capability (to compete with Ardis and Mobitex, and maybe CDPD and maybe GSM—what an alphabet soup)

Has had a rough (perhaps ongoing) time becoming a reliable system with acceptable voice quality.

The hope is that the more efficient channel usage for dispatch will justify the technology and that the additional capabilities (such as paging integrated with a cellular telephone) will make it more desirable than other technologies. Expected to be most competitive for users who need more than one service (cellular telephone with mobile dispatch or radio paging, for example).

See *AMPS*, *Ardis*, *CDPD*, *GSM*, *Mobitex*, *Motorola*, *SMR*, *PCS*, *PCTS*, and *TDMA*.

ESP
Enhanced Serial Port

A PC serial port technology intended to handle bit rates faster than 38,400 bits/s.

Developed by Hayes Microcomputer products to handle higher-speed serial communications. It uses a standard 16550 buffered UART (and powers on to act as a standard 16550 serial port), but has an on-board processor and includes the following features:

- 1 kbyte receive and transmit buffers each. This reduces the number of times the PC's CPU must get involved with the data communications (this reduces processor loading)
- Support for DMA transfers between the ESP and PC's memory (this reduces the CPU time and the bus loading required to transfer the data)

Requires special communications drives (which are available for both OS/2 and Windows).

Not widely implemented.

More information is at *http://www.hayes.com/esp.htm*.

See *16550A*, *DMA*, *EIA/TIA-232*, and *UART*.

Ethernet

The predecessor to the IEEE's 802.3 CSMA/CD local area network standard.

Differs in many minor (but often crucial) ways, for example, the type of grounding for the transceiver cable and the use of the type/length field of the frame.

Named after the "ether" which was thought to be the medium through which electromagnetic waves propagated. The story goes that in the 1800's, learned people figured out that sound couldn't go through a vacuum; some medium such as air or water was needed. They then wondered what medium the light and heat from the sun needed. While they knew that there was no air in space, they drew an analogy and decided that there had to be *something* up there and called it the ether. Learned people now know that electromagnetic waves *can* propagate through a complete vacuum, and there is no "ether." As a play on this concept, the name Ethernet was chosen for the LAN. The medium was initially a thick (about 1 cm in diameter) coaxial cable, usually yellow, and specially designed for the purpose.

See *10BASE-T*, *100BASE-T*, *802.3*, *Cable*, *Encoding*, *LAN*, *Switched LAN*, and *Token Ring*.

Ethernet II

The frame format usually used by DECnet and LAT on 802.3 LANs.
See *802.3* and *LAT.*

Extended Binary Coded Decimal Interchange Code   See **EBCDIC.**

Extended Capabilities Port   See **ECP.**

Extended Data Out Random Access Memory   See **EDO RAM.**

Extended Graphics Adapter   See **XGA.**

Extended Industry Standard Architecture   See **EISA.**

Extended Superframe   See **ESF.**

Extremely Low Frequency   See **ELF.**

Facsimile   See **Fax.**

FAQ
Frequently Asked Questions

A file on an online service of the most frequently asked questions and their answers. It is good etiquette to read this before posting questions (which may have already been frequently asked—and patiently and expertly answered).

Many Internet Usenet FAQs are on the ftp site *ftp://rtfm.mit.edu/pub/usenet-by-group/* which is often too busy; a mirror of it is at *ftp://ftp.uu.net/usenet/news.answers/*.

The uu.net site compresses such text files using a UNIX program called compress, and such compressed files have the filename extension .Z (for example, noodle.Z). To view these files from a PC, you need an uncompress program. Many such freeware and shareware programs are available, such as decomp2.zip at *ftp://ftp.uu.net/pub/OS/msdos/simtel/compress/*. Unfortunately, this file itself is compressed using pkzip (you need pkunzip or a work-alike). After you finally get the file uncompressed, you find that each line of a UNIX text file is terminated by a line feed only (which they call an end of line), not by carriage return *and* line feed (which is what PCs typically expect). Either import the ASCII file into a word processor (which usually fixes the line feed problem), or use a utility like crlf.com (you can search for the pkunzip and crlf utilities on CompuServe, using the GO IBMFF forum).

Of course, you can avoid this entire headache and get the FAQs from *http://www.cis.ohio-state.edu/hypertext/faq/usenet/FAQ-List.html*, where they are uncompressed and don't have the line feed problem.

FAQs are very highly recommended reading (if there is one there for your topic).

See *RTFM.*

Fast20   See **SCSI-3**.

Fast ATA

An interface that is used to connect a computer to its hard disk drive.

A faster IDE-type hard disk interface promoted by Seagate Technology that has a maximum transfer rate of 11.1 Mbytes/s (when using PIO Mode 3) and 13.3 Mbytes/s (when using *Mode 1 Multiword DMA* transfers).

These rates are specified by the *Small Form Factor Committee*.

Supports drives larger than the IDE limitation of 504 Mbytes.

Competes with Enhanced IDE.

Seagate has a WWW server at *http://www.seagate.com*.

See *E-IDE*, *Fast ATA2*, *PIO*, *SCSI*, and *Small Form Factor Committee*.

Fast ATA2

An enhancement to Seagate's Fast ATA, which supports PIO Mode 4 and Mode 2 Multiword DMA, both of which transfer data at a burst rate of 16.6 Mbytes/s.

See *Fast ATA*.

Fast IDE

Same as Enhanced IDE.

See *E-IDE*.

Fast Ethernet   See **100BASE-T**.

FAT
File Allocation Table

DOS's disk-based file system.

By using DOS's `fdisk` utility, a physical disk can be divided in one or more *partitions* (or *volumes*). DOS supports up to four partitions per physical disk.

A partition is represented by a single drive letter and has a *file allocation table* (in fact there is usually also a backup copy of the FAT), which is a sequence of up to 65,536 16-bit pointers (or *entries*).

A DOS disk is formatted into 512-byte *sectors*, and 2^n (4, 8, 16, 32, etc.) sequential and contiguous sectors are grouped into a *cluster*. A cluster is the smallest amount of disk space that can be allocated to a file.

Each of the FAT entries (the first of the sequence through to the last, up to number 65,535) corresponds to the first through to the last of the clusters in the partition. The 16-bit value stored in each of the FAT entries points to the cluster that is the next part of the file.

Some FAT entries are reserved for other uses:

- All zeros mean that the cluster is unallocated
- All ones (except for the last 4 bits) means it is the last cluster of the file

Because a partition can be a maximum of (only) 65,536 clusters, the larger the partition, the larger the cluster size must be.

For example, a disk with a cluster size of 8,192 bytes (that is, each cluster is 16 sequential 512-byte sectors) can have up to (8,192 bytes per cluster × 65,636 clusters per partition =) 536,870,912 bytes (which is 512 Mbytes) per partition.

On average, each file will waste half a cluster (since, depending on the exact file size, the last cluster in a file could have anywhere from 1 byte to a full cluster of data). Therefore, a smaller cluster size is usually desirable. As the partition size increases, the amount of disk space wasted per file also increases. If the files stay the same average size, then the percentage of larger-partition disks that is wasted increases at the same rate that the partition size increases.

This means that partitioning a large disk into several smaller partitions (so that DOS can use smaller clusters) is usually desirable (though many disk compression programs can use this otherwise-wasted space, providing better disk utilization).

Other reasons for partitioning a disk into more than one partition include using a different type of file system for some partitions (to support a different operating system that can be booted) and reducing the area over which the disk's read/write head must seek for files on a partition, which speeds access time.

A reason for not wanting a small partition size is that the smaller the partition, the smaller the cluster size and therefore the more pieces a file will be stored in—and each piece can be stored in a different part of the partition (rather than all sequentially), slowing file access. This is called disk or file fragmentation.

A file's *directory entry* is a 32-byte data structure that has the file's:

- 11-character (which is displayed in 8.3 format) name
- Pointer to the first cluster of the file
- Size (in bytes)
- Date and time of creation (or last modification)
- Attribute byte (starting at bit 0, the six attribute bits are read-only, hidden, system, volume label, subdirectory, and archive).

A partition's root directory (files in D:*.*, for example) is usually a fixed size of 16 kbytes (which allows for 512 file and subdirectory entries in the partition's root directory).

Subdirectories (D:\WP60*.*, for example) are like normal files and can be extended in size (as more files or subdirectories are created), one cluster at a time.

DOS cluster sizes are listed in the following table.

Partition Size[a] (Mbytes)		Cluster Size	Average Wasted per File
From	To	(bytes)	
1.44 (diskettes)		512	256
	<16[b]	4,096	2,048
16	<128	2,048	1,024
128	<256	4,096	2,048
256	<512	8,192	4,096
512	<1,024	16,384	8,192
1,024	<2,048	32,768	16,384
2,048	<4,096	65,536	32,768

[a] Including the space used by directories.

[b] Before DOS 3.0, the FAT had only 12 bits per entry, allowing for a maximum of 2^{12} clusters (though actually only 4,078 clusters could be used, as 18 of the 4,096 cluster values are reserved for other uses) per volume. Even for current DOS versions, floppy diskettes and hard disk volumes smaller than 16 Mbytes use a 12-bit FAT. 12-bit FAT hard disks usually use 4,096-byte clusters. A 16-bit FAT also reserves 18 cluster entries, leaving $2^{16} - 18 = 65,518$ clusters for data storage.

Therefore it is best to use a partition size of just under 512 or 256 Mbytes:

- Equaling those sizes exactly would double the space wasted per file
- Sizes smaller than those would be inconveniently small (except, perhaps, for a partition that will store only smaller user data files, not application or operating system software)
- Sizes larger than those would waste too much space per partition

Newer hard disk formats, such as OS/2's *High Performance File System* (HPFS) and Windows NT's *NT File System* (NTFS) have the following:

- Filenames that are up to 254 characters and can contain lowercase letters (and even spaces and multiple periods)
- 512-byte clusters, regardless of the disk size
- *Lazy Writes* (also called *Write-behind* or *Write-back Caching*), which accept the data from an application immediately (making it believe that the disk write has been completed) and later write them to disk (if the disk write later fails, the file system writes to a different location on the disk, marking the first one so that the file system does not attempt to use it again)

- A smarter disk–space allocation algorithm, to reduce disk fragmentation

Note, however, that these operating systems file systems' support for floppy diskette drives always uses the DOS FAT system (8.3-style filenames, etc.).

Therefore (for hard disks), the average disk space wasted per file, for HPFS and NTFS, is only 256 bytes. NTFS supports clusters of up to 4,096 bytes (which are more efficient than 512-byte clusters but are used only for full clusters).

Windows 95 uses a *Virtual File Allocation Table* (VFAT) as its file system. Some features are the following:

- 255-character filenames (including both upper-case and lower-case characters and multiple periods)
- FAT-compatibility (by storing an 8.3-style filename for each file, which is used for DOS access)
- A smarter disk space allocation algorithm, which reduces disk fragmentation (a file being stored in noncontiguous clusters, which results in longer file access times)

See *Cache*, *Disk Drive*, *Disk Formatting*, *Stac*, and *Time-stamp*.

Fax
Facsimile

Those amazing machines (or boards in PCs) that can send and receive images of letters and drawings over a telephone line.

Currently, Group III machines are the most common (though other types of machines are standardized). The *group* specifies the digitization and compression scheme, as shown in the following table.

Group	CCITT Standard	Year Released	Transmission Time per Page[a]
			Many nonstandard systems were used before Group I, primarily by the newspaper industry.
I	T.2	1968	4 to 6 minutes (depending on the length of the page), plus 30 seconds between pages (to change the page); sends 180 lines per minute, since the drum (on which the page to be sent was mounted) rotated 180 times per minute; scans at 98 lines per inch.
II		1976	2 to 3 minutes, plus 30 seconds between pages; sends 360 lines per minute and scans at 100 lines per inch.

(table continued on next page)

Group	CCITT Standard	Year Released	Transmission Time per Page[a]
III	T.4 and T.30	1980	9 to 50 seconds (at 9,600 bits/s), plus 15 seconds negotiation before first page.
IV	T.6	1984	3 to 12 seconds (at 64,000 bits/s).

[a] Depends on resolution selected and the image sent.

Group III machines use the following modem modulations:

- V.29 9,600 (with fallback to 7,200) bits/s
- V.27*ter* 4,800 (with fallback to 2,400) bits/s
- Sometimes V.17 14,400 (with fallback to 12,000) bits/s

Also, half-duplex V.21 is used for the initial negotiation phase, as specified in T.30 and described below. Finally, 64,000-bits/s transmission over ISDN lines may become an option soon.

The basic Group III resolutions are as follows:

- 1,728 pels in a scan width of 215 mm (this is about 8.5 inches and so is about 203 pels per inch)
- 3.85 or optionally 7.7 scan lines per mm (this is about 98 or 196 per inch)

These are summarized in the table below.

Mode	Resolution		Bits per Square Inch	Relative Size of Image Data
	Horizontal (pels/inch)	Vertical (lines/inch)		
Standard	203	98	19,894	1
Fine	203	196	39,788	2
Super Fine	203	392	79,576	4
Ultra Fine[a]	406	392	159,152	8

[a] Standardized only for smaller page sizes, such as A6.

A scan width of 2,560 pels is optional. This would support a width of up to 12.6 inches (for example, to fax a B size 11" × 17" page).

Here is a summary of the sequence of a fax call:

- After dialing the called fax machine's telephone number (and before it answers), the calling Group III fax machine (optionally) begins sending a *calling tone* (CNG). This is a repeated ½-second duration 1,100-Hz tone, with a 3-second pause between tones, which can be used by an automatic Voice/Data/Fax switch to connect the call as required.

- When the called fax machine answers, it replies with a 3-second 2,100-Hz tone, the *Called Station Identification* (CED).
- The two fax machines then communicate using 300-bits/s, V.21 modulation. This is an old, slow, reliable, full-duplex modem modulation that uses *Frequency Shift Keying* (FSK). FSK which uses one tone to send a "1" and another for a "0"—this produces a distinctive warbly sound when carrying data. HDLC framing is used, with a 16-bit CRC and 256 (the default) or (optionally) 64-byte frames.
- The communication begins with the called (answering) fax machine sending the calling fax a 20-character identifying message. The standard allows this message to carry only the numbers, "+", and a space, but some fax machines support letters as well. This message is called the *Called Subscriber Identification* (CSI). It is manually programmed into each fax machine and is supposed to be the answering fax machine's telephone number in international format (for example +1-416-555-0641). The calling fax machine usually shows this on its LCD display.
- The called fax machine then sends a 32-bit *Digital Identification Signal* (DIS), which requests the following:
  - Bit rate to be used for fax transmission
  - Time required to print a scan line (defaults to 20 ms but can also be specified as 0, 5, 10, or 40 ms; 0 ms is specified if the receiving fax machine can receive into buffer memory, to speed up the fax transmission)
  - Fax resolution
  - Maximum paper size; support for specifying the A5 and A6 paper size is included in a larger (40-bit instead of 32-bit) DIS
- The calling fax sends the called fax a *Calling Subscriber Identification* (CIG, though sometimes people make up new acronyms, and call this a *Transmit Station Identification*, or TSI). It is (typically) a 25-character company or user name (as configured in advance through cryptic button-pushes on the calling fax). The receiving fax may show this information on its LCD display and include it in a log that can later be printed. Along with other information, such as time, date, and page count, the calling fax usually includes the CIG in the fax image sent to the called fax; this is called the TTI. U.S. law may soon require displaying the date and time sent and the sending business's or individual's name and telephone number at the top of each received fax page (though the significance of this with portable PCs with fax modems is questionable).
- The calling fax then sends the called fax machine a *Digital Command Signal* (DCS), which confirms which options requested in the DIS will be used for the call; that is, the called and calling fax machines do a one-round-trip negotiation to agree on the options. These options are based on those requested and the capabilities of the called fax machine.

- A test data transmission is then done at the agreed bit rate, and the fax machines switch back to 300-bits/s mode to confirm that the transmission was successful. If not, then a lower speed is used. Otherwise, page transmission begins.

After each page, the fax machines switch back to 300-bits/s mode to determine whether there are more pages to be sent.

Group III fax machines usually negotiate a scan width of 1,728 pels per row, which is used for a scan width of 215 mm (this is about 8.46"). This is used for both North American standard A-size 8½" × 11" paper and Metric A4 (210 mm × 297 mm) paper.

These 1,728 pels are compressed using a data compression scheme that first looks for sequences of pels set to the same value in the horizontal raster scans of the source document and produces a count of the number of repetitions of that value (this is called *Run Length Encoding*—RLE).

Then a lookup table is used that produces bit patterns that are shorter to represent the more commonly expected counts. This is called *Modified Huffman Encoding* and is often called MH in fax machine specifications. Almost all fax machines support this.

The table is designed to compresses long sequences of white space better than black (since this is what documents typically have). For example, an all-white row requires only nine bits. This is called *one-dimensional* compression. At *fine* Group III resolution, a single page is about 3,800,000 bits (464 kbytes). By using only one-dimensional compression, this can be compressed to 20 to 50 kbytes, depending on the image.

Group III fax machines can also use *two-dimensional* compression (though not all machines implement it), in which only the difference between the current and the previous (one-dimensional compressed) scan row is sent. This is called *Modified Read* (MR) or *Modified Modified Read* (MMR) in fax specifications. To reduce the impact of scan rows lost due to line noise, this is limited to two rows for standard resolution and four rows for fine resolution (following a one-dimensionally compressed row).

For example, at *standard* Group III resolution, a single page is about 250 kbytes; by using two-dimensional compression, this can be compressed to about 25 to 80 kbytes (10:1 to 3:1 compression).

Since Group IV fax machines always use error correction, there is no limit to the number of rows that can be two-dimensionally compressed (this is specified in T.6).

Both one-dimensional and two-dimensional compression are examples of *lossless data compression*.

At the receiving end, if after decompressing each row of received data, the receiver does not get exactly 1,728 pels, then it knows that a data transmission error occurred. The corrupted row is ignored, and in its place, either the previous (good) row is repeated or a blank (white) row is used.

Some fax machines will request a retransmission of the entire page if that page had more than 32 or 64 (depending on the implementation) corrupted rows. Most transmitting fax machines ignore these requests (since the paper has already been scanned and the fax did not keep a copy to retransmit).

The T.30 standard also specifies an optional *Error-Correcting Mode* (ECM), which supports retransmitting corrupted rows (rather than the entire page).

Since ECM slightly increases fax transmission time and most fax calls have very few errors, most fax machines with ECM can be set to disable the feature.

Group IV machines require 56,000- or 64,000-bits/s communications (a switched 56 or ISDN B channel), and have selectable resolutions of 200 × 200, 300 × 300, and 400 × 400 dots per inch.

A fax board's *service class* specifies how much of the work is done by a Group III fax board (the rest being done by the PC) and is also an extension to the *Hayes AT command set*, since it describes the commands supported by a fax modem.

Class 1 fax boards are defined in EIA/TIA-578 (*Service Class 1 Asynchronous Facsimile DCE Control Standard*) and the subsequent EIA Technical Systems Bulletin 43 (TSB-43). ITU-T's T.31 is an international version of the standard but includes some extra functions. Class 1 fax boards perform only the simplest functions such as:

- Converting the *asynchronous* data from the PC to *synchronous* HDLC data
- Generating and detecting the handshaking tones before a fax transmission
- Generating and checking for HDLC flags and performing HDLC zero-bit stuffing and deletion

The PC does everything else, such as the image rasterization and data compression. Many fax protocol functions are very timing-sensitive, which can be a problem for PCs with multitasking operating systems—especially UNIX, which is usually not good at meeting such *real-time* requirements.

However, Class 1 fax boards are the most flexible, since almost all functions are done in software on the PC, such as the following:

- Error-correcting mode (which is specified in T.30)
- *Adaptive answering*, in which the fax board (which also has a data modem) decides whether an incoming call is a fax or data call and handles it accordingly (this function usually can be performed only by a Class 1 fax board)

In addition to the Class 1 functions, *Class 2*–based fax boards perform the following functions (so the PC does not need to):

- *Line supervision* (that is, establishing and clearing the call)
- Support of error-correcting mode (though this is not widely implemented)

Note that not all Class 2 fax boards provide a Class 1 software interface (that is, they do the Class 1 functions, but automatically).

Because of the long time between the availability of the first drafts of the Class 2 standard (SP-2388, document TR-29/89-21R8, dated March 21, 1990, and a later version released August 1990) and the final approved standard (EIA/TIA/ANSI-592, released November 1992, with first products available in 1994), many fax boards (still) support only the draft. To distinguish these (there were changes made to the final standard), conformance with the draft standard is indicated by "*Class 2*" (there are many undocumented variations of the implementation of this *de facto* Standard), and conformance with the final standard is indicated by "*Class 2.0*" (this is not widely supported, with the significant exception of USRobotics and ZyXEL).

The ITU-T's international version of Class 2.0 is called T.32. It includes more functions, though, such as the data link functions described in TIA/EIA-602.

In addition to the Class 2 functions, *Class 3* boards were expected do the rasterization, based on higher-level information from the PC (such as text in ASCII and graphics data in TIFF format).

Initially, it was expected that offloading more functions to the fax board would result in Class 2 (and greater) fax boards making Class 1 boards obsolete. However, today's faster PCs can easily handle all the tasks necessary for faxing, even when using a "dumb" Class 1 fax board. Since the PC has the necessary processing power anyway, why waste money building more power into the fax board? It is likely that the Class 3 standard will never be approved.

There are three incompatible specifications to support *Binary File Transfer* (BFT) between fax boards, so that they can send the original file (in the original file format), not a rasterized version of it:

- CCITT's T.434 (and the similar TIA/EIA-614)
- Microsoft's *At Work Fax* (which also supports *public key encryption*, which provides *authentication* and *encryption*)
- Intel's not-very-popular CAS, which includes a BFT capability (which works only with CAS)

Only Class 1 (and not Class 2 or 2.0) fax boards can implement BFT or ECM.

A summary of fax options is shown in the figure below.

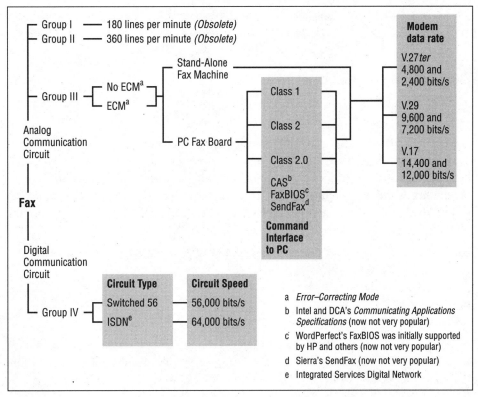

Fax—1

The Group III fax capabilities are specified in the following:

- ITU-T T.4 (which is the same as EIA/TIA-465). This describes the page widths, scan resolutions, transmission times per line, and one-dimensional compression scheme that are supported.
- ITU-T T.30 (which is the same as EIA/TIA-466). This covers the negotiation method and options that are negotiated at connection time and the protocol that is used to manage the session.

A pointer page to fax information on the Internet is at the site *http://www.faximum.com/FAQs/fax.*

A copy of the T.4 Standard is at *gopher://wiretap.spies.com:70/00/Library/Techdoc/Standard/ccitt.t4.*

A copy of the test pages used for fax transmission speed testing is at *http://www.cs.waikato.ac.nz/~singlis/ccitt.html.*

Some additional information is at *http://www.grayfax.com/faxsminar.html* (they make fax test equipment) and in the Usenet newsgroup *comp.dcom.fax.*

See *Asynchronous, AT Command Set, Authentication, CAS, Data Compression, DID, DN, Encryption, HDLC, ISDN, Modem, Paper, Pixel, RLE, Synchronous,* and *Usenet.*

FCC
Federal Communications Commission

The U.S. regulatory body that is responsible for the use of radio frequency transmissions and allocating frequency spectrum.

Having realized that the government was losing a revenue opportunity by giving away frequencies (initially by first-come, first-served, then by lottery), the FCC now auctions some services. The recent notable auction resulted in a total of $7 billion being bid for 99 licenses by 18 companies for PCS frequencies Blocks A and B to cover the 51 largest cities ("major trading areas"). Details are on the FCC's ftp server at *ftp://ftp.FCC.gov/pub/Auctions/PCS.*

The FCC has an ftp server at *ftp.fcc.gov* and a WWW site at *http://www.fcc.gov.*

See *CATV, CRTC, PCS, PUC,* and *V.21.*

FCS
Frame Check Sequence

A generic term for the extra bits (usually a multiple of 8, such as 8 or 16 bits) added to a frame of data to assist in detecting errors (frames that had one or more bits changed because of noise on a data link, for example).

Several types are popular; they are listed in the following table.

Type of FCS	Generation	Length (bits)
BCC (Block Check Character)	Another generic term, like FCS. Is likely a checksum or CRC.	8 or 16
Checksum	Least significant 8 bits of the binary addition of the message. Usually generated in software.	8
CRC (Cyclic Redundancy Code)	Remainder of binary division of message by the generator polynomial. Usually generated in hardware.	Usually 16 or 32
Hamming Code	Usually generated in hardware for ECC memory.	Depends on message length

See *Checksum, CRC, ECC,* and *Parity.*

FDDI
Fiber Distributed Data Interface

A high-speed (and usually local) networking technology.

A 100 Mbits/s user data rate, dual ring (for redundancy), connectionless LAN.

The fiber-PMD option supports up to 2 km (single-attached multimode fiber with 1,300-nm LED source), or 60 km (single-attached, single-mode fiber with high-power laser diode light source) between concentrator and workstation.

Each ring can have up to 500 nodes (or 1,000 if repeaters are used) and up to 200 km total fiber length (circumference)—though to allow for wrap-around during failure recovery, ring circumference is limited to 100 km.

Dual-attached stations on the main ring can be up to 2 km apart (62.5/125 μm or 50/125 μm multimode fiber) or 30 km (single-mode fiber).

With these great distances, some would say that this is also a MAN technology.

The TP-PMD (*Twisted Pair Physical Medium Dependent*) option supports up to 100 m over category 5 UTP.

Future media options may include 850-nm multimode fiber and STP (sometimes called SDDI—an informal *de facto* standard for this is called *Green Book*).

Frame size is up to 4,500 bytes (4,478 bytes information field bytes plus the header and trailer).

The type of fiber-optic cable connector that is used is called a *Media Interface Connector* (MIC).

The main ring requires *Dual Attachment Stations* (DAS) to support the secondary ring which is used to provide a wrap-around for a cable break or failed station. Through a concentrator, *Single Attachment Stations* (SAS)—which are less expensive but have no redundancy—can be attached to the network. Each DAS port is either an A or a B port, as shown in the accompanying figure.

SAS (and, optionally, DAS) stations are connected to the main ring through *concentrators*. The concentrator ports are designated the M (Master) ports, and the station ports are S (slave) ports. Therefore A ports connect to B ports, and M ports connect to S ports. Connectors are keyed to ensure that these requirements are met.

DAS stations (or concentrators) connected to two different SAS concentrators (one pair of fibers to each) provide *Dual-homing* redundancy (if either SAS connection fails, the other provides connectivity).

Most FDDI networks will have few DAS on the main ring (mostly concentrators), most devices being connected to the main ring concentrators or on second-level concentrators (which are connected to the main ring concentrators). This is called

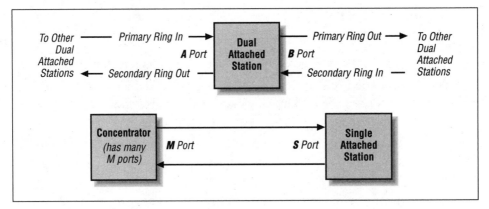

FDDI-1

a *dual ring-of-trees* architecture. Smaller LANs would often have a collapsed backbone (*ring-in-a-box*) architecture, in which all stations connect to a single concentrator or all stations would be directly on the main ring (*dual-ring*).

The cable bit rate is actually 125 Mbits/s, since each 4 bits of information are *encoded* as 5 NRZI bits (called a *symbol*) to provide features such as:

- Data transparency
- Frame delimiting
- Clock recovery

Target Token Rotation Time (TTRT) is usually set to 8 ms. To ensure fair access, stations can transmit only for their *Token Holding Time* (THT, which is derived from the TTRT).

There has been some experimentation with a synchronous option that provides less network latency (8 to 16 ms, rather than standard FDDI's 10 to 200 ms). It is designed to support multimedia and to be compatible with standard asynchronous FDDI. Bandwidth is preallocated to stations with time-sensitive requirements. Bandwidth that they don't require is available to the asynchronous FDDI stations.

The *Station Management Layer* (SMT) provides features such as the following:

- Neighbor identification
- Fault detection and reconfiguration
- Insertion in, and deinsertion from, the ring
- Traffic statistics monitoring

The parts of the FDDI standard are shown in the following table.

OSI Reference Model			FDDI Standard	
Layer	Name			
2	Data Link	LLC[a]		
		MAC	MAC	
1	Physical		PHY	SMT
			PMD	

[a] Logical Link Control.

Each FDDI standard covers the features shown in the following table.

FDDI Standard		Covers
MAC	Media Access Control	Controls access to fiber or cable
		Token handling
		Frames the data, generates the CRC
		Recognizes addresses
PHY	Physical Layer	Encodes and decodes
		Converts serial to parallel
		Clock recovery
PMD	Physical Medium Dependent	Specifies cable and connectors
		Specifies transceivers and optical bypass switch
SMT	Station Management	Controls all layers of the FDDI model
		Ring monitoring and management
		Connection management
		Generates and responds to SMT frames

Some people try to pronounce it as *fi*dee.

Initially standardized in ANSI X3T9.5 (released in 1989). The international standard is ISO 9314.

See *ANSI*, *Baud*, *Encoding*, *FDDI-II*, *FFDT*, *FFOL*, *LAN*, and *MAN*.

FDDI-II
Fiber Distributed Data Interface II

An incompatible superset of the original FDDI that better supports multimedia, video, and voice, since bandwidth can be reserved for *isochronous* (regularly occurring, delay-sensitive) traffic. Divides the 100 Mbits/s into 16 6.144-Mbits/s circuits that can be allocated to carry asynchronous or isochronous traffic. Each of the 16 circuits can be subdivided into 96 separate 64-kbits/s channels.

A *synchronous bandwidth allocation* scheme uses a time-slicing algorithm to allow end-stations to reserve bandwidth.

Not widely implemented. Many people believe that it will never be popular, since FDDI is too slow for broadcast-quality video (ATM will be better suited, because of its greater speed), and compressed video is bursty anyway (so isochronous service is of little use).

See *FDDI* and *Isochronous*.

FDDI Follow-On LAN   See **FFOL.**

FDDI Full-Duplex Technology   See **FFDT.**

Federal Communications Commission   See **FCC.**

FEP
Front End Processor

A $100K to $1M box that provides communication services for IBM mainframes.

Sometimes called a *communications controller*.

Services include data link activation, polling, and error detection and correction. Links to users include EIA-232, V.35 (which then goes to a 3274 to the users), and Token Ring. The link to the mainframe is either the IBM *bus and tag channel* or *Escon*.

In increasing order of size and newness, IBM FEP model numbers are as follows:

- 3704 and 3705 (really old, no longer manufactured)
- 3720 and 3725 (somewhat old)
- 3745 and 3746 (the most common, cost about $300,000)

Runs NCP. Can also run NPSI (which proves support for X.25).

See *3174 and 3274, Channel, ESCON, Mainframe, NCP (Network Control Program), NPSI, PU 2, PU 4,* and *WAN*.

FFDT
FDDI Full-Duplex Technology

A software method, proposed and patented by Digital Equipment Corporation, to enable two directly connected FDDI-equipped computers to communicate full-duplex (which some people say then has 200 Mbits/s of capacity—and it does, but only if exactly half of that traffic needs to go in each direction at the same time).

DEC expects applications will include connecting disk subsystems to high-performance workstations.

Competes (or at least it could compete, if FFDT were standardized and available) with fibre channel.

See *DEC*, *FDDI*, *Fibre Channel*, and *HiPPI*.

FFOL
FDDI Follow-On LAN

The proposed name of a standard that might replace FDDI some day. Operates at up to 2.4 Gbits/s.

See *FDDI*.

Fibre Channel

A very high-speed (up to more than 1 Gbits/s), low-latency (10 to 30 μs —which is better than ATM), full-duplex data communications scheme that is optimized to carry large blocks of data for both channel- and LAN-type connections (simultaneously, on the same medium).

Supports both:

- *Dedicated* media (also called *switched*, since each device gets its own switch port and does not share the media's bandwidth with other devices)
- *Shared* media

Three potential uses are:

- I/O device connections, for example, channels to disk drives, such as the SCSI interface and IBM's Escon
- Clusters of workstations
- Switched LANs, supporting computers from many vendors, using multiple protocols and interfaces, such as TCP/IP and ATM

Six speeds are defined (because of protocol overhead, the payload data rate is lower than the bit rate on the cable), as shown in the following table.

Cable Bit Rate (Mbits/s)	Payload Data Rate	
	Mbytes/s	Mbits/s
132.8125	12.5	100
265.625	25	200
531.25	50	400
1,062.5	100	800
2,125	200	1,600
4,250	400	3,200

The specified distances for the various media and data rates are given in the following table.

Media	Speed (Mbytes/s)			
	12.5	**25**	**50**	**100**
Single-mode fiber (long-wave laser)	10 km			
50/125 μm multimode fiber (short-wave laser)	a	2 km	1 km	a
62.5/125-μm fiber (long-wave LED)	500 m	1 km	a	a
Video coax	100 m	75 m	50 m	25 m
Miniature coax	40 m	30 m	20 m	10 m
Shielded twisted pair	100 m	50 m	a	a

[a] Not defined in the standard.

The connector types are listed in the following table.

Media	Connector	Requires
Fiber	Duplex, polarized SC	One strand for transmitting, one for receiving
Coax	TNC (receiver) and BNC (transmitter)	One coax for transmitting, one for receiving
STP	9-pin D-subminiature	One pair for transmitting, one for receiving

Note that UTP is not a supported medium.

Frame size is up to 2,148 bytes, as shown in the following table.

Bytes	Function
4	Start of frame delimiter
24	Frame header, including 24-bit source and destination addresses and sequence numbers to support windowing and flow control
0 to 2,112	Higher-layer data (payload), may include a 64-byte optional header, reducing payload to 2,048 bytes
4	CRC
4	End of frame delimiter

Higher-level addresses are assigned to switch ports (stations then inherit these) and have a three-level hierarchy (domain, area, and port number).

Fibre channel has five layers (which are expected to be implemented as physically separate components), as shown in the accompanying figure.

FC-4	Upper–layer protocol and application interfaces					
	TCP/IP	HiPPI	ATM	SCSI	Escon	
FC-3	Common services and feature selection					
FC-2	Framing, flow control, service classes					FC-PH
FC-1	8B/10B encoding and decoding					
FC-0	133 Mbits/s	266 Mbits/s	531 Mbits/s	1.062 Gbits/s	Future higher speeds	
	Rate–specific media interfaces and transmission speeds					

Fibre Channel—1

The lower three layers are called the *fibre channel physical* standard and define all the physical transmission characteristics.

FC-1 is the transmission encoding and decoding layer and uses IBM's patented Escon 8B/10B coding.

FC-2 is where most fibre channel functions take place. The FC-2 layer performs the following functions:

- Signaling—that is, establishing connections between originators and responders. The originator specifies the destination address (IEEE Ethernet-type addresses are used—these are 48 bits in length). The responder receives messages and sends back responses.
- Frame segmentation, reassembly, and sequencing functions. Fibre channel frame sizes are negotiated between each pair of communicating stations, and are from 36 bytes to 2 kbytes in length.
- Flow control (using a sliding window scheme), error detection (using a 32-bit CRC), and correction.
- The implementation of the four service classes (see below).

FC-3 provides features for special situations (which are expected to be important in the future), such as how data written to disk drives will be "striped" (split, with each part written to a different drive, to speed up the reading and writing), and multicast functions to deal with a video server (a device storing digitized video).

FC-4 (also called *multiple service interconnect*) handles interfaces with other (legacy) network protocols and applications, such as ATM AAL5, ESCON, HiPPI, IPI, SCSI, and TCP/IP.

The *Fibre Channel Systems Initiative* (consisting of Hewlett-Packard, IBM, and Sun Microsystems) promotes fibre channel interoperability. They have defined three *profiles* to ensure interoperability for specific uses, as listed in the following table.

Profile	Use
Storage	Point-to-point connections to data storage subsystems (based on SCSI or IPI) for use such as backing up data
Networking	How to encapsulate IP packets over fibre channel and the design of switches
Internetworking	Interfaces between fibre channel and Ethernet, Token Ring, and FDDI networks, as well as LAN and WAN versions of ATM

Four *service classes* are defined, as shown in the following table.

Class	Configuration
1	Configures switches so that a dedicated, circuit-switched, connection-oriented, guaranteed delivery (through the use of acknowledgments) channel is set up between source and destination. No other devices can connect to the source or destination ports. Best for sustained, high-throughput, time-critical, nonbursty transactions such as real-time graphics, mass storage, and links between supercomputers.
2	A connectionless (with guaranteed delivery through the use of acknowledgments), frame-switched service that supports multiplexing to share bandwidth from many ports into others. Best for bursty and interactive traffic. Does not guarantee that the data will be delivered in the original sequence (as each frame can be delivered over any available route—even a single fibre channel switch can have multiple paths), but sequence numbers in the frames permit the receiving station to present the frames in the correct sequence to the upper layers. Frames lost due to congestion or port contention are replied to with a *busy signal* and are retransmitted until they successfully get through the network and are acknowledged.
3	Same as Class 2, but no guaranteed delivery (since there is no frame acknowledgment). Good for sending messages rapidly from one source to many destinations (emulating a broadcast) or when the round-trip delay is large. Has higher throughput (again, since there is no waiting for frame acknowledgments).
4	Isochronous (also called constant bit rate, or guaranteed fractional bandwidth) and guaranteed latency and original sequence of frames service for digitized voice and video. Will be specified in an addendum to the standard (*fibre channel enhanced physical*).

A fifth class—*Intermix*—is a mix of Class 1 and Class 2. The Class 1 frames get priority access to the full fibre channel bandwidth, and Class 2 frames are carried when capacity is available.

Three topologies (or types of *fabric*) have been defined, as shown in the following table.

Topology	Characteristics
Switched fabric	This will likely be the most common and requires that users (either a small workgroup or a campus–wide network) be connected to others through a switch. The switch can provide different speed accesses on different ports, and the communicating devices negotiate to ensure that the faster device does not send data faster than the receiver can accept it. This is called *dynamic rate conversion*.
Point-to-point	Two users are directly connected by a fibre channel connection. Both devices must be at the same speed.
Arbitrated loop (FC-AL)	A method of connecting more than two (and up to 127) users without requiring a switch (therefore reducing the cost). For this topology, only coaxial cable can be used for the media. Disadvantages are that bandwidth is shared and that coaxial cable distances are much less than distances for fiber-optic cable. All devices must be at the same speed. The loop can handle only a single connection (between two stations) at a time. That connection must be cleared before another connection can be established. A loop can be connected to a port on a switch. If multiple devices are contending for use of the loop, then the device with the lowest address wins.

Some topology notes:

- All stations support all three topologies (they look the same to the stations)
- Devices on one topology can communicate with devices on the other topologies
- Station capabilities are the same regardless of the topology used (for example, all service classes are available to all topologies)
- Topologies can be mixed in a single fibre channel network

Fibre channel defines many types of ports, as shown in the following table.

Port	Used on	IEEE Addresses Assigned[a]
Fabric port or F port	Fibre channel switch (connects to N Port)	
Node port or N port	End-station (disk array, computer, etc.) directly connected to a Switched F Port	Highest addresses
FL port	Fibre channel switch (connects to a Loop)	Middle addresses
NL port	End station (connects to a loop)	Lowest addresses

[a] When contending for control of a loop, the device with the lowest address wins. Therefore loop-connected end-stations have the highest priority.

The mapping of LAN and higher-layer protocols (including Ethernet and Token Ring, SCSI, TCP/IP, ATM AAL5, and 802.2) to Fibre Channel will be included as part of the specification.

Still under development, much of it by Hewlett-Packard (which bought the technology from Canstar). An ANSI standard, soon to be an ISO standard as well.

See *8B/10B, ATM, ESCON, FFDT, HiPPI, HP, Isochronous, LAN,* and *SCSI.*

Fiber Distributed Data Interface   See **FDDI.**

Fiber-optic Inter Repeater Link   See **FOIRL.**

Field   See **Interlaced and NTSC.**

File Allocation Table   See **FAT.**

File Transfer, Access and Management   See **FTAM.**

File Transfer Protocol   See **ftp.**

Finger

A utility available on UNIX computers and included with many TCP/IP protocol suites (for other operating systems) that provides information about users with accounts on the local computer or a remote computer. Most of the information comes from the /etc/passwd file. Finger commands are listed in the following table.

Command	Displays
`finger user@host`	If user is a valid `login name` (exactly matching, including the case) or a complete first or last name (exactly matching one but the case need not match), as entered in the user's `given name` entry, then the following will be displayed: `Login name:` (the username the user logs in to `host` with) `In real life:` the user's given name `Directory:` the user's home directory `Shell:` the user's default shell `Last login` (if the user is not currently logged in) or `On since` (if the user is currently logged in): the time and date when the user last logged in to `host` and the port from which the user logged in `Project`[a] : the contents of the file `.project` in the user's home directory `Plan`[a] : the contents of the file `.plan` in the user's home directory
`finger user`	As above, but for user on the local host
`finger @host`	The `login name`, `given name`, `port`, `idle time`, `login time` and `date`, and other information from the `passwd` file for each `user` currently logged in to `host`
`finger`	As above, but for the local host

[a] For these files to be displayed, they must have `world read` and `execute` permissions.

The destination host must be running a `finger` server, usually called `fingerd` (finger daemon) for the `finger` utility to display information for a given host.

Called "finger" because it is like putting your finger on someone to get information.

Specified in RFC 742.

See *RFC* and *UNIX*.

Firewall

A device (or software in a router) that links an organization's internal TCP/IP network to the Internet and restricts the types of traffic that it will pass, to provide security.

Popular products include SEAL from Digital Equipment Corporation and Interlock from Advanced Network Services, Inc. (ANS).

Restrictions can be based on the the following:

- Type of access (email, telnet, ftp, etc.)
- Contents of the data (attempting to be) accessed
- Direction
- Source or destination IP address (host)
- Time of day

Older firewalls require you first to log in to them (usually using telnet) and then to request a service (such as an ftp session) to the intended destination.

Newer firewalls do this in one step, using a facility called *quoting*, which passes command-line parameters, such as a username, password and service required, to the firewall. User applications (such as a WWW browser) may need to support a *proxy server* (that is, the firewall) to be able to transparently provide service to the user while communicating through the firewall.

See *ANS*, *CERT*, and *Internet*.

FireWire

Apple Computer's name for IEEE 1394.

See *1394*. pg. 10

Flame

The email equivalent of raising your voice and criticizing or insulting someone. Most people think that flaming someone is seldom a mature thing to do.

Called "flame" because it is like blasting someone as an angry fire-breathing dragon might. (Of course, I've never actually seen a dragon toasting someone, but I don't expect it would be a pretty sight.)

FOIRL
Fiber-Optic Inter Repeater Link

An 802.3 option for linking repeaters over fiber-optic cable.

See *10BASE-F*.

Folders

The Apple Macintosh and Windows 95 operating systems' name for disk subdirectories. Also used to refer to the subdirectory-like method used for filing electronic mail messages in many email programs.

Font

Usually refers to a *face*, which is the entire family of letters (and numbers, punctuation, etc.) of a particular shape or design.

There are two broad categories:

- *Bitmap* or *raster fonts*
- *Scalable* or *outline fonts*

While scalable fonts are usually more desirable (because you can adjust the size while maintaining the proportions and smooth edges), bitmap fonts are required for raster devices, such as computer monitors and dot matrix printers.

Software such as *Adobe Type Manager* (ATM, for *PostScript Type 1 Fonts*) and Microsoft's *TrueType* (for its *TrueType Fonts*) can convert scalable fonts to bitmap fonts. The accompanying figure shows the common types of fonts currently available.

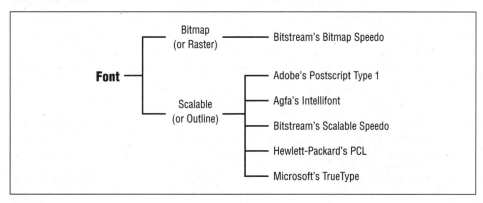

Font—1

See *ATM* (*Adobe Type Manager*), *Bitmap Font*, *Outline Font*, *PCL*, *Point*, and *Typeface Family*.

foo.bar
F _ _ _ _ _   *Up Beyond All Recognition*

During the Second World War, the term "fubar" was used in status reports and on repair tags to indicate (likely unrepairable) defective machinery and equipment.

The (to many people) meaningless two-syllable word somehow came to people who need an example filename when producing program manuals and documentation. The spelling changed, and the two syllables were used as the separate file name and file extension.

See *NFG* and *RTFM*.

Fractional T1   See **FT1**.

Frame

A unit of data exchanged within a network or subnetwork. An ISO/OSI Layer 2 (link layer) protocol data unit.

See *802.3*, *Frame Relay*, and *HDLC*.

Frame   See **Interlaced and NTSC**.

Frame Check Sequence   See **FCS**.

Frame Relay

A variable-length (up to about 8,000 bytes, more commonly implemented as up to 4,096 bytes) shared-bandwidth WAN. Uses a subset of HDLC called LAPD.

Frame relay is optimized for use over higher-speed (such as T1) and very low error-rate data circuits. For example, to reduce the processing load on, and latency through, frame relay networks, the switches do not perform any error correction (other than discarding corrupted frames) nor flow control (other than setting the Forward Explicit Congestion Notification and Backward Explicit Congestion Notification bits in the frame header). If the user equipment does not react fast enough (or at all) to the flow control, then the network discards frames when it gets congested. Whether due to corrupted frames or a congested network, discarded frames must be retransmitted by the user-equipment (which is typically a router).

Since frames can take different paths through a network, the receiving equipment (usually a stand-alone router) also must perform frame reordering at the receiving end.

Initially only PVC-based—you choose where each virtual circuit is connected, when the service is set up (that is, at *subscription time*).

Port speeds (the speed of the physical data circuit *access line* from the user to the service provider's frame relay switch and the speed of the switch port) are typically between DS-0 and T1, though there are usually only two choices:

- 56,000 or 64,000 bits/s (whichever is offered)
- T1 (1.544 Mbits/s)

Some service providers offer a fractional T1 option.

As was stated above, the network does not use conventional window-based flow control (which only lets end-stations transmit a predetermined number of messages before they are acknowledged). Instead, carriers commit to being able to carry a prespecified data rate (the *committed information rate*) for each PVC. The

CIR (which will usually be up to one-half of, but could be equal to, the speed of the access line) is specified as a bit rate averaged over a 1-second period. Carriers charge more for higher CIRs.

Users can always send data at up to the speed of the access line, and if the carrier's network has extra capacity, then the network will carry these "*burst*" data (that is, data coming in, in excess of the CIR). Otherwise, the network can discard the burst data.

The frame relay header includes a *discard eligibility* bit, which indicates which frames to choose first when frames must be discarded.

Some carriers offer PVCs with zero CIR (at a cost savings to the user). Users find that these services drop less than 0.01% of traffic and so are often a cost-effective choice.

A single access line can have many PVCs (logical connections to different locations), and the CIRs for those PVCs can be configured to exceed the speed of the access line; this is called *oversubscribing*.

Oversubscribing is usually in the user's interest, since the user's data are likely to be very bursty (that is, the user won't be sending at the full CIR on all PVCs simultaneously). Oversubscribing ensures a high data rate to each PVC's destination when needed, while reducing the cost of the access line. Carriers typically allow oversubscribing of 200% to 400%. For example, a 64-kbits/s access line carrying four PVCs with CIRs of 32 kbits/s each would be oversubscribed 200%.

Other types of frame relay services are beginning to be offered, for example:

- Switched virtual circuits (SVCs—you can select who to call, just like a telephone or X.25 call)
- *Simplex* service—data go only in one direction. This is useful for broadcasting, such as a stock price feed. Or, two simplex circuits (in opposite directions) could be used, each with a different CIR. This would be useful for data communications where a high volume of data go in one direction (such as large file transfers), but very little in the other direction (the protocol's acknowledgments). In contrast, standard duplex frame relay circuits require the same CIR in both directions.

Other types of access, such as asynchronous dial-up (perhaps using SLIP), switched 56, and ISDN BRI (useful for disaster recovery sites), are becoming available from some service providers.

An optional *local management interface* supports statistics and other communication between the network and the end user.

MCI Communications Corp. and Stentor call their service *Hyperstream*. AT&T calls its service *Interspan*. Unitel calls its service *DataVPN Interspan*.

A problem with frame relay service is that carriers are just beginning to establish connections between each other. While a technical specification exists (*Network-Network Interface* (NNI) which covers the signaling aspects), it does not address *operational issues* such as billing and troubleshooting. Other aspects, such as harmonizing billing rates and policies, how retransmissions are billed, performance guarantees, and troubleshooting procedures will need to be negotiated between all interconnected carriers.

The *Frame Relay Forum* "is an association of Corporate members comprised of Vendors, Carriers, Users and Consultants committed to the implementation of Frame relay in accordance with National and International Standards." It was formed in 1991, and maintains chapters in North America, Europe, Australia/New Zealand, and Japan. It promotes and develops standards for frame relay, and has a WWW server at *http://frame-relay.indiana.edu/.*

Frame relay is rapidly being accepted, but only recently have SVC (switched connections) and public-dial started to become available.

Encapsulation of other protocols is defined in RFC 1490.

In addition to the WWW references in the entry for standards, there is a good frame relay pointer page at *http://www.mot.com/MIMS/ISG/tech/frame-relay/resources.html.*

Also, additional information is available from equipment vendors, a major one being StrataCom Inc. at *http://www.stratacom.com.*

See *BRI, DS-0, Encapsulation, FT1, HDLC, NNI, Standards, Switched 56, T1, WAN,* and *XModem.*

Frequently Asked Questions   See **FAQ.**

Front End Processor   See **FEP.**

FT1
Fractional T1

A (usually) 128-, 256-, 384-, 512-, or 768-kbits/s point-to-point digital data communications channel (which corresponds to 2, 4, 6, 8, or 12 channels of a T1). The physical circuit is a full 1.544 Mbits/s T1 line with CSU/DSUs, but only some (that is, a *fraction*) of the 24 slots are used.

See *CSU, DSU, HDSL, T1,* and *WAN.*

FTAM
File Transfer, Access, and Management

An OSI-compliant standard for file transfer, remote creation and deletion, and setting and reading attributes. The standard also describes the format of files to be transferred (for example, it supports stream, flat records, binary/text, indexed, and disk directory formats).

The analogous TCP/IP service is ftp.

See *ftp* and *OSI*.

ftp
File Transfer Protocol

An interactive file transfer capability that is often used on TCP/IP networks. Requires users to log in to (have an account on) the remote computer.

Anonymous ftp allows users to log in using the *username* anonymous. It is then polite to use your email address as your *password* so that the administrators of the remote computer can keep a record of who accessed their computer.

See *TCP/IP* and *tftp*.

FUD
Fear, Uncertainty, and Doubt

A marketing tactic (which many used to accuse IBM of using) to discourage buying from the competition.

The allegation is that starting (possibly exaggerated) rumors of products or features that don't yet exist (usually because they are not yet ready) would scare potential purchasers into delaying purchasing decisions (or deciding not to buy from the competition at all) for fear that they will purchase the wrong product.

See *IBM* and *Microsoft*.

Full-duplex

Communications in which both sender and receiver can send at the same time. Communications on a point-to-point WAN link between two routers is full-duplex (since the routers are likely connecting two buildings full of people, each of whom will be sending or receiving simultaneously).

See *Simplex* and *Half-Duplex*.

Frame User to Network Interface   See **DXI.**

FWIW
For What It's Worth

A common email abbreviation.

<g> or <grin>
Grin

A common email expression that is used when something is stated with a smile (for example, to indicate a joke).

G.723

Also called MP-MLQ. (I don't know which name is worse or more forgettable.)

See *MP-MLQ*.

Generic Security Service—Application Program Interface   See **GSS-API.**

GIF
Graphics Interchange Format

A file format developed by CompuServe Information Service (in 1987) for storing 256 color, raster (as opposed to vector) graphical images. Based on the LZW data compression algorithm.

See *CompuServe* and *LZW.*

Global Positioning System   See **GPS.**

Global System for Mobile Communications   See **GSM.**

GMT
Greenwich Mean Time

The time in Greenwich, England, the location of which defines where the *prime meridian* (that is, 0° longitude) is. The rest of the world's time zones (and longitude) are referenced to this meridian.

No longer used as a time reference, since time is no longer referenced to the stars (the world doesn't rotate consistently enough for this, it apparently wobbles and slows too much).

See *Satellite* and *UTC*.

Gopher

A method of snooping through the Internet for files and retrieving them. Easier to use than the `ftp` utility (though gopher actually retrieves files using `ftp`), but not nearly as much fun, and not as powerful as the WWW.

A series of menus (on destination machines) provide pointers to resources, which the gopher client software (running on your local machine) displays, or uses as a trigger to launch other applications, such as telnet or WAIS.

Many WWW browsers can also be gopher clients (for example, enter *gopher://internic.net/* into Netscape).

The name comes from the system's function: to "go fer" things. Also, it was developed at the University of Minnesota, and its Twin Cities campus athletic teams are called the Gophers.

The gopher FAQ is at *ftp://rtfm.mit.edu/pub/usenet/news.answers/gopher-faq*.

See *ftp*, *WAIS*, and *WWW*.

GOSIP
Government OSI Profile

Government specifications of the OSI standards and options to use to implement various computer communications functions. The U.S. and U.K. both have a GOSIP with the same intent, but the specifications are different. COSAC is the Canadian equivalent specification.

See *COSAC* and *OSI*.

GPS
Global Positioning System

A system of 24 satellites, each of which orbits the earth every 12 hours at a height of 20,200 km. Four satellites are located in each of six planes inclined at 55° to the plane of the earth's equator.

When receivers "see" three satellites simultaneously, they can calculate their *latitude* and *longitude* (with an accuracy of 100 m for public use and 16 m for military use) and *velocity* (accuracy to 0.1 m/s), and *time* information is provided (with an accuracy better than 1 μs). When a fourth satellite is in view, *altitude* information is also available.

Fearing that enemies could use GPS's positional information to help target bombs, the higher-accuracy GPS information is encrypted, so it is available only to the U.S. military.

Some points on accuracy:

- These accuracies are measured as *Spherical Error Probable* (SER); that is, 95% of all location fixes will be within (for example) a sphere of 16 m radius.
- If only the horizontal accuracy is of concern (usually the case for things that don't fly), then the accuracy is stated as "*2DRS*" (twice the distance, *root mean square*), which produces a slightly different number (21 m for this example).

Differential GPS (DGPS) uses a second GPS receiver (for example, at an airport or harbor) that has a precisely known location and involves calculating the difference in location between the two receivers. This method can provide positional information (for the first receiver) that is accurate to 1 to 3 m (or a few centimeters for the military use).

Initial position information is available within about 2 minutes after powering on a GPS receiver, and updates are then available every ½ second.

Officially called *Navstar*.

See *CDMA* and *Navstar*.

Graphical User Interface   See **GUI**.

Graphics Interchange Format   See **GIF**.

Greenwich Mean Time   See **GMT**.

GSS-API
Generic Security Service—Application Program Interface

An IETF-approved API for securely passing *authentication* information (determining who can run which programs) between application programs in a distributed computing environment.

See *API*, *Authentication*, and *IETF*.

GSM
Global System for Mobile Communications (previously Groupe Spécial Mobile)

The current (1992), and rapidly gaining acceptance, Pan-European (and Pacific Rim and South Africa) digital cellular telephone standard developed by the European Telecommunications Standards Institute's (ETSI) *Groupe Spécial Mobile*. Also used in some Middle Eastern countries and parts of Australia.

The frequencies allocated to the service are divided into 200-kHz blocks, each of which supports eight simultaneous users (by using a form of TDMA that lets a handset transmit a few bytes of data or digitized voice, 217 times per second).

Each user gets a 13-kbits/s service, which is divided into two channels:

- A 9,600-bits/s channel (the *Bm* channel) for user asynchronous or synchronous data or digitized voice. This is circuit-switched, taking 20 to 30 seconds for a call setup.
- A 382-bits/s channel (the *Dm* channel), which is used for signaling (setting up and clearing the Bm channel's calls).

  Since the Dm channel can carry messages of up to 160 characters, it can also be used for *Short Message Services* (SMS), such as providing caller identification, notifying users of waiting voice mail messages or received (and stored on a server for later retrieval) faxes, stock price changes, and weather reports for cities keyed in by the caller.

Supports encryption of voice and data. Less frequency-efficient than the North American TDMA (IS-54) method, but very robust.

Is analogous to North American (analog) AMPS Cellular, as it uses cells and hand-offs (though not all operators track users, so some GSM operators only offer outgoing service (originated from the mobile phones).

An advantage over North American cellular is that GSM was initially designed to handle data.

GSM supports two data modes:

- *Transparent* provides a raw data channel, complete with whatever errors occur.
- *Nontransparent* uses a GSM-specific error-correcting protocol, which usually provides better throughput than end-user error correcting protocols, though some say that the GSM error-correction is not robust enough.

Support for fax, ISDN, and X.25 access is either available or in development. Some operators assign multiple phone numbers to a phone to differentiate incoming calls to the phone as voice, data, or fax.

While all GSM services and telephones are compatible, much work remains to be done before users will be able to use their telephones anywhere and receive the same services. For example:

- Roaming agreements between operators (for billing purposes) are required before operators will provide services to other operators' customers.
- Many operators are just beginning to offer data services (which require the addition of modem connections to land-line services).

- Network design may need to be modified to offer all services. For example, voice traffic requires low delay but can tolerate brief communication problems (such as noise), whereas data service can tolerate delays but brief transmission problems are often unacceptable.

Initial installations all use the 900-MHz frequency band.

In some countries, GSM is being expanded to *Digital Communication System*. This is usually called DCS 1800 (it uses the 1,800-MHz frequency band). DCS 1800 supports more users, but has smaller cells (so more base stations are needed to cover a given area). The smaller cells allow the telephones to use lower transmit power, so they can have smaller batteries and therefore be lighter and/or last longer between recharging.

A version designed for the 1.9-GHz North American PCS frequency band is called PCS 1900. It is being implemented by Bell South and Pacific Bell.

Most European countries have earlier and incompatible (that is, country-specific) analog systems, which use technology similar to North America's AMPS. For example, England has a system called TACS, and the Scandinavian countries have a system called NMT.

See *AMPS, Ardis, CDMA, ESMR, Mobitex, PCS (Personal Communications Service), RBOC, RDS,* and *TDMA*.

GUI
Graphical User Interface

The two main (and incompatible) UNIX GUIs are *OPENLOOK* and *Motif*.

See *Motif* and *OPENLOOK*.

H.261

A digitization and data compression scheme for analog video, typically used for video conferencing. Uses multiples of 64-kbits/s communication channels and so is sometimes referred to as P×64 ("P times 64").

See *H.320* and *Video*.

H.320

The standard for integrating voice, digitized video, and control messages on one or more 64-kbits/s channels (usually on ISDN circuits). Two video formats are specified:

- The full screen *Common Intermediate Format* (CIF) is 352 horizontal × 288 vertical pixels
- The *Quarter CIF* (QCIF) option is 176 × 144 pixels

Both are at 30 frames per second.

One or two 64-kbits/s channels are usually adequate for QCIF. This shows the power of data compression—uncompressed CIF would require 73 Mbits/s at 30 frames per second.

ISDN, switched 56, or fractional T1 circuits can be used.

The input could be a video camera or a portion of a PC's screen (so that everyone can see what is being displayed).

Future work will support LANs.

H.32P is an effort to support video conferencing over POTS.

See *ISDN*, *FT1*, *PCS (Personal Conferencing Specification)*, *POTS*, *Switched 56*, *Video*, and *WAN*.

Half-Duplex

Communications that can go both to and from all parties but in only one direction at a time.

The classic analogy is a narrow country bridge. Cars can cross in either direction, but only one direction at a time.

Spoken communications between two (polite) people and data communications on traditional Token Ring and Ethernet LANs are half-duplex (though full-duplex versions have been implemented—of LANs, that is).

See *10BASE-T*, *Simplex*, and *Full-duplex*.

HDLC
High-Level Data Link Control

A *bit-oriented*, synchronous, link layer, data-framing, flow control, and error detection and correction protocol.

Uses a header with control information and a trailing *cyclic redundancy check* character (which is usually 16 or 32 bits in length).

Implementations are both standard subsets (see below) or vendor-specific (such as that used for the 56,000-bits/s interfaces on a vendor's remote bridge or router). IBM calls HDLC *SDLC*.

Some standard subsets are listed in the following table.

	HDLC Subset	Used for
802.2	Logical link control	FDDI, Token Ring, and some Ethernet LANs
LAP	Link Access Procedure	Early X.25 implementations
LAPB	Link Access Procedure, Balanced	Current X.25 implementations
LAPD	Link Access Procedure for the ISDN D channel	ISDN D channel and frame relay
LAPM	Link Access Procedure for Modems	Error-correcting modems (specified as part of V.42)

BISYNC is (was) an older method of synchronous data communications.

See *802.2*, *BISYNC*, *CRC*, *DLC*, *Frame Relay*, *ISDN*, *MNP*, *SDLC*, *Synchronous*, *V.42*, and *XModem*.

HDSL
High-Bit-Rate Digital Subscriber Line

A technology developed by Bellcore that provides full-duplex T1 service (using two twisted pairs of cable) over greater distances than the *alternate mark inversion* encoding that is traditionally used by T1.

Also, full-duplex *fractional T1* service can be provided over a single pair of wires.

Uses:

- Two copper twisted pairs (same as T1) but runs each full-duplex at 784 kbits/s on each (the lower bit rate reduces cross-talk)
- ISDN's 2B1Q line coding—2 bits encoded into a four-state (*quaternary*) symbol
- *Echo Cancellation* (which permits use on lines with *bridge taps*)
- *Adaptive Equalization* (automatically adjusts to permit operation over poorer-quality lines)

Maximum repeaterless cable distance is:

- 12,000 feet for 24-gauge cable (more than 80% of all T1 customer loops are less than 12,000 feet, and T1 links over 6,000 feet require a repeater)
- 9,000 feet for 26-gauge cable

ADSL provides a similar service.

See *ADSL*, *B8ZS*, *Bellcore*, *Encoding*, *FT1*, *Full-duplex*, and *T1*.

HDTV
High-Definition Television

A digital television (and more) broadcasting method to be an enhancement to the current standard NTSC broadcast and cable TV television signals used today.

Some features are the following:

- Will initially (for at least 15 years) use the 6 MHz channels that were left unassigned (to reduce interference) between currently assigned TV broadcast channels (that is, if channels 3 and 5 are assigned and used in a coverage area for standard NTSC broadcast television, then channel 4 will be available and will be used for HDTV).
- Provides a 16:9 (horizontal:vertical) aspect ratio, like a movie screen that is showing a standard 35-mm (called *Academy format*) or 70-mm movie film. This is wider than the 4:3 ratio of current standard televisions.
- Provides up to a 60-frames/s screen writing rate.
- Uses a subset of MPEG-2 data compression (and the *discrete cosine transformation* method that it specifies) to compress the source information (which has a data rate of 1.2 Gbits/s) by a factor of more than 60:1, to a broadcast data rate of less than 20 Mbits/s per TV channel.

- Using something called *digital vestigial sideband* modulation (wow, now if that doesn't impress you, they hope the picture quality will), this still fits into the current standard 6-MHz bandwidth television channels.

  In fact, for cable TV broadcasting, a single 6-MHz channel can carry two HDTV signals, since the HDTV signal can be simplified because the CATV environment is very (electrically) quiet.

Several frame rates and formats are defined, as shown in the following table. All yield "square pixels," that is, the number of pixels per inch is the same horizontally and vertically. This facilitates conversions between HDTV formats and also to common PC monitor resolutions (such as VGA, which also use square pixels). NTSC does not have square pixels.

Formats, in number of ...		Scanning	Frame Rates (frames/s)	
Active samples[a] (horizontal pixels)	Active Lines (vertical pixels)		HDTV[b]	NTSC[c]
1,280	720[d]	Progressive	24, 30, and 60	23.976, 29.97, and 59.94
1,920	1,080[d]	Progressive	24 and 30	23.976, 29.97, and 59.94
		Interlaced	30[e] (60 fields per second)	23.976, 29.97, and 59.94

[a] *Active* means that they are visible (for example, NTSC has 481 active lines out of the total of 525; the remaining 44 occur while the scanning beam is blanked during its retrace to the top-left corner of the screen).

[b] Movies are 24 frames per second, computer video and graphics are usually 30 frames per second, and 60 frames per second would be best suited to sports and other fast-action programming.

[c] These frame rates are provided in case they simplify using existing NTSC-format programming.

[d] Note that the numbers of lines in the two formats are in the exact ratio 3:2, which facilitates conversions between the formats. The ratio between the number of lines in a standard PC's VGA display and the HDTV 720 line format is also 3:2—for the same reason.

[e] This single interlaced format is useful for compatibility with existing interlaced program sources.

Noninterlaced (progressively scanned) 60-frame/1,080-line mode may be supported in the future if more bandwidth is available or compression technology advances further.

Uses Dolby Laboratories AC-3 multichannel digital sound system, which provides the following audio channels:

- Left
- Center
- Right
- Left-surround

- Right-surround
- Low-frequency enhancement

All this audio is encoded into a 384-kbits/s bit stream and provides compact-disc-quality audio. Other audio features are provided, such as the following:

- A constant volume level when switching channels
- Using the multiple audio channels for different languages or for services for the visually or hearing impaired

The digitized video, audio, and auxiliary information are packaged in 188-byte packets (only one type of information per packet). A 4-byte header in the packet:

- Includes an 8-bit synchronization byte
- Identifies (using 13 bits) what type of information the 184-byte packet payload carries
- Provides encryption (scrambling) control (to support pay-per-view and other premium services)

Information that is sent periodically in the payload provides synchronization between the different data streams, for example, to ensure lip-sync between the voice and video.

Added to each 188-byte packet are 20 bytes of Reed-Solomon *forward error correction* bytes to enable many (hopefully most) errored packets to be corrected by the receiver. (Packets that are too corrupted to be corrected are ignored.)

HDTV televisions will likely be sold only in very large sizes (and therefore be expensive) so that viewers will be able to see the benefit of the improved picture resolution.

Currently being developed by the *Digital HDTV Grand Alliance*, which was formed in 1993. The members started out as competitors, each proposing its own system to be accepted by the FCC, but the huge development expense, need to share technology (none had the best system overall), and threat of "winner-take-all—and the rest lose all" were too great to continue competing.

The members (and their contributions) are the following:

- AT&T and General Instrument (video encoder)
- The Massachusetts Institute of Technology
- Philips Electronics North America (video decoder)
- The David Sarnoff Research Center and Thomson Consumer Electronics (transport subsystem and system integration)
- Zenith (modulation subsystem)

All initial HDTV work used analog technologies. Early work (1968 to 1987) developed a system called MUSE (*Multiple Sub-Nyquist Encoding*), but it:

- Required two standard 6-MHz channels per HDTV channel
- Was susceptible to ghosting and other interference
- Was developed in Japan, and many in the United States thought HDTV was an important technology to keep the United States competitive in both technology and manufacturing

Then, in 1990, General Instrument proposed a digital system. This was a dramatic surprise. It was previously thought that digital would be too expensive and would not offer any user-perceived benefits, given the bandwidth restrictions. Digital's feasibility and advantages were demonstrated, and all analog development work was abandoned.

May be called *Digital Television* (DTV) in the future, to emphasize the flexibility of the technology to simply be a high-speed wireless data transport—possibly used (also) for broadcasting electronic newspapers, stock prices, or even an ATM data feed.

See *CD-ROM*, *FCC*, *Interlaced*, *MPEG*, *NTSC*, *PAL*, *SECAM*, *VGA*, and *Video*.

Hewlett-Packard Company   See **HP**.

High-Bit-Rate Digital Subscriber Line   See **HDSL**.

High-Definition Television   See **HDTV**.

High-Level Data Link Control   See **HDLC**.

High Level Language API   See **HLLAPI**.

High-Performance Routing/Advanced Program-to-Program Communications   See **HPR/APPN**.

HiPPI
High-Performance Parallel Interface

A connection-oriented (you have to establish a call before you can send data), circuit-switched (the entire link is dedicated to the connection for the duration of the connection), point-to-point (only two connections can be on a link, one at each end), somewhat expensive, and really high-speed networking technology.

Some characteristics are the following:

- Speed:
  - 800 Mbits/s or 1.6 Gbits/s (either implementation can be Simplex or Full-duplex)
- Distance:
  - 25 m over copper cable (either directly between two end-stations or from an end-station to a switch—switches can be cascaded to provide a total distance of up to 200 m)
  - 300 m on multimode fiber-optic cable
  - HiPPI-serial can go 10 km over single-mode fiber-optic cable (using SONet)
- Cable:
  - 62.5/125 multimode fiber-optic cable
  - A 50-pair STP copper cable (using 100-pin connectors) provides a simplex, 800-Mbits/s (total throughput), 32-bit-wide data link. A second cable can be used to provide either a 1.6-Gbits/s capacity or a full-duplex link. An additional two cables (four total) can be used to provide a 1.6 Gbits/s, full-duplex data link (sounds a bit expensive and bulky to me).
- Delays:
  - Connections established in less than 1 μs.
  - Latency averages 160 ns
- Protocols:
  - HiPPI specifies a frame format, which can be used directly
  - The HiPPI frames can carry TCP/IP or IPI-3 (*Intelligent Peripheral Interface*, a protocol used to communicate to RAID disk subsystems)
- Switching:
  - HiPPI uses 24-bit addresses, and each switch's ports each require a unique address
  - The number of cascaded switches is limited by the addressing (for example, up to six 16-port-in/16-port-out switches can be cascaded, since each switch port requires a 4-bit address, so six switches would use up all 24 address bits)

Initially developed for connections between mainframes, supercomputers, disk drives, and tape drives.

Standards for interconnecting with ATM, SONet, and fibre channel (which is similar in goal and is also an ANSI standard but has many more implementation options) are in development.

Standardized by ANSI and promoted by the *HiPPI Networking Forum* (HNF). RFC 1347 covers HiPPI and IP.

Further information is at *http://www.esscom.com/hnf/*.

See *ATM (Asynchronous Transfer Mode)*, *FDDI*, *FFDT*, *Fibre Channel*, *Full-duplex*, *RAID*, *Simplex*, and *SONet*.

High-Speed Serial Bus   See **1394.**

High-Speed Serial Interface   See **HSSI.**

HLLAPI
High-Level Language API

IBM's PC-based API for communication between a program and 3270 terminal-emulation software.

Enables an application program running on a PC to communicate with a main-frame, though in a very awkward way—by reading and writing characters on a computer terminal's screen. This is often called "screen scraping."

LU 6.2 is a much better way of doing this. It is a peer-to-peer-oriented successor that (don't things always go this way?) requires much more RAM on the PC (possibly leaving less for the PC's application program).

See *3270*, *API*, and *LU 6.2*.

Home Page

An ASCII file (which is in HTML format) typically accessed over the Internet from client computers running Web browser programs such as Netscape. The file is called a home page since it is typically a starting point, as the home page usually has references to other HTML pages on the same computer, or computers connected to that one (typically over the Internet).

The address of the home page file is called a URL, for example, *http://ourworld.compuserve.com/homepages/Mitchell_Shnier*. This specifies that on the host ourworld.compuserve.com, in the directory /homepages/Mitchell_Shnier there is a file (the name typically defaults to something like HOMEPAGE.HTM or Welcome.html), which is accessed using the HTTP protocol. The host computer runs a program called an http daemon (typically called httpd), and the host is then called a Web Server, since the cross-links to other home pages built in to this home page creates a Web (like a spider's web) of interconnections, between the Web servers interconnected through the Internet.

The Web server listens (usually on TCP port 80) for page requests from clients, and replies with the contents of the requested page.

See *ASCII*, *Client/Server*, *HTML*, *HTTP*, *Internet*, *TCP*, *URL*, and *WWW*.

Host

The name for any device on a TCP/IP network that has an IP address. Also any network-addressable device on any network.

HP
Hewlett-Packard Company

A humongous big company started by two nice guys (guess what Bill and Dave's last names were) in 1939 to make electronic test equipment. The first product was a relatively low-cost but high-quality audio sine-wave oscillator—the HP 100A. (The story goes that eight of these were used to test the sound system developed to make the Walt Disney Studios movie *Fantasia*.)

In addition to laser printers (and test equipment), Hewlett-Packard makes over 10,000 other products, such as lots of really complicated medical equipment and scientific test equipment.

Hewlett-Packard has a WWW server at *http://www.hp.com*, and Interex (the International Association of Hewlett-Packard Computing Professionals) has a WWW server at *http://www.interex.org/*.

See *COSE*, *HPUX*, *IrDA*, *OSF*, *P7*, *PA-RISC*, *PCL*, and *SNMP*.

HPUX

Hewlett-Packard's older UNIX-like operating system.

See *HP* and *UNIX*.

HPR/APPN
High-Performance Routing/Advanced Program-to-Program Communications

A new version of APPN that supports a connectionless network-layer service.

See *APPN*.

HSSI
High-Speed Serial Interface

A 52-Mbits/s link used for connecting an ATM switch to a T3 DSU/CSU (for example).

See *ATM (Asynchronous Transfer Mode)*, *CSU*, *DSU*, *Fibre Channel*, *HiPPI*, and *T3*.

HTML
Hypertext Markup Language

The language used to describe WWW pages so that font size and color, nice backgrounds, graphics, and positioning can be specified and maintained (though users can change how these are actually displayed by their own browsers).

A tag-based ASCII language that is used to specify the content and *hypertext links* to other documents on *World Wide Web* servers on the Internet. *Browsers* (such as Netscape and Mosaic, which can be made for any operating system, hardware platform, monitor resolution, etc.) can then be used to view the prepared documents and follow links to display other documents.

For example,

```
<HTML>
<HEAD>
<TITLE>This is the title</TITLE>
</HEAD>
<BODY>
<H1>This is a first-level heading</H1>
This is a paragraph with <B>bold</B> and
<I>italic</I> words.<P>
</BODY>
</HTML>
```

would display something like this:

This is a first-level heading
This is a paragraph with **bold** and *italic* words.

HTML–1

The *title* is used to update the title bar of Web browser displays and is the name stored as the *bookmark*. The *body* of the text is what is displayed to the person reading the page. The ends of paragraphs are marked with a <P> (or sometimes, paragraphs are surrounded by <P> and </P>).

The first popular versions of HTML were 0.9 and 1.0, since they were supported by Mosaic v1.0.3 (which is widely available and used on the Internet). It supports the following types of commands:

- Basic document delimiters, such as <HTML>, <HEAD>, <TITLE>, and <BODY>
- Section headings, <H1> through <H6>, which use a bold font, in decreasing size for each level of heading
- Lists, using either bullets ("•") or sequential numbers
- Paragraphs, indenting, and spacing, such as the <P> above, a hard-return
 (the viewer normally automatically wraps text according to the font and screen size used for display), and <HR>, which displays a horizontal separator line

- Character attributes, such as **bold**, `monospaced`, and *italic*
- Special characters, such as "é," or characters used by HTML, such as "<"
- Graphics images to be displayed within the document. (These images are separate files, which can be located anywhere on the Internet and are usually in JPEG or .GIF format.)
- "Anchor" commands, which specify text or images that can be clicked on, to load another HTML document. (Again, these can be anywhere on the Internet.)

Everything in HTML v1.0 is "one way only," that is, users can only display documents. There is no way to send information back to a WWW server.

HTML version 2.0 (which is supported by Netscape Navigator 1.0) adds commands for interactive forms. That is, users can fill in forms from their browsers, and send the information back to the WWW server (which then handles the received information by running a CGI script).

HTML version 3.0 (some of which was called HTML+ for a while) is supported by Netscape Navigator version 1.1. The main enhancement is support for tables.

Further information is available at *http://www.w3.org/pub/WWW/*.

Tools are used to prepare the *home pages* and linked documents. For example, see *http://www.sq.com*. Initially developed as a research project at the European Laboratory for Particle Physics (CERN).

Modeled after, but much less powerful and not interchangeable with, SGML.

See *CGI, Home Page, HTTP, Internet, SGML, VRML*, and *WWW*.

HTTP
Hypertext Transfer Protocol

The protocol used to carry WWW traffic between a WWW browser computer and the WWW server being accessed.

The protocol is documented at *http://www.w3.org*.

See *GIF, Home Page, HTML, S-HTTP, SSL, URL*, and *WWW*.

Hypertext Markup Language   See **HTML.**

IAB
Internet Architecture Board

The coordinating committee for Internet design, engineering, and management. Oversees the health and evolution of the Internet (in practice by withholding the approval of new standards) and approves new standards. Previously called the *Internet Activities Board*.

See *IETF* and *Internet*.

IAP
Internet Access Provider

Same as *Internet Service Provider*.

See *ISP*.

iBCS
Intel Binary Compatibility Standard

A standard for Intel-based implementations of UNIX to permit *binary portability*. That is, the same compiled and linked program executable can run on more than one UNIX—for example, SCO and Interactive UNIX.

A newer version of the standard is iBCS2.

See *Portability*, *SCO*, *Solaris*, and *UNIX*.

IBM
International Business Machines

A really big company.

IBM has (or had) more to do with current computing than most people realize:

- IBM developed the technology on which SCSI is based.
- IBM owns part of the company that runs the Internet backbone.
- IBM developed SQL.
- IBM invented the RISC concept.
- IBM designed the original PC and chose to license (and not ignore or buy outright) MS-DOS from Microsoft, thereby giving Microsoft a start.
- IBM developed HDLC (which it calls SDLC).

IBM operates a WWW Server at *http://www.ibm.com*.

See *ANS*, *COSE*, *Internet*, *HDLC*, *Mainframe*, *OSF*, *PC*, *RISC*, *SCSI*, *SDLC*, and *SQL*.

ICMP
Internet Control Message Protocol

An IP protocol that permits routers to inform other routers or hosts of IP routing problems or suggested better routes.

See *Host*, *IP*, *Ping*, *RIP*, and *TTL* (*Time-To-Live*).

iComp
Intel Comparative Microprocessor Performance Index

A benchmark for comparing the relative power (that's processing power, not heat dissipation) of Intel processors.

Intended to highlight how fast the CPU executes instructions, because Intel thought that consumers were paying too much attention to the clock speed—which is measured in megahertz, or millions of cycles per second (MHz)—of processors. Intel knew that new processors would be much more powerful while possibly having a lower clock speed (for example, because of clock doubling, a math coprocessor, or *superscalar* design).

A 25-MHz 486SX is given the rating of 100, and all other ratings are relative to this.

A weighted average, based on the instruction mix that Intel expects to be representative for operating systems and applications for the next 3 to 5 years (which are, for example, expected to have a growing emphasis of 32-bit applications). This is an important distinction and assumption, as Intel's P6 (for example) is so optimized for 32-bit operations that it is only slightly faster (and can actually be slower) when executing 16-bit applications (which will continue to be widely used for years to come).

The current iComp rating is made up of four industry-standard benchmarks (which measure both 16-bit and 32-bit processor performance for integer, floating-point, graphics, and video performance), each weighted as shown in the following table.

Benchmark	Percentage Weighting	Benchmark Measures
SPECint92	25	Integer math performance
SPECfp92	5	Floating-point math performance
PCBench	68	Ziff-Davis' DOS CPU performance (only the *processor harmonic* measurement is used)
Whetstone	2	Floating-point math performance
Total	*100*	

The rating does not include tests of disk or video system performance, nor other important aspects of a system, such as the number of expansion slots or type and speed of the system bus.

That is, the iComp rating is only one of many important metrics in comparing computer systems. For example, throughput of a file server is usually limited mostly by the disk subsystem and the bus. Usually, CPU processing power is not the most important factor in determining capacity.

Intel says that it will revise the method of calculating the rating to keep it relevant to the current and expected applications and operating systems.

Some actual iComp ratings are listed in the following table.

Processor	Clock Speed (MHz)[a]	iComp Rating
486SX	20	78
486SX	25	100
486DX or SL	25	122
486SX	33	136
486DX or SL	33	166
486DX2	25/50	231
486DX2	33/66	297
DX4	25/75	319
DX4	33/100	435
Pentium P60	60	510
Pentium P66	66	567
Pentium P75	50/75	610

(table continued on next page)

Processor	Clock Speed (MHz)[a]	iComp Rating
Pentium P90	60/90	735
Pentium P100	66/100	815
Pentium P120	60/120	1,000

[a] If clock-multiplying technology is used (clock doubling, etc.), then the external/internal clock speeds are both shown.

See *Intel*, *P6*, *PC*, *SPEC*, and *Superscalar*.

IDE
Integrated Drive Electronics

A very popular (even the Macintosh supports it now) industry-standard hard disk drive interface developed by Western Digital and Compaq (in 1986) as an improvement on IBM's ST-506 and ST-412 (which were the popular PC disk drive interfaces at the time).

IDE uses the PC BIOS's interrupt 13^{16} to provide an interface to the operating system.

To reduce the cost, the electronics that are needed to run the disk drive are part of the disk drive, not the disk controller—hence the name. An IDE disk drive "controller" or "adapter" basically directly connects the PC's (usually) ISA bus to the 40-pin IDE disk drive connector, and is so simple it is sometimes called a *paddle card*.

A maximum of two standard hard disk drives (the master and one slave—as selected on the drives) can be driven by one controller.

Typical maximum sustained transfer rates are 1 to 3 Mbytes/s, limited mostly by the ISA bus (though IDE is typically implemented on lower-performance disk drives that transfer data at no more than about 5 Mbits/s, so the IDE interface is not a bottleneck).

Since the BIOS allows up to 1,024 cylinders and 63 sectors per track, and IDE allows up to 16 heads and DOS supports 512 bytes per sector, maximum IDE drive capacity is therefore 504 Mbytes ($512 \times 63 \times 1,024 \times 16 = 528,482,304$ bytes), where a Mbyte is ($1,024 \times 1,024$ bytes =) 1,048,576 bytes.

Western Digital's newer *Enhanced IDE* competes with Seagate's *Fast ATA*.

Western Digital has a WWW server at *http://www.wdc.com*.

See *AT*, *ATA*, *ATASPI*, *BIOS*, *Disk Drive*, *Fast ATA*, *FAT*, *E-IDE*, *Interrupt Request*, *ISA*, *PC*, *PIO*, *SCSI*, and *Winchester*.

IDEA
International Data Encryption Algorithm

An algorithm for encrypting data, making it well-nigh impossible for others to read your message.

A *single-key* encryption algorithm (as is the much better-known DES). IDEA was selected (not DES or RSA) for use in certain parts of PGP because IDEA:

- Has a much longer key (128 bits, rather than 56 bits), making it much more secure
- Runs much faster than DES when implemented in software (DES was designed to run slowly in software, to make decrypting messages without the key more difficult)
- Runs about 4,000 times faster than RSA
- Is not export restricted from North America (as DES is)—in fact, IDEA was developed in Switzerland at ETH (Eidgenössische Technische Hochschule, which is the Swiss Federal Institute of Technology, at Zürich)
- Is much more secure than RSA for a given key size (the 128-bit idea key is apparently as secure as a 3,100-bit RSA key—and 1,024 bits is the current maximum RSA key size)

No license fee is required for noncommercial use of IDEA.

See *DES*, *Encryption*, *PGP*, and *RSA*.

IEC
Interexchange Carrier

Same as IXC.

See *IXC*.

IEEE
Institute of Electrical and Electronics Engineers

The group that (among many other things) produced the standards for Ethernet and Token Ring (which is done by the 802 Committee, so-named because it was formed in February of 1980).

The IEEE maintains a WWW site at *http://www.ieee.org*.

See *10BASE-T*, *10BASE-F*, *100BASEFX*, *100BASE-T*, *100BASE-T2*, *100BASE-T4*, *100BASE-TX*, *1284*, *802.1h*, *802.2*, *802.3*, *802.5*, *802.6*, *802.9a*, *802.10*, *802.11*, *802.12*, *802.14*, *LAN*, *POSIX OSE*, and *Standards*.

IETF
Internet Engineering Task Force

The group (formed in 1986) that determines new protocols and application requirements for the Internet, with the following characteristics:

- The protocol engineering and development arm of the Internet
- A large open international community of network designers, operators, vendors, and researchers who are concerned with the evolution of the Internet architecture and the smooth operation of the Internet
- Supervises the development of RFCs
- Reports to the IAB

The IETF has a WWW server at *http://www.ietf.cnri.reston.va.us/home.html.*

See *IAB, InterNIC,* and *RFC.*

IGP
Interior Gateway Protocol

A protocol (such as RIP or OSPF) that is used for routing within a TCP/IP *autonomous system.*

See *OSPF* and *RIP.*

IGRP
Interior Gateway Routing Protocol

A proprietary, router-to-router, intradomain protocol that was developed by Cisco Systems for routing TCP/IP and OSI CLNP.

One of the main functions of a router is to choose the "best" path between a source and a destination. Since each path might comprise many links, a method of comparing the links is required. Rather than characterizing each link along the path with only one metric (as does RIP—it counts only hops), IGRP uses five (count 'em, folks) metrics.

The metrics evaluated are the link's speed (or available bandwidth), delay, packet size, loading, and reliability.

In networks with diverse data link types, this can be an important improvement. Of course, then the problem is what you mean by "best"—the fastest or the most reliable. And what if sometimes you mean one (for example, for file transfers), and other times you mean another (for email)? Application programs and protocols usually have no way of communicating their individual requirements to the router.

Enhanced IGRP supports TCP/IP, IPX, and AppleTalk and provides many of the benefits of link-state router-to-router protocols, such as the following:

- Fast convergence (more quickly propagating updated routing information to the entire network)
- Variable-length subnet bit masks
- Updates sent as soon as connectivity changes take place
- No periodic router-to-router broadcasts

See *Cisco Systems*, *Link-state*, *QOS*, *RIP*, and *Subnet Bit Mask*.

ILSR
IPX Link State Router

Novell's proprietary enhancement to its RIP distance-vector-based routing protocol.

See *Link-state*.

IMAP
Internet Mail Access Protocol

The newer type of Internet mail server. It allows connected stations to first view message headers and choose which, of the mail messages for them, they wish to receive. (The others remain stored on the mail server.)

Can work with the older POP2 and POP3 mail servers, only offering the POP functionality (for example, you need to accept all mail messages once a connection is established to the mail server).

See *Internet*, *POP*, and *SMTP*.

IMHO
In My Humble Opinion

A common email abbreviation.

In-Band

As in *In-bandwidth*, that is, using the same bandwidth (wires or data channel) for *signaling* (sending control information) as for data transmission.

Examples of in-band signaling include the following:

- On an EIA-232 interface, sending and receiving the x-on and x-off flow control characters (11_{16} and 13_{16}) on pins 2 and 3—that is, as part of the sent and received data (this means that the data cannot have any x-on or x-off characters in them)

- On a standard touch-tone (DTMF) telephone or service type II switched 56 data set, sending the phone number dialed to the central office on the same pair of wires that the voice or data communications uses

While usually less expensive to implement than an out-of-band signaling method, in-band signaling is usually undesirable, since it restricts or disrupts the data that can be sent.

Also, in-band signaling leaves the possibility that users can inadvertently (or purposely) affect the signaling. For example, on standard telephone connections the telephone company uses a 2,600-Hz tone to indicate that a long-distance call is completed, and sending one at the right time can provide free long-distance calls. People who often call themselves *"phone phreaks"* make or buy *blue boxes*, which can generate this tone. Mind you, this is *theft of telecommunications services*, a bad thing to do. The Usenet newsgroup `alt.2600` has many people trying to fool others that they have done this, trying to entrap people that do this, and claiming that others are trying to entrap others.

Much of this "fun" changed with the advent of the *Common Channel Signaling System Number* 7 (CCS #7). This is an out-of-band signaling method (initially only within the phone network, later out-of-band to the customer site too, using the ISDN D channel) that prevents users from messing with the phone company's signaling and enables the phone company to offer new features, such as Caller ID.

Another example of in-band signaling is that pay phones indicate how much money has been deposited by sending a 2,200-Hz tone to the central office for each 5¢ deposited; a nickel is a 60-ms tone pulse, a dime is two 60-ms tone pulses, separated by 60-ms, and a quarter is five 15-ms tone pulses.

Since the tones are sent on the same pair of wires as your voice is, what stops you (other than the law) from making a device that can generate these tones and holding it to the telephone mouthpiece?

While I never got my *red box* working, sometimes you get a pay phone that doesn't mute the earpiece when you drop in the money, and you can hear these tone pulses.

See *ASCII, DTMF (Dual Tone Multi-Frequency), EIA/TIA-232, ISDN, Out-of-band, Switched 56,* and *Usenet.*

IND$FILE

A program that runs on an IBM mainframe (which is running TSO, CICS, or VM/CMS) that provides the mainframe side of a file transfer capability from 3270-type terminals (or PCs emulating them). Many third-party PC-based terminal-emulation software packages provide the terminal side of this file transfer capability.

Also called *SEND/RECEIVE*.

See *3270*, *CICS*, *Mainframe*, and *VM*.

Industrial Design

In Canada, a *registered industrial design* receives protection against others copying the aesthetics and appearance of the product.

Covers the shape, pattern, or ornamentation (either of the entire product or of a component part of it) of a useful mass-produced article, regardless of how the article is actually manufactured. That is, an infringement would look as though it (or an important part of it) came from the same mold (more than it looks as though it came from some other *prior art*).

In the United States, a *design patent* provides similar protection.

The design must have features that are specifically included for visual appeal (though their quality and merits are not judged). For example, users should be able to see the article when the product is used normally, and the article should be a substantial and important part of the product.

Products that are created as a work of art are automatically protected by *copyright* (no *registration* required), but if a product is used (or intended to be used) as a model or pattern to produce more than 50 single useful articles or sets of articles it becomes an *industrial design*, which can be protected only if it is registered as an industrial design.

Some products (a distinctive package, for example) can be covered by both an industrial design (initially) and later (after the product has been put on the market), a *trademark*.

An industrial design must be original and produced in quantity (or there must be an intention to do so).

The following cannot be registered as industrial designs:

- Designs for articles that serve no useful purpose, are utilitarian only (and are not intended to provide visual appeal), have no fixed appearance (they can change shape, such as a bean bag), or are normally hidden by other parts of the article
- A manufacturing process, an article's construction method, or the materials used in the construction
- An idea
- The function, useful purpose, or functional features of the article
- The particular colors used for an article

An *industrial design application* (for registration) must be filed within one year of publicizing the design or offering the product for sale (and preferably before the design has been so "published"). If you wait longer than one year, you cannot get industrial design protection. As for patents, some countries do not permit publicizing before applying for protection of an industrial design.

Registration is required (to get any protection), and it enables the owner to prevent others from making, using, renting, or selling the design in Canada for 10 years from the registration date.

The application must cover the distinctive, important and original visual features of the design (and not the functionality of the resulting article). If the description does not cover the details, then the resulting registration will not provide the coverage needed. Too broad a description will be impossible to enforce. Detail should be provided to differentiate the design from others that are known to exist.

The application must include drawings or photographs (showing how the industrial design will be used on the product to be manufactured) that correspond to the description.

In addition to the *examination fee* required for registration (and the fees for the *patent agent* who usually prosecutes the application), a one-time maintenance fee must be paid before five years have elapsed (if it is not paid, the registration expires, and others may freely use the design, just as if the 10-year period had expired).

The proprietor of an industrial design is usually the creator, but industrial designs done for an employer are the property of the employer. Designs done under contract (that is, not in an employer-employee relationship) are the property of the person who pays the contractor (it is the other way around for copyrights).

The ownership of industrial designs may be permanently transferred (*assigning* some or all of the rights), as that of any property can.

A proprietor of a registered industrial design can also *license* the use of the industrial design for a specific use, for a period of time, and for a specified geographic area.

Marking a registered industrial design with the name of the proprietor (for example, Ⓓ Mitchell Shnier Designs) on the article, its label, or packaging, is not required. However, if a court finds that someone has been infringing, and the article is not marked, the only remedy is an *injunction* preventing further infringement; if it is marked, a court can also award a remedy of financial compensation.

In Canada, industrial designs are administered by the Industrial Design Office, which is part if the CIPO.

Intellectual property protection documents are available from Micromedia Limited, at *http://www.mmltd.com.*

See *CIPO, Design Patent, Intellectual Property Protection*, and *Patent*.

Industry Canada

The current name for the Canadian federal government agency that is responsible for licensing radio frequency spectrum.

Was previously called the Department of Communications, and before that, Communications Canada, and before that, the Department of Communications. (My, but they are busy over there.)

Industry Canada is also responsible for *intellectual property protection*.

See *CATV*, *CIPO*, *CRTC*, *FCC*, and *Intellectual Property Protection*.

Industry Standard Architecture   See **ISA.**

Infrared Data Association   See **IrDA.**

Initial Program Load   See **IPL.**

Institute of Electrical and Electronics Engineers   See **IEEE.**

Integrated Circuit Topography Act

The Canadian act that provides protection from others copying an integrated circuit (IC) design. It covers both the three-dimensional and per-layer design for up to ten years. The design must be original, but can be based on *reverse-engineering* other designs (obviously most everyone agreed that reverse engineering is a normal part of engineering design—incrementally improving on earlier work).

Registration is required.

Since protection of integrated circuit designs is dramatically different in different countries, international protection is difficult to obtain.

The U.S. act that provides similar protection is the *Semiconductor Chip Protection Act*. There is some information at *http://www.law.cornell.edu/topics/copyright.html*.

See *Intellectual Property Protection*.

Integrated Drive Electronics   See **IDE.**

Integrated IS-IS

DEC's proprietary link-state, interdomain, *and* intradomain routing protocol based on OSI's IS-IS. One advantage of DEC's implementation is that it currently handles DECnet Phase IV, OSI CLNP, and IP. Also, IPX and AppleTalk are handled by encapsulating them into IP.

See *Link-state*.

Integrated Services Digital Network   See **ISDN.**

Intel

Inventor of the first microprocessors (starting with the 4004, which was designed as a flexible solution to calculator innards). The Intel processor architecture remains the basis of all PCs, though other companies have developed clones of it.

The following table lists Intel processors and their features.

Processor	Clock Speed (MHz)	MIPS	Transistors (thousands)	Bus Width (bits)[a] Internal Data Bus/ External Data Bus/ Address Bus			Introduced
4004		0.06	2.3	4	4		1971
8008				8	8		
8080	2	0.1	6	8	8	16	1974
8086	5	0.33	29	16	16	20	1978
8088	5	0.33	29	16	8	20	1979
80286	8	1.2	134	16	16	24	1982
80386DX	16	6	275	32	32	32	1985
80386SX	16	2.5	275	32	16	24	1988
486DX	25	20	1,200	32	32	32	1989
486SX	20	16.5	1,185	32	32	32	1991
486DX2	50	40	1,200	32	32	32	1992
486DX2	66	54	1,200	32	32	32	1992
486DX4	100			32	32	32	1994
Pentium	66	112	3,100	32	64	32	1993
Pentium	100	170	3,300	32	64	32	1994
P6	133	250	5,500[b]	32	64	32	1995
P7		500	10,000				1997

[a] The external data bus width is (for example) the number of bits in each read from Level 2 cache.

[b] Not including the 15.5 million transistors for the 256-kbyte Level 2 cache that is in the same IC package as the CPU.

Because of competitive pressure, the development work for recent Intel processors has started before predecessor processors have been finished, as shown in the accompanying figure (yes, data for 1996 dates and beyond have been estimated). This has accelerated the release of new processors to faster than every 4 years (as shown in the table).

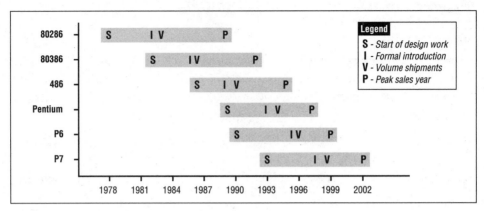

Intel−1

Intel maintains a WWW server at *http://www.intel.com*.

See *486DX, 486DX2, 486DX4, 486SX, 486SX2, 80386DX, 80386SX, DX4, iComp, MIPS, OverDrive, PC, Pentium, P6, P7,* and *VLIW*.

Intel Binary Compatibility Standard   See **iBCS**.

Intel Comparative Microprocessor Performance Index   See **iComp**.

Intellectual Property Protection

The purpose of *intellectual property protection* is to protect owners of intellectual property while promoting creativity and the orderly exchange of ideas.

Many forms of protection are available, as shown in the following table

Protection	Protects	Requires	Lasts
Copyright	Artistic and creative works—the expression of an idea	Automatically covered, though a © serves as a reminder. Works can be registered as well.	The lifetime of the author, plus 50 years
Canadian Industrial Design	The shape, pattern, or ornamentation (aesthetics and appearance) of a useful manufactured article	Registration in each country	10 years from registration
U.S. Design Patent			14 years from registration

(table continued on next page)

Protection	Protects	Requires	Lasts
Patent	The idea itself (functionality, processes, and techniques)	Filing and granting of a patent in each country	20 years from the date of application
Integrated Circuit Topography	Integrated circuit designs	Registration	Up to 10 years from registration
Trademark	Distinguishing words and symbols	Can be covered automatically after a period of use, but registration is recommended	15 years after registration, renewable in 15-year periods thereafter

Ideas and concepts can be covered by *copyright* or *patent* protection only after being translated into a tangible form (such as a written description or a built unit).

The Geneva-based *World Intellectual Property Organization* (WIPO, which has about 120 member countries) promotes intellectual property protection through *international treaties* and technical assistance to developing countries. It administers several international treaties, such as the *Paris Convention for the Protection of Industrial Property*, which was developed in 1883, and covers patents, *trademarks*, and *industrial designs*.

The Paris Convention provides for *national treatment*, which means that member countries grant the same level of intellectual property protection and remedies against infringement to each others' citizens as they grant to their own.

Patent and copyright protection is more similar in different countries than are industrial design and (especially) integrated circuit design protection.

The Cornell Law School's Legal Information Institute has a WWW page with (among other things) intellectual property protection information at *http://www.law.cornell.edu/topics/topic2.html#intellectual property* (wow—there is space between intellectual and property; I've never seen that before).

See *CIPO, Copyright, Design Patent, Industrial Design, Integrated Circuit Topography Act, Patent, Trademark,* and *Trade Secret.*

Interexchange Carrier   See **IXC.**

Interior Gateway Protocol   See **IGP.**

Interior Gateway Routing Protocol   See **IGRP.**

Interlaced

A lower-cost way of producing high-resolution images on a video monitor while reducing *flicker*.

Flicker is an observation that the display is quickly turning on and off (which is more apparent when the displayed image has a light-colored background or when the room lighting is fluorescent, which itself flickers).

A monitor's *electron beam* scans across the screen (left to right), being turned on and off by the video adapter to illuminate dots (called *picture elements*, *pixels*, or *pels*). At the end of each horizontal *raster scan*, the beam is turned off, and it returns back to the left side of the screen (this is called *horizontal retrace*) and moves one row (or *line*) down. This continues until all rows are displayed, then the beam is returned back to the top of the screen (*vertical retrace*).

It can be less expensive, especially for televisions and higher-resolution computer displays, to use an *interlaced* display. In this case, during the first *display refresh cycle*, the odd-numbered (1, 3, 5, etc.) rows are scanned (illuminated). This is called a *field*. During the next cycle, the even-numbered rows (2, 4, 6, etc., each of which is between the just-displayed odd-numbered rows) are scanned. This is the next *field*. The two fields comprise a *frame*.

A fast display cycle can then be used, which reduces flicker and permits faster-moving objects to be displayed, while reducing the cost of the monitor and adapter (since the electron beam has to write only half the pixels per display cycle).

Higher-quality monitors don't do this interlacing trick. They have a *noninterlaced* (or *progressively scanned*) display. The entire screen is rewritten each display cycle, which must occur at 70 Hz or more to eliminate flicker.

Standard broadcast television (NTSC) uses interlacing. It has a frame rate of 29.97 frames per second, and a field rate of 59.94 fields per second.

See *Color*, *NTSC*, *Pixel*, *Rasterize*, and *Video*.

Intermediate System   See **IS.**

International Business Machines   See **IBM.**

International Data Encryption Algorithm   See **IDEA.**

International Organization for Standardization   See **ISO.**

International Telecommunication Union   See **ITU.**

internet

A (usually private) network of networks, such as a network interconnecting a company's many in-house networks. Often, TCP/IP is the one protocol common to all networks.

See *Internet*.

Internet

The largest network in the world, which consists of many networks, such as NSFNet and the Defense Data Network, along with *gateways* to others, such as BITnet.

A TCP/IP-based network linking more than 20 million users (160,000 new ones per month) and 1.5 million computers on more than 45,000 networks in 46 countries. These numbers are completely out of date (and were never very accurate), because each subnetwork is administered by its owner, and the number of hosts on the Internet doubles every 7 months (15% growth per month). 120 new commercial network IDs are registered per day.

The largest backbone (which used to be called NSFNet and is funded by the U.S. government) has about 4,000 networks and 1 million hosts). The backbone currently runs at T3 speed, soon to be OC-3. Officially called the *National Research and Education Network*.

The T3 backbone was installed and is administered by a joint venture (of IBM, Merit Network, and MCI) called Advanced Network and Service, Inc. (ANS). The routers that are used are based on IBM RS/6000 RISC workstations.

The part of the backbone that is funded by the U.S. government is called NSFNet, and traffic on it is subject to the *acceptable use policy*. The rest of the backbone is called the *Commercial Information Exchange* and is funded by the commercial *Internet service providers*. There are no restrictions on the traffic it can carry.

Although the Internet is officially called the National Research and Education Network, NREN will soon apply only to the restricted-use (that is, noncommercial) part of the backbone, which will be used to support research on protocols, RPCs, large file transfers, and other advanced applications.

A volunteer-based organization, the *Internet Society* (ISOC) has the ultimate authority for the future of the Internet. Anyone can join the ISOC, which has the purpose of promoting global information exchange through Internet technology. The ISOC appoints a council called the *Internet Architecture Board*, which regularly meets to sanction standards and allocate resources, such as addresses. The IAB decides when a standard is required, determines what the standard should be, and announces it.

Internet users provide input through the *Internet Engineering Task Force* (IETF, also a volunteer-based organization). It meets regularly to discuss operational and near-term technical problems of the Internet. IETF working groups are formed to address significant problems.

Other networks (for example, BITnet and the UUCP network) are physically connected to the U.S. Internet but may offer more limited services (in general, these are switching to *full Internet access* so that they can offer their users all the popular capabilities, such as ftp, telnet, and WWW). Still other networks (such as Canada's CA*net) have always had full Internet access (and have multiple connections for greater reliability and throughput).

See *ANS, ARPAnet, AUP, BITnet, CA*net, CERT, CIX, DNS (Domain Name System), Gopher, Home Page, IAB, IETF, Internet, InterNIC, IP Address, IMAP, IRC, ISP, Host, NREN, NSFnet, Ping, POP, TCP/IP, uucp, WAIS,* and *WWW.*

Internet Access Provider (IAP)   See **ISP.**

Internet Architecture Board   See **IAB.**

Internet Control Message Protocol   See **ICMP.**

Internet Engineering Task Force   See **IETF.**

Internet Mail Access Protocol   See **IMAP.**

Internet Network Information Center   See **InterNIC.**

Internet Packet Exchange   See **IPX.**

Internet Protocol   See **IP.**

Internet Relay Chat   See **IRC.**

Internet Service Provider   See **ISP.**

InterNIC
Internet Network Information Center

InterNIC Information Services is an initiative that is partially funded by the National Science Foundation to:

• Provide Internet information services
• Supervise the registration of Internet addresses and DNS names

- Assign RFC numbers
- Help users make use of, and obtain access to, the Internet

Contacts are listed in the following table.

email	info@internic.net
ftp	ftp.internic.net
phone	1-800-444-4345 and 619-455-4600
www	http://internic.net

See *CA*net*, *DNS (Domain Name System)*, *Internet*, and *RFC*.

Interrupt Request See **IRQ.**

Inverse Multiplexer

Usually, a *multiplexer* is used to provide many users (typically low-speed asynchronous terminals, such as DEC VT100s, or PCs emulating them) with access to a single higher-speed connection (since it is less expensive to provide one higher-speed link than many lower-speed links).

An *inverse multiplexer* works the other way around. It solves the problem that high-speed (greater than 64 kbits/s), switched (you choose who you want to connect to, just before you send data) WAN services are not (yet) widely available.

The inverse multiplexer provides a high-speed switched service by establishing many (typically) 56- or 64-kbits/s switched connections simultaneously (and handling the splitting and combining of the data). For example, if you needed a 384-kbits/s service for a two-hour video conference, the inverse multiplexer would make six simultaneous 64-kbits/s calls (perhaps using several ISDN BRI connections). If the connection was long-distance, you would pay six times the rate for a single 64-kbits/s call.

Inverse multiplexers are an interim technology (they're a kludge), which will be replaced by *Multirate ISDN*, frame relay SVCs, ATM, and other cleaner solutions in the near future.

See *800*, *ATM (Asynchronous Transfer Mode)*, *Bonding*, *Digital 800*, *Frame Relay*, *ISDN*, *PPPML*, *Switched 56*, and *WAN*.

IP
Internet Protocol

UNIX's internetworking protocol (OSI layer 3). Includes information for fragmentation/reassembly and Time-To-Live and identifies the encapsulated protocol (for example, TCP). Routers use this information.

IP routers drop packets to handle congestion (the sending router is supposed to detect the congestion by the high rate of retransmit requests from the receiver and slow down).

The currently used version is Version 4, or IPv4.

See *CSLIP, DNS (Domain Name System), ICMP, Internet, InterNIC, IP Address, IP Multicast, IPng, Link-state, Mobile IP, RIP, SLIP, TCP, TTL (Time-To-Live)*, and *UNIX*.

IP Address

All network-layer protocols have an address format, and for the 32-bit IP addresses of the TCP/IP protocol, addresses are of the form "`199.12.1.1`". This is called *dotted decimal*, and each of the four sections is a decimal number from 0 to 255, representing 8 bits of the IP address. Part of the address specifies a *network*, and the rest of the *address* specifies a specific host on that network.

Since there are only 32 bits to the entire IP address and some networks have many more hosts than others (and there are fewer larger networks), there are different *address classes*. These allocate different numbers of bits to the network and host portion of the address.

The address classes are summarized in the following table.

IP Address Class	Address Range[a]	Comments
	0.0.0.0	The local host[b] also used to signify the default router
A	0.*x.x.x*	Host *x.x.x* on the local network
	1.0.0.1 *to* 126.255.255.254	2^7-2 (126) *Class A* networks total, each with $2^{24}-2$ (16,777,214 to be exact) hosts
	127.*x.x.x*	Used for internal host loopback
B	128.0.*x.x*	Reserved
	128.1.0.1 *to* 191.254.255.254	$2^{14}-2$ (16,382) *Class B* networks, each with up to $2^{16}-2$ (65,534) hosts
	191.255.255.*x*	Reserved
C	192.0.0.*x*	Reserved
	192.0.1.1 *to* 223.255.254.254	$2^{21}-2$ (2,097,150) *Class C* networks, each with up to 2^8-2 (254) hosts
	223.255.255.*x*	Reserved
D	224.0.0.0 *to* 239.255.255.254	Reserved for multicast groups

(table continued on next page)

IP Address Class	Address Range[a]	Comments
E	240.0.0.0 *to* 254.255.255.254	Reserved for experimental and future use
	255.255.255.255	Broadcast to all hosts on the *local* network

[a] The network number (or ID) part of the IP address is set in **bold** in this chart.

[b] By convention, setting the network or host part of the address to zero refers to the *local* ("*this*") network or host (respectively). Setting the host part to all ones refers to *all* hosts on the specified network. Therefore, a network or host address of all ones or all zeros cannot be used as a specific network or host ID.

Because all Class A addresses have been used and there are very few Class B addresses left, new addressing schemes are required for networks that have more than 254 hosts.

Efforts to handle this addressing problem include *Classless Inter-Domain Routing* (CIDR), IPng, and RFC 1597.

See *CIDR*, *DNS* (*Domain Name System*), *Host*, *IP Multicast*, *IPng*, *RFC 1597*, and *Subnet Bit Mask*.

IP Multicast
Internet Protocol Multicast

Video conferencing, electronic whiteboards, and other anticipated multimedia uses for networks will need *one-to-many* and *many-to-many* communication capability, which is substantially different from the traditional *one-to-one* or *point-to-point* connections that most current LAN and WAN applications use. Other possible uses for multicasting capability include nonmultimedia applications, such as updating mail server databases.

In addition to being able to send a single message to many destinations at once (current technology would require the same message to be sent many times, once to each destination), requirements are as follows:

- Routers must be able to efficiently locate routes to many networks at once
- Only a single copy of each packet should be sent on any shared link
- Traffic should be sent only on links that have at least one recipient (this addresses both network loading and security concerns)

IP multicast requires destination hosts wanting to receive a multicast to *subscribe* (also called "register"), using the *Internet group management protocol* (which supports other related functions, such as leaving a multicast group). Subscribing is done by specifying the Class D IP address used for the particular multicast (just like tuning to a particular television channel). All of this is defined in RFC 1112.

Routers track such IGMP requests and build a *connectivity tree* for each possible sender to each registered receiver. When multicast traffic is received from a particular sender, the router then uses its tree for that sender to determine on which ports traffic needs to be forwarded.

There are three potential router-to-router protocols to support routers dynamically learning which multicast group's data need to be sent out which ports (that is, the building of the trees):

- *Protocol Independent Multicast* (PIM, supported by the IETF and Cisco), which works with more protocols than just TCP/IP
- *Distance Vector Multicast Routing Protocol* (DVMRP, used by MBONE and supported by Bay Networks)
- *Multicast Open Shortest Path First* (MOSPF, supported by Proteon)

Apple's *Simple Multicast Routing Protocol* (SMRP) provides similar capabilities but currently only for AppleTalk traffic from applications such as QuickTime Conference.

See *IP Address, MBONE, Multimedia, PIM, QTC,* and *SMRP*.

IPL
Initial Program Load

See *Bootstrap*.

IPng
Internet Protocol Next Generation

It is anticipated that the current implementation of TCP/IP's *Internet protocol* will run out of addresses within the next few years (since all hosts that are directly on the Internet require a worldwide unique address). IPng is to be the next version of IP and is to support a larger address.

A committee of the IETF is developing standards for the migration of IP to support larger addresses and other features required for the future. The address field will likely increase from the current 4 bytes to 16 or 64 bytes and will allow users to use the same IP address even when they physically connect to a different place on the Internet.

It is to include support for:

- Encryption
- User authentication (using a 32-bit *security association ID* and a variable-length field that carries authentication data in the header, hosts negotiate the type of encryption algorithm and the key size for each session)
- Automatic network configuration (automatically assigns IP addresses to hosts)
- The ability to handle delay-sensitive traffic (through a 24-bit *Flow ID* in the header that identifies delay-sensitive traffic to routers)

Also called IPv6.

It is a new protocol, not backward-compatible with IPv4 (which is the current version).

See *Authentication, DHCP, Encryption,* and *IP Address*.

IPv6
Internet Protocol, version 6

See *IPng*.

IPX
Internet Packet Exchange

The network layer (OSI layer 3) datagram-based protocol usually used by Novell's NetWare network operating system.

Supports any window size—and packet sizes up to 64 kbytes. Novell's NCP and SPX both use IPX.

The higher-layer workstation shell (NCP, as implemented in NetX, for example) controls the *window* size, the number of frames that can be outstanding (sent but not yet acknowledged), and the *frame* size (the number of bytes per frame).

Since NetX was based on XNS, it has several of its limitations, such as a window size of 1 and a frame size up to only 576 bytes. These significantly reduce performance for longer-delay and lower-speed data links, such as most WAN links between routers.

Novell's newer shell software (VLMs) supports a window size of up to 16 and a frame size of up to 4,096 bytes.

The protocol includes several periodically sent packet types as shown in the following table.

Packet Type	Use
Router Information Protocol	Multicasted every 60 seconds by routers (which may be stand-alone or built in to file servers) to keep other routers current about open paths.
Service Advertising Protocol	Multicasted every 60 seconds by all servers (such as file servers, print servers, and communication servers) so that clients can learn the names, services, and MAC addresses of the servers. These messages are usually offset from a file server's RIPs by 30 seconds.

(table continued on next page)

Packet Type	Use
Watchdog Packets	Sent by servers (an ASCII "?" is sent at least every 4 minutes and 57 seconds) to confirm that clients (which respond with a "Y") are still up and connected.
Serialization Packets	Servers multicast their NetWare license number to confirm that the same copies of the servers' software are not (illegally) installed elsewhere on the network.

Has nothing to do with the Internet.

See *NCP*, *Novell*, *RIP*, *SAP*, and *XNS*.

IPX Link State Router   See **ILSR.**

IRC
Internet Relay Chat

A multiuser chat system (that is, the messages that everybody types are displayed to everyone else). It is often used on the Internet, was originally written by Jarkko Oikarinen in 1988, and was first used in Finland.

As on a citizens band radio, there are different *channels* to support simultaneous conversations and topics.

Client software (which runs on your PC) can be downloaded from *ftp://cs-ftp.bu.edu/irc/clients/pc/windows* (this is a Windows version) and is used to connect to an IRC server (such as *irc.bu.edu, mickey.cc.utexas.edu*, or *irc.mcgill.ca*).

IRC commands start with "/", so /help provides some local help. Once the user is on-line with IRC, on-line help is available on channel #irchelp (channel names are preceded with a "#"). /list provides a list of available channels.

The IRC FAQ is at *http://www.kei.com/irc.html* and *ftp://cs-ftp.bu.edu/irc/support/alt-irc-faq.*

RFC 1459 describes IRC.

See *Internet*, *RFC*, and *UNIX.*

IrDA
Infrared Data Association

A method for communication between electronic devices, using 880-nm infrared light (this is a longer wavelength than people can see).

TV remote controls also use infrared light but use a different "color"—880 to 950 nm wavelength.

As a side point, if you aim your TV remote control at a wall (from a distance of a few inches) and hold down a button while viewing the wall through a video camera, you'll see the infrared light. (Well, it's not X-ray vision, but I thought it was neat.)

Anyway, back to our regularly scheduled program . . .

For IrDA, the distance between sender and receiver can be anywhere between 0 and 1 meter (though up to 3 meters are optionally allowed by the specification). Typical maximum distances for actual products are 4 to 6 feet.

Eight-bit data are sent LSB first, half-duplex (so that transmitters can easily ignore their own reflections). The initial default speed is 9,600, but devices can negotiate to use 2,400, 19,200, 38,400, 57,600, or 115,200 bits/s.

Some vendors, such as IBM, also support a nonstandard transfer rates of 1.15 Mbits/s. Rates of 1 to 4 Mbits/s will likely be standardized soon.

Bits are sent as as follows:

- A binary 0 is a pulse of infrared light, sent at the beginning of the bit-time. The pulse can be either a fixed-length 1.6 μs pulse (regardless of the bit rate) or a 3/16 bit-time pulse (this is a lower-cost implementation that unfortunately requires more power).
- A binary 1 is no pulse.

An HDLC-like protocol is used, which guarantees that there will never be more than five sequential ones in the data stream.

The error rate is expected to be better than 10^{-9} (no more than one bit in error, out of 1,000,000,000 bits). Based on Hewlett-Packard's SIR (*Serial Infrared*) scheme, of which several parts are patented. The most popular initial application is for printing from laptop PCs.

See *1284*, *Color*, *HDLC*, and *HP*.

IRQ
Interrupt Request

The name of the hardware interrupt signals that PC peripherals (such as the serial or parallel ports) can use to get the processor's attention.

For example, interrupts are used to drag the processor away from whatever interruptible task it is currently doing and give it a byte of received data that just can't wait (otherwise another byte of data will overwrite that one, therefore losing data).

The original 8-bit IBM PC and PC/XT used a single *interrupt controller* IC, which supported eight hardware interrupts (of which two were used on the CPU motherboard and are not brought out to the bus). Other interrupts were reserved for controllers and ports.

The later IBM PC/AT 16-bit ISA bus extended this to another eight interrupts by cascading a second interrupt controller to the first interrupt controller's IRQ 2 input (making IRQ 2 unavailable for use), though the new interrupt 9 was mapped to appear as interrupt 2.

Other peripherals that use interrupts include LAN adapters, sound boards, scanner interfaces, and SCSI adapters. Interrupts usually cannot be shared, so each must be (usually manually) assigned a unique interrupt (sometimes called an interrupt vector).

The lower interrupt numbers have higher priority.

The following table shows the ISA bus interrupt assignments.

IRQ	Use
0	System timer (provides 18.21-ms ticks to the operating system). Since lower IRQs have higher priority (if two interrupts are signaled at the same time), this has the highest priority.
1	Keyboard.
2	Not available on the 16-bit ISA bus, since it is used to connect to the output of the interrupt controller for interrupts 8 through 15. The interrupt 2 pin on the 16-bit ISA bus is connected to the interrupt 9 input of the interrupt controller. The PC is configured to call the interrupt handler for interrupt 2 when interrupt 9 is activated.
3	Serial communications port 2 (COM2) and sometimes 4 (COM4), if installed.
4	Serial communications port 1 (COM1) and sometimes 3 (COM3), if installed
5	First used for the hard disk controller in the PC/XT, then reserved for a second parallel printer port (LPT2) in the PC/AT. Since it is rare to have more than one parallel printer port in a PC (and the PC's BIOS usually does not use interrupts for printing anyway), IRQ is usually available for use. Often used by a sound board (for example, SoundBlaster often requires interrupt 5) or LAN adapter.
6	Floppy diskette controller.
7	First parallel printer port (LPT1). While WordPerfect (if using the `Print to Hardware Port` option for better performance) and Novell's `RPrinter` (and a few other programs) use interrupts for printer output, most programs (and DOS) do not. Therefore interrupt 7 may be available to use even if LPT1 is present (and used) in the PC. This is the lowest priority interrupt.

(table continued on next page)

IRQ	Use
8	A PC's real-time clock IC (which contains both the battery-backed-up CMOS memory and the time-of-day clock, which is read when the PC is powered on) can be set to generate an interrupt 8, in binary multiples from two per second to 8,192 per second.
	Interrupt 8 has a lower priority than interrupt 1 but a higher priority than interrupt 9.
9	Used to handle boards that generate interrupt 2 (that is, interrupt 2 on the ISA bus is wired to the interrupt controller input for interrupt 9), since the real interrupt 2 is used for the cascade of interrupts 8 through 15. The ISA bus therefore has no interrupt 9 pin.
10	Available.
11	Available.
12	May be used by the IBM bus mouse, but usually available.
13	Reserved for math coprocessor errors. Not available on the ISA bus.
14	Used by the non-SCSI hard disk controller (usually IDE) in PC/AT (and later) PCs.
15	Often used by SCSI disk controllers, but there is no "standard" setting for a SCSI disk controller interrupt.
	Has a lower priority than interrupt 14 but a higher priority than interrupt 3.

See *Bus*, *DMA*, *Intel*, *ISA*, *PC*, *PIO*, *PnP*, and *Shared Memory*.

IS
Intermediate System

A router on an OSI network.

See *ES*, *IS-IS*, and *OSI*.

IS-54   See **TDMA.**

IS-95   See **CDMA.**

IS-IS
Intermediate System to Intermediate System

The OSI router-to-router protocol. It is a link-state (as opposed to distance-vector) based algorithm that works only with OSI's network-layer protocol CLNP.

See *CLNP*, *IS*, *Link-state*, and *OSI*.

ISA
Industry Standard Architecture

The bus used in standard IBM-compatible PCs to provide power to add-in boards and communication between the add-in boards and to the motherboard (into which the boards plug).

Since IBM did not publish timing specifications, there were initially compatibility problems. This was resolved in 1987, when the IEEE produced a complete bus specification (including timing).

Since the Intel 8088 CPU (used in the first 4.77-MHz PCs introduced in 1982) had an 8-bit data bus, the bus in the original PC also had an 8-bit data bus (the *8-bit PC* or *PC/XT Bus*), and data were transferred 8 bits at a time. This 62-pin bus supported the following:

- 8 data lines (allowing for 8 bits of data to be transferred at a time)
- 20 address lines (1 Mbyte of addressing, though the video adapter was assigned 128 kbytes, starting at address 640 kbytes, and this created the now-infamous DOS memory limitation)
- Interrupts 2 through 7 (separate signal for each interrupt)
- DMA channels 1, 2, and 3 (two signals for each channel, request and acknowledge). The original PC's motherboard used DMA channel 0 for memory refresh, and since the DMA controller and the memory were on the motherboard, the signals were not brought to the bus.

The other pins are used for power and timing signals.

The 80286 used in the IBM PC/AT ("*advanced technology*," which it was when it was introduced in 1984) had a 16-bit data bus, so IBM (then still the sole standards-setter for PCs) added 36-pin connector which provided the following:

- Eight more data lines (allowing for 16-bit data transfers)
- Four more address lines (allowing 16 Mbytes of addressing)
- Interrupts 10, 11, 12, 14, and 15 (interrupt 13 is reserved for a math coprocessor, which would be on the motherboard, so interrupt 13 is not brought out to the bus)
- DMA channels 0, 5, 6, and 7 (DMA channel 4 is used to link the new DMA channels to the original ones). Unlike the original PC, the PC/AT uses a dedicated memory refresh circuit, so DMA Channel 0 is available for use, and it is brought out to the bus.

This is the *16-bit PC/AT bus*, or, more commonly (and simply), the *ISA bus* which is provided in most PCs (older PCs only support ISA; newer PCs typically support both ISA and PCI).

The ISA bus has a *theoretical* maximum transfer speed of 16 Mbytes/s (more commonly stated as 8 Mbytes/s, since it usually requires one bus cycle for the address and another for the 16 bits of data). The *typical* maximum speed is 1 to 2.5 Mbytes/s (which is 8 to 20 Mbits/s). This speed is so variable because of bus contention with other devices (mainly memory) and buffering delays due to the asynchronous nature of the bus (the processor speed is different from the bus speed).

See *Bus*, *DMA*, *EISA*, *IEEE*, *IRQ*, *PC*, *PCI*, and *PIO*.

ISDN
Integrated Services Digital Network

A WAN-oriented data communication service provided by telephone companies.

The most popular types of channels provided are the following:

- *B channels* (bearer):
  - Circuit-switched (the whole connection is switched to one destination, as a telephone call is)
  - 64,000 bits/s each
  - Full-duplex (data can be sent and received simultaneously)
  - Carry digitized voice or data
- *D channels* (delta)
  - Packet-switched (each frame of data can go to a different destination, like on a LAN or X.25 network)
  - 16,000 bits/s (for basic rate ISDN) or 64,000 bits/s (for primary rate ISDN) each
  - Full-duplex (data can be sent and received simultaneously)
  - Carry both signaling (dialed digits, ring the telephone, etc.) and data (typically, up to 9,600 bits/s on basic-rate ISDN)

ISDN is unique among WAN services in that it provides access both to the circuit-switched *public switched telephone network* and to packet-switched services, such as X.25 and frame relay.

Basic-rate ISDN provides two B channels and one D channel.

Primary-rate ISDN provides 23 B channels and one D channel, though by using *Nonfacility Associated Signaling* (NFAS), a single 64 kbits/s D channel can provide signaling for up to eight primary rate ISDN lines, so the second through eighth primary rate ISDN lines typically provide 24 B channels and 0 D channels.

Because B channel calls are established digitally (by signaling the D channel), call set-up time is typically 1 to 3 seconds (since there is no need for the slow process of sending and decoding DTMF tones, and no need to wait for modem negotiations). In contrast, a typical analog modem call requires 30 to 60 seconds to establish. Another neat feature of ISDN D channel signaling is that if both your BRI B channels are being combined to provide faster access to your Internet service provider and an incoming voice call is signaled, one B channel can be hung up to accept the incoming call (slowing your Internet access to half-speed during your voice connection). When finished talking, the B channel can be automatically reconnected for your full-speed surfing pleasure.

Multirate ISDN will allow a specified number of B channels to be combined to provide higher-speed dial-up circuit-switched digital connections, using digital 800 service.

When used for video conferencing, the H.320 standard is usually used.

The ISDN FAQ is at *ftp://rtfm.mit.edu/pub/usenet/news.answers/isdn-faq,* and some ISDN information is at *http://www.bellcore.com/demotoo/ISDN/ISDN.html.* Dan Kegel's ISDN page is at *http://alumni.caltech.edu/~dank/isdn.*

While we are on the topic of ISDN people with WWW pages—Scott Adams (creator of Dilbert and Dogbert) used to work for Pacific Bell in its ISDN Lab as an applications engineer and has a Dilbert home page at *http://www.unitedmedia.com/comics/dilbert/.* (While employed there, he claimed that he didn't need the job but that it was a good source of material for his cartoon strip.)

See *B-ISDN, BRI, Bonding, Digital 800, DTMF (Dual Tone Multi-frequency), H.320, In-Band, Inverse Multiplexer, Narrowband ISDN, NI-1, NI-2, NI-3, NT-1, Out-of-band, PCM, PRI, V.25bis, V.120, WAN, Wideband ISDN,* and *WinISDN.*

ISO
International Organization for Standardization

An international standards-setting organization with the mandate of fostering trade between countries.

The ISO has a WWW server at *http://www.iso.ch/welcome.html.*

See *Standards.*

ISO 900x
International Organization for Standardization 9000 Certification

ISO certifications of quality systems that help manufacturers and service providers develop a quality-conscious approach for their research, testing, manufacturing, and support operations.

Addresses how products and services are put together, not how well those products and services work. Each standard applies to different types of processes, as shown in the following table.

ISO	Certifies Facilities That Handle ...
9001	Research and development, product manufacturing, and product installation and maintenance
9002	Product manufacturing and installation only
9003	Product testing and final inspection of products

ISO 9001 includes requirements for 20 basic elements that affect quality, such as customer service, engineering, and manufacturing.

Registration is granted by independent, third-party organizations, such as *Bureau Veritas Quality International* and *Det Norske Veritas*, and is valid for 3 years, subject to periodic audits.

Many European countries now require suppliers to have ISO certification.

While the ISO 9000 certification emphasizes the management of process, the U.S. National Institute of Science and Technology's Baldridge Program emphasizes more organizational issues, such as management leadership, analysis of comparative quality measurements, and strategic quality planning.

See *ISO* and *Six-σ Quality*.

Isochronous

A characteristic of a (usually high-speed) data service that can accept data at guaranteed intervals (such as from one B channel of a 2B+D circuit-switched ISDN service, which produces 8 bits of data every 125 μs). Is therefore suitable for digitized voice and video.

Sometimes called a *constant bit rate* service.

ATM and fibre channel can provide this service, so they are suitable for multimedia.

Packet-switched services (such as X.25) and standard Ethernet cannot support isochronous traffic, since other traffic may briefly prevent the isochronous traffic from being carried.

See *802.9a*, *ATM (Asynchronous Transfer Mode)*, *Fibre Channel*, and *Multimedia*.

Isochronous Ethernet   See **802.9a**.

ISP
Internet Service Provider

A company that provides end users (such as you, me, and big companies) access to the Internet.

The computer equipment at an ISP will typically include the following:

- The incoming telephone lines (typically 20 to a few hundred) each connect to a V.32*bis* or (very much preferably) a V.34 auto answer modem.
- Each modem's EIA-232 serial port runs at 115,200 bits/s and is connected to a cable to a terminal server (which is often made by Cisco).
- A terminal server is a device with (usually) 8 to 32 EIA-232 ports and one Ethernet port. The terminal server (initially) converts the asynchronous data from the EIA-232 ports to the TCP/IP telnet protocol on the Ethernet.
- In addition to the above, there will usually be a router with incoming ISDN and dedicated 56-kbits/s circuits, which will also be connected to the Ethernet. These lines support users accessing the Internet service provider at higher speeds than analog telephone lines and V.34 modems can support.
- The connections from the router's ISDN lines and the terminal server's modems are configured to initially be established with a workstation (usually made by Sun). The workstation handles the following functions (actually, there will often be two or more workstations for increased capacity and reliability):
  - Security (storing and prompting for usernames and passwords)
  - Billing (tracking and reporting on the duration of connections)
  - Receiving, storing, and forwarding USENET news (usually dedicating a 1- or 2-Gbyte disk drive to that function)
  - Receiving, storing, and forwarding email
  - Storing WWW home pages (built by both the ISP themselves and by users)
  - Being a Web and ftp server
- If the dial-in users (after logging in) choose a menu item to run the SLIP or PPP protocol (as is usually the case), then the Sun workstation sends commands to the terminal server to have the terminal server run the SLIP or PPP protocol on the asynchronous port to the user.
- The dial-in user's WinSock (or whatever TCP/IP protocol stack they are using) TCP/IP packets are then encapsulated into SLIP or PPP frames by their PC's dialing program. When the terminal server receives these frames from the users, it strips off the SLIP or PPP frames from the TCP/IP packets, encapsulates them in Ethernet frames, and forwards them onto the Ethernet at the ISP.
- Connected to the ISP's Ethernet is a router (often made by Cisco) which has a T1 (or faster, or slower, depending on the number of simultaneous users to be supported) connection to the Internet. The T1 will either go directly to an Internet backbone router (for example, at ANS in Elmsford, New York), or through a closer router—which then connects to the Internet backbone (likely through a higher-speed link, such as a T3).

- The dial-in user is now a node on the Internet, and can run any program and TCP/IP protocol they wish (ftp, http, etc.). Packets are then forwarded directly from the terminal server's Ethernet port to the router to the Internet. They no longer go to the Sun workstation (unless the dial-in user specifically connects to the workstation, for example, by running their mail program).

Two large ISPs are Netcom On-Line Communication Services, Inc. (see *http://www.netcom.com*) and Performance Systems International (which has much more interesting stuff on its WWW server, which is at *http://www.psi.net*).

IBM and CompuServe provide Internet access from a local telephone call in hundreds of cities all over the world (*http://www.ibm.net* and *http://www.compuserve.com*).

See *ANS*, *Cisco Systems*, *CIX*, *EIA/TIA-232*, *Ethernet*, *FT1*, *Internet*, *ISDN*, *Modem*, *Ping*, *PPP*, *SLIP*, *Sun*, *T1*, *telnet*, *TCP/IP*, *Usenet*, *V.32bis*, *V.34*, *WinSock*, and *WWW*.

ITU
International Telecommunication Union

The oldest organization in the United Nations.

ITU's headquarters is in Geneva, Switzerland, and ITU has the following mandate (guess whether these are my words or not):

- To maintain and extend international cooperation for the improvement and rational use of telecommunication of all kinds
- To promote the development of technical facilities and their most efficient operation with a view to improving the efficiency of telecommunication services, increasing their usefulness, and making them, as far as possible, generally available to the public
- To harmonize the actions of nations in the attainment of those common ends

In 1993, the ITU was reorganized into three *sectors* (plus the coordinating *general secretariat* from the previous structure) as shown in the following table.

Sector	Abbreviation	Responsibilities
Telecommunication Standardization	ITU-T	All standards development activities of the previous CCITT and CCIR
Radiocommunication	ITU-R	Other activities of the previous CCIR and previous International Frequency Registration Board (IFRB), such as radio regulatory issues and frequency assignments
Telecommunication Development	ITU-D	Telecommunication support for developing countries, for example by offering technical cooperation and assistance

The ITU has a WWW server at *http://www.itu.ch.*

See *CCIR, CCITT, ITU-T,* and *Standards.*

ITU-T
International Telecommunication Union, Telecommunication Standardization Sector

The new name for the CCITT—though some say that standards that were created before the name change (and not modified since) continue to be called CCITT standards. Along with the name change is a substantial change in the *standards approval* process. It can now be conducted by correspondence (typically within 3 months), provided that the study group is in consensus. Previously, this approval could be finalized only at the Plenipotentiary Conferences, which are held every 4 years.

Only *countries* are members (no companies or standards organizations, such as the IEEE).

However, a country can designate a standards organization to be its representative in certain areas. For example, the United States has designated ANSI to be its ITU-T representative for telecommunications matters.

Two-thirds of the member countries must vote "yes" for a recommendation to be accepted.

See *H.261, H.320, ITU, Standards, T.120, X.400,* and *X.500.*

IXC
Interexchange Carrier

A long-distance phone company, usually using its own long-distance facilities (rather than only *reselling* others'). Provides voice and data services between LECs (one or both of the LECs involved may be one of the RBOCs).

The three largest IXCs are listed in the following table.

IXC	Market Share (percentage)
AT&T Corp.	60
MCI Communications Corp.	20
Sprint Corp.	10

The remaining 10% is divided among more than 300 smaller providers. (No one knows exactly how many there are.)

For each long-distance call, IXCs pay the LEC that owns the cable to the destination telephone an *access fee* to route the call to its destination.

IXCs establish a *Point Of Presence* (POP) within each LEC's service area (physically a termination point in the LEC's central office, often caged-in to ensure that they don't fiddle with each other's equipment).

See *Carrier, LATA, LEC,* and *RBOC.*

JPEG
Joint Photographic Experts Group

The name of a standard for *lossy data compression* of digitized still images.

JPEG can also be used for motion video compression (which MPEG was designed for) and has some advantages over MPEG, such as the following:

- Suitable for frame-by-frame editing, since *frame interpolation* is not used for compression
- Does not remove the information in the blanking intervals (which may be needed for synchronization)
- Digitizes the color information at the full rate

See *Data Compression, Lossy Data Compression, MPEG,* and *Video.*

Kaleida

The Apple-IBM joint venture to develop multimedia software, technology, and standards. Seems to have gone away. Too bad—it had such a nice name.

See *Apple-IBM Alliance*.

Kerberos

A security system for client/server computing.

Entirely software-based and can have multiple secure areas (or *realms*, usually delimited by administrative boundaries) in an Enterprise network. Its uses are:

- Encryption to secure network transmissions
- A password-authentication service to verify a user's right to access a given host or server

Also supports time-based limits for accesses.

The *Kerberos server* (a "trusted third-party server") consists of two parts:

- An *authentication server*, which verifies identities (and has the user ID and password for all users)
- A *ticket-granting server*, which gives clients permission to access various servers and applications on the network

The Kerberos server is used to validate the verification procedures between all clients and servers. Clients must (and servers optionally) prove their identity for each service invoked.

All servers (file servers, database servers, etc.) must be registered in the authentication server's *database*, and share a secret key with the authentication server.

Users first log in to the authentication server (by providing their user ID), requesting a *ticket-granting ticket*. The authentication server then looks up the user's password and provides a ticket-granting ticket and a session key (valid for the current log-on only), both of which have been encrypted using the user's password. At the user's workstation, the user is then prompted for his or her password, which is then used to decrypt the received message (note that the user's password was never sent over the network).

The decrypted ticket-granting ticket includes the following:

- The user's ID
- A time stamp
- Duration (specified by the network administrator, perhaps half an hour to 8 hours) for which the session is valid
- A ticket-granting server's ID

The ticket-granting ticket is DES-encrypted using a key that is known only by the authentication server and the ticket-granting server, so the workstation cannot tamper with the ticket-granting ticket, and only the specified ticket-granting server can use it.

For the allowed period of time (the duration), the workstation can use this ticket-granting ticket to request access to another server or device on the network (to actually get some work done—you gotta do that once in a while), using a similar process.

Kerberos version 4 has been in use for several years. MIT's Project Athena recently released version 5, which includes support for:

- Security algorithms other than DES
- One server to access another server on the user's behalf (for example, a print server getting a specified file from a file server)

Intended to be highly portable across operating systems and hardware platforms.

The name is from the three-headed dog that guards the gates of Hades in Greek mythology.

See *Authentication*, *Client/Server*, *DES*, *Encryption*, *RSA*, *PGP*, and *SESAME*.

Kermit

A copyrighted but shareware file transfer and terminal emulation program that can be freely reproduced and shared (as long as you don't try to sell it, and a manual is purchased for each end-user). Also, a file transfer protocol that is often implemented by commercial data communication software packages.

Other than being an extremely flexible, customizable, and powerful data communications program, a major feature is that a version of Kermit is available for virtually every computer, including PCs, UNIX computers, Macintoshes, VAXes, Data General, Honeywell/Bull, IBM mainframes, Cray supercomputers, and on and on.

The source code is also available (including a C version), so it can be compiled for new machines or modified and enhanced.

The early versions of Kermit were somewhat like XModem in that the file transfer protocol had a small frame size (94 bytes) and a Window size of 1, resulting in slow transfer times.

Newer versions of Kermit support the following:

- Frame sizes up to 9,024 bytes
- Window sizes up to 31 frames
- TCP/IP (telnet) and NetBIOS
- COM3 and COM4 at any interrupt and port address and support for LANs (Ethernet, Token Ring, etc.)
- Server mode, in which a host machine can be left waiting (unattended) for a call and the calling machine can send and receive files and issue DOS commands to the server machine.

Many bulletin board systems and commercial data communication programs (SmartTerm, ProComm, etc.) support the Kermit file transfer protocol (so they can transfer files to and from people using the Kermit program). However, these programs often implement older versions of the Kermit protocol that don't support the larger frame and window sizes (or the user has not configured the software to use the larger frame and window sizes). Many people therefore erroneously think that Kermit is a slow protocol.

Kermit is named after Jim Henson's Muppet *Kermit the Frog* (the idea was that the program would be easy to work with and fun, just like Kermit). The name is used with permission (from Henson Associates, not from Kermit the Frog).

The software is maintained at Columbia University in New York. Contacts are listed in the following table.

email	kermit@columbia.edu
fax	212-663-8202
ftp	kermit.columbia.edu
Phone (ordering)	212-854-3703
Phone (technical)	900-555-5595 or 212-854-5126
Usenet	comp.protocols.kermit.announce comp.protocols.kermit.misc
WWW	http://www.columbia.edu/kermit http://www.cc.columbia.edu/kermit/

See *BBS*, *EIA/TIA-232*, *NetBIOS*, *TCP/IP*, *telnet*, and *XModem*.

LAN
Local Area Network

A limited-distance (typically under a few kilometers) high-speed network (typically 4 to 100 Mbits/s) that supports many computers (typically two to thousands).

The popular standard LANs are shown in the accompanying figure.

The table below shows four options for upgrading Ethernet and Token Rings (which would prove the old saying that the nice thing about standards is that there are so many to choose from).

Technology	Benefit
100Base-T (Fast Ethernet)	Easy upgrade from 10Base-T Ethernet (same drivers, hopefully using the same cabling) Low cost
100VG-AnyLAN	Uses existing cabling Has upgrade path for Ethernet *and* Token Ring Suitable for multimedia Low cost
FDDI	Most mature technology (wide vendor support, proven interoperability) Fault tolerance option (*dual homing*) Medium cost
ATM	Most future-proof (speeds from 25 Mbits/s to more than 2.4 Gbits/s—whatever you can afford) Is already a switched technology (dedicated bandwidth to each user) Suitable for multimedia Highest cost

(table continued on next page)

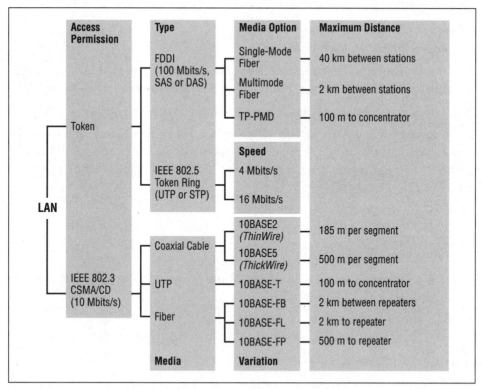

LAN–1

Technology	Benefit
802.9 (Isochronous Ethernet)	Easy upgrade from 10BASE–T (but not Token Ring)
	Supports multimedia and links to ISDN
	Uses existing cabling
	Low cost
Switched LAN	Easily added to existing Ethernet or Token Ring LANs
	Uses existing cabling and workstation LAN adapters
	Low cost

See *100BASE-T, 100VG-AnyLAN, 10BASE-F, 10BASE-T, 802.3, 802.9a, ATM (Asynchronous Transfer Mode), Cable, Coax, Ethernet, FDDI, Fibre Channel, HiPPI, HSSI, MAN, STP, Switched LAN, Token Ring,* and *UTP.*

LAN Network Manager   See **LNM.**

LAPM
Link Access Procedure for Modems

One of the two error detection and correction protocols specified in V.42 to correct data communication errors occurring on the link between two modems.

Each frame of data holds up to 128 bytes of data and has a 16- or 32-bit CRC.

Up to 15 (which is also the default value) frames can be sent before an *acknowledgment* is required (that is, the *window size* defaults to 15). Therefore, 1,920 bytes of memory must be reserved for storing unacknowledged frames (since they may need to be retransmitted).

See *CRC*, *MNP*, and *V.42*.

LAST
Local Area Systems Technology

A simple and fast DEC protocol used by Pathworks for disk and printer access over a LAN from DOS PCs. Built on LAT.

See *LAT* and *Pathworks*.

LASTport
Local Area Storage Transport

Same as LAST.

See *LAST*.

LAT
Local Area Transport

A DEC protocol for interactive, asynchronous terminal traffic over a LAN (typically between a DECserver *terminal server* and a VAX minicomputer).

Operates at the transport layer. Does not have a network layer and so is not routable.

See *DEC*, *Encapsulation*, *Ethernet II*, and *VMS*.

LATA
Local-Access Transport Area

The geographic area within which telephone calls can be handled without going through a long-distance carrier.

Telephone calls between different LATAs must go through a long-distance carrier (that is, an IXC, such as AT&T or MCI).

Short-hop (or local) toll telephone calls (that is, calls within LATA) can be handled by a LEC (usually an RBOC) or (in most states) by an IXC (though extra digits must usually be dialed to select a carrier other than your LEC for these short-hop toll calls).

See *Carrier, IXC, LEC,* and *RBOC.*

Latency

The *time delay* of data traffic through a network or switch.

Interactive multimedia, database, and other applications usually require short round-trip delays. Since the traffic will likely pass through many networking components in the "big grey cloud" between the users and computers, each component must have a short (and often predictable) *latency*. That is, if there are three switches between a client and server, then there will be six switch delays in a round-trip message.

As the bit rates of networks get faster (so the time taken to shift the bits out of one computer and into another is shorter), the tolerable network delays get smaller (since the network's internal delays become more apparent). Also, new applications, such as MPEG-2 video compression, can be more adversely affected by variable delays.

Other metrics are still important, such as bits, frames, or packets per second, and lost data.

Some typical latencies are listed in the following table.

Component	Typical Latency (μs)
ATM switches	10 to 130
Ethernet switches	20 to 100
Ethernet bridges	250 to 500
Routers	1,200

See *Multimedia, MPEG,* and *QOS.*

LBX
Low Bandwidth X

An option in the X11R6 *X Window* specification that supports operation over low-speed (preferably 9,600 bits/s or faster) asynchronous (usually dial-up) communication lines. LBX would run over TCP/IP over PPP.

See *Asynchronous, TCP/IP, PPP,* and *X.*

Least Significant Bit (or Byte)   See **LSB.**

LEC
Local Exchange Carrier

In the U.S., the "local phone company." If it used to be part of the Bell System (that is, owned by AT&T), then the LEC is owned by one of the seven RBOCs. Otherwise, the LEC is one of the hundreds of rural telephone companies that were never part of the Bell System and typically have under a few thousand subscribers each (though some have 500,000 or more).

LECs own the central office(s) and the *local loop* (the cable from the C.O. to each of their subscribers) to provide communications services within a limited geographic area (called a LATA).

After the AT&T divestiture, LECs were restricted from providing long-distance services (and the IXCs were restricted from providing local service), though this is changing. LECs can charge (that is, the call is a *toll call*) for longer-distance calls within their own territories.

See *AT&T, Carrier, C.O., IXC, LATA,* and *RBOC.*

Legacy System

A traditional (usually IBM) mainframe system.

This term is usually used by the TCP/IP and UNIX community as a polite reference to big old dinosaur IBM environments (FEPs, CICS, SNA, sDLC, 3270-type dumb terminals, and the like).

See *3270, CICS, FEP, Mainframe, SDLC,* and *SNA.*

Lempel-Ziv-Stac   See **LZS.**

Lempel-Ziv-Welch   See **LZW.**

LEN
Low-Entry Networking

The most basic subset of APPN functionality for an *end node.*

See *APPN* and *PU 2.1.*

Link Access Procedure for Modems   See **LAPM.**

Link-state

A method used by routers to determine the best path between two hosts that wish to communicate.

A type of *routing algorithm* (OSPF and IS-IS are example implementations) that improves on RIP methods by including more factors in the calculation of shortest path, according to the upper-layer *type of service* requested.

For example, the path with the best delay, relative throughput, and/or reliability.

Communication between routers is more efficient than with RIP, since only changes in network connectivity are sent as they occur, rather than periodically exchanging entire routing tables. Another advantage of link-state is that routers will load-share over equally "short" links, whereas RIP will choose only one of the links.

A problem with link-state is that the router's CPU and memory requirements grow as the network size increases. If network changes occur too often (before new paths can be calculated), there will be routing problems.

Most protocols have a new link-state protocol, as shown in the table below, to (eventually) replace their RIP-based protocol.

Protocol	Link State Router to Router Protocol	Acronym
AppleTalk	AppleTalk Update-based Routing Protocol	AURP
DECnet Phase V	Integrated IS-IS	Integrated IS-IS
IP	Open shortest path first	OSPF
IPX	NetWare Link Services Protocol (uses the IPX link state router)	NLSP
OSI	Intermediate System to Intermediate System	IS-IS

See *AURP*, *IGRP*, *ILSR*, *Integrated IS-IS*, *IS*, *IS-IS*, *NLSP*, *OSPF*, *RIP*, and *SPF*.

Little Endian

Specifies that the *least significant byte* is stored in the lowest-memory address, which is the address of the data.

The Intel 80X86 and Pentium and DEC Alpha RISC processors are Little Endian.

Windows NT and OSF/1 are Little Endian.

Little Endian is the less common UNIX implementation.

See *Big Endian*, *MS*, and *UNIX*.

LLC2
Logical Link Control 2

The frame format used to carry 3270 traffic on Token Ring LANs.

As a *connection-oriented* link layer protocol, acknowledgments are required to each frame sent. Also, IBM implements *keep-alive* messages to ensure that both ends of a connection are still up.

When sending LLC2 frames over a WAN, these acknowledgments and keep-alive messages waste WAN bandwidth. Other technologies (such as DLSw) can spoof (produce the required responses locally) these messages to conserve WAN bandwidth.

See *Connection-oriented*, *DLC*, *DLSw*, and *Spoofing*.

LNM
LAN Network Manager

IBM's software for managing Token Ring LANs.

Polls stations for logged errors, such as bad CRCs.

See *CRC*, *Token Ring*, and *SNMP*.

Local Access Transport Area   See **LATA.**

Local Area Network   See **LAN.**

Local Area Storage Transport   See **LASTport.**

Local Area Systems Technology   See **LAST.**

Local Area Transport   See **LAT.**

Local Bridge

A bridge that is directly connected to the LANs it serves. (In contrast, a pair of remote bridges have a WAN link between them.)

See *Remote Bridge*.

Local Bus

A bus that provides full processor clock–speed and processor bus–width access directly to a 486 (or higher) PC's processor, rather than going through the 8- or 16–bit-wide ISA bus (which always runs at 8 MHz, even when the processor runs faster).

VESA's VL-bus and Intel's PCI are competing local bus standards (although there's not much competition left—VL-bus lost). PCs will usually also have an ISA, EISA, or MCA bus for lower-speed peripherals, such as sound boards.

See *Bus*, *MCA*, *PCI*, *VESA*, and *VL-Bus*.

Local Exchange Carrier   See **LEC.**

Logical Link Control 2   See **LLC2.**

Logical Unit   See **LU.**

Lossy Data Compression

A data compression scheme that loses some information (that is, the reconstructed data will have lower quality) in order to provide the most compression possible.

Used where the loss of information will not be a problem (such as video conferencing, where providing smooth motion and color is more important than very fine detail). In contrast, *lossless data compression* uses a method that enables the original data to be reconstructed exactly (for example, by calculating the difference between successive pictures).

See *CD-ROM*, *Data Compression*, *H.261*, *MP-MLQ*, and *Video*.

Low Bandwidth X   See **LBX.**

Low Entry Networking   See **LEN.**

LSB
Least Significant Bit (or Byte)

The lowest-order bit. For example, the least significant bit of 01000111 is a 1 (er, that's the 1 on the very right). The *most significant bit* is a 0 (yep, that's the 0 on the very left).

See *Big Endian* and *MS*.

LU
Logical Unit

An individual session between an IBM computer terminal (which may support more than one LU at a time—that is, the actual terminal can support more than one logical terminal) and a mainframe.

See *3270*, *LU*, *LU 0*, *LU 1*, *LU 2*, *LU 3*, *LU 4*, *LU 6.1*, *LU 6.2*, *LU 7*, *Mainframe*, *PU*, *PU 2*, *PU 2.1*, *PU 4*, and *PU 5*.

LU 0
Logical Unit Type 0

A non-architected (you can interpret the data any way you want to), peer-to-peer (program-to-program) type of data communications and API that is more flexible but has fewer built-in capabilities than LU 6.2.

Used for applications, such as file transfers, in which the protocol is defined by the file transfer programs running at each end of the link, and all that is needed is a reliable transport.

See *LU 6.2*.

LU 1
Logical Unit Type 1

The LU type used for sending *SNA Character String* (SCS) data streams from host-based applications to remote terminals, such as 3270 printers or 3770 RJE terminals.

See *3270* and *RJE*.

LU 2
Logical Unit Type 2

The LU type used for communications to 3270-type computer terminals.

See *3270*.

LU 3
Logical Unit Type 3

The LU type used for communications with 3270-type printers.

See *3270*.

LU 4
Logical Unit Type 4

A peer-to-peer communications method now made obsolete by LU 6.2.

See *LU 6.2*.

LU 6.1
Logical Unit Type 6.1

The LU type used for program-to-program communications, in which the program at one end is IBM's CICS or *Information Management System* (IMS).

See *CICS*.

LU 6.2
Logical Unit Type 6.2

IBM's recent (well, not that recent, but more recent than the original SNA), open networking standard and API enhancement to SNA. Supports peer-to-peer communication—for example, either side can initiate a connection, and both sides can be user workstations (typically PCs). Also supports program to program communications, in that the programs running on the peers can send binary data (that is, any 8-bit pattern per byte) directly between them. In contrast, the original SNA only supported sending printable EBCDIC characters (that is, screen images and print jobs) from a mainframe to a printer or fixed-function terminal (more commonly called a dumb terminal).

While (the much less popular) LU 6.1 also supports program-to-program communication, LU 6.1 is not peer-to-peer since one side must be a mainframe. A *logical unit* is a session on a terminal. Defines the operations and responses for one *half-session* (which may be a terminal or a program in a PC or mainframe) that communicates with another half-session elsewhere. Requires so much RAM that LU 6.2 is not feasible under DOS.

Sometimes called APPC. Is part of SAA.

HLLAPI is a simpler and terminal-emulation-based predecessor.

See *APPC*, *APPN*, *CPI-C*, *HLLAPI*, *SAA*, and *SNA*.

LU 7
Logical Unit Type 7

The LU type used for communications between an application program and a 5250-type terminal.

See *5250*.

Luminance (Y), Chrominance (UV)   See **YUV.**

LZS
Lempel-Ziv-Stac

A data compression algorithm developed by Stac Electronics and often used by routers.

Multiple *compression dictionaries* can be maintained so that when a certain type of data is detected, the best dictionary can immediately be used without first building it and sending it to the receiver.

See *CCP*, *Data Compression*, *LZW*, and *Stac*.

LZW
Lempel-Ziv-Welch

A data compression algorithm that builds a dictionary of frequently repeated groups of (8-bit) characters (such as ASCII "the") on a per-file basis and represents these frequent character-strings as shorter bit patterns. Before compressed data transfer, the sender's compression dictionary must be sent error-free to the receiver (so an error correcting protocol must already be established on the data link).

The method is therefore good at compressing text files but not as good at other types of files (such as graphics files, which may have repeating patterns at intervals that are not multiples of 8 bits). *RLE* is another type of compression.

Patented (in 1985) by Sperry Corp., which is the predecessor company to Unisys Corp. Used by the .GIF file format (developed by CompuServe), and a similar scheme is used by the V.42*bis* modem data compression standard. CompuServe paid a one-time licensing fee to Unisys (rumored to be $125,000), and most V.42*bis* modem manufacturers pay a royalty to Unisys.

Based on the *Lempel-Ziv* (named after Abraham Lempel and Jacob Ziv) universal data compression algorithm, which is in the public domain.

See *CompuServe, Data Compression, GIF, LZS, RLE,* and *V.42bis.*

Mach

Carnegie-Mellon University's extension of AT&T System V Release 2.2 UNIX. See *OSF/1* and *UNIX*.

Magnetic Ink Character Recognition See **MICR**.

Mainframe

The classic multimillion-dollar huge (and usually IBM) computer handling the accounting or inventory functions for a huge organization. Security and procedures surround it, as does an air-conditioned, raised-floor, power-conditioned computer room, staffed by 24-hour-per-day operators reading the local tabloid-sized daily newspaper.

Common IBM mainframes (in increasing size) are System/370 (now that's an old family), 9370, 43*xx* (4361, 4381), 303*x*, 308*x*, 3090, and ES/9000. All recent IBM mainframes are part of the System/390 family.

Mainframes used to be IBM's stranglehold on the business community and government, but newer computing technologies are reducing most corporations' emphasis on mainframes:

- PCs: IBM invented these in 1981 but lost its commanding market share when IBM did not innovate or drop prices fast enough
- Microsoft DOS and Windows: IBM gave Microsoft its start by using Microsoft DOS and Basic for IBM PCs; now Microsoft dominates the PC software industry—something IBM would have preferred to have done themselves
- Apple Macintoshes: these used to be IBM's enemy; now IBM cooperates with Apple on the PowerPC to compete with Intel (and IBM made Intel famous by using Intel's CPUs in the PC)

- UNIX workstations: IBM has its own RS/6000, but these are not in first or second place
- Minicomputers: here IBM has a winner, the AS/400

See *AIX, Channel, CICS, DASD, DLC, EBCDIC, FEP, IBM, IND$FILE, Legacy System, LU, LU 0, LU 1, LU 2, LU 3, LU 4, LU 6.1, LU 6.2, LU 7, MVS, PU, PU 2, PU 2.1, PU 4, RJE, SDLC, TSO, VM,* and *VTAM.*

MAN
Metropolitan Area Network

A high-speed network that covers more than a few kilometers (that is, larger than a LAN) but less than any arbitrary distance (that is, smaller that a WAN).

The IEEE 802.6 standard was supposed to be a (the?) standard MAN, but you don't hear much about it anymore.

Although FDDI is usually considered a LAN technology, it could also be considered a MAN technology, since FDDI can have up to a 200-km circumference.

See *DQDB, FDDI, LAN, SMDS,* and *WAN.*

Management Information Base   See **MIB.**

Manufacturing Message Specification   See **MMS.**

MAPI
Messaging API

Microsoft's API for messaging. A standard way of providing communication services to applications (making them *mail-enabled*) so that they can send and receive "mail" (blocks of data, documents, files, etc.), directly from within applications.

The APIs are independent of platform, mail system, and transport protocol.

MAPI is the most popular messaging API for the PC environment. Backed by Microsoft, Novell/WordPerfect, and Lotus.

Two levels are defined:

- *Simple MAPI* does basic mail functions (such as sending and receiving messages).
- *Extended MAPI* has a *Service Provider Interface* (SPI), which will interface to software that provides an interface to other mail services, such as CompuServe—so that any application using the extended MAPI will be able to use CompuServe as a message carrier.

Competes with VIM (though VIM is used mostly for Lotus applications running under Windows or OS/2) and XAPIA's CMC (which is used more for cross-platform use).

See *CMC*, *MHS* (Message Handling System), *VIM*, and *XAPIA*.

Massively Parallel Processing   See **MPP**.

MBONE
Multicast Backbone

One method of supporting multicast traffic (for example, for video conferencing) on LANs and the Internet.

Since the Internet does not currently support multicast traffic, "tunnels" (predefined paths across the Internet, between routers running the *distance-vector multicast routing protocol*) are used.

See *IP Multicast* and *PIM*.

MCA
Micro Channel Architecture

The 32-bit bus used in most IBM PS/2 PCs and the RS/6000 workstations. Introduced in 1987. Some characteristics are:

- It runs at 10 MHz
- The theoretical maximum data transfer rate is 20 or 40 Mbytes/s (depending on the mode)
- The connector has 112 pins
- It supports up to 16 bus masters

Two types of slots are defined:

- 16-bit slots have a 16-bit data bus and a 24-bit address bus and support for video and audio
- 32-bit slots support separate 32-bit data and address buses.

Was never accepted as widely as expected, perhaps because IBM (at least initially) charged too high a royalty for its use, or because existing PC adapter cards could not be used (requiring that customers buy all new cards and that manufacturers design new cards).

See *Bus* and *Bus Master DMA*.

Message of the Day   See **MOTD**.

Message Transfer Agent   See **MTA.**

Messaging

A loosely coupled method of communication between platforms.

Uses *mailboxes* rather than RPCs. Mailboxes permit asynchronous interprocess communication.

The Message-Oriented Middleware Association (MOMA) has a WWW server at *http://www.sbexpos.com/sbexpos/associations/moma/home.html.*

See *API, MAPI, VIM,* and *RPC.*

Messaging API   See **MAPI.**

Metropolitan Area Network   See **MAN.**

MHS
Message Handling Service

An OSI-compliant standard for electronic mail, as described in the X.400 standard.

See *X.400.*

MHS
Message Handling System

Novell's support for electronic mail (and files and notifications) management, storage, exchange, forwarding, and routing.

The idea is that a third-party mail program (such as Microsoft Mail or cc:Mail) delivers mail to Novell's MHS, which then gets the message to the destination server. The destination server then delivers the message to the mail program for delivery to the destination user.

Based on Novell's *standard message format* messaging APIs.

Unrelated to the X.400 MHS.

See *CMC, MAPI, Novell,* and *VIM.*

MIB
Management Information Base

The variables stored by an SNMP agent.

See *SNMP.*

MICR
Magnetic Ink Character Recognition

The method that is used to automatically read account numbers and bank transit numbers from checks.

Micro Channel Architecture   See **MCA.**

Microcom Networking Protocol   See **MNP.**

Microsoft

What can be said? Microsoft is big, hires enthusiastic programmers who work around the clock, and has a WWW server at *http://www.microsoft.com.*

Middleware

Software that facilitates cross-platform distributed computing (that is, getting computers from different vendors and running different operating systems to communicate).

APIs that shield developers from underlying transport protocols and operating systems, along with a mechanism (such as *message passing* or *remote procedure calls*) for cooperating applications to communicate (over a LAN or WAN or within the same machine).

See *API*, *Messaging*, and *RPC*.

MIDI
Musical Instrument Digital Interface

A standard for mixing computers and music.

A daisy-chained (each component has a MIDI In and a MIDI Out connector), serial communications (at 31,250 bits/s), and messaging scheme to connect electronic musical instruments (usually *synthesizers* of some sort) to a *controller*. The controller may be an electronic keyboard, a *sequencer* (which stores sequences of keyboard commands), or a PC running a game.

The sequencer is usually a PC.

Messages are typically 1 to 3 bytes in length. A typical message would be as follows:

- Byte 1: *Message type* (such as `Note On`)
- Byte 2: *Key number* (which note, out of 128 possible notes)
- Byte 3: *Velocity value* (how fast the key was pressed)

Specifies Big Endian transmission and storage (MS bytes first).

A five-pin DIN connector is used, but only three of the pins are used (current loop data out and return plus a shield).

The MIDI minimum requirement is to be able to create 128 pitched instruments, each able to produce 24 notes on 16 different channels.

The MIDI capability of PC sound cards producing musical instrument sounds can be provided by one of two methods:

- *FM* (Frequency Modulation) *synthesis* is an older and inexpensive method that uses combinations of (usually four) sine waves (as specified in the sound card's ROM or RAM) to imitate the instrument's sound.

- The better-sounding *wavetable lookup synthesizer* method uses actual prerecorded samples of instrument sounds, which are modified according to the MIDI commands.

See *Big Endian*, *MPC*, *Polyphony*, and *Scale*.

Milnet

A government military network run by the U.S. Defense Communications Agency.

MIME
Multipurpose Internet Mail Extension

A standard method for sending and receiving attachments to Internet mail (usually called "email" or simply "mail") messages. Attachments are typically non-ASCII files, such as a spreadsheet or word processing document, or a graphical image. The attachment is usually either too large to be pasted into the sender's email message or is binary (which is not directly supported by Internet email). The following steps describe how MIME mail messages are handled:

- An option in the sender's email program allows the sender to specify the file-name of the file to be attached to the mail message. The file may have graphical or multimedia (images, video, sound) information.

- The file's extension (.doc or .wri, for example) indicates what the file's format and content are.

- If the file is binary (that is, it has other than the printable ASCII characters in it), it is automatically converted to ASCII (prior to MIME, this required a separate step, often using the uuencode and uudecode programs). This file conversion increases the length of the attachment (not a surprise—you can't get something for nothing).

- The mail message and attached file are mailed to the recipient.

- The recipient's mail program (which must support MIME) converts the file back to binary, and displays an icon (for WordPerfect or Word, for example) in the received mail message (according to the attached file's filename extension).

Clicking on the icon starts the application (WordPerfect or Word), so the attached file can be viewed (or edited, printed, etc.).

Works across different computing platforms.

See *OLE* and *SMTP*.

Mini-Disk

A re-writable 60-mm diameter CD-ROM (standard CD-ROMs are 120 mm in diameter) that uses *magneto-optical technology* to store up to 140 Mbytes per disk.

Data can be directly overwritten, no separate erase pass is required. Can be used for both audio and data. Developed by Sony.

See *CD-ROM*.

MIPS
Millions of Instructions Per Second

A measure of CPU processing power that is often used to compare computer processing speed. Often called "*Mythical Instructions Per Second*," as many consider the measure to be too simplistic to be meaningful (if nothing else, you have to specify which instructions are being executed).

The legendary DEC VAX-11/780 is used as a basis (it was popular in the late 1970s and early 1980s) and is defined to be a one-MIP machine.

Since VAXes (or, as VAX lovers like to pluralize them, VAXen) are fair to compare to each other (more so than to computers with other architectures), DEC uses the term VUP (VAX unit of processing power)—with one VUP equal to one MIP.

Because of the poor definition of what type of instructions to use to measure it, MIPS is seldom used today. Intel developed iComp, and workstation manufacturers use SPEC and other benchmarks, such as Dhrystone and Whetstone.

A processor's MIPS rating is typically somewhere between its SPECint92 rating and twice its SPECfp92 rating.

See *DEC*, *iComp*, *Intel PC*, and *SPEC*.

MIPS Computer Systems

A company (now owned by Silicon Graphics) that makes RISC processors (R3000 and R4000 and now newer ones) to compete with Sun's SPARC (and other workstation CPUs).

For a while, DEC, Silicon Graphics, Toshiba, NEC, Siemens and Sony were designing workstations using the processor. (The deal was that each vendor could design a chip for a specialized market.)

Also, Microsoft (Windows NT), SCO (ODT), and USL (SVR4) were working (separately) to produce a Little Endian version of their operating systems for the R4000 (a 100-MHz chip). Currently the only ACE-compatible processor (which really doesn't matter anymore, now that that effort has fallen apart).

Silicon Graphics has a WWW server at *http://www.sgi.com*.

See *ACE*, *Little Endian*, and *RISC*.

MIRS (Motorola Integrated Radio System)   See ESMR.

MMS
Manufacturing Message Specification

An effort to use OSI protocols for industrial applications, such as electric utility equipment monitoring and control. Replaces the manufacturing automation (MAP) effort.

See *OSI*.

MNP
Microcom Networking Protocol

A series of data communication–enhancing protocols that are usually embedded into modems (rather than being part of a PC's communication software).

MNP levels 1 through 11 support features such as error correction, using a 16-bit CRC (MNP 4) and data compression (MNP 5). MNP 10 can keep a connection open during the handoff time on a cellular telephone connection and adjust packet size according to communications circuit quality (packet size starts small at the beginning of a call, and is rapidly increased if line conditions are good). During idle times, the two MNP 10 modems exchange link management idle packets to monitor line quality.

MNP levels 4 and 5 use a block size of up to 256 characters.

The following points apply to data communication links using modems which use MNP 5 data compression:

- MNP 5 compresses data at up to a 2:1 ratio (so you can feed data at 19,200 bits/s into an MNP 5 9,600-bits/s modem), but the actual data compression ratio depends on the data—ASCII text (which is only 7-bit data, and has lots of "e"s, for example) will be much more compressible than an executable program file (which is 8-bit data and will likely have almost random bytes).
- You should set the PC's (or whatever is sending the data) ports (at both ends of the link) to at least twice the modem data-pump speed (the bit rate at which the modems actually are sending data). Otherwise, you don't get the full (or any) benefit of data compression.

- You must configure the PC's serial port for flow control (either `x-on/x-off` or RTS/CTS) so that the PC does not send data too fast when the data are not very compressible and to stop the data from the PCs while the modems retransmit during error correction. If the data are not compressible at all (for example, because they were already compressed with a program such as `pkzip` or `lharc`), then MNP 5 actually makes the data bigger. (V.42*bis* is smart enough to shut itself off if it detects that the data are not compressible.)

MNP 4 and 5 are superseded by LAPM (which is part of the V.42 standard) and V.42*bis*. That is, you use MNP 4 and 5 only if they are all the modem at the other end supports.

Microcom has an WWW server at *http://www.microcom.com.*

See *CRC*, *HDLC*, *LAPM*, *Modem*, *V.42*, and *V.42bis*.

Mobile IP
Mobile Internet Protocol

An effort to enable a (likely wireless) TCP/IP device to roam (as cellular telephones do) across different subnets of an IP network.

This is handled by forwarding packets from the device's *home router* to its current (or *away*) *router*. As the mobile device finds it is in a different router's territory, it tells that router the address of the device's home router. The away router then sets up a connection to the device's home router and acknowledges to the device that the away router can forward packets between the device and its home router.

Changes to the standard TCP/IP protocol stacks in both the devices and the routers are required.

Developed by IBM.

See *IP*.

Mobitex

Ericsson's Eritel subsidiary's cellular land-radio-based packet-switched data communication system. Used by RAM mobile data.

The raw data transmission bit rate was originally 8,000 bits/s (using 512-byte packets) for all installations, which provides a user data throughput of about 2.4 to 5 kbits/s, but this has been upgraded to 19,200 bits/s in some larger cities.

Usage charges are per kilobyte.

More open that the competing Ardis system, since all specifications are developed by the *Mobitex Operators Association.*

Was designed by L.M. Ericsson and Swedish Telecom. Uses 896 to 901 MHz and 935 to 940 MHz. Cantel offers the service in Canada.

Available in about 11 countries, but different frequencies are used, so roaming is complicated.

L.M. Ericsson has a WWW server at *http://www.ericsson.nl/*.

See *Ardis*, *CDPD*, *ESMR*, *GSM*, and *RAM Mobile Data*.

Modem
Modulator/Demodulator

An electronic device that converts binary data (for example, the ±12 V EIA-232 signals from a PC's COM port) to analog tones and voltages that are suitable for transmission over standard dial-up or *leased line* telephone lines.

Given the fixed 3,000-Hz bandwidth of typical POTS analog lines and the increasing power of *Digital Signal Processing* (DSP) ICs, newer modems use more complex types of modulation to provide faster data rates. The following table summarizes the types of dial-up (in contrast to leased line) modems.

Modulation	Data Rate (bits/s)	Comments
Bell 103	300	
Bell 212A	1,200	Usually compatible with V.22
V.22*bis*	2,400	
V.32	9,600	
V.32*bis*	14,400	
V.terbo	19,200	Pre-V.34, nonstandard modulation, with fewer features than V.34
V.FC	28,800	
V.34	28,800	Was called V.*fast* during development
V.34*bis*	33,600[a]	Not yet standardized

[a] The maximum speed has not yet been determined.

Current *external dial-up modems* (they are separate boxes that connect to your PC's serial COM port, through an EIA-232 cable) will usually handle both *synchronous* (as required by X.25 and IBM 3270 and 5250 protocols) and *asynchronous* (as used by standard PC serial COM ports and most bulletin board systems) data communications.

Internal modems (which are *printed circuit boards* that mount inside a PC and include a built-in serial COM port) are often asynchronous only.

Most current modems have both built-in V.42 error correction and V.42*bis* data compression.

Many current modems also have fax capability:

- Fax machines (and PC fax modems) use different types of modems than data modems; since a fax transmission is basically one-way during a call, half-duplex modems are used (they are less expensive).
- All current fax machines and modems that use standard telephone lines are *Group 3*. Most have an *Error Correction Mode* (ECM).
- Fax boards require a command interface for the PC to communicate with the fax modem. There are several such interfaces, but the most common is *Class 1*, which requires the host PC (and not the fax modem's on-board processor) to do most of the work (this provides the most flexibility and features, the lowest cost, and usually the best performance, since the PC's processor is far faster than any fax modem's dinky little single-chip controller).

At connection time, modems send tones to each other to negotiate the fastest mutually supported modulation method that will work over whatever quality line has been established for that call.

If you wanted the best modem on your block, you would want one with the following:

- *V.34 modulation*, which sends data at up to 28,800 bits/s, depending on how good a phone connection you get and whether the other end has an equally fast modem.
- *V.42 error detection and correction*, which specifies both LAPM and MNP 4 so that you will be compatible with whatever the modem at the other end may support.
- *V.42 bis data compression* and maybe MNP 5 data compression too—in case that's all the modem at the other end has.
- *V.17 fax modulation*, which sends fax images at 14,400 bits/s (if the fax machine or modem at the other end has this modulation and the connection is good enough) or slower (most commonly V.29 9,600 bits/s).

  The fax modem or software should also implement ECM.

The "universe" of dial-up modems and features is shown in the accompanying figure.

Most modems are based on ICs made by Rockwell International.

See *Asynchronous, Baud, CAS, DCE, DTE, EIA/TIA-232, EIA/TIA TSB-37a, Fax, Full-duplex, MNP, PCM, POTS, Rockwell International, RPI, Synchronous, V.8* through *V.120*, and *WAN*.

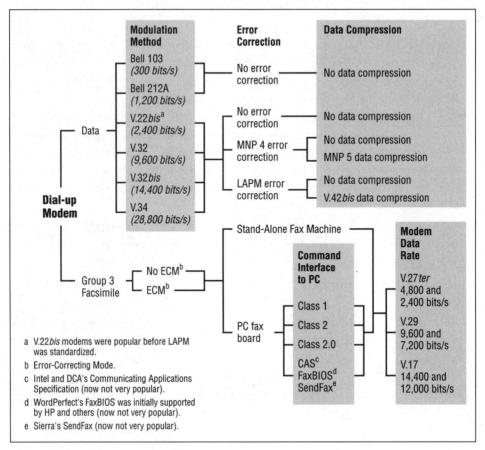

Modem—1

Monitors

UNIX workstations usually have 16- or 20-inch monitors, with a resolution of 1,152 × 900 or 1,280 × 1,024 (horizontal × vertical). For comparison, a PC's VGA is 640 × 480, and Super VGA (SVGA) is 800 × 600.

See *HDTV*.

MOTD
Message of the Day

A (hopefully) brief message displayed to users after they log in to a UNIX computer. The text is stored in the file /etc/motd and typically concerns system administration announcements such as new features or procedures.

See *UNIX*.

Motif

OSF's (which developed it) *graphical user interface* (therefore sometimes called OSF/Motif), widely licensed by OSF to others. It is both a standard API (and GUI) and a GUI alone (the "look-and-feel" to the end user), since there are other APIs, such as Tcl/Tk, that can provide a Motif-like user interface (almost the same appearance and behavior).

The Motif API is a standard tool kit for GUI applications that works at the level of menus and icons.

Motif is based on work by Hewlett-Packard and DEC and is also promoted by IBM. (These three companies are therefore major proponents of the technology.)

Motif uses the *X Window System* as its communication protocol and low-level (that is, drawing boxes and the like) display interface.

Competed with, and won out over, OPENLOOK, perhaps because Motif:

- Is not controlled by a single company
- Always had solid support (Sun initially supported something else called NeWS and then OPENLOOK)
- Looks more like Microsoft Windows
- Has always had a nicer, three-dimensional look
- Can have keyboard keys assigned to specific functions
- Had a single set of APIs (which was an advantage while it competed with OPENLOOK)

The OSF has some Motif information at *http://www.osf.org/motif/index.html*.

See *API*, *CDE*, *COSE*, *GUI*, *HP*, *OPENLOOK*, *OSF*, *Tcl/Tk*, *X/Open*, and *X*.

Motion Picture Experts Group   See **MPEG**.

Motorola

A really big company with a WWW server at *http://www.mot.com*.

See *88open*, *AMPS*, *Ardis*, *ESMR*, *PowerPC*, and *Sun*.

Motorola Integrated Radio System (MIRS)   See **ESMR**.

MPC
Multimedia PC

A certification from the *Multimedia PC Marketing Council* that a PC meets minimum requirements suitable for multimedia. The initial specifications (*Level 1*, released in 1990) were often criticized as not being powerful enough, hence the *Level 2* MPC specification. The following table lists the features of the two levels.

	MPC Level	
	1	**2**
CPU	16 MHz 80386SX	25 MHz 486SX minimum
RAM	2 Mbytes	4 Mbytes (8 Mbytes recommended)
Hard disk	30 Mbytes	160 Mbytes minimum (340 Mbytes recommended)
CD-ROM	150-kbytes/s transfer rate, seek time under 1 second	400-ms maximum access time, 300-kbytes/s (double-speed) average transfer rate using no more than 60% of CPU time, XA-ready, multisession-capable
Sound	8-bit; MIDI sampling in and out at 11,025 samples/s and 22,050 samples/s	16-bit per sample, 44,100 samples/s stereo sound, .WAV digital audio and MIDI recording and playback; also XA-sound recommended
Video	16-color VGA (640 × 480 pixels)	65,536-color VGA (640 × 480 pixels), 1.2-Mpixels/s writing speed with less than 40% CPU utilization recommended[a]

[a] Provides 15 frames per second motion video at 320 × 240 pixel resolution and 256 colors.

Multisession-capable means that the CD-ROM can read files added incrementally, such as those produced by Kodak's Photo-CD system.

CD-ROM XA-ready (extended architecture) means that the CD-ROM drive can read XA CD-ROM files (a standardized way of playing back video clips synchronized with compressed audio).

See *CD-ROM*, *MIDI*, *Multimedia*, *PCM*, and *Video*.

MPEG
Motion Picture Experts Group

A committee of the ISO that has produced a standard for *lossy data compression* and storage of full-motion video.

Interpolating between frames is used to provide better compression than the JPEG method, but this prevents the MPEG method from being used in frame-by-frame applications, such as editing and switching.

MPEG-1 is intended for computers, games, and set-top boxes (that is, a box that sits on top of your television, perhaps bringing video from the information highway—whatever that turns out to be). The video has a resolution of 352 × 240 pixels (horizontal by vertical) at 30 frames per second. Using specialized hardware (an MPEG decompression IC), it can provide near VHS-quality desktop video (that is, it is almost as good as playing a rented videotape on a home VCR) at a data rate of 150 kbytes/s (which is the data rate from a standard single-speed CD-ROM player).

MPEG-2 is intended for use with broadcast-quality (that is, really expensive and very high-quality) applications and defines a transport (protocol) that supports functions such as adding closed-captioning and different language channels.

MPEG compression uses three types of frames:

- *I* (*Intra*) key frames are compressed by using JPEG and used to support quickly scanning through a file and as reference points for B and P frames.
- *P* (*Predicted*) frames are generated by comparing redundancies in images that are several frames apart (that is, looking for blocks of video data that are the same as portions of previous I frames).
- *B* (*Bidirectional Interpolated*) frames are generated by looking for redundancies in the immediately preceding and also succeeding P or I frames.

MPEG-1 competes with AVI video.

For normal home use, MPEG-2 encodes at 3 Mbits/s, so an average 2-hour movie would require 2.7 Gbytes of storage.

See *AVI*, *CD-ROM*, *HDTV*, *JPEG*, *Lossy Data Compression*, *VHS*, and *Video*.

MP-MLQ
Multipulse-Maximum Likelihood Quantization

A standard for voice digitization and compression that uses a data rate of 5,300 or 6,300 bits/s and is well-suited to multiple compression/decompression cycles.

Standardized in G.723.

See *Lossy Data Compression* and *PCM*.

MPP
Massively Parallel Processing

At least 64 processors (each with local memory) grouped together to work on a large computational problem.

For very specialized applications (such as searching databases or processing graphical images), this can produce huge performance gains. For applications that cannot be so easily split into separate tasks, the communications required between processors usually result in this not being the best computing technology choice.

See *SMP*.

MPR II

A standard limiting the electromagnetic field that can be emitted by computer equipment.

A voluntary standard specified by the Swedish government limiting *Very Low Frequency* (VLF—more than 300 Hz and up to 30 kHz) EMF emissions to less than 0.25 μT (millionths of a tesla) at 50 cm distances in any direction from a computer monitor.

Initially released in 1987, revised to include *Extremely Low Frequencies* (ELF—up to 300 Hz) in 1991. Another standard (which permits only even lower EMF emissions) is TCO.

See *ELF*, *EMF*, *TCO*, *T*, and *VLF*.

MPTN
Multi-Protocol Transport Network

IBM's software that translates transport-layer software from one protocol to another transport protocol so that only one transport protocol need be supported on WANs.

Initial uses will be to translate (rather than the less-efficient *encapsulate*) TCP/IP to SNA and SNA to TCP/IP.

Support for NetBIOS, AppleTalk, IPX, and DECnet IV is expected.

MPTN can be software on end-systems or on gateways. MPTN does not translate higher-level protocols (such as CPI-C or RPC), so end-systems must still be compatible at layers above the transport layer.

MPTN is supported under OS/2 and on IBM's 6611 multi-protocol router.

See *CPI-C*, *Encapsulation*, *RPC*, and *TCP/IP*

MS
Most Significant

The upper bytes or digits. For example, the MS digit of the number 832 is 8.

See *Big Endian*, *Little Endian*, and *LSB*.

MTA
Message Transfer Agent

A computer that transfers X.400 messages between mail systems.

See *UA* and *X.400*.

Multicast

An important capability for supporting conferencing. Many networks (such as frame relay) and protocols (such as TCP/IP) are being augmented with the capability.

See *Frame, IP Multicast, MBONE, Multimedia, PCS (Personal Conferencing Specification)*, and *T.120*.

Multicast Backbone   See **MBONE**.

Multimedia

Literally "many media," for example, using sound, pictures, and text to (hopefully) make a more effective, understandable, or memorable presentation or conference.

To support multimedia, networks must provide:

- *Scalable* bandwidth (as new users and applications require connectivity, the network must support ever-increasing traffic loads)
- Consistent *Quality of Service*; that is, the error rate (usually due to dropped packets), network latency (typically less than 400 ms, round-trip), and network throughput must be selectable (according to the needs of the application) and predictable
- *Multicast* routing, to efficiently support *one-to-many*-type traffic

While ATM is designed to provide these features, other technologies (such as IP multicast, routers with support for priority queuing, and RSVP) can (hopefully) support multimedia over existing networks and at lower cost.

Multimedia traffic has characteristics such as:

- *One-to-one* (point-to-point) or *one-to-many* (point-to-multipoint)
- Interactive (bidirectional) or playback (one-way)

Some example uses, and the quality of service required to provide the required data communications, are shown in the table below.

		Playback	**Real-Time Interactive**
Point-to-Point	Example use	Multimedia mail	Self-paced training
	Quality of service required	Available bit rate	Variable bit rate
Point-to-Multipoint	Example use	LAN TV	Desktop conferencing
	Quality of service required	Constant bit rate	Variable bit rate, low latency

Some further characteristics of the types of traffic are the following:

- *Constant bit rate*: traffic such as that from digitized audio and video that requires a certain minimum data rate (the digitization rate) and does not benefit from additional bandwidth
- *Variable bit rate*: traffic such as interactive terminal sessions (telnet traffic), which are very bursty in nature
- *Available bit rate*: file transfers, and other applications that simply run, and likely complete, faster as they get more bandwidth

See *802.9a, ATM (Asynchronous Transfer Mode), IP Multicast, Isochronous, FDDI, FDDI-II, Latency, MIME, Multicast, MPC, PACE, PCM, Prioritization, RSVP, QOS,* and *QTC.*

Multimedia PC   See **MPC.**

Multiple Master

Adobe Systems, Inc.'s extension to its *Type 1* font format that supports very flexible font modification (for example, reducing the serifs, compressing the text, making the stroke slightly bolder) while maintaining high quality.

The intent is to facilitate document distribution and maintain the look and paging of documentation without having to distribute all the fonts.

See *Acrobat, Outline Font, PostScript Type 1 Fonts,* and *SuperATM.*

Multi-Protocol Transport Network   See **MPTN.**

Multipulse-Maximum Likelihood Quantization   See **MP-MLQ.**

Multipurpose Internet Mail Extension   See **MIME.**

Musical Instrument Digital Interface   See **MIDI.**

MVS
Multiple Virtual Storage

IBM's mainframe operating system for heavy-duty large-database and high-transaction-rate support.

Predecessors in this *OS* family of operating systems are (were) VS2, VS1, and DOS (not the PC kind).

Multiple MVS *virtual machines* can run under VM.

See *Mainframe, TPC,* and *VM.*

Narrowband ISDN

Basic rate 2B+D ISDN service. For a while was criticized as "too little, too late." Too little, because of too slow a data rate and because B channels are only circuit-switched (requiring the full line to be used for one purpose, and the time required for call set up may be a problem for some applications). Too late, because that level of performance is available with more conventional services.

However, it now seems well suited to video conferencing, dialing-in to LANs and the Internet, and disaster recovery site connectivity.

Some would say that narrowband ISDN includes *primary rate ISDN*—and some would say that primary rate ISDN is *wideband ISDN*.

See *B-ISDN*, *H.261*, *ISDN*, *WAN*, and *Wideband ISDN*.

NAS
Network Application Support

DEC's API (that is, the development environment) for its *Advantage Networks*. The set of functions that are available to application programs to use the network services.

See *Advantage Networks* and *DEC*.

National Institute of Standards and Technology Automated Computer Telephone Service   See **NIST ACTS.**

National ISDN   See **NI-1, NI-2, and NI-3.**

National Research and Education Network   See **NREN.**

National Television System Committee   See **NTSC.**

National Science Foundation See **NSF.**

Native Signal Processing See **NSP.**

Navstar

The U.S. Air Force's official name for GPS. (They run the system, so they get to choose the official name.)

See *GPS.*

NCP
NetWare Core Protocol

Novell's NetWare client/server protocol.

Runs on top of IPX. Traditionally has had a window size of 1, but Novell's recent *packet burst mode* shells (BNetX and the VLMs) support larger window sizes.

See *IPX* and *Novell.*

NCP
Network Control Program

The software running on an IBM FEP.

See *FEP* and *IBM.*

NDIS
Network Device Interface Specification

A software interface between driver software supplied by a LAN adapter manufacturer and protocol stacks (such as DEC's PathWorks or Wollongong's TCP/IP) above it, as shown in the accompanying figure.

Also, simultaneously using more than one protocol stack usually requires an NDIS (or the competing ODI) interface.

Developed by Microsoft. Supported by 3Com, Banyan (in VINES), and DEC (for Pathworks). It is usually considered more open than the competing ODI, since ODI is controlled only by Novell.

See *API, NDIS,* and *ODI.*

NDS
NetWare Directory Services

Novell's method of distributing resource information to LAN clients.

The global (spans an entire enterprise), distributed (databases are kept close to users, rather than in a single, central location), replicated (for fault-tolerance)

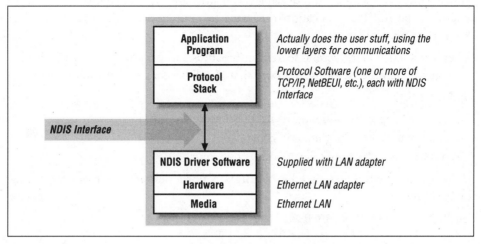

NDIS-1

database that keeps track of users and resources and provides controlled (by system administrators) access to network resources (such as files and printers).

All network objects (users and resources) are grouped into *containers*, which are organized hierarchically (like a disk's subdirectory structure). The hierarchy may be geographic or organizational.

Also stores the MHS database.

Replaces the *Bindery* of NetWare 3.*x*.

See *MHS* (*Message Handling System*), *NetWare 4.x*, and *X.500*.

NetBEUI
NetBIOS Extended User Interface

A nonroutable LAN protocol.

An extension to NetBIOS. Used for IBM's OS/2-based LAN Manager and Microsoft's LAN Manager and Windows for Workgroups.

NetBEUI (and NetBIOS, on which it is based) is nobody's favorite protocol (small packet and window size, nonroutable, not open), so Microsoft has selected WinSock as its choice for preferred communications API.

See *NetBIOS*, *WinSock*, and *WOSA*.

NetBIOS
Network Basic Input/Output System

An IBM-developed (initially for IBM's Sytek PC LAN program) standard software interface (API) to a network adapter. Has become a standard interface supported (either natively or with an additional layer of software) by most network operating systems to permit PC application programs to communicate directly with other PCs at the transport layer.

When the NetBIOS software is loaded, it broadcasts its proposed (up to 15-character) name to all other stations to ensure that it will have a network-unique name.

NetBIOS:

- Does not support windowing (it has a Window size of 1)
- Has a small packet size (under 678 bytes)
- Does not have a network layer (so it is not routable)

These are among the reasons why NetBIOS is not a desirable protocol (especially for WAN links).

See *BIOS*, *DLSw*, and *NetBEUI*.

Netscape

A WWW browser.

See *SSL* and *WWW*.

netstat

A UNIX program to confirm IP addresses and port numbers for a connection. The *-n* option leaves addresses in numerical (not name) form.

See *DNS* (*Domain Name System*) and *IP Address*.

NetWare 4.x

A processor-independent version of Novell's NetWare file server software.

Versions run directly on a SPARC or PA-RISC processor (no UNIX underneath it). A *NetWare system interface* provides the interface between each processor's hardware and NetWare. NLMs will need only be recompiled to run on it.

A major enhancement over NetWare 3.x is the *NetWare Directory Services*, which provides resources according to network-wide permissions, rather than file server–specific permissions. For example, to print a file on a printer, only the name of the printer (and permission to print on it) is required, rather than having to first log in to (and having a username and password for) the file server that controls that print server and then printing the file.

See *NDS*, *NLM*, *Novell*, *Operating System*, and *SPARC*.

NetWare Core Protocol   See **NCP.**

NetWare Directory Services   See **NDS.**

NetWare Link Services Protocol   See **NLSP.**

NetWare Loadable Module   See **NLM.**

Network Application Support   See **NAS.**

Network Basic Input/Output System   See **NetBIOS.**

Network Control Program   See **NCP.**

Network Control Program Packet-Switching Interface   See **NPSI.**

Network Device Interface Specification   See **NDIS.**

Network File System   See **NFS.**

Network Information Center   See **InterNIC.**

Network Information Service   See **NIS.**

Network Interface Card   See **NIC.**

Network Termination Type 1   See **NT-1.**

Network Time Protocol   See **NTP.**

Network-to-Network Interface   See **NNI.**

NeXTStep

The object-oriented operating system that originally only ran on NeXT workstations. NeXTStep 486 runs on Intel platforms as well.

Developed by NeXT Computers, Inc. as part of the NeXT computer (the company eventually gave up on the hardware side of the business). The company was started by Steve Jobs, cofounder of Apple Computer, after he left Apple Computer (in 1980) because he didn't like how John "Sugar-water" Sculley was running it (and Apple's board lost confidence that Steve could run a company that size).

NeXT Computers has a WWW server at *http://www.next.com.*

See *Intel* and *Operating System.*

NFG
No F_ _ _ _ _ _ Good

An abbreviation that is often used to label defective (and probably not repairable) electronic equipment.

See *foo.bar.*

NFS
Network File System

A method of mapping (technically called "mounting") shared remote disk drives so that they appear to be local. Developed and licensed by Sun Microsystems.

Uses UDP, not TCP.

Defined in RFC 1094.

See *NIS, ONC, RFS, RFC, Sun,* and *UDP.*

NI-1
National ISDN-1

While ISDN is a great idea, the many incompatible implementations have adversely affected its acceptance. The national ISDN effort is a successful effort to have a common implementation standard.

A consistent North American implementation of basic rate ISDN, as specified by Bellcore. Features that must be included are the following:

- Call forwarding
- Automatic callback
- Call hold
- Calling number identification

Euro–ISDN is the homologous pan–European effort.

See *Bellcore, BRI, ISDN, NI-2,* and *PRI.*

NI-2
National ISDN-2

Extends NI-1 to include the following:

- Universal feature operations
- Some aspects of primary rate ISDN

See *NI-1* and *NI-3.*

NI-3
National ISDN-3

Extends NI-2 to include the following:

- Further primary rate features
- Calling name delivery
- Music on hold
- Improved testing capabilities

See *NI-2*.

NIC
Network Information Center

See *InterNIC*.

NIC   [Controller" in Bonsai]
Network Interface Card

A name for the LAN adapter (printed circuit board), installed in a PC, that enables it to communicate over a LAN. The term is used more often by IBM customers and Token Ring people.

See *TIC*.

NIS
Network Information Service

Along with NFS, results in a method of providing a distributed database system to centralize (storing one copy, each on a single computer) common configuration files, such as the password file (/etc/passwd) and the hosts file (/etc/hosts). The advantages of centralizing such files are:

- Files do not need to be replicated—which would invite administration problems in keeping the copies identical.
- Users in a (usually UNIX-) distributed computing environment all see a familiar and consistent system (for example, network mounted file systems, application programs and development tools, host and file access rights, and so on) regardless of which machine they log in to.

NIS servers manage copies of the database files, and NIS clients request information from them, instead of using their own local copies (which would be an administrative impossibility to keep consistent and current). For example, when running NIS, the TCP port numbers (normally kept in /etc/services) are served over the network from a central machine.

NIS was developed by Sun Microsystems, and they have licensed it to about 300 companies and universities.

Since NIS was formerly called *Yellow Pages* (unfortunately, that name is trade-marked—somebody else thought of it first), many commands and directory names still start with yp.

See *NFS*, *ONC*, *Sun*, *TCP*, *Trademark*, and *UNIX*.

NIST ACTS
National Institute of Standards and Technology Automated Computer Telephone Service

A dial-up data service (303-494-4774 at 1,200 bits/s) that provides the accurate time.

NIST does lots of standards and research stuff. It has a WWW server at *http://www.nist.gov*.

NLM
NetWare Loadable Module

The shared programs, drivers, and function libraries that a Novell NetWare 3.*x* file server runs to perform some of its functions (especially when it is for an optional feature or one that may require updates), as shown in the following table.

NLM Filename Extension	Use
.DSK	Disk drivers
.LAN	LAN adapter drivers
.NLM	All other programs (such as install) and libraries (such as clib.NLM, which is analogous to a Windows or OS/2 dll)

NLMs can be loaded and unloaded from the system console, while the server is running, with users logged in. NLMs are automatically loaded when one NLM references another that is not yet loaded into the file server's memory.

See *API* and *Novell*.

NLSP
NetWare Link Services Protocol

A link-state protocol based on OSI's IS-IS, and developed by Novell to:

- Replace its use of RIP (a *distance-vector* router-to-router protocol that involves broadcasting routing tables every 60 seconds)
- Change the way SAP (server broadcasts every 60 seconds identifying their name, service, and address to potential clients) is used

Has lower network overhead and faster convergence—especially useful over slow (9,600-bits/s) WAN links.

Each NetWare router maintains two databases:

- The *Adjacency Database* tracks the router's direct network links and immediate neighbors
- The *Link State Database* is the connectivity map for the entire network, which will allow all NLSP devices to determine (or converge on) the same, best route for each possible source-to-destination pair of communicating nodes.

Costs (the metric used to determine the best path) can be manually changed for each link to direct traffic toward or away from particular links (for example, faster or more expensive WAN communications links).

As with all such *link-state* algorithms, rather than broadcasting every router's entire table every 60 seconds, NLSP sends only the changes.

NLSP routers will detect RIP/SAP routers and act as traditional RIP/SAP routers on those links.

See *IS-IS*, *Link-state*, *OSI*, *RIP*, *Novell*, and *WAN*.

NNI
Network-to-Network Interface

Frame relay's and ATM's (completely different, but similar in goal) specification for the interface between two networks.

Similar in intent to X.75 for X.25 networks, in that it is an extension to the protocol to permit two networks to be interconnected.

See *ATM (Asynchronous Transfer Mode)* and *Frame Relay*.

Novell

Novell, Inc. has over 65% (by nodes) of the network operating system market. The next largest competitors (Banyan, DEC, IBM, and Microsoft) have about 4% each.

Novell has a WWW server at *http://www.novell.com.*

See *IPX*, *MHS (Message Handling System)*, *NCP (NetWare Core Protocol)*, *NCP (Network Control Program)*, *NDS*, *NetWare 4.x*, *NLM*, *NLSP*, *ODI*, *Operating System*, *Univel*, and *VLM*.

NPSI
Network Control Program Packet-Switching Interface

IBM's FEP software that supports X.25.

See *FEP*, *NCP (Network Control Program)*, *QLLC*, and *X.25*.

NREN
National Research and Education Network

The official name for the Internet, because of the 1991 U.S. Congress act by this name says so. Intended to link research communities in government, industry, and higher education.

See *Internet*.

NSF
National Science Foundation

The U.S. agency that provides some Internet funding—initially only for the backbone, now for routing support ($20 million over 5 years to Merit, Inc. and the University of Southern California Information Sciences Institute; this work used to be done by ANS).

See *ANS*, *NSFnet*, and *Internet*.

NSFnet
National Science Foundation Network

The part of the Internet backbone that is funded by the U.S. government.

Because of the substantial commercial use of the Internet and the change in its funding, NSFnet disappeared on April 30, 1995.

The Internet backbone is now privately run (on a for-profit basis by ANS), and the small amount of government-funded work will use the private backbone using government grants.

See *ANS* and *Internet*.

NSP
Native Signal Processing

Another effort by Intel to get the processor (which is likely made by Intel— and they would like to give you a reason to want a faster one) rather than specialized ICs, such as *digital signal processors* (that might not be made by Intel) to handle tasks such as simple sound playback and mixing.

The effort includes the PCI chip sets, software drivers, and APIs to encourage manufacturers and application developers to use the technology for (at least) the following:

- Sound (special effects, speech synthesis and recognition)
- Telephony

- Video (video conferencing)
- Handwriting recognition

See *API*, *PC*, *PCS* (*Personal Conferencing Specification*), and *PCI*.

NT-1
Network Termination Type 1

A device needed to connect an end user's ISDN equipment to the pair of wires from the phone company.

The device that connects the ISDN *U interface* (the single pair of copper conductors from the telephone company's central office) to a building's internal ISDN *S bus*. The ISDN S bus is the four-pair cabling (with 8-pin modular jacks) used to interconnect ISDN devices, and may also be used to power them. An ISDN S bus has nothing whatsoever to do with Sun's "*SBus*."

The NT-1 gets its power from a connection to the building's 110-V A.C. and usually also has a built-in rechargeable battery so that telephone service is available during power failures (unlike standard POTS telephones, ISDN telephones have active electronic devices in them and need power). Of the four pairs of wires of the *S bus*, two are for data, and the other two can be used to send power from the NT-1 to the ISDN telephones and other devices.

The NT-1 may be built in to a *terminal adapter*. The single "terminal adapter/NT-1" unit is then all that is needed to connect (for example) a PC's standard EIA-232 COM1 port to the *basic-rate* ISDN U interface from the telephone company.

See *BRI*, *Bus*, *Connector*, *EIA/TIA-232*, *ISDN*, and *POTS*.

NTP
Network Time Protocol

A protocol for communicating the time from time servers to other hosts on an IP network.

See *TCP*.

NTSC
National Television System Committee

The name for the method used to transmit television signals in North America.

Actually, the name of the group that sets the broadcast television standards in North America. Originally formed to standardize the method for color television broadcasting. The method chosen (augmenting the existing monochrome *composite video signal*) was standardized in 1953 and is still the standard for North America and Japan.

The *frame rate* is 29.97 frames per second (0.1% slower than the original 30 frames per second, to avoid interference with the color subcarrier part of the NTSC television signal). In contrast, computer video usually runs at 30 frames per second, since it does not use NTSC.

Each frame is made up of two *fields*, with the second field writing between the lines of the first, to provide more displayed lines per frame (the *persistence* of the CRT phosphor is long enough that the first field remains displayed while the second is being written).

Each frame is made up of 481 horizontal lines (240.5 lines per field) that are visible (sometimes called "*active*") plus another 44 lines (22 per field) that are *blanked* (the electron beam is turned off), since they occur while the scanning beam returns to the upper-left corner of the screen. This makes a total of 525 lines per frame.

Such *interlaced* scanning was necessary to fit the screen resolution desired into the video bandwidth available. Newer technologies (such as computer monitors and HDTV) usually use noninterlaced (also called *progressive*) scanning.

The term "NTSC" is also used to refer to the standard video signal that is used (for example) between a *video cassette recorder* (a standard home VCR) and television (it uses what is often called an RCA connector).

When broadcasted, an NTSC signal requires a *6-MHz bandwidth*. That is, channel 2 is 54 to 60 MHz, channel 3 is 60 MHz to 66 MHz, and so on. To reduce interference, adjacent television channels (for example, channels 3 and 4) are not assigned in the same coverage area, and the transmitting antennas of transmitters that are assigned to the same frequency must be at least 155 miles apart.

For each 6-MHz channel:

- The main (sometimes called video) carrier frequency is 1.25 MHz above the base frequency (of 54 MHz for channel 2, for example—so the video carrier is at 55.25 MHz).
- This carrier is *amplitude modulated* (AM) by the *composite video signal* (which has all of the picture and synchronization information).
- The (left+right) sound information is sent by *frequency modulating* (FM) a sound subcarrier that is 4.5 MHz above the video carrier frequency (so the sound for channel 6 is at 87.75 MHz—which explains why you can usually hear broadcast TV audio on a standard FM radio, since FM starts just above this, at 88 MHz).
- For stereo signals, an FM left–right audio signal is also sent, at a pilot frequency above the sound subcarrier.

Standard television has a 4:3 (horizontal:vertical) aspect ratio. Regular *monochrome* (black–and–white) television broadcasts began in 1936 in Britain and in 1939 in the U.S.

NTSC video can produce the changes per horizontal line listed in the following table. (These limitations are due to the modulation methods and frequencies chosen.)

Value	Changes per Line	Used for
Luminance (intensity)	267	Fine monochrome detail
Orange–blue color	96	Flesh tones and other colors
Purple–green color	35	Other colors

PAL and SECAM are similar–technology systems that are used outside of North America.

A higher-quality (than NTSC) standard is called *S-Video* and is supported by some VCRs and televisions.

See *CATV*, *Color*, *Composite Video Signal*, *HDTV*, *Interlaced*, *PAL*, *SECAM*, *VHS*, and *Video*.

NWay   See **100BASE-T.**

Object Linking and Embedding   See **OLE.**

Object Request Broker   See **ORB.**

OC-x
Optical Carrier

The standard speeds used for high-speed data transmission (typically used for ATM) in North America.

The standard for SONet data transmission over optical fiber. Common speeds are OC–3 (155.52 Mbits/s) and OC–12 (622.08 Mbits/s).

See *ATM (Asynchronous Transfer Mode)*, *SONet*, and *STS*.

ODBC
Open Database Connectivity

Microsoft's effort to provide a single API for database (called *data sources*) access.

Data sources with ODBC interfaces include:

- XBase (*.DBF) files
- SQL databases
- Microsoft Access and Excel
- Paradox
- Novell Btrieve files
- IBM DB2

Since it is a general-purpose interface (not tailored to a specific database), it provides only a subset of most database vendors' capabilities.

Part of Microsoft's WOSA and an implementation of *CLI 1992* (*Call-Level Interface*), which was created in 1992 by the *X/Open Group* and the *SQL Access Group*.

See *DBA*, *SQL*, *WOSA*, *XBase*, and *X/Open*.

ODI
Open Data-Link Interface

A software interface between driver software supplied by a LAN (such as Ethernet) adapter manufacturer and protocol stacks (such as Novell's IPX or Wollongong's TCP/IP), as shown in the accompanying figure.

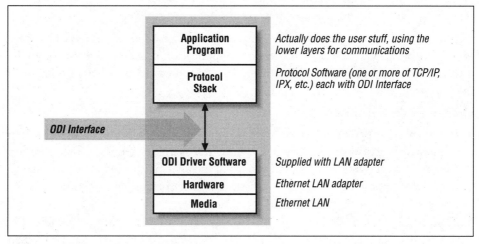

ODI–1

Using more than one protocol stack simultaneously usually requires an ODI (or the competing NDIS) interface.

Replaces the previous network-specific IPX drivers.

Developed by Novell. Also supported by Apple.

See *API*, *NDIS*, and *Novell*.

ODT
Open Desktop

SCO's OSF/1-compliant UNIX, licensed from DEC, will run DEC applications. Based on Carnegie-Mellon's Mach kernel, which is based on 4.2 BSD. Communication initially is TCP/IP and NFS. Has a graphical user interface.

See *OSF*, *OSF/1*, *SCO*, and *UNIX*.

OLE
Object Linking and Embedding

A method used by Microsoft's Windows products to integrate the output from one program as data into another (for example, a drawing into a word processing document).

The appropriate program (the drawing package) is automatically run to edit the data (when you select the drawing with the mouse).

The newer version 2.0 of OLE supports *in situ* editing (as does HP's NewWave), so that rather than opening or moving you to a new window, it lets you edit the embedded object without hiding the rest of the document (clicking starts the required application and changes only your menus and tools).

Documents that contain links to the output from other applications are called *compound documents*. An *OLE client*, or *container*, application contains objects. An application can also produce embedded objects, in which case it is called an *OLE server* or *component*.

Other possible uses are as follows:

- Utility programs that won't be used by themselves but are very useful when integrated with other programs. The favorite example here is a spell checker. Everyone would like to use their own spell checker (with their own customizations) with all of their programs (email, database, spreadsheet, desktop publishing, etc.).
- Conversion utilities (for example, to convert a word processing or graphics file format to a different format—WordPerfect to Word or `.tif` to `.bmp`), accessed by mouse-clicking a selection from the file icon's properties. No need for a new user interface for the conversion program, as it uses the already-familiar properties-setting method built in to whatever operating system is being used.

Pronounced "ol-*é*".

Developed by Microsoft and generally a more powerful feature than its predecessor, DDE. Competes with Apple's *OpenDoc* and IBM's *System Object Model* (SOM).

See *DDE* and *OpenDoc*.

OLTP
On-line Transaction Processing

Handling real-time *transactions* such as those that stock exchanges and airline reservation systems require. Such systems require transaction management, extensive audit trails, routing, scheduling, and administration.

See *SQL* and *TPC*.

ONC
Open Networking Computing

Sun's networking protocols to support distributed computing. Includes NFS, NIS, and RPC.

A newer version (ONC+) is part of Sun's Solarix 2.*x* operating system and includes security and performance enhancements.

See *NFS*, *NIS*, *RPC*, *Solaris*, *Sun*, and *UNIX*.

Open Database Connectivity   See **ODBC.**

Open Data-Link Interface   See **ODI.**

Open Desktop   See **ODT.**

Open Shortest Path First   See **OSPF.**

Open Software Foundation   See **OSF.**

Open Systems Interconnection   See **OSI.**

OpenDoc

A method of integrating the outputs of more than one application program into a single document.

A vendor-neutral (unlike OLE), cross-platform (DOS, Windows, UNIX, OS/2, and Macintosh) open standard for the APIs to create and edit *compound documents* (which are documents that can be composed of tables, charts, text, video, sound, and graphics—all in one file). Different programs can be used to edit each component (or *part*) of the file.

Promoted by Microsoft competitors such as Apple, Borland, IBM, Novell/WordPerfect, Sun, and Taligent.

Originally developed by Apple but now owned and controlled by *Component Integration Laboratories*.

Competes with, but will also work with, OLE.

See *DDE* and *OLE*.

OPENLOOK

The graphical user interface developed by Sun.

Uses the *X Window System*'s X11 communication protocol (as does the competing *Motif*) but presents a different user interface (look-and-feel) than Motif.

Even though OPENLOOK had some neat features—for example, it was cheaper (included with Sun workstations for free) and had nicer scroll bars (they show how far through the document you are)—Motif is now the industry standard. Even Sun (who now supports COSE and CDE) no longer includes OPENLOOK with its operating systems), and the only place you find OPENLOOK now is in Linux (which is a public-domain UNIX).

See *CDE, GUI, Motif, X,* and *UNIX.*

OpenVMS

DEC's new name for their VMS operating system, now that they will license it to run on other platforms. (It's amazing what a little serious competition will do—Apple has done the same previously unimaginable thing with their Mac OS operating system).

See *Alpha AXP, DEC, Operating System,* and *VMS.*

Operating System

The software that runs user applications and provides an interface to the hardware. Hardware that runs more than one operating system is becoming more popular (or perhaps it would be better to say that there are fewer hardware platforms now but more companies with operating systems). The following table shows which hardware platforms run what operating system(s).

Hardware Platform	Operating System					
	IBM		Microsoft		NeXTStep	Other
	AIX	OS/2	DOS	Windows NT		
DEC Alpha				✓		DEC OpenVMS, OSF/1
HP PA-RISC					✓	HP-UX
IBM/Apple/Motorola PowerPC	✓	✓		✓		Apple Macintosh Mac OS, Windows 3.1, Novell NetWare, Sun Solaris, PowerOpen
IBM RS/6000	✓					

(table continued on next page)

Hardware Platform	Operating System					
	IBM		Microsoft		NeXTStep	Other
	AIX	OS/2	DOS	Windows NT		
Intel Pentium		✓	✓	✓	✓	Banyan VINES, Novell NetWare, Sun Solaris, SCO UNIX, Windows 3.1
Motorola 68000					✓	Apple Macintosh
Silicon Graphics MIPS R4x00				✓		Silicon Graphics IRIX, SVR4
Sun Super-SPARC				✓	✓	SunOS, Sun Solaris

See *Alpha AXP*, *Intel*, *PA-RISC*, *PC*, *PowerPC*, *RISC*, *SPARC*, and *UNIX*.

Optical Carrier See **OC-x.**

ORB
Object Request Broker

An effort to standardize schemes for sharing and using object-oriented information in distributed computing environments. The *Object Management Group* sponsors this work.

OS/2
Operating System/2

IBM's preemptive multitasking (tasks are interrupted when their time-slice has expired or when there is a more important task to do), PC-based (initially, then PowerPC was to be supported) GUI operating system that competes with Microsoft Windows.

Version 2.0 was released in Spring 1992. Version 3.0 (internally, then externally, called Warp) was released in late 1994.

See *IBM* and *Operating System*.

OSF
Open Software Foundation

A nonprofit research and development organization that was formed in 1988 and devoted to open software (that is, software with standardized and publicized interface specifications).

DEC, HP, and IBM formed the OSF when Sun and AT&T (which then owned UNIX) formed a partnership (this caused more than a bit of concern to the rest of the UNIX industry), though many other companies are now members.

The goal is to develop OSF/1 (which is a merging of System V, BSD, and Mach) as competition to UNIX International's SVR4 UNIX and to develop other standards, such as DCE and the X Window System, that facilitate multivendor, distributed computing.

DEC has implemented OSF/1 on their Alpha processor.

Initially, Sun felt that OSF's only purpose was to work against Sun (Scott McNealy termed it "Oppose Sun Forever"). However, OSF was reorganized in 1994 to Sun's satisfaction, and Sun joined.

OSF oversees COSE's work.

The OSF has a WWW server at *http://www.osf.org/*.

See *DCE, DEC, DME, Mach, Motif, ODT, OSF/1, Sun, SVR4, X/Open,* and *X*.

OSF/1

OSF's UNIX-like operating system. It was to have been based on AIX, but the Mach version 2.5 kernel was used instead (and is now based on Mach 3.0). Includes POSIX 1003.1 and XPG features. DEC's implementation for their Alpha AXP processor is *binary compatible* with their Ultrix.

See *AIX, Alpha AXP, Mach, ODT, Operating System, OSF, Portability, POSIX OSE, SVR4, UNIX,* and *XPG*.

OSI
Open Systems Interconnection

A suite of protocols and standards sponsored by the ISO for data communications between otherwise incompatible computer systems.

Unfortunately (for the many people and companies that spent so much time and money on the effort), the TCP/IP suite of protocols has eclipsed OSI, and you don't hear much about OSI anymore (except for a few applications, such as the X.500 directory service).

When work began (in the late 1970s) on providing a standard method for communications between different hardware platforms, TCP/IP was not considered an option for serious commercial applications, since TCP/IP:

- Required you to run UNIX (which, at the time, was not used for commercial applications and had only a command-line user interface)
- Had poor security and management features
- Had too small an address size

Therefore the ISO promoted development of OSI (how palindromic).

Although all major (and many minor) computer vendors now have OSI products, the OSI protocols were never widely implemented, and TCP/IP has become the first choice for multivendor networking, because of its:

- Lower-cost and more-efficient implementation (less CPU time required, smaller programs)
- Availability for most operating systems
- Fast standardization and development cycle (usually using the Internet to facilitate communications) when a new requirement is identified
- Familiarity among college graduates (universities use TCP/IP, so once out of school, a graduate's first choice when designing a system is to use TCP/IP)
- Easier-to-access (and zero-cost) documentation and standards (they are all available on the Internet)

The following table shows the OSI name for the protocol, standard, or function of the homologous TCP/IP-based networking component.

TCP/IP Name	OSI Equivalent	
FTP	FTAM	File Transfer, Access, and Management
Host	ES	End System
IP	IP	Internet Protocol
OSPF	IS-IS	Intermediate System to Intermediate System
Router	IS	Intermediate System
SMTP	X.400	ITU-T's Electronic Mail Standard
SNMP	CMIP	Common Management Information Protocol
TCP	CONP	Connection-oriented Protocol
TELNET	VTS	Virtual Terminal Service
UDP	CNLP	Connectionless Protocol

See *COSAC, CLNP, CONP, COS, COSAC, ES, FTAM, ftp, GOSIP, IP, IS, IS-IS, ISO, MMS, OSInet, OSPF, RFC, SNMP, SPF, Standards, TCP, TCP/IP, telnet, UDP, X.400,* and *X.500.*

OSInet

A test network set up by a consortium of North American OSI software vendors and users that offers the *Network Registration Service* (NRS) database of successful interoperability testing.

OSPF
Open Shortest Path First

A newer protocol for the communication of network connectivity and status information between TCP/IP routers.

A link-state, intradomain routing algorithm that is becoming a replacement option for RIP. Handles only TCP/IP's IP. As shown in the following table, OSPF produces much less router to router network traffic, and provides faster connectivity updates too.

Method of Sending	RIP	OSPF
Changes in network connectivity	Not supported	Multicasted (to routers only) as they occur
Full network connec-tivity table	Broadcasted to all stations every 60 seconds	Multicasted (to routers only) every 30 minutes

Each router learns the status of all links within an *autonomous system* and calculates the shortest path (based on hops, link speed, and other factors) to the destination as a tree, with that router at the *root* and each possible path to the destination as a path on the tree.

The shortest path calculated may depend on the requested *type of service*.

The router then sends the packet the one hop to the next router, which then repeats the calculation to send the packet one hop closer to the final destination, again along the shortest calculated path for the tree built by that router, with that next router as the root.

See *IP Multicast*, *Link-state*, and *RIP*.

Outline Font

A method of storing the definitions of font shape. Also called a *scalable* or *vector font*.

It is a scalable font because the *outline* of each character is described by vectors that can be scaled (adjusted to any size). The curves between the end-points of the vectors are usually specified by using a *bezier spline* (which has a pleasing curve).

Outline fonts need to be rasterized before use by raster-oriented printers (for example, dot matrix and laser). This can be done in the printer (for example, if the printer supports PostScript) or by the PC (for example, if it uses Adobe Type Manager).

Since the scaling process may produce asymmetric characters (because of round-ing), *hinting* is often used to specify requirements (such as that both legs of an "M" be the same width).

The major formats of outline fonts are listed in the following table.

Font Format	Defined by	Used by
Intellifont	Agfa Division of Miles, Inc.	PCL 5 (HP LaserJet printers)
Speedo	Bitstream, Inc.	Many software packages
TrueType	Apple Computer, Inc., Microsoft Corporation	Microsoft Windows
Type 1	Adobe Systems, Inc.	PostScript printers and displays

An older technology is the bitmap font.

See *ATM (Adobe Type Manager), Bitmap Font, Font, PostScript Page Description Language, PCL, PostScript Type 1 Fonts, PostScript Type 3 Fonts, Rasterize,* and *Typeface Family.*

Out-of-band
Outside of bandwidth

Using a separate channel for signaling (than the voice or data channel).

The separate channel may be physically separate wires, or may be a time-multiplexed channel (such as an ISDN D channel). While this often costs more it ensures that the full bandwidth is available for the voice or data.

For example, an EIA-232 interface using RTS/CTS (*Request to Send/Clear to Send*) flow control is out-of-band flow control, since these signals (pins 4 and 5) are separate from the data.

See *EIA/TIA-232, In-Band,* and *ISDN.*

OverDrive

Intel's name for the upgrade CPUs that usually plug into an extra socket on a PC's motherboard, which is intended for that use (to add functionality), or that entirely replaces the existing CPU.

A 169-pin socket in most 486SX and 486DX-based PCs, which can accept a version of a 486 CPU that runs internally at double the system clock speed while running externally at the normal system clock speed. This permits a (for example) 33-MHz 486-based system to be upgraded by simply plugging an OverDrive chip into the socket. (This disables the original 486, and all processing is performed by the OverDrive chip.) The system will then run at 66 MHz when doing internal operations (such as math and register operations and processing out of its internal Level 1 cache), while having "normal" external timing, so no modifications are required to the standard 33 MHz 486 motherboard. Systems that are *initially designed* with speed-doubled processors use the similar 486DX2.

The Pentium processor upgrade for a 486 motherboard is called a P54C. The clock-doubled 3.3-V Pentium processor upgrade for a Pentium motherboard is called a P54CT (a regulator on the chip converts the motherboard's 5 volts to the 3.3 volts).

See *486SX, 486SX2, Intel, PC,* and *Pentium.*

P6

Intel's successor to the Pentium processors. The P6 is now called the Pentium Pro.

Has 5.5 million transistors. Initial versions run at 133 MHz internally and 66.5 MHz externally. Gives almost twice the performance of the 100-MHz Pentium.

The Pentium can process two instructions at once; however, if the processing of one instruction must wait (for example, if a branch took an unexpected path so the next instruction has not yet been fetched), then the processing of the other instruction is also stopped. This avoids the complicated situation of instructions being executed out of the original order.

The P6 can process three instructions at once (and three instructions per clock cycle—wowzers!), and if the processing of one instruction must wait, then the other instructions can continue being processed. (I guess that's what uses up the additional 2.2 million transistors.) Intel calls this *dynamic execution.*

Runs at a new lower voltage of 2.9 V and (still) dissipates 15 to 20 watts (hot). Has built-in multiprocessor support for up to four processors per computer.

Can use a clock multiplier (the ratio of internal to external clock speed) of 2:1 (which is used by the initial version of the processor), 3:1, or 4:1 (which will presumably be used later, when they figure out how to get the innards running lots faster).

Has the same size on-chip *Level 1* cache as the Pentium (8 kbytes for instructions, 8 kbytes for data).

The 256-kbyte *Level 2* cache (which has 15.5 million transistors) is on a separate die (the actual eeny-weeny little chippy) but is mounted in the same package as the processor die (making for faster access than the external Level 2 cache of the Pentium).

See *Cache, iComp, Intel, Pentium, PC, SMP,* and *Superscalar.*

311

P7

Intel's successor to the P6.

May include RISC capabilities developed as part of Intel's work with Hewlett-Packard and their PA-RISC architecture. May have a 64-bit-wide instruction set. May be introduced about 1998.

See *Intel*, *HP*, *P6*, *PA-RISC*, *RISC*, and *VLIW*.

PABX
Private Automatic Branch Exchange

Another name for Private Branch Exchange.

See *PBX*.

PACE
Priority Access Control Enabled

3Com's proposed method of supporting multimedia over Ethernet. Both 10- and 100-Mbits/s Ethernet are supported. Standard Ethernet adapters are used in the user workstations, but Ethernet switches replace conventional concentrators. The switches use a technique called *interactive access*, which anticipates the behavior of the standard Ethernet adapters to provide different *classes of service* (time-sensitive and not time-sensitive) so that the Ethernet link can be shared between different types of traffic.

3Com expects that ATM (which supports various classes of service, for the same reasons) will be a *backbone* technology, and 3Com's PACE technology will make it possible to use Ethernet to bring multimedia capability (cost-effectively) to the desktop.

See *10BASE-F*, *10BASE-T*, *100BASEFX*, *100BASE-T*, *100BASE-T2*, *100BASE-T4*, *100BASE-TX*, *802.3*, *Ethernet*, and *Multimedia*.

Packet

A (OSI layer 3) unit of data exchanged between end systems (host computers).

See *Frame*.

Packet Ensemble Protocol   See **PEP**.

Packet Internet Groper   See **Ping**.

PAL
Phase-Alternation Line

The broadcast color television standard used in Western Europe (including the U.K.) and Australia.

Compared to North America's NTSC, PAL:

- Is not as well standardized (many countries use slightly different implementations)
- Usually has better resolution (625 lines, compared to NTSC's 525 lines)
- Usually has a slower *frame rate* (25 rather than 29.97 frames per second—therefore often showing noticeable *flicker*)
- Uses a similar method of adding the color information (using a *subcarrier*)—though the color (often called the *hue* or *tint*) is automatically calibrated and so does not need adjustment, as North American televisions do
- Has the same 4:3 aspect ratio

Many countries have slightly different implementations of PAL, with names such as PAL-M (which is used in Brazil and is similar to NTSC in that it requires 6 MHz for each channel, has 626 lines per frame, and uses 60 Hz scanning) or PAL-I1 (which requires 8 MHz per channel, has 625 lines per frame, and uses 50 Hz scanning—and can provide a better picture because of it).

See *HDTV*, *NTSC*, *SECAM*, and *Video*.

Paper

Did you ever wonder:

- How big an E-size drawing is
- What the dimensions of a "standard A4" piece of paper are
- What "20-pound bond" paper is and why it is almost the same weight as 50-pound book or envelope paper

Well I did, and here is what I found.

Nonmetric paper sizes are listed in the following table.

Size	Width	Height	Comments
	Inches		
A	8.5	11	Standard North American *letter size* paper.
Legal	8.5	14	Lawyers love this stuff.
B	11	17	Sometimes called *ledger* (accountants love this stuff)
C	17	22	
D	22	34	
E	34	44	
F	28	40	

(table continued on next page)

Size	Width	Height	Comments
	Inches		
G	11	42	These sizes are intended to be stored rolled, rather than flat.
H	28	48	
J	34	48	
K	40	48	

Metric paper sizes (as standardized by the ISO) are listed in the following table.

Size	Width	Height	Width	Height
	mm		inches	
2A0	1,189	1,682	46.81	66.22
A0	841	1,189	33.11	46.81
A1	594	841	23.39	33.11
A2	420	594	16.54	23.39
A3	297	420	11.69	16.54
A4	210	297	8.27	11.69
A5	148	210	5.83	8.27
A6	105	148	4.13	5.83
A7	74	105	2.91	4.13
B0	1,028	1,456	40.48	57.32
B1	728	1,028	28.66	40.48
B2	514	728	20.24	28.66
B3	364	514	14.33	20.24
B4	257	364	10.12	14.33
B5	182	257	7.17	10.12
B6	128	182	5.04	7.17

Metric A4-size paper is the size that is supposed to replace standard 8½" × 11" office paper (A4 is slightly narrower and taller).

Other than size, the most common distinguishing factor for paper is its weight. (Note that the paper's actual thickness depends on many factors, such as whether the paper is *coated* to give it a shiny and smooth surface.) This weight is expressed as the number of pounds for 500 sheets (one *ream*) of paper in its *basis size*—and this size depends on the type of paper (!), as shown in the following table.

Type of Paper	Basis Size (inches)	
	Width	**Height**
Bond	17	22
Book paper	25	38
Book cover	20	26
Vellum Bristol	22.5	28.5
Index	22.5	30.5
Tag	24	36

This explains why an 8½" × 11" piece of 20-pound bond weighs a different amount than an 8½" × 11" piece of 20-pound book paper—these papers have different basis sizes.

Perhaps the most common papers are standard *20-pound office bond* (the type you use in your photocopier and laser printer) and *60-pound book*, also called *offset* (the type used in softcover books). Since these papers have different basis sizes, the metric measurement (grams per square meter) is a better way to compare weights, as shown in the following table.

Paper Type		Common Paper Weights				
Bond	pounds	16	20	24	28	36
	g/m^2	60.2	75.2	90.2	105.3	135.4
Book (or offset)	pounds	40	50	60	70	90
	g/m^2	59.2	74.0	88.8	103.6	133.2

As shown, 20-pound bond paper is almost the same weight as 50-pound book paper (just another reason why metric is a good idea). The weights for other papers can be calculated by scaling these numbers linearly. For example, 32-pound bond would be ($32/28 \times 105.3 =$) 120.3 g/m^2.

See *Ream* and *SI*.

Parallel Port

A PC's standard, traditional parallel printer port is a female DB-25 connector. The interface has 8 data bits to the printer, plus 5 control signals to the printer, and 5 control signals from the printer.

The pin-out is shown in the table below.

The interface uses TTL (*Transistor-Transistor Logic*) voltages which are *unbalanced* signals (all signals are referenced to a common ground and are therefore very susceptible to electrical noise).

With standard printer cables, the maximum cable length is about 15 feet. With well-shielded cable, this can be extended to about 50 feet but is not recommended.

The interface and the 36-pin connector was first defined by the implementation by the Centronics Data Computer Corporation, on their printers (beginning in the mid-1960s). The interface is therefore sometimes called a *Centronics interface*.

Typical actual transfer rates are up to 100 kbytes/s.

There are two competing efforts (ECP and EPP, now both merged into the IEEE 1284 standard effort) to define higher-speed and better bidirectional capabilities.

The table below shows several details of PC parallel printer ports. Included are the pin numbers (for both the DB-25 on the back of a PC and the Centronics connector on the printer), and the signal name, function, and direction of the signal.

Pin Number		Pin Name	Direction		Pin Function
DB-25	Centronics		PC	Printer	
1	1	/Strobe[a]		→	The data to printer is valid when this signal is low (and for at least 0.5 μs before and after this). The printer should read the data on the signal's falling edge.
2	2	Data bit 0		→	
3	3	Data bit 1		→	
4	4	Data bit 2		→	
5	5	Data bit 3		→	Data to printer
6	6	Data bit 4		→	
7	7	Data bit 5		→	
8	8	Data bit 6		→	
9	9	Data bit 7		→	
10	10	/Ack		←	Acknowledge—the printer finished processing the byte of data and is ready for more when this signal goes high.
11	11	Busy[a]		←	When this signal goes high, the printer has accepted the byte of data and is processing it (and will not accept another byte of data) until this signal goes low (and /Ack goes high).

(table continued on next page)

Pin Number		Pin Name	Direction		Pin Function
DB-25	Centronics		PC	Printer	
12	12	PE		←	Paper Empty (the printer is out of paper when this signal is high), or maybe there is a paper jam—there is no single definition.
13	13	Slct		←	Select (or on-line)—when this signal is high, the printer confirms that it is selected and on-line.
14	14	/Auto Fd[a]		→	Auto Line Feed—when this signal is low, the PC has requested that the printer insert a line feed after each line (carriage return) sent from the PC.
15	32	/Error or /Fault		←	The printer is saying that an error condition has occurred (when this signal is low).
16	31	/Init		→	Initialize Printer—when this signal goes low, the PC has requested the printer to do an internal reset (clear the input buffer, reset printer logic, and return the print head to the left margin) to initialize itself.
17	36	/Select In[a]		→	Select Input—when this signal is low, the PC has selected the printer, which should then accept subsequent data from the PC.
18-25	16, 19-30, 33	Ground		↔	Signal ground.

[a] Note that these signals are inverted between the PC's I/O port registers and the PC's parallel port. This table presents the information as it appears on the PC's parallel port.

In the preceding table, signals prefaced by a slash indicate that the signal is *negative logic*; that is, it is considered asserted when the signal is low.

See *1284, ECP, EPP,* and *TTL.*

PA-RISC
Precision Architecture-RISC

Hewlett-Packard's RISC architecture, used in their HP 9000 servers and workstations and introduced in 1986.

Has *Bi-Endian switching* (can be either *Little Endian* or *Big Endian*).

Successor to the HP 3000 minicomputer architecture.

See *Alpha AXP*, *Big Endian*, *HP*, *Little Endian*, *P7*, *RISC*, and *SPEC*.

Parity

A weak method of error detection (but not correction) in which the sender generates extra data bits (that are appended to the data) so that the receiver can determine whether the data have been corrupted (with a somewhat low confidence, since an even number of bits in error in the same byte will not be detected).

In *serial data communications*, communications software can configure a PC's UART to add (for example) an odd parity bit to each transmitted character. The UART will then set the parity bit to either a binary 1 or 0, as required to ensure that the total number of ones (that is, bits that are set to binary 1) in the character (including the parity bit) is an odd number.

Other serial data communications parity settings are:

- *Even*—the total number of ones is an even number
- *Mark* or *1*—this is a silly setting, since the parity bit is always set to binary 1, which does not provide any error detection and just reduces the throughput of the communication line by about 10%
- *Space* or *0*—the parity bit is always set to a binary 0, also a silly thing to do
- *None*—no parity bit is sent

Generally, parity is not used (it is set to none), since for interactive use it is usually obvious when there is data corruption (junk characters are displayed on your screen) and file transfers use a protocol (such as `ZModem` or `Kermit`) that is much better at detecting errors, through the use of CRCs, and in both cases, error correcting modems are usually used.

A PC's memory usually uses parity. It stores 9 bits for each byte (8 bits) to be stored, the ninth bit being an even parity bit for the byte. When each byte of data is retrieved from memory, a hardware circuit checks the parity, and, if it is incorrect, generates a hardware interrupt (which requests the operating system to do something, such as display a message to the user).

Since memory is becoming more reliable and implementing parity is expensive—it requires ⅛ (12.5%) more bits, costing 12.5% more—many newer PCs don't use parity RAM. Therefore memory errors would go undetected (perhaps causing the

PC to hang the once every few years it is predicted memory errors would occur). Macintoshes have used nonparity memory for several years.

Rather than only detecting (some) errors, high-end servers (for which cost is less of a concern, relative to reliability) often use ECC (*Error Correcting Code*) memory, which can detect and correct some errors. The method requires adding several "redundant" bits to each (usually) 32-bits of memory. Typically, single-bit errors can be corrected, and 2- or 3-bit errors can be detected.

Communications between a PC and its keyboard use a form of serial communications (using 1 start bit, 8 data bits, an odd parity bit, plus a stop bit), at about 10,000 bits/s—the keyboard sets the transmission rate (the four-wire interface between a PC and its keyboard has 0 V/+5 V power supplied by the PC and bidirectional clock and data wires). So parity can detect keyboard-to-PC errors too.

See *AT Command Set*, *Checksum*, *CRC*, *ECC*, *FCS*, *MNP*, *RPI*, *UART*, and *V.42*.

Patent

A federally-administered legal protection against others manufacturing and selling your product.

Patents will be granted only if they are:

- *New*: first in the world—though the *Paris Convention Treaty* allows some time for patents filed in one country to be filed in some other countries, and still be considered new
- *Novel*: show inventive ingenuity and not be "obvious to someone skilled in the technology"—they should be thinking "now why didn't I think of that?"
- *Useful*: passes the "utility test"—it has to really work and solve a real problem

Patents can be any of the following:

- *New technologies*: mechanical, electrical, or chemical inventions or discoveries
- *Techniques*: such as manufacturing methods or processes
- *Equipment*: mechanical or electrical products, devices, tools, or apparatus (which may in turn be used to make other products
- *Compositions*: chemical compounds
- An improvement on any of these (90% of patents are improvements to other existing patented inventions)—to use the new patent may require a license from the original patent holder.

Patents do not cover the artistic or aesthetic qualities of an article (though other forms of intellectual property protection may).

A patent is granted only for the *physical embodiment* of an idea (not the idea itself), for example, a description of a product's construction, or a process that produces something tangible or of value.

Patents will not be granted for a scientific principle, idea, abstract theorem, method of doing business, computer program, or medical treatment.

In the U.S. and Canada, a *patent application* must be made within one year of publicizing the patent (though preferably before publicizing it—especially since most other countries require that the patent application be made before any publicity or use anywhere—that is, it must have *absolute novelty*). The U.S. and Canada's one-year grace period enables you to go to a trade show or do some market research before committing the resources to the patent process.

It is up to the owner of a patent to find patent *infringers* and take legal action. Typically, a patent will cost $4,000 to $6,000 (mostly for assistance in preparing the documentation) per product per country. A worldwide patent may cost only $12,000 if only major English-speaking countries need to be covered and the required legal work is small. These costs can escalate rapidly if the patent application requires a great deal of research or refinement. Prosecuting an infringer can cost $250,000. It is worth patenting something only when there is real and lasting business value in having a patent. Devices that can be made in many ways or will be obsolete before the year or two (minimum) required to obtain a patent are not good candidates for patents.

The core of a patent is the *claims* section that describes the uniqueness of the patent.

The purpose of a patent is to both protect the owner and "promote the creation and implementation of technological information, so that all can share in the benefit from the advance in technology and knowledge" (nice chunk of words).

A patent application consists of the following:

- *An abstract*—a brief summary of the contents of the specification.
- *A specification*, which has two parts: a clear and complete description of the invention and its usefulness (this cannot be expanded with *new matter* after the application has been filed), and the *claims*, which set out the *essential features* and define the *boundaries* of patent protection being sought. (Information provided in the patent that is not covered by the claims can be used by anyone immediately, but if the claims are too broad, then the patent will likely be refused for overlapping existing patents.)

    A test of the specification's clarity is that it should enable anyone with average skill in the technology to make or use the invention (after all, that's the deal; you describe the technology for the benefit of others, and the government gives you exclusive use of the technology for 20 years).

- *Drawings* (if the invention can be shown by one; possible exceptions include chemical compositions and processes) showing all features of the invention, as defined by the claims.

As most countries do (except the U.S., though this is expected to change), Canada uses "first to file," rather than "first to invent." But don't file too soon, or you might not yet have all of the important details for a working, useful invention worked out—and you will need to file a second patent (more fees, please).

In the U.S., the Patent Office keeps a patent application secret until the patent is issued or rejected, at which point it becomes public information.

In contrast, the Canadian Patent Office publishes patents 18 months after they are filed, which is most likely before the patent would be awarded. Therefore most people prefer to apply for a U.S. patent before applying for a Canadian patent. This publicizing would make it impossible to get patent protection in countries (many of those other than the U.S. and Canada) that require that the invention not be publicized before filing for their patent protection.

The information contained in patents may be used by anyone if the patent is later rejected (when they get around to examining it).

If the patent is formally *abandoned* before 18 months (in Canada) or before being awarded or rejected, then the information will be kept secret.

In Canada and the U.S., patent protection lasts 20 years from the date of application. (In the U.S. this was, until recently, 17 years from the date of approval.)

While patent protection does not begin until a patent is granted, inventors may use the term "*Patent Pending*" once an application has been filed (even without requesting the patent be examined; this creates up to a 1-year *priority period*). This provides no legal protection, but gives the inventor time to assess the feasibility or marketability of the invention and may discourage potential infringers.

Among other things, examiners check for *prior art*; that is, whether something too similar has already been patented. While a new patent will not be awarded for something that is almost entirely based on one or more previous patents, combining such prior art in a new and novel way can be patentable. There is no requirement that patented products be *marked* "Patented," but it is certainly a good deterrent to potential infringers to let them know that a product is patented.

It is illegal to mark unpatented products as patented.

In addition to the *filing* and *examination fees* that are required to get a patent (not to mention the fees of a *patent agent*, which most inventors choose to use), an annual *maintenance fee* is required. (If you don't pay it, your patent lapses, and anyone can use it as if it were expired.) When a patent expires, anyone can freely make, use, or sell products based on the invention and the information in the patent.

Many standards (such as those for Ethernet and Token Ring) specify the use of patented technologies. Standards-setting organizations permit this only if the patent owner agrees to license the technology to any company requesting it, for a reasonable licensing fee.

The rules for the U.S. and Canadian patent process and protection are somewhat similar (that is, if you can get a U.S. patent, you will likely be able to get a Canadian one as well), except for coverage of life forms (for example, laboratory rats with special features) and computer programs.

To support improvements and next generation products, the U.S. patent system allows *continuation in part*, so that a patent that has already been applied for can be modified without being considered to be new matter.

The *Canadian Patent Act* provides that independent contractors own the patents for their inventions (even when the development work is paid for by the contractee) unless there is a written agreement otherwise. However, the *Integrated Circuit Topography Act* states the opposite (for integrated circuit topographies); the principal owns the work, not the contractor (unless there is a written agreement otherwise).

The *Canadian Patent Office* is part of the CIPO. In the U.S., the *Patent and Trademark Office* administers patents. The following table shows the names for the similar types of intellectual property protection in Canada and the U.S.

Canada	United States
Industrial Design	Design Patent
Patent	Utility Patent

The U.S. Patent and Trademark Office has a Web site at *http://www.uspto.gov*. Some of their patent database can be searched from there.

The Cornell Law School has some U.S. Patent Law information at *http://www.law.cornell.edu/topics/patent.html*.

See *CIPO*, *Intellectual Property Protection*, and *Trade Secret*.

Pathworks

DEC's marketing name for their LAN data communications software.

DEC's implementation of Microsoft's LAN Manager for VMS.

But can also refer to DEC's LAN servers and protocols for VMS on Ethernet (LAST), VMS on Token Ring (DECnet or NetBEUI), Ultrix (DECnet or optional TCP/IP), SCO/UNIX (TCP/IP), DOS (NetBEUI or optional IPX), OS/2 (NetBEUI), and Macintosh. Also supports LAT and OSF's Motif GUI. Optional IPX support is available. Pathworks for DOS can be run out of high memory (DOS 5 or Windows).

See *DEC*, *LAST*, and *VMS*.

PBX
Private Branch Exchange

The telephone switch that is used at a (typically) small to medium-sized company. Has a separate pair of wires to each user's telephone (or possibly more than one pair per telephone if the phone has fancy features, such as an LCD display or a speaker-phone) and to the nearest central office, for each outside trunk.

When you pick up your handset, the dial-tone that you hear is generated by the local PBX. If you dial "9," the PBX selects an outside line for you (connects your extension to an outside trunk that goes to the nearest central office), and you then hear the dial-tone from the C.O.

Sometimes called a Private Automatic Branch Exchange (PABX).

See *C.O.*, *DMS*, and *POTS*.

PC
Personal Computer

A computer that is run by an Intel (or Intel-compatible) processor.

Some characteristics of recent such processors are listed in the following table.

Processor	Speeds (MHz)[a]	Voltage[b]	Internal (L1) Cache		Math Co-processor[e]
			Size (kbytes)[c]	Type[d]	
8080[f]	2, 2.5, 3.0	5.0	0	None	External
8088	4.77, 8, 10	5.0	0	None	External
80286	6, 8, 10, 12	5.0	0	None	External
80386SX	16, 20	5.0	0	None	External
80386DX	16, 20, 25, 33	5.0	0	None	External
Intel 486SX	16, 20, 25, 33	5.0	8	Write-thru	External
Intel 486SX2	25/50, 33/66	5.0	8	Write-thru	External
Intel 486DX	25, 33, 50	5.0	8	Write-thru	Internal
Intel 486SL	25, 33	5.0, 3.3	8	Write-thru	Internal
Intel 486DX2	25/50, 33/66	5.0	8	Write-thru	Internal
Intel DX4	25/75, 33/100, 50/100	3.3	16	Write-back	Internal
Intel Pentium OverDrive (P24T)	25/63, 33/83	5.0	16/16	Write-back	Internal
Intel Pentium	60, 66	5.0	8/8	Write-back	Internal
	50/75, 60/90	3.3, 2.9			
	66/100, 60/120, 66/133	3.3			

(table continued on next page)

| Processor | Speeds (MHz)[a] | Voltage[b] | Internal (L1) Cache | | Math Co-processor[e] |
			Size (kbytes)[c]	Type[d]	
Intel P6	133	2.9	8/8	Write-back	Internal
AMD Am486SX	33, 40	5.0, 3.3	8	Write-thru	External
AMD Am486SX2	25/50	5.0	8	Write-thru	None
	33/66	3.0		Write-back	
AMD Am486SX4	33/100	3.0	8	Write-back	None
AMD Am486DX	33, 40	5.0, 3.3	8	Write-thru	Internal
AMD Am486DX2	25/50, 33/66	5.0	8	Write-thru	Internal
	40/80	3.0	8	Write-back	Internal
AMD Am486DX4	33/100, 40/120	3.0	8 or 16	Write-back	Internal
AMD K5	100	3.3	16/8		Internal
Cyrix Cx486SLC2	25/50	5.0	2	Write-thru	External
Cyrix Cx486DX	33, 50	5.0, 3.3	8	Write-back	Internal
Cyrix Cx486DX2	25/50, 33/66	5.0/3.45	8	Write-back	Internal
Cyrix Cx486DX2	40/80	3.45	8	Write-back	Internal
Cyrix Cx486DX4	33/100	3.45	8	Write-back	Internal
Cyrix M1	50/100	3.3	16		Internal
IBM 486SLC2	25/50, 33/66	5.0, 3.3	16	Write-thru	External
IBM "Blue Light-ning"	25/50, 25/75, 33/66, 33/100	5.0, 3.3	16	Write-thru	External
IBM 486DX2	33/66	3.3/3.45	8	Write-back	Internal
	40/80	3.45			
NexGen Nx586[g]	35/70, 37.5/75, 42/84, 46.5/93	4.0	16/16	Write-back	Optional

[a] The external memory bus speed and internal CPU speed are shown separately ("25/50") for clock–doubled (and tripled, etc.) processors. Processors with memory bus speeds of 50 MHz or faster (for example, all of the Pentiums) run the expansion bus (PCI, etc.) at half the memory bus speed, so a 120 MHz Pentium runs the memory bus at 60 MHz and the expansion bus at 30 MHz.

[b] Recent version of newer processors operate at lower voltages to reduce power consumption (for longer battery life or Energy Star compliance), which reduces heat dissipation (no need for a fan).

[c] Rather than a single *unified* cache, some processors have separate code and data caches (indicated by a "16/8" for example).

[d] Write-back caches store both reads and writes. Write-through caches store only reads, so write performance is slower.

[e] Processors before the 486DX had no built-in math coprocessor.

[f] Being an 8-bit processor, the 8080 could not run DOS (so could not be used in a PC)—it is included for comparison only.

[g] A separate bus to the L2 Cache runs at the full CPU speed.

Typical recent processor speeds are given in the following table.

Processor	Clock Speed (MHz)	>MIPS (Drystones v1.1)	PC Magazine PC Bench 8.0 Processor Score	Relative Speed
80486SX	25		18	1.0
80486DX	25	20		
80486SX	33	27.2	24.5	1.2
80486DX	33		29	1.3
80486DX2	25/50	41	27.7	1.8
80486	50		35	1.9
80486DX2	33/66	53.9	46.7	2.2
DX4	33/100	70.7	64.3	3.5
Pentium	60	100	72.7	4.0
Pentium	66	112	78	4.3
Pentium	60/90	150	102	5.7
Pentium	66/100	166	120.2	6.7
Pentium	60/120			
P6	66/133	250		

A main reason for the PC being so popular (especially as compared to Apple's Macintosh) has been the documentation and standardization of the PC's bus—so *printed circuit boards* (or *cards*) could be added to provide new capabilities. These boards plug into the PC's *bus*. So that the processor can individually address each board, each board must be configured to have unique settings for the items in the table below. (Most boards don't use all of these communication methods, so they don't require all these settings.)

Setting	Typical Settings	Function
DMA Channel	0 through 7	DMA is used for high-speed data transfers between peripherals and memory. See *DMA*.
I/O Address	$02E8_{16}$	Input/output ports are the addresses at which peripherals exchange data with the CPU. See *PIO*.
IRQ	2_{10} through 15_{10}	Interrupts interrupt whatever the CPU is doing so that time-critical information can be transferred when needed. (For example, data from a modem will be read before another character comes in and overwrites the first.) See *IRQ*.

(table continued on next page)

Setting	Typical Settings	Function
Memory Address	$D000_{16}$	Each byte of a PC's 640 kbytes of RAM has a unique memory address. Some peripherals communicate with the PC's CPU by using a block of memory addresses (the memory is actually on the peripheral). PC RAM and other peripherals must not be configured to have memory at the same addresses. See *Shared Memory*.

The original IBM PC had the capability to use a standard color television as a display, and it therefore had to have a 3.579545 MHz oscillator (see *NTSC*). The PC designers decided to put an oscillator of four times this frequency (14.31818 MHz) into the PC, since this frequency could be divided by 4 for the color television signal and by 3 (producing approximately 4.7727267 MHz) to produce a clock signal for the 8088 processor (which had a maximum clock speed of 5 MHz). While this resulted in the processor being run at slightly less (4.5%) than its maximum speed, it was close enough that the cost savings (of not having to use a second oscillator) were apparently considered worth the performance loss.

A hardware counter IC in the PC used the 4.7727267 MHz processor clock signal divided by 4 (which is 1.19318167 MHz) to drive a 16-bit counter, which divided this by 65,536 to produce a hardware interrupt (IRQ 0) at approximately 18.2065 Hz. DOS uses this "tick" to keep track of the time of day (as ticks since midnight) *once the PC has been told what the current time is.*

Since the PC's ticks only enable the PC to track the accumulated time since the PC was powered on, starting with the PC/AT, PCs have had a battery-backed-up *Real-Time Clock* (RTC) IC, which keeps track of the time and date even when the PC's power is off. The RTC is read when the PC is (re)started to set the operating system time. The RTC IC also has 64 bytes of battery-backed-up CMOS RAM (*Complementary-Symmetry Metal-Oxide-Semiconductor Random Access Memory*) to store:

- The time and date (10 bytes)
- RTC control and status (4 bytes)
- System settings (50 bytes), such as the type of diskette drives installed

The PC's BIOS has a program (usually started by pressing Ctrl-Alt-Esc or Ctrl-Alt-Ins) to examine and change these CMOS settings.

The real-time-clock IC uses a 32,768-Hz oscillator, which easily divides to exactly 1 second.

A recent trend is to reduce the cost of providing new PC functions by using the main CPU for functions that used to be off-loaded to smaller processors on other add-in boards, such as those in the following table.

Effort	PC's Resources Used for	Instead of
Class 1 fax modem	Fax image rasterizing	Class 2 fax modem
Controllerless modem	Interpreting the AT command set	Modems with controllers (processors)
DCI and GDI	Video processing	Video adapter
LAN adapter PIO	Replacing DMA	LAN adapters with DMA and bus master DMA.
NSP	Audio processing	Sound boards with dedicated DSP ICs (Digital Signal Processing Integrated Circuits)
PCS	Desktop video conferencing image compression	Video boards with dedicated compression hardware
RPI	Serial data communications error correction and data compression	Modems with processors that handle V.42 and V.42*bis* onboard
USDA	Video memory	Dedicated memory on video adapter

Advanced Micro Devices, Inc. (AMD) and Intel have WWW servers at *http://www.amd.com* and *http://www.intel.com*, respectively.

See *AT, BIOS, Bus, Cache, DCI, DMA, EDO RAM, Energy Star, Fax, iComp, Intel, IRQ, MIPS, NSP, NTSC, Pentium, PnP, PCS (Personal Conferencing Specification), PIO, RPI, RAM, Shadowed BIOS, Shared Memory, SPEC, Superscalar, Tick,* and *USDA.*

PC 95

A designation Microsoft dreamed up to define the minimum requirements for a PC to run Microsoft's Windows 95 operating system:

- 80386 or better CPU
- 4 Mbytes or more RAM
- 640 × 480 display (standard VGA) with 256 colors (or more)
- Dedicated mouse (or other pointing device) port (that is, don't use up a serial port for it) or an integrated pointing device
- One serial port
- One parallel port

See *Operating System, PnP, PC,* and *Windows 95.*

PC Cards

The new name for PCMCIA cards. The organization that defines the standard is still the PCMCIA.

See *PCMCIA*.

PCCA
Portable Computer and Communications Association

A group that is developing extensions for NDIS and ODI so that these interfaces (which previously supported only wired media) can also be used between protocol stacks and hardware that supports wireless transmission.

The same group has also developed an extension to the *AT command set* called SWATS.

See *802.11*, *Mobile IP*, *NDIS*, *ODI*, *SWATS*, and *WinSock*.

PCI
Peripheral Component Interconnect

Intel's *local bus* standard.

Introduced in 1992 (the first version) and 1993 (Release 2.0). Supports up to 16 physical slots—an addressing limitation, which won't be reached because of the electrical limitation of 10 *loads* (which will typically amount to three or four plug-in PCI cards) residing on each PCI bus. PCs can have two or more PCI buses, so there can be six or more PCI cards per PC.

32- and 64-bit-wide bus implementations are defined. 64-bit support uses an additional in-line connector (similar to the AT bus's extra connector).

32- and 64-bit cards can be installed in 64- and 32-bit slots (and the other way around too—the cards and buses detect this and work properly). When a 64-bit card is installed in a 32-bit slot, the extra pins just overhang, without plugging into anything.

Implementations have a separate (from the processor's) clock, running at D.C. to 33 MHz (though usually at 33 MHz). Slowing the bus's clock speed is needed to reduce PC power consumption when the PC is not being used.

Since the bus is *multiplexed* (the same pins carry address and data), two *bus cycles* (one to send the address, the next to send the data) are required per 32- or 64-bit transfer.

A *burst mode* is defined for reads and writes (though the 486 supports only read bursts), which allows any number of data cycles to follow a single address cycle.

A 32-bit, 33 MHz PCI bus implementation would have a nonburst peak transfer rate of 66 Mbytes/s and a burst peak transfer rate of up to 132 Mbytes/s. 32-bit

PCI has a typical sustained burst transfer rate of 80 Mbytes/s—enough to handle 24-bit color at 30 frames per second (full-color, full-motion video).

Supports bus mastering DMA, though some PCI implementations may not support bus mastering DMA for all PCI slots. The CPU can run concurrently with bus mastering peripherals.

Is called a *mezzanine* (or *intermediate*) bus, since it is not the processor's bus. This is good, since processor buses tend to match (and be limited to) that particular processor. (Witness the fast decline of VL-bus when the 486 became old news.)

ISA, EISA, and MCA buses can be driven by a PCI (using a *bridge* chip set), so non-PCI peripherals can be used in the same PC.   ⌐ not defined in this book

Since PCI is not processor-specific (VL-bus is 486-specific), it can be used for other processors, such as DEC's Alpha and the PowerPC (so Macintoshes can use PCI peripherals).

PCI is the first bus to support both 3.3- and 5-V cards. Keys in the connector ensure that the (single-voltage and non-interchangeable) cards are not plugged into the wrong voltage slot (smokers!).

Dual-voltage cards and slots can be made, which automatically try 3.3-V operation first and then try 5-V if that is not supported.

Competes with (but is generally faster than and better suited to processors better than the 486) VESA's VL-bus.

PCI boards support:

- Automatic configuration (they don't require manual assignment of BIOS extension addresses)
- Parity checking of the data and address bus signals
- *Scatter/gather DMA* (up to four 4-kbyte blocks of data that are scattered because of virtual memory management schemes can be transferred with a single DMA operation)

PCI cards have from 64 to 256 bytes of configuration memory:

- 16 bits are reserved for a vendor identification code (each vendor gets a unique number)
- 16 bits are reserved for a device identification (vendors assign a unique number to each of their products)
- The remainder of the first 64 bytes are reserved for future use

The rest of the memory is available for vendor-specific use.

Competes with EISA, but PCI:

- Has a much faster transfer rate (both providing faster operation and leaving more bus time for other peripherals)
- Has lower-cost cards (for example, because PCI is fast enough to transfer data from a LAN—and LAN adapter—to a PC's memory at full LAN speed, less buffer memory is needed on the LAN adapter)
- Supports *Plug and Play*
- Is faster to install (EISA's irritatingly slow configuration procedure is not needed)

Future PCI enhancements will include 66 MHz operation. The PCI standard is developed by the PCI Special Interest Group.

See *Alpha AXP*, *Bus*, *Bus Master DMA*, *DMA*, *Energy Star*, *Local Bus*, *PnP*, *PowerPC*, *Video*, and *VL-Bus*.

PCL
Printer Command Language

Hewlett-Packard's language for controlling their printers (though many competitor's printers are compatible with it).

Competes with Adobe's PostScript *Page Description Language* (in the sense that the commands sent to a printer are usually one or the other—but PostScript is a more powerful language).

PCL commands are *escape sequences* (a few characters starting with the ASCII escape character—which is $1B_{16}$ or 27_{10}). For example, PCL5 includes commands for specifying the following:

- Number of copies, page size, source paper tray, and output bin
- Print resolution
- Page margin and orientation
- Cursor positioning
- Font, line spacing, character spacing and height, stroke weight
- Downloadable font and pattern data
- Rectangle draw and fill commands
- Switch to HP-GL/2 mode (HP Graphics Language, originally developed for HP plotters, which are vector-oriented—they draw with pens)

PCL has evolved over time, and each new version supports all previous features, plus the new features, as shown in the following table.

PCL Version	Used for	Example New Features
1		Basic printing and spacing functions, suitable for single-user printers
2		Adds multiuser printing tools
3		Adds high-quality office printing support
4	LaserJet Series II	Page formatting functions
5	LaserJet III and 4	Scalable fonts and HP-GL/2 support
5e[a]	LaserJet 4L	Power-down modes

[a] The "e" is for "enhanced."

See *ASCII*, *HP*, *PostScript Page Description Language*, and *TrueType*.

PCM
Pulse Code Modulation

A method of digitizing audio (turning it into those ones and zeros that computers love so much).

Periodically (8,000 times a second for telephone systems, 44,100 times a second per right and left channel for audio CDs) samples the input and produces (for example) an 8-bit (for telephone systems) or 16-bit (for audio CDs) value representing the amplitude of the audio input at that instant in time.

Since digitizing assigns a specific (binary) number for any input amplitude, and only a given number of amplitudes are available (for example, 256 for 8-bit digitizing), chances are that the assigned number will be a little bit too high or a little bit too low compared to the actual input. This error is called *quantization error* and produces *quantization noise* at the output.

Since better accuracy is required for lower signal levels (since the quantization error is more significant compared to the signal), digitization values are assigned closer together for lower signal levels. This type of nonlinear *Analog-to-Digital converter* (or A/D) is called a CODEC (*Coder/Decoder*).

There are two such nonlinearities standardized:

- *μ-law* (pronounced "moo law" or "mew law"), used in North America, Japan, and South Korea
- *A-law*, used in the rest of the world

Converters are therefore required to interconnect these two types of PCM-digitized voice channels.

The digitized audio can be carried by ISDN B channels or E1 or T1 channels.

Analog signals passing through one or more PCM digitizations will have some level of *nonlinear signal distortion*, which may affect the maximum data rate that modems using the channel can achieve.

See *ADPCM, CD-ROM, CODEC, E1, ISDN, MP-MLQ, Multimedia,* and *T1.*

PCMCIA
Personal Computer Memory Card International Association

The name of the group that produced the specification for the credit card–sized plug-in boards (initially) for laptop computers.

Initially, the cards were called that too, but it was decided that nonpronounceable six-letter acronyms just don't cut it. So the cards are now called *PC cards* (which is an ambiguous but nonintimidating name).

The PC (that is, *Personal Computer,* not *Printed Circuit*) cards are 85.6 mm deep × 54 mm wide and have a 68-pin connector (two rows of 34 pins on 1-mm centers).

The predecessor cards were developed by the *Japan Electronics Industry Development Association* (JEIDA) to store keyboard parameter sets for music synthesizers and sampling keyboards and were therefore only memory cards.

Several different height PC cards are defined, as shown in the table below.

Type	Height (mm)	Common Use
I	3.3	Memory (RAM or Flash RAM)
II	5	LAN adapters and modems
III	10.5	Hard disks
IV[a]	15.5	Hard disks

[a] Not standardized

Although JEIDA had specified a Type IV card slot, PCMCIA rejected it as part of the PCMCIA standard, and only a few manufacturers (for example, Toshiba) use this type of slot.

Thinner cards can be plugged into thicker slots (for example, a Type II slot will accept a Type I or Type II card).

The cards can provide up to 64 Mbytes of memory or be I/O (Input/Output)- or file-transfer-oriented devices.

The interface supports only one interrupt (which can be a limitation for multiple-function cards, such as LAN adapters and modems).

There are several versions of the specification:

Version 1.0 (the standard was released in 1989, first products appeared in 1990) of the standard defined only Type I cards and did not define I/O capability or software drivers (as the cards only had some form of memory and so did not need drivers).

Version 2.0 defined I/O but still no software drivers (vendors provided proprietary drivers with their cards). The interface to the PC is a 16-bit data path with a bus speed of 6 MHz.

Version 2.1 finally provided a good level of standardization and features. For example, v2.1 PCMCIA cards provide the following:

- *Host Independence*—they work in any type of computer with a PCMCIA slot
- *Plug and Play*—no manual configuration is required
- *Hot Swapping*—no need to power off or reboot the computer (the connector pins at the outside edges are the power pins and are longer than the rest—ensuring that the card gets power before data, so it can power up in an orderly way)
- *Execution in Place* (XIP)—programs run directly from the ROM in the PCMCIA card, so there is no need to transfer the memory contents to the computer's RAM first

Also, v2.1 defined:

- Software drivers called *card services*, which is a higher-level Application Program Interface (API)
- *Socket services*, which is a BIOS-level interface which has standard calls regardless of how a vendor implements the function

The card services can be either:

- Separate drivers, which are loaded by `config.sys` (for MS-DOS and OS/2 v2.1)
- Built in to newer operating systems, such as OS/2 Warp version 3 and Windows 95, as part of their plug and play support

These standard software interfaces have made the PCMCIA much simpler and more useful.

The next version of the standard ("3.0") is called the *PC Card Standard* (that is, it is not called PCMCIA anymore—no one liked that abbreviation), *February 1995 Release* (in their wisdom, they stopped using version numbers) and refers to the cards as *PC cards*.

This PC Card Standard now includes specifications for the following:

- 32-bit bus mastering DMA support (called *CardBus*) at a bus speed of 20 to 33 MHz (thereby offering performance similar to EISA or PCI)
- Multifunction adapters (for example, a combination Ethernet/Modem adapter)
- 3.3-V (instead of 5-V) operation (this reduces the power requirements— important for battery-operated laptop PCs)

Each card has a *Card Information Structure* (CIS), which specifies the card's:

- Manufacturer and model number
- Voltage and current requirements
- I/O configuration information (for example)

It is a linked-list (resident in the *attribute memory* of the card) of information stored in *tuples*, which are three-part data structures (information type, link to next tuple, and information).

The standard does not define the external connectors for user equipment (such as a cable to a telephone line), only the interface to the PC.

See *Bus Master DMA*, *DMA*, *EISA*, *IRQ*, *PCI*, and *PnP*.

PCS
Personal Communications Service

The name for a proposed new wireless voice and data communications system.

Lower transmit power (than standard AMPS cellular telephones) is to be used, so the telephones can be smaller and lower-cost (since smaller batteries and less-powerful components are needed).

Also, the intent is to provide one phone number per person, which would be used for home (personal), office (business), paging, and mobile communications. Is supposed to offer a "follow-me" service, in which the one phone number always finds you—regardless of where you are.

A *personal agent* (software) would be programmed to (for example) pass business calls home only if they were urgent and to forward them to your voice mail if not.

140 MHz (120 MHz for use, 20 MHz for research and expansion) in the 2-GHz band has been reserved in North America (specifically 1,850 to 1,910 MHz for use, 1,910 to 1,930 MHz reserved, and 1,930 to 1,990 MHz for use).

The U.S. has split this 120 MHz into three 30-MHz blocks (called Blocks A, B, and C) plus three 10 MHz blocks (called Blocks D, E, and F).

Each block is then auctioned off (by the FCC) for each geographic area.

Other services are already using these frequencies (mostly phone company terrestrial microwave links—the huge four-legged towers offering long-distance telephone service for thousands of simultaneous conversations). In Canada alone, there are 1,400 such transmitters, which must be relocated to other frequencies before PCS can be offered in those areas.

The similar effort in Canada is called PCTS, and that in Japan is called PHS (*Personal Handiphone Service*).

See *AMPS*, *CT2*, *DECT*, *FCC*, and *PCTS*.

PCS
Personal Conferencing Specification

A cross-platform (Windows, OS/2, Macintosh, and UNIX) desktop (that is, to the PC, not a conference room) conferencing communications standard intended to facilitate global workgroups sharing video, voice, text, and graphics over LANs, ISDN, and analog phone lines.

Version 1.0 (released in December 1994) supports mixed audio (digitized voice), video (from cameras), and document (shared PC monitor screens, for example, showing a spreadsheet in real-time) conferencing over LANs and over ISDN and switched 56 WANs.

Version 2.0 is to add specifications for multimedia (LANs only), network administration, LAN/WAN gateways, and video conferencing over analog phone lines.

Builds on Microsoft's TAPI and Novell's TSAPI.

Promoted by Intel. Some would say that Intel is big on video technology because it requires faster processors (likely from Intel—what a surprise!).

Competes with H.320 (though H.320 initially defines only WAN-connected users) and T.120 (for document conferencing).

Future versions will support H.320.

See *H.320*, *ISDN*, *NSP*, *PC*, *PCWG*, *T.120*, *TAPI*, and *TSAPI*.

PCTS
Public Cordless Telephone Service

The name for the Canadian digital cordless telephone service for both private (residential and business) and public (pay a *common carrier* for air time) use.

Very low power (10 mW) results in very small cells. Private base stations will provide service for private use, and public base stations will communicate with the same handsets when they are in serviced public areas, such as shopping malls.

The digital technology offers many advantages, including noise-free and secure communications, calling number identification, and numeric paging. Many varieties of cordless services are defined, as shown in the following table.

Name	Capability	Comments
CT1	Standard residential-type analog cordless phones. Use separate frequencies for transmit and receive. Only 10 frequency pairs are assigned in North America, so interference with neighbors is common. Maximum range is about 50 m.	Very noisy service because of analog technology
CT2	Uses frequency division multiple access—each channel uses a 100-kHz bandwidth, out of a total bandwidth of 4 MHz. Speech is digitized at 32 kbits/s, and "full-duplex" conversations are supported over a single channel using *time division duplexing* (also called "*ping-ponging*," since the direction of transmission is changed 500 times per second). There is no location tracking, so mobiles cannot receive calls, only generate them.	Developed for use in Britain; is currently also in use in parts of Asia and Europe
CT2Plus	CT2 with the addition of common-channel signaling for faster call delivery, automatic location registration to provide both incoming and outgoing service, and up to 40 MHz of total bandwidth for greater call-handling capacity. Cell sizes are from 30 m to 200 m in diameter and so are called *pico-cells*—these can be linked to form *zones*, which support handoffs between pico-cells for uninterrupted service while moving. CT2Plus systems can operate in CT2 environments.	The Class 2 technology has been approved for use in Canada. The 944 to 948.5 MHz band has been allocated. This provides 40 full-duplex 100-kHz speech channels and 60 signaling channels. 948.5 to 952 MHz is being held for possible future allocation.
CT3	Similar to DECT	Developed by L.M. Ericsson for high-capacity wireless-handset PBXs
DECT	Digital European Cordless Telecommunication standard was created by the Council of European PTTs for both public and private use. Uses *time division multiple access* which is more efficient than FDMA (*Frequency Division Multiple Access*, where the frequencies available are divided among the simultaneous users). Uses the 1.88 to 1.90 GHz band and supports up to 10 times more traffic in this 20 MHz than CT2Plus handles in 8 MHz.	

While CT2Plus (30 MHz in the 944-MHz band) was selected by Canada, the U.S. later selected the "2-GHz band" (the frequencies are actually just above 1.9 GHz), and Canada realized that to get economies of scale in manufacturing equipment and to support roaming, the Canadian PCTS service had to be compatible with the U.S. service. Therefore the Canadian public effort is on hold (though Northern Telecom still uses CT2Plus for its office cordless telephone service, which they call Companion) until the U.S. determines how PCS will be implemented.

One difference from cellular is that all handsets will work with all base stations—whichever service provider's is closest. In cellular, your handset communicates only with base stations from your service provider (either the local wire-line or the non-wire-line carrier).

Several technologies are being evaluated, including CDMA, PCS 1900, and PACS.

The equivalent U.S. service is called PCS.

See *AMPS*, *Carrier*, *GSM*, and *PCS* (*Personal Communications Service*).

PCWG
Personal Conferencing Work Group

A group promoted by Intel (and consisting of over 150 vendors) to develop a desktop video conferencing standard called PCS.

See *PCS* (*Personal Conferencing Specification*).

PDA
Personal Digital Assistant

A small, hand-held, battery-operated, microprocessor-based device that is expected to do things such as:

- Store telephone numbers, addresses, and reminders
- Send and receive email and faxes (wirelessly)
- Receive pages (just like an alphanumeric pager)
- Recognize handwriting

See *PowerPC*.

PEL
Picture Element

The term used for *pixel* by many IBM people and in fax documentation.

See *Fax* and *Pixel*.

Pentium

Intel's name for their 273-pinned, *superscalar* (it can execute more than one instruction per clock cycle—about two per clock cycle to be specific) successor to their 486 processor.

Was not called "586" because Intel found out (the hard way) that numbers cannot be trademarked.

Pentiums have the following:

- 64-bit data bus, though internal registers and the address bus are both 32 bits wide
- A built-in floating-point unit
- Separate (nonunified) 8-kbyte (each) write-back data and instruction caches
- A programmable clock generator, which supports internal-to-external frequency ratios such as 3:1, 2.5:1, 2:1, 1.5:1, and 1:1

Initial versions (called P5):

- Run at 60 and 66 MHz (some say that the 60-MHz versions were simply 66-MHz chips that couldn't run at full speed)
- Have no clock doubling
- Use 5 volts

The standard desktop PC 90- and 100-MHz versions (called the P54C):

- Run at 60 and 66 MHz externally (therefore using a clock multiplier of 1.5)
- Use 3.3 volts (rather than the 60-MHz Pentium's 5 volts)—therefore using about ¼ of the power of the 60-MHz Pentiums

The Pentium version for the 237- or 238-pin *OverDrive* socket of 25- and 33-MHz 486 systems is called the P24T. Such upgraded 486 Pentiums:

- Are slower than same-clock-speed native Pentium systems because of the narrower bus (486 systems have only a 32-bit external data bus)
- May not support other Pentium features such as *burst-mode* reads and writes (depends on the existing PC's bus)
- Have a nifty built-in fan, and you run a TSR that monitors the fan's speed. If the fan doesn't run fast enough or the chip detects a heat problem, then a message pops up, and the CPU is slowed to the 25- or 33-MHz system clock speed. A slower clock speed dissipates less heat, since most heat is generated when the clock signal changes state—from high to low or from low to high (funny things are everywhere).
- Almost triples the processing power of a 25-MHz 486 and almost doubles the processing power of a clock-doubled 486DX2/50. Uses a 2.5:1 internal-to-external clock speed.

A 75-MHz version (which runs at 50 MHz externally) uses Intel's SL technology, which enables the processor to be stopped when it is not needed, to save power. The actual integrated circuit die (the unencapsulated chip, which is directly bonded to a portable PC's printed circuit board) weighs less than 1 gram.

Pentium support for *dual processing* (two Pentium processors sharing system RAM and *Level 2* cache) requires adding a P54CM Pentium to a P54C-based system. The P54CM is identical to the P54C but has a pin that ensures that the system starts in single-processor mode, letting the operating system enable the second processor when it is ready.

Both the 75- and 90-MHz versions support a *Voltage Reduction Technology* (VRT) that provides a 3.3-V (which is somewhat of a standard voltage) external interface (to the CPU's input and output pins) while operating the innards of the CPU at 2.9 V. This substantially reduces the power required (important for battery-operated portable PCs), and the heat dissipation (reducing or eliminating the need for cooling fans (an important reliability, noise, and power consideration).

Often referred to as P*xxx*, where *xxx* is the internal clock speed—for example, a P100 would be a 33-MHz (externally)/100-MHz (internally) Pentium processor.

See *Branch Prediction*, *Cache*, *EDO RAM*, *iComp*, *OverDrive*, *P6*, *PC*, *SMP*, *Superscalar*, and *Trademark*.

Pentium Pro   See **P6.**

PEP
Packet Ensemble Protocol

A previously popular (especially in the UNIX community) proprietary high-speed (23,000 bits/s, half-duplex) modulation method used by dial-up modems from Telebit Corporation.

Obsolete now that standard high-speed modem modulation methods are available (such as V.32*bis* and V.34).

See *Modem* and *V.8* through *V.34*.

Peripheral Component Interconnect   See **PCI.**

Perl
Practical Extraction and Report Language

A scripting language that is often used under UNIX.

It provides access to all operating system calls but is interpreted (not compiled), so it is faster to code and easier to debug than writing in C (for example) but runs more slowly (this is usually not a concern for the type of work for which scripts are usually used).

See *Tcl/Tk*, and *UNIX*.

Personal Communications Service   See **PCS.**

Personal Computer   See **PC.**

Personal Computer Memory Card International Association   See **PCMCIA.**

Personal Conferencing Specification   See **PCS.**

Personal Conferencing Work Group   See **PCWG.**

Personal Digital Assistant   See **PDA.**

Phigs
Programmers' Hierarchical Graphics Standard

An ANSI three-dimensional graphics description and manipulation standard that is well suited to hierarchical structures (something made up of parts, each of which is made up of other parts). Each level of detail can be described separately.

PGP
Pretty Good Privacy

A freeware, *public-key* authentication and encryption method based on the *IDEA single-key* and RSA public-key encryption algorithms.

Well suited to electronic-mail communications (email), *Electronic Data Interchange* (EDI), and *Electronic Funds Transfer* (EFT). It does not require the secure exchange of encryption keys (even initially), yet messages that are exchanged will be authenticated (so both the sender and receiver can be assured that the message was not changed) and encrypted (so only the intended receiver can read the message), and the receiver can be assured that the sender really did send the message. Neat, huh?

Has other features too, such as:

- Key management and distribution
- Data compression (using an algorithm compatible with `pkzip`)

Here is how the method works:

- Each sender and receiver needs a copy of the PGP software. Versions for PCs (DOS, Windows, and OS/2), Macintoshes, VAXes, Amigas, and most UNIX workstations are available.

- Using the software, each user generates a pair of long, binary numbers (each up to 1,024 bits); one is the public key, and the other is the *private* (or *secret*) key. The numbers are stored in a file called a *key ring*, but to distribute the public key, it can be written to an (optionally) ASCII file (so that the keys can be sent through email systems that cannot handle binary files).

  The public key file includes the owner's name (and usually email address) and can be viewed with the PGP software. The public key file (when typed directly to your screen) with only one entry might look like this:

  ```
  -----BEGIN PGP PUBLIC KEY BLOCK-----
  Version: 2.6.2i
  iQCVAwUAL6KYxbCfd7bM70R9AQFfrgP/ZnxreHTVXc
  zO69bJav3FGjfTiVxGEOqbE4EgbYvKgfc60=
  =Qmmk
  -----END PGP PUBLIC KEY BLOCK-----
  ```

  There—now you can say you've seen a key.

  The secret key is kept secret. You don't give it to anyone. You keep it on your own key ring file. In fact, it is encrypted before you store it in your own key ring file (in case anyone snoops through your files or steals your computer).

- Everyone who wants to exchange messages sends a copy of their public key to everyone else who may want to exchange messages with them. This exchange can be done by diskette, by email, or using Internet-accessible *public keyservers*. There is no need to keep your public key secret, since all it is good for is encrypting messages (that only you can decrypt—because only you have the secret key) and authenticating messages from you. It is of no help in attempting to decrypt messages from you.

- There are now two ways to use the PGP software to send messages:

  - *Authentication* (so that the receiver can be sure the message was from you and that it has not been tampered with). Using your secret key, PGP can be used to encrypt your message. While everyone can decrypt the message (using their copy of your public key), they can be sure it was sent by you (since your public key is the only way to decrypt your message, they know that that message could only have been encrypted by using your secret key—and only you have your secret key). This provides authentication (a "digital signature"), nonrepudiation (it *had* to be from you, and you can't deny that you sent it—unless you let someone else have your secret key), and assurance that the message was not tampered with (nobody changed it).

  - *Encryption* (so that only the intended recipient can read the message). Using the intended recipient's public key, you can encrypt your message so that only the intended recipient can read the message (only the recipient's secret key can decrypt it). This provides encryption so that no one else can read your message.

One, the other, or both of these can be used for every message—depending on what you want: authentication, encryption, or both.

That is basically the story, but here are some implementation notes that show why things need to be just a little bit more complicated. (Isn't software always like that?)

- The secret key is an impossible-to-remember (up to) 1,024-bit number. Even if it is coded into ASCII, it will still be impossible to remember. (Could you remember the public key shown above?) How do you keep a copy of something that is too long to be remembered and too secret to be written down or stored on a computer? What happens is the following:

  - PGP prompts you for a *pass phrase* (as opposed to a pass*word*), that is, for *many* words (including punctuation and numbers), perhaps a short meaningless sentence that you can remember and not write down anywhere.

  - The pass phrase is used in a single key encryption of the secret key, and only the encrypted secret key is stored on your key ring.

  - When the secret key is needed (to decrypt a received message, for example), PGP prompts you for your pass phrase, uses it to decrypt your secret key, and then uses the secret key to decrypt the received message.

- The RSA public key encryption method runs too slowly to be used to encrypt or decrypt messages longer than a few words. To encrypt a message using the public key, here is what actually happens:

  - For each message to be sent, the PGP software creates a random one-time 128-bit-long number called a *session key* (which has nothing to do with the RSA public and secret keys discussed already). This session key is used to encrypt the message, using the IDEA single key algorithm (which encrypts messages 4,000 times faster than the RSA public key method). That is, your message is actually encrypted by using a conventional single key algorithm, *not* RSA.

  - The public key actually is used only to RSA-encrypt the one-time session key (since this session key is only 128 bits, it RSA-encrypts fast enough).

  - The IDEA-encrypted message is sent to the recipient, along with the RSA public-key-encrypted one-time session key.

  - The receiver uses its RSA secret key to RSA-decrypt the session key, which is then used to IDEA-decrypt the message.

The PGP software does all this stuff for you, and users don't normally know (or care) that their messages are not actually encrypted by using RSA.

That is, because it runs so much faster, conventional single key encryption is used for the actual message. The RSA public key encryption is used only to get the conventional single key securely to the other end.

- For authentication, using the RSA secret key to encrypt a message would take too long (as above, the RSA algorithm runs too slowly) and would require the receiver to have the PGP software to decrypt the message, even if the receiver doesn't happen to need authentication.

Therefore the following is what is actually done to digitally sign a message (that is, for authentication):

  - A hashing algorithm (currently one called MD5, from RSA Data Security, the same company that developed the RSA algorithm itself) is used to produce a 128-bit *message digest* of the message that requires authentication.

  - The MD5 hashing algorithm is designed so that if the message is changed in any way, the message digest will also change (and it would be extremely difficult to find a way to change the message while still producing the same message digest).

  - The message sender's RSA secret key is used to RSA-encrypt the message digest, which is then converted to ASCII and called a *PGP signature*. This "digital signature" is placed at the end of the *plaintext* (unencrypted) message that requires authentication. For example:

    ```
    -----BEGIN PGP SIGNED MESSAGE-----

    This is the plaintext ASCII message we want to
    ensure is authentic.

    -----BEGIN PGP SIGNATURE-----
    Version: 2.6.2
    iQCVRonqMX0U1eysqYqjcUtm0rvbrXoYUy8a9vJzj4
    WuyfGtoLVxsfTjNNTrY0810SXx/yOMYtBW7mq+zNmq
    EykGFZTdfsVKFEyFw6AJ//BAh+LQNb01Xo=
    =aW2m

    -----END PGP SIGNATURE-----
    ```

  - In addition, if desired, the message can now be encrypted by using the intended receiver's public key (this ensures that no one else can read the message). The recipient will then decrypt the received message, using his or her secret key, with the comfort of knowing that no one else has been able to read it.

  - If it was decided not to encrypt the message, then all recipients of the message can simply read the actual plaintext message (which will be above the line ---BEGIN PGP SIGNATURE---).

  - If desired, any recipient of the message can authenticate it, using the PGP software. The software will prompt for the sender's public key, which will be used to decrypt the received message digest, and compare this with a message digest calculated from the received plaintext message.

- If you can't trust the method through which you received someone's public key (for example, you did not get it directly from a trusted keyserver), you might want to verify that your copy of someone's public key is authentic. Use the PGP software to generate a *key digest*—a shorter (16-byte), hashed version of a public key—and phone the key's owner and compare key digests (reading the ASCII hex digits to each other).

PGP was designed, and the first version written (in 1991), by Philip Zimmermann, a Colorado-based consultant who for a while was in big heckers with the U.S. government, which claimed he might have exported munitions (in this case, the encryption algorithms embedded in the PGP software, which someone else posted on some bulletin board systems and eventually were posted on Internet-accessible computers).

For personal, noncommercial use, the software (source code, documentation, and compiled executables) are freeware, and the primary source is the Massachusetts Institute of Technology's ftp site `net-dist.mit.edu`, in the `/pub/`PGP subdirectory.

For PCs the file has a name like `p262i.zip`, which means version 2.6.2.i, where the "i" means *international version*. The only difference between this and the U.S. noninternational version is that some parts of the international version use code that may be patented in the United States, so the U.S. version was written with the same functionality but avoids infringing the patent.

For commercial or government use in Canada or the U.S., a version (which is completely compatible with the freeware version) is available from ViaCrypt in Phoenix, Arizona (*viacrypt@acm.org*).

More information is at *http://web.mit.edu/network/pgp.html* and *http://www.mantis.co.uk/pgp/pgp.html*.

See *Authentication*, *DES*, *EDI*, *Encryption*, *IDEA*, and *RSA*.

Phase-Alternation Line   See **PAL.**

Physical Unit   See **PU.**

Picture Element · See **PEL and Pixel.**

PIM
Protocol-Independent Multicast

A router-to-router protocol that supports multicast traffic over existing unicast routing protocols, such as IGRP, IS-IS, OSPF, and RIP.

Two modes have been defined:

- Dense-mode PIM:
  - Intended for networks in which most LANs need to receive the multicast (such as LAN TV and corporate and financial information broadcasts).
  - Uses *reverse-path forwarding*, in which the traffic is initially *flooded* (sent to) all router interfaces (except the one on which it arrived). Downstream routers that do not need a traffic feed (either because they have no receivers on their interfaces or because they are already receiving the feed from another port) reply with a *prune* message, asking to be removed from the forwarding list (*tree*).
- Sparse-mode PIM:
  - Intended for networks in which several different multicasts (each going to a small number of receivers) are typically in progress simultaneously (such as desktop video conferencing and *collaborative computing*).
  - Senders and receivers first *register* with a single router, which is designated the *rendezvous point*.
  - Traffic is sent by the sender to the rendezvous point, which then forwards it to the registered receivers.
  - As intermediate routers see the source and destination of the multicast traffic (it is unlikely that the best path from source to destination goes through the rendezvous point), they optimize the paths so that the traffic takes a more direct route (likely bypassing the rendezvous point).
  - Traffic is still sent to the rendezvous point, in anticipation of new receivers registering.

Supported by Cisco.

See *IGRP*, *IP Multicast*, *IS-IS*, *OSPF*, and *RIP*.

Ping
Packet Internet Groper

A TCP/IP diagnostic program that sends one or a series of *ICMP* (*Internet Control Message Protocol*) `echo` packets to a user-specified IP address. The echo packet requests the receiver to reply with an `echo reply` packet. The `ping` program typically measures and displays the round-trip time and percentage of returned packets.

Very useful to confirm:

- Network connectivity (whether the address is considered valid)
- That the destination host is operational

- Network loading and speed (how long it takes the replies to return)
- Network errors (percentage of packets that are lost)

Good `ping` utilities will let the user specify the size of the `ping` packets, number sent, time to wait between each packet, and time to wait for a reply (before giving up and sending the next) and will display the minimum, average, and maximum response times and the number (and preferably percentage) of responses not received (presumably because the outgoing `ping` or the corresponding response was lost by the network or the destination host).

Like other acronyms that are memorable, meaningful, and pronounceable ("PCM-CIA"—not!), this one was likely made up after the term was in common use. The idea is that you are "bouncing a packet off of some computer" and listening for (and timing) its return—just like radar and sonar (which stand for *Radio Detecting and Ranging* and *Sound Navigation and Ranging*).

See *ICMP*, *IP*, *PCMCIA*, *SPOOL*, and *UDP*.

Pink

A new object-oriented operating system that is being developed by Taligent.

See *Taligent*.

PIO
Programmed Input/Output

A (usually) slower-response-time (but lower-cost and lower-CPU-overhead) method of transferring data from, or to, a peripheral (such as a disk drive controller or LAN adapter).

The PC's CPU does an input or output operation for each byte or word of data either:

- After the CPU has determined that data are available, by polling (checking periodically) the hardware to determine its status
- During a hardware interrupt (which was triggered by the availability of data)

Since the CPU must perform several instructions (many bus accesses) for each transfer, this method is usually slower than the *shared memory*, *DMA*, or *bus master DMA* methods.

An advantage is that neither a DMA channel nor upper memory space is required (maybe no interrupt either). This simplifies installation and reduces conflicts with other peripherals. Also, PIO is the only method supported by the BIOS routines (which are also called Int 13, as these routines are accessed by using a call to software interrupt 13_{16}) built in to PCs. For a PC to use DMA, *drivers* (which are typically DOS TSRs or Windows VxDs) must be loaded (which is a headache).

First introduced with their 3C509, 3Com uses a very fast implementation of PIO (which they call *parallel tasking*—the data are transferred to the PC while the Ethernet frame is being received). Since the Ethernet bytes arrive (Ethernet cable to Ethernet adapter) slower than the PIO transfers data (Ethernet adapter to PC memory), this implementation of PIO is no slower than DMA—and can be faster, since the transfer starts when the Ethernet frame begins to arrive, not after it has completely arrived (as a DMA transfer would typically require).

See *BIOS*, *Bus*, *Bus Master DMA*, *DMA*, *E-IDE*, *IDE*, *IRQ*, *PC*, *PIO*, and *Shared Memory*.

Pixel
Picture Element

The smallest unit of resolution, usually measured separately for horizontal (the number of dots across) and vertical (the number of rows).

For monochrome display or output, a pixel requires 1 bit of storage. For color displays, a pixel will represent many bits of storage. For example, 24-bit color (8 bits each for red, green, and blue) requires 3 bytes of storage.

Also called *pel* (especially by IBM people and in fax specifications).

See *Fax*, *Interlaced*, and *Video*.

Plain Ordinary Telephone Service   See **POTS**.

PMFJI
Pardon Me for Jutting in

A common email abbreviation, used by a person adding a message to an ongoing conversation (that is, a series of messages on a particular topic, which is called a *thread*).

PnP
Plug and Play

An effort initiated by Microsoft (first supported in Windows 95) and Intel to make adding adapter boards to PCs simpler.

The goal is that once a new adapter board is plugged in and the PC is powered on (or a notebook computer is plugged into its docking station or a wireless PC comes into range of its network), the boards would be automatically configured (DMA channel, interrupt, memory, and I/O port addresses are all set to valid, unique values)—no need to manually set jumpers or switches on the boards—and drivers would be automatically loaded (no need to manually type commands into `config.sys` or `autoexec.bat`).

Plug and Play device drivers support *dynamic reconfiguration*, so they can be loaded and unloaded while a system is running. Therefore a Plug and Play laptop PC could be removed from, or inserted into, a docking station, and PCMCIA boards can be inserted and removed without powering down the system.

On power-up, a *configuration manager* calls software components called *enumerators* (one for each type of bus, for example, ISA, PCI, and PCMCIA) to identify the installed devices (*enumeration*).

Software called *resource arbitrators* then determine a nonconflicting configuration of resources, which is then sent to each device and device driver, which configure themselves accordingly. This configuration information can be stored so that the enumeration step can be skipped next boot time.

For new boards (so that there is a better chance that systems can be configured with no conflicts), Microsoft strongly recommends that they can be automatically set to any of:

- Eight IRQ lines
- Three DMA channels
- Eight I/O port base addresses
- Eight memory addresses

To get completely automatic operation, support must be built in to the adapter boards, PC's BIOS, and operating system.

For systems that don't have all of this support:

- For existing (non–Plug and Play) ISA boards, and using a Configuration Utility, a Plug and Play PC will provide *plug and tell* capability to specify how the board should be manually configured.
- For existing operating systems (DOS and Windows 3.1), a PnP utility (ISA configuration utility—`icu`) is used to gather information from PnP boards, keep track of available resources, and manually reserve resources for non-PnP boards.
- For existing PCs (with no PnP BIOS), a utility (configuration assist—`cassist`) tries to determine what resources are already used by non-PnP boards and writes this information to a file (which `icu` can read).

SCAM provides Plug and Play support (and other features as well) for SCSI devices.

VESA's DDC will provide Plug and Play support for monitors.

In addition to Microsoft and Intel, Plug and Play is being promoted by Compaq and Phoenix Technologies.

See *BIOS, DDC, DMA, IRQ, ISA, PC, PC 95, PCI, PCMCIA*, and *SCAM*.

Point

In computer-based typesetting, 1/72 of an inch. In traditional typesetting, slightly less than this (1/72.27", to be exact).

See *Font*.

Point-to-Point Protocol   See **PPP**.

Polyphony

The number (or capability) of simultaneous sounds or notes (typically at least 24 or 32) that can be produced by a sound board or MIDI synthesizer.

See *MIDI*.

POP
Point of Presence

The communications equipment located in (for example) a multi-tenant building that provides an alternative communications service. Connection to this point of presence could then provide communication service using (for example) the local cable TV provider's coaxial cable or fiber-optic cable (presumably at lower cost), rather than the local telephone company's facilities.

See *Carrier*, *CATV*, *Coax*, and *IXC*.

POP
Post Office Protocol

The older type of Internet mail server.

Most new servers are IMAP. POP downloads all mail to a user as soon as the user connect to the mail server.

See *IMAP* and *SMTP*.

Port Number   See **TCP**.

Portability

The capability of running software that (usually) was designed and developed on one platform (type of CPU, hardware, and operating system) on another platform (for example) to standardize on the software across an enterprise or to have a larger market for the software.

Some people make a verb from the word: "to port the software to another platform" or "ported from the Sun environment."

- *Source-code portability* means that recompilation is necessary. For example, you get the C language source code and compile it using the compiler for the *target system* (new computer platform). Ideally, the software can now be run on that target system. Usually, small problems are encountered (often because operating system functions work slightly differently) that need to be isolated, and the source code needs to be changed.
- *Object-code portability* means that the software needs to be relinked (but not compiled).
- *Binary portability* implies that the executable code is ready to run on any compatible machine. The most common example of this is PC programs that can be run on any processor from the 8088 to the Pentium and clone processors as well (such as Cyrix, AMD, etc.).

See *CDE, iBCS, PC, POSIX OSE, PowerPC*, and *RISC*.

Portable Computer and Communications Association   See **PCCA**.

POSIX OSE
Portable Operating System Interface (UNIX-like) Open Systems Environment

IEEE-sponsored work to define standard interfaces for APIs and many other functions so that applications will be source-code (but not object-code) portable between different hardware/software platforms. There are several efforts, as shown in the following table.

POSIX-related standard	Covers
1003.1	Basic file and I/O APIs (kernel), now includes 1003.4
1003.2	Shell and utilities
1003.2a	Extension utilities for time–sharing systems
1003.4	Threads extension to support real-time features, such as timers, priority scheduling asynchronous event notifications, and I/O (now included as part of 1003.1)
1003.5	1003.1 APIs for Ada
1003.6	Security extensions such as access control lists
1003.7	System administration support, such as adding users and checking device status
1003.8	Transparent network file access (NFS-like features)
1003.9	1003.1 APIs for FORTRAN
1003.12	Protocol-independent communication services
1003.15	Batch (noninteractive) support

(table continued on next page)

POSIX-related standard	Covers
1003.17	Distributed name space and directory service
1201.1	Window GUI
1224	X.400 message-handling interface
1238.0	Lower-layer OSI support
1238.1	OSI file transfer access method

Both SVID and BSD4.3 UNIX proponents are working on POSIX compliance for their systems (though POSIX is more similar to SVID). System administration will likely continue to be very product-specific.

Many non-UNIX systems (such as Windows NT) are POSIX-compliant, especially for non-user-interface efforts, such as 1003.1.

IEEE POSIX standards are made into ISO standards, such as ISO IS 9945.

The ISO has a WWW server with POSIX information at *http://www.dkuug.dk/ JTC1/SC22/WG15,* and the IEEE has some POSIX information at *http://stdsbbs.ieee.org:70/1/pub/PASC/*

See *IEEE, ISO, Portability, SVVS, UniForum,* and *UNIX.*

Post Office Protocol See **POP.**

PostScript Page Description Language

Adobe Systems, Inc.'s device-independent, ASCII language sent to a printer (which has a PostScript interpreter) to describe where to draw lines, circles, and other graphics. The printer then prints these at whatever its resolution is. Includes font selection and scaling commands.

PostScript *Level 2* interpreters (the software in the printer that converts the PostScript language into printer commands) are more advanced than *Level 1.* For example, Level 2 supports *dynamic memory allocation,* which can usually avoid *limitcheck* memory errors, which Level 1 interpreters encounter when a path has more than 1,500 points, and Color.

TrueImage was Microsoft's abandoned attempt to compete with PostScript.

Adobe receives about 3% of the price of any PostScript printer as a royalty.

There are "clone" PostScript interpreters available, presumably because the suppliers charge less than Adobe does. These would be used by printer manufacturers and built in to their printers (so the printers can be controlled by the PostScript output of application programs). For example, Phoenix Technologies (famous for

IBM PC-clone BIOSes and now owned by Xionics Document Technologies) has a clone PostScript interpreter called PhoenixPage.

The PostScript FAQ is at *http://www.cis.ohio-state.edu/hypertext/faq/usenet/postscript/ faq/top.html*.

See *ATM (Adobe Type Manager)*, *EPS*, *Multiple Master*, *Outline Font*, *PCL*, *PostScript Type 1 Fonts*, *PostScript Type 3 Fonts*, *Speedo*, and *TrueType*.

PostScript Type 1 Fonts

Adobe and several other *Type Foundries* produce *Type 1* fonts, which are described by a subset of the *PostScript Page Description Language*.

Type 1 fonts were the first *hinted* outline fonts—that is, the font descriptions include information on how to print on lower-resolution devices while maintaining print quality (such as character symmetry and shape). PostScript is widely supported, especially for professional typesetting work.

Competes with TrueType (which is oriented to the mass market and Microsoft's Windows).

See *ATM (Adobe Type Manager)*, *Font*, *Outline Font*, *PostScript Page Description Language*, and *PostScript Type 3 Fonts*.

PostScript Type 3 Fonts

Unhinted fonts that can be printed on PostScript printers but cannot be used by *Adobe Type Manager* (to be displayed or printed on non-PostScript monitors or printers).

See *ATM (Adobe Type Manager)*, *Font*, *PostScript Page Description Language*, and *PostScript Type 1 Fonts*.

POTS
Plain Ordinary Telephone Service

The only type of telephone service you could get 20 years ago. A simple analog telephone (and the corresponding service from the phone company) on which you can dial and receive calls.

The lowest common telephone service available everywhere.

A pair of copper conductors (a *twisted pair* of wires, called the *local loop*) connects your telephone to the nearest *central office*. It is estimated that there are about 560 million such local loops in the world, so there is a substantial effort to provide higher speed services (such as ADSL, ISDN, and switched 56) to work over these existing local loops.

Newer services include Caller ID, ISDN, and switched 56, which some people call *Pretty Amazing New Stuff*—that is, a change from POTS to PANS. (Har har har, ho ho ho, he he—look at that—those telephone guys can make better acronyms than the computer guys.)

See *800, ADSL, C.O., DID, DN, Carrier, CPE, CTI, DTMF (Dual Tone Multifrequency), Fax, In-Band, ISDN, Modem, PBX, RBOC, SIT, Switched 56, TAPI, TSAPI,* and *Tip and Ring.*

PowerOpen

A new UNIX-like operating system created by the Apple-IBM Alliance.

Will run on the PowerPC platform. Combines IBM's AIX and Apple's AUX and will have a Macintosh-like GUI.

See *AIX, Apple-IBM Alliance, A/UX, GUI, PowerPC, Operating System,* and *UNIX.*

PowerPC

The RISC-based processor created by Apple, IBM, and Motorola all working together. (They realized that they could not compete with Intel by continuing to work separately, competing with each other.)

Based on IBM's RS/6000 and manufactured by Motorola. The points and table below describes the various versions:

- 601: the first PowerPC processor, executes three instructions per clock cycle. First versions ran at 50 MHz. Can emulate a Motorola 68000 processor, so PowerPC-based Macintoshes can run software compiled for pre-PowerPC Macintoshes (which used Motorola 68000-family CPUs). That is, software has *binary portability* between the older Macintoshes and the new PowerPC-based Macintoshes. First used in the IBM RS/6000 model 250, which was introduced in September 1993, and later used in Apple Macintoshes (such as the Performa 6110 and Power Mac 6100, 7100, and 8100 series), starting in March 1994.
- 602: for consumer multimedia applications, such as games and PDAs (which need fast integer multiplication and logarithms for handwriting recognition and other advanced functions)
- 603: low-power version with power management features, for battery-operated portable computers
- 603: an improved 603 that has a faster 68040 emulator
- 604: high-speed
- 620: really-high-speed

Proc-essor	Clock Speed (MHz)	Transistors (Millions)	Width (bits)			L1 Cache (kbytes)		Pins
			Register	Address Bus	Data Bus	Code	Data	
601	80	2.8	32	32	64	32		304
601v	100	2.8	32	32	64	32		304
602	66	1.0	32	32	64^a	4	4	144
603	66	1.6	32	32	32/64	8	8	240
	80	1.6	32	32	32/64	8	8	256
603e	100	2.6	32	32	32/64	16	16	256
604	100	3.6	32	32	64	6	16	256
620	133	7.0	64	40	128	32	32	625

^{a} 32-bit bus time-multiplexed to provide 64-bit transfers.

Runs Apple's Mac OS, IBM's AIX and OS/2, Microsoft Windows NT, PowerOpen, and Sunsoft's Solaris operating systems.

Apple Computer, Inc and International Business Machines Corporation (IBM) have WWW servers at *http://www.apple.com* and *http://www.ibm.com.*, respectively.

See *88open*, *ACE*, *AIX*, *Cache*, *CHRP*, *Motorola*, *Operating System*, *PDA*, *Portability*, *PReP*, *RISC*, *Somerset*, *SPEC*, and *Superscalar*.

PowerPC Reference Platform   See **PReP.**

PPP
Point-to-Point Protocol

A protocol for (most commonly) TCP/IP routers and PCs to communicate over dial-up and leased-line WAN connections.

Establishes a standard way for routers and computers connected over a synchronous or asynchronous WAN link to establish, monitor, and terminate a session (and, of course, exchange data in between).

The WAN connections can be either of the following:

• *Dial-up*, for example, a V.32*bis* "Hayes-compatible" auto-dial, auto-answer modem on a standard "POTS" analog telephone line (just like you have at home) or an ISDN connection

• *Leased Line*, for example, a 56-kbits/s point-to-point link

PPP also defines how to encapsulate packets into HDLC frames for transmission over the serial communication lines.

Usually used for IP, but (unlike SLIP) is protocol-independent (a 16-bit field identifies the protocol—such as IP, IPX, AppleTalk, DECnet, OSI, or transparent bridging).

Other advantages over SLIP include:

- IP header compression
- Data compression (see CCP)
- Error correction
- Packet sequencing
- Authentication

Includes a *link control protocol* that initiates, configures, tests the data link connection, and handles feature negotiation at call setup time. Also includes a set of network control protocols that determines how to handle network-layer transactions.

Even with the negotiation phase, there are enough implementation subsets that interoperability problems often occur. The RFCs include those shown in the following table.

	Specification	**Supports**
BCP	Bridge Control Protocol	Transparent bridging
IPCP	IPX Control Protocol	Routing of IPX encapsulated in PPP
NBCP	NetBEUI Control Protocol	Routing of NetBEUI encapsulated in PPP
ATCP	AppleTalk Control Protocol	Routing of AppleTalk encapsulated in PPP

Defined in RFCs 1331 through 1334.

See *Asynchronous, Authentication, CCP, Encapsulation, HDLC, ISDN, POTS, PPPML, SLIP, Synchronous, V.8* through *V.120*, and *WAN*.

PPPML
Point-to-Point Protocol Multilink

A specification for combining (*inverse multiplexing*) multiple ISDN B channels to provide a higher-speed service.

Defined in RFC 1717.

See *Inverse Multiplexer, ISDN*, and *PPP*.

Practical Extraction and Report Language   See **Perl.**

Precision Architecture-RISC   See **PA-RISC.**

PReP
PowerPC Reference Platform

An attempt by IBM (alone) to specify a standard hardware platform that would be able to run OS/2, AIX, Windows NT, and Apple's Macintosh operating system. The requirements were the following:

- 8 Mbytes (minimum) and 16 Mbytes (standard) of RAM, with room for 32 Mbytes of RAM
- 4 kbytes (minimum) nonvolatile configuration RAM
- 120 Mbytes (minimum) hard disk, either local (expandable to 200 Mbytes) or network-accessible
- 1.44-Mbyte 3½" floppy diskette drive
- CD-ROM drive (strongly recommended)
- SCSI-2 (preferred method of attaching additional peripherals)
- Keyboard and mouse
- 16-bit audio
- 1,024 × 768 resolution monitor
- Serial communication ports

But Apple and Motorola wanted some say in the specification, so it has been replaced by CHRP.

See *CHRP* and *PowerPC*.

Pretty Good Privacy   See **PGP.**

PRI
Primary Rate ISDN

An ISDN service that provides (for example):

- In North America and Japan, Primary Rate ISDN service can be any of the following:
  - 23 B channels plus one D channel (but sometimes 24 B channels and no D channels if the D channel information can be carried over another circuit)
  - One H_{11} channel (1.544 Mbits/s) and no D channel
  - Three H_0 channels (where each H_0 is 384 kbits/s) plus one 64-kbits/s D channel
- In Europe and Australia, Primary Rate ISDN can be any of the following:
  - 30 B channels plus one D channel
  - One H_{12} channel (1.920 Mbits/s) plus one 64-kbits/s D channel
  - Five H_0 channels (where each H_0 is 384 kbits/s) plus one 64 kbits/s D channel

The H_0 channel's bit rate is equal to the aggregate of six 64-kbits/s B channels and fast enough to support full-motion, full-color video conferencing. The H_{11} (pronounced "H, 1, 1") and H_{12} channels are a full "unchannelized" T1 (or E1).

Note that these rates each add up to a full (or almost full) T1 (or E1).

In North America, PRI is implemented using a standard T1 circuit which uses B8ZS to provide *clear channel* 64,000-bits/s channels. The actual link between the customer premises and the telephone company central office will typically be either a two-pair copper link (one pair receives, the other pair transmits) or fiber-optic cabling (two strands per T1).

Typical uses are for connecting PBX (Private Branch Exchanges) to central office switches, and receiving multiple, simultaneous ISDN calls at:

- Companies supporting telecommuting, through dial-in routers accessing their in-house LAN
- *Internet service providers* supporting callers who use ISDN to access the Internet.

See *B8ZS, BRI, ISDN, ISP, PBX, T1*, and *Video*.

Printer Command Language   See **PCL.**

Prioritization

A feature implemented in multiprocotol router software that ensures that time-critical protocols do not time-out when there is a temporary peak in the traffic load on the WAN link.

Usually needed most for *legacy* protocols (such as SDLC), which were designed to work on dedicated, single-protocol links—where the delays are known and predictable. When a router combines many protocols onto a single WAN link (to reduce communication costs), the delay between networks will depend on the WAN loading (due to the other protocols). Since some protocols cannot tolerate delays, (at best, there may be retransmissions, needlessly further loading the WAN link, and at worst, users may be unceremoniously disconnected), a method is needed to give them priority over other protocols.

Two methods are common:

- *Bandwidth Reservation* (sometimes called *Custom Queuing*), in which each protocol is assigned a percentage of the total WAN bandwidth, so that regardless of the total WAN traffic load, a predetermined amount of bandwidth is available for the time-critical protocol. When a protocol does not need all of its reserved bandwidth, then other protocols can use it. A problem is that if a time-critical protocol temporarily needs more than its assigned priority (and the other protocols also need all of theirs), then the time-critical protocol may still time-out.

- *Protocol Priority* or *Priority Queuing*, in which each protocol is assigned a relative priority. The most time-critical protocol gets the highest priority. A problem is that if the time-critical protocol needs all of the bandwidth, the other protocols get no bandwidth.

Of the two methods, bandwidth reservation is best for most applications, as long as the amount of bandwidth reserved for each protocol is the minimum required to provide acceptable service.

See *Legacy System*, *RSVP*, and *SDLC*.

Priority Access Control Enabled   See **PACE**.

Private Branch Exchange   See **PBX**.

Programmed Input/Output   See **PIO**.

Programmers' Hierarchical Graphics Standard   See **Phigs**.

Protocol-Independent Multicast   See **PIM**.

PU
Physical Unit

An IBM data communications device that is physically connected to an FEP (typically through Token Ring or an EIA-232 connection) and directly takes part in SNA protocols (such as responding to SDLC polling).

Also referred to as a *Node Type*.

See *FEP*.

PU 2
Physical Unit Type 2

IBM's traditional 3274- or 3174-based *cluster* (or *communication*) *controller* and the protocol for communication between it and the *front end processor* driving it.

See *3174 and 3274* and *FEP*.

PU 2.1
Physical Unit Type 2.1

A simple implementation of IBM SNA's APPN, also called *Low Entry Networking* (LEN). Used by the AS/400.

See *5250*, *APPN*, and *LEN*.

PU 4
Physical Unit Type 4

An IBM SNA *front end processor* (such as a 3745). Used to communicate to other FEPs or to *communication controllers* (such as a 3174). Also called an *SNA intermediate network node*.

See *3174 and 3274, Channel*, and *FEP*.

PU 5
Physical Unit Type 5

An IBM SNA mainframe (such as a System/370, System/390, or 3090). Runs VTAM to handle data communications.

See *Mainframe* and *VTAM*.

Public Cordless Telephone Service   See **PCTS.**

PUC
Public Utilities Commission

The U.S. agencies (one for each state) that regulate telephone tariffs, electric power rates, and other utility rates.

See *CRTC* and *FCC*.

Pulse Code Modulation   See **PCM.**

QLLC
Qualified Logical Link Control

IBM's method of supporting SNA over X.25 packet-switching networks. Usually, NPSI will be installed on the FEP to provide the X.25 support.

SNA frames are mapped to X.25 packets. For SNA frames that do not have corresponding X.25 packets, the X.25 Q bit is set to indicate a nonstandard use of the packet.

See *DLC*, *FEP*, *NPSI*, *SNA*, and *X.25*.

QOS
Quality of Service

The network requirements (latency, maximum packet loss, etc.) to support a specific application.

Different types of multimedia traffic have different requirements. It is important for networks to know these so that the networks can be efficiently used (some applications require guaranteed bandwidth, some need only to use bandwidth that is left over after all guaranteed traffic has been carried). Therefore, protocols must support carrying this QOS information so that applications can specify it and networks can know what is required.

See *ATM*, *Multimedia*, *IGRP*, *IP Multicast*, *RSVP*, and *WinSock*.

QTC
QuickTime Conference

Apple Computer's cross-platform, video conferencing, collaborative computing, and multimedia communications technology.

Supports sharing, over LANs and WANs, of real-time (that is, not necessarily instant response time but predictable response time) data, images, and sound.

Three types of connections can be established:

- Point-to-point: two people interactively communicate
- Multipoint: many people interactively communicate
- Multicast: one person broadcasts to many

See *Apple*, *IP Multicast*, *Multimedia*, and *SMRP*.

Radio Data System   See **RDS.**

RAID
Redundant Array of Inexpensive Disks

A disk subsystem (that appears as a single large, fast, super-reliable disk drive) composed of more than one (usually equal-sized) disk drives (called an *array*) to provide improved reliability, response time, and/or storage capacity.

Several techniques are used:

- *Spanning* or *Software Striping*: splits the data from a single file or database onto several disk drives—this permits many simultaneous (up to as many disk drives as are used) accesses to the data
- *Mirroring*: duplicates the data from one disk onto others so that the data are still available if a drive fails
- *Duplexing*: duplicates both the disks and the disk controllers (the printed circuit board that goes between the PC's bus and the disk drive)

All of these techniques speed response times during periods of heavy loading, since more than one physical disk drive is supplying data simultaneously.

RAID arrays may also support the following:

- *Hot Swapping*: a failed disk drive can be removed and replaced, and the data can be automatically restored to the new disk while the subsystem is powered up and continues to operate in production service
- *Hot Sparing*: an extra disk drive in the array is automatically put into service (no need to manually plug in a new one) when a failure occurs
- *Spindle Synchronization*: synchronizes the rotation of all drives in an array, making it easier for the controller to track which disk sectors can be read soonest

Five *RAID levels* are defined (six if you count what some people call Level 0) and described in the table below.

RAID Level	Functionality	Comments
0	Data are striped across available disks (to improve access times), with no redundancy.	Not part of the original RAID definition. Not RAID, since there is no redundancy.
1	Two disk drives are mirrored (both store the same data), using a single disk controller. Data can be read off both drives simultaneously (either drive can service any request), providing improved performance.	Often implemented in software. Doubles the number of disk drives required, therefore suited only to smaller storage requirements. Provides faster write times than RAID 4 or 5.
2	Data are spanned across multiple disks, and additional disks are used to store *Hamming codes* (to detect and correct errors or recover from failed drives). Four data disks would require three additional error detection and correction disks.	Offers the greatest redundancy but is not currently commercially available because of the high cost.
3	Data are *striped* byte by byte across two or more (four is apparently best) data disks (first byte to first disk, second byte to next disk, and so on—written in parallel to all disks). A parity byte is constructed from the corresponding bytes on the data disks and is written to one additional disk, which is dedicated as a *parity disk*. The contents of a failed disk can be reconstructed from the other disks.	Considered best for larger transfers, such as graphics or imaging files.
4	Same as RAID 3, but data are striped (and parity is constructed) in disk *sectors* rather than bytes.	Has lower performance than RAID 5; is seldom used or available.
5	Data are striped sector by sector across two or more disks. Parity information sectors are striped along with the data on each disk, and there is no dedicated parity disk.	Considered best for smaller transfers. Offers better write (and the same read) performance as RAID 4.

See *Disk Drive*, *ECC*, and *SLED*.

RAM
Random Access Memory

A type of computer memory that can be quickly (we're talking nanoseconds here) written and read.

The "random" is in contrast to linear types, such as tape drives, in which you cannot read any location at any time (you need to spin the tape to where your data are stored).

As processors get faster, faster types of RAM (such as EDO RAM) are required.

See *Cache*, *DRAM*, *ECC*, *EDO RAM*, *PC*, *RAMDAC*, *Shadowed BIOS*, *Shared Memory*, and *VRAM*.

RAM Mobile Data

A company jointly owned by RAM Broadcasting, Inc., Ericsson, and BellSouth Corp. that provides a cellular-radio-based packet data service called *Mobitex*.

Competes with Ardis and CDPD. Ericsson encourages others to manufacture compatible equipment (people prefer an open standard).

See *Ardis*, *CDPD*, and *Mobitex*.

RAMDAC
Random Access Memory Digital-to-Analog Converter

The integrated circuit that converts the digital information stored in a video adapter's *frame buffer* (which has an image of what is to be displayed on the screen) to the analog signals needed to drive the monitor.

At a refresh rate of 75 Hz (that is, the entire screen must be rewritten 75 times per second), a resolution of 1,024 × 768 pixels, and 24-bit color (3 bytes of RAM per pixel), the RAMDAC must be able to handle (75 × 1,024 × 768 × 3 =) 176,947,200 bytes per second over 170 Mbytes/s. The frame buffer RAM must be able support this data transfer rate plus the CPU accesses needed to create and change the display.

See *Color*, *RAM*, *VESA*, and *Video*.

Rasterize

The process of converting an image which may be described by a series of straight-line segments (often called vectors) or curves (described with an equation) to a raster image (which is a series of horizontal lines of varying intensity and possibly color).

Many display devices (such as laser printers and television and computer screens) create their output by scanning a beam from left to right across each row (starting at the top left corner), and then repeating this process for each row down the screen.

- For television and computer screens, the beam is a focused stream of electrons that bombards and excites colored phosphors. This causes them to glow briefly—the *persistence* of the phosphor is chosen so that the glow lasts until the next scan (which is typically 1/30 to 1/70 of a second). The beam is moved using precisely-controlled electromagnets.
- For laser printers, the beam is often a red or infrared (770 to 795 nm wavelength) high-intensity (5 mW) light beam produced by a *laser diode* (hence the name "laser printer"). The beam is focused by lenses and reflected off of a rotating mirror—this creates the required scanning. The paper is advanced by an accurately-controlled motor.

By electronically varying the intensity of the beam as it scans, any image can be displayed.

While a raster is a very efficient method of displaying an image, it is often not the best way to store (it requires too much memory) or create the image (raster images scaled to other resolutions only look nice if the other resolutions are integral multiples of the original).

For example, fonts are best described using mathematical descriptions of the shape of their outlines. Once the font has been scaled to the desired size (and the color and pattern to be used to fill the outline has been generated), a rasterizing process (such as that done by the Adobe Type Manager) is then used to create the image needed for the display device.

See *ATM (Adobe Type Manager)*, *Interlaced*, and *Outline Font*.

RBOC
Regional Bell Operating Company

One of the seven U.S. holding companies (also called *Baby Bells*) that were formed to own the *Local Exchange Carriers* (LECs) created by the *divestiture* of AT&T (also called *the breakup of Ma Bell*), which occurred in 1984.

Each owns the previously AT&T-owned telephone companies in a specific geographic region, as shown in the following table.

RBOC	Owns These Local Exchange Carriers	Which Are in These Geographic Areas
Ameritech	Illinois Bell, Indiana Bell, Michigan Bell, Ohio Bell, and Wisconsin Telephone	Illinois, Indiana, Michigan, Ohio, Wisconsin

(table continued on next page)

RBOC	Owns These Local Exchange Carriers	Which Are in These Geographic Areas
Bell Atlantic	Bell of Pennsylvania, Chesapeake and Potomac of Maryland, C&P of Virginia, C&P of Washington, D.C., C&P of West Virginia, Diamond State Telephone, and New Jersey Bell	Delaware, Maryland, New Jersey, Pennsylvania, Virginia, Washington, D.C., West Virginia
BellSouth	South Central Bell, Southeastern Bell, and Southern Bell	Alabama, Florida, Georgia, Louisiana, Kentucky, Mississippi, North Carolina, South Carolina, Tennessee
Nynex	Southern New England Telephone and New York Telephone	Connecticut, Massachusetts, Maine, New Hampshire, New York, Rhode Island, Vermont
Pacific Telesis Group	Nevada Bell and Pacific Telephone	California, Nevada
SBC Communications (was Southwestern Bell Communications until 1994)		Arkansas, Kansas, Missouri, Oklahoma, Texas
U.S. West	Mountain Bell, Northwestern Bell, and Pacific Northwest Bell	Arizona, Colorado, Idaho, Iowa, Montana, Minnesota, Nebraska, New Mexico, North Dakota, Oregon, South Dakota, Utah, Washington, Wyoming

Greater-distance calls within an RBOC's territory may be *toll calls*, but RBOCs are currently prevented from offering long-distance services (that is, calls between different RBOCs or to other countries). Similarly, the IXCs are generally restricted from offering local service.

However, these restrictions are being reduced. For example, some RBOCs are offering to give up their monopoly on providing local telephone service in exchange for being allowed to offer long-distance telephone services.

As is the case with a company deciding to support the development of a standard, most RBOCs have decided that it is better to have some of a big thing (where you can always fight for more market share), rather than all of a little thing (where the market growth potential is low, and stagnant things seldom prosper).

The RBOCs maintain a WWW server at *http://www.bell.com.*

See *AT&T*, *Bellcore*, *Carrier*, *IXC*, *LATA*, *LEC*, and *POTS*.

RBHC
Regional Bell Holding Company

Another name for RBOC, since an RBOC can be considered a holding company for the telephone companies (also called Local Exchange Carriers) which it owns.

See *LEC* and *RBOC*.

RDS
Radio Data System

A method of transmitting data simultaneously with a standard FM stereo (or monophonic) radio broadcast. Possible uses include sending song titles and signaling when traffic or weather reports are being broadcast.

Bits are continuously sent at 1,187.5 bits/s (chosen partly because the data's 57-kHz carrier frequency and the standard 19-kHz *stereo pilot* frequency are integral multiples).

The data are sent in blocks of 26 bits: 16 data bits plus 10 *forward error correction* bits (the error correction code used can correct an error burst of 5 or fewer bits in each block of 26 bits without requiring a retransmission). *Groups* of four blocks of 26 bits are used, each group therefore contains 64 data bits, and 104 bits total.

Four bits are reserved to designate the *group type* (which identifies what the subsequent data are). Some defined group types are:

- Station name (the four *call letters*)
- Time and date (in UTC format, sent on the zero-second each minute)
- Radio paging (rather than using a separate transmitter, why not use an existing radio station's?)
- Emergency warning messages
- Program type (drama, rock, etc.)
- Text messages (called *radio text*) of up to 64 characters, sent as 4 characters per group

Another bit sent in every group indicates whether music or speech is currently being broadcast.

Originally developed by Swedish Telecom (and called MBS) in 1976 as a method of sending data to radio pagers. Developed by the European Broadcasting Union (in the early 1980s) into RDS. Standardized in 1993 by the U.S. National Association of Broadcasters (Washington, D.C., phone 202-429-5373).

See *ECC*, *GSM*, and *UTC*.

Ream

Now defined as 500 sheets of paper, but some related definitions are shown in the following table.

Number of Sheets of Paper	Called	Comments
480	Short ream	Old definition of ream
500	Ream	Used to be called a long ream
516	Printer's ream	Also called a perfect ream

See *Paper*.

Recommended Standard 232   See **EIA/TIA-232.**

Red, Green, Blue   See **RGB.**

Reduced Instruction-Set Computer   See **RISC.**

Redundant Array of Inexpensive Disks   See **RAID.**

Regional Bell Operating Company   See **RBOC.**

Registered Jack 45 (RJ-45)   See **Connector.**

Remote Bridge

One of (usually) a pair of (usually Ethernet) bridges that connects two (or more) LANs over a WAN. Token Ring remote bridges are usually called *split bridges*.

See *LAN*, *Local Bridge*, *Token Ring*, and *WAN*.

Remote File System   See **RFS.**

Remote Imaging Protocol Script Language   See **RIPscrip.**

Remote Job Entry   See **RJE.**

Remote Network Monitoring MIB   See **RMON.**

Remote Procedure Call   See **RPC.**

Resource Reservation Protocol   See **RSVP.**

RFC
Request for Comments

The process for defining new UNIX and TCP/IP standards is (briefly) to:

- Detail the proposed standard in a document
- Make the document available on the Internet for all to download and read
- Request comments

The document is therefore called a *Request For Comments* and is given a number (RFC numbers are assigned by the Network Information Center—InterNIC), for example, RFC 1149 (which is titled *A Standard for the Transmission of IP Datagrams on Avian Carriers*—a hint: this particular document's date is April 1, 1990). After comments have been considered and the document has possibly been changed, the resulting standard (after approval from the IETF) retains the original name (such as RFC 1149).

From *http://www.cis.ohio-state.edu/hypertext/information/rfc.html*, RFCs can be searched (by keyword or RFC number), and viewed or retrieved. A chronological listing of all RFCs (beginning with the most recent) is at *http://www.cis.ohio-state.edu/htbin/rfc/rfc-index.html*. Any specific RFC can be viewed at, for example, *http://www.cis.ohio-state.edu/htbin/rfc/rfc1882.html* for RFC 1882.

Using ftp, RFCs are available from *ftp://ds.internic.net/rfc,* or by using a WWW browser from *http://ds.internic.net/rfc/*. When using this method, RFC 1597 (for example) is file `RFC1597.txt` (in ASCII text) and `RFC1597.ps` (in PostScript format—these look nicer, but you need a PostScript printer or viewer).

A list of all RFCs and their length and status (for example, many are obsolete) is at *http://ds.internic.net/rfc/rfc-index.txt* (this file is about 250 kbytes).

See *IETF*, *InterNIC*, and *PostScript Page Description Language*.

RFC 1597

A method for dealing with the problem that no more worldwide unique Class A IP addresses and very few Class B addresses are available for new networks.

While lots of Class C addresses are available (for a while anyway), many (most?) organizations have more than 254 hosts (which is all that a single Class C IP address can address).

Sounds like a problem, doesn't it? Lots of large companies need lots of addresses, but large blocks of addresses are not available. One solution is based on the observation that while an organization may need a large number of IP addresses for internal use (one per host computer) the following is also true:

- Only a small number of users (that is, hosts) will need to simultaneously access the outside world (the Internet)—most of a company's TCP/IP traffic is between hosts within a company's network

- While everyone needs to be able to send and receive Internet mail, this only requires that one host for an entire organization (and not each individual user) needs a worldwide unique IP address.
- Most companies use a *firewall* between the Internet and their internal network. When using a firewall to access the Internet, all internal users' ftp, telnet, and WWW (for example) traffic usually shares the single IP address of the firewall. Each user does not need their own external IP address, since the connections are initiated by the users, who need only a unique *socket number*, not IP address.

The approach described in RFC 1597 is for the organization to obtain a (usually Class C) worldwide unique (or "external") address for each host that requires direct communication with the Internet (for example, to provide a WWW or ftp server). Internally, the organization uses any IP addresses it wishes. An *address translation gateway* (which is usually part of the software in a router) then translates the worldwide unique external addresses from the Internet to the internal addresses used by the organization.

RFC 1597 reserves some IP addresses for this private internal use. Since these particular addresses can never be valid Internet addresses, routers know whether to do a translation or not.

These reserved addresses are listed in the following table.

Bits in Address Range	Address Range Size and Type	IP Address Range	
		From	To
24	One *Class A*	10.0.0.0	10.255.255.255
20	16 *Class B*	172.16.0.0	172.31.255.255
16	256 *Class C*	192.168.0.0	192.168.255.255

A problem with this method is the administration required for the address translation gateway (manually mapping the reserved, internal RFC 1597 addresses to the registered external addresses).

Another method of handling the Class A and B IP address shortage is called CIDR.

See *CIDR*, *IP Address*, and *Socket Number*.

RFS
Remote File System

The capability of locally mounting a disk drive which is physically located elsewhere on a network. That is, the remote disk drive appears to be part of the local computer system—and files can be created, opened, and deleted (subject to the access permissions) on the remote disk, using the same commands as if it were a disk on the local computer.

Developed by AT&T for their implementation of UNIX. Not as flexible as Sun Microsystems' (far more widely used) NFS.

See *NFS* and *Sun*

RGB
Red, Green, Blue

A method of sending or specifying color video information, typically to a video monitor.

Uses a separate cable for each of the red, green, and blue color signals (the connectors are the RCA-type or, more commonly, a BNC-type connector—especially in professional video equipment). Typically, the green also carries the synchronizing and blanking information, but this may be on a fourth cable.

RGB provides more accurate color than composite video does, since the color is usually generated as three separate signals in the first place, so the signals don't need to be converted (which would reduce the quality—as they say, "something always gets lost in the translation").

See *BNC, Color, Composite Video Signal,* and *Video.*

RIP
Routing Information Protocol

A method that routers use to communicate network connectivity status and determine the best path over which to send traffic.

Many protocols have their own incompatible implementation, as shown in the following table, so DECnet's RIP is incompatible with TCP/IP's RIP, which is incompatible with Novell's RIP, and so on.

Protocol	RIP Router to Router Protocol
AppleTalk	Routing table maintenance protocol
DECnet	Routing information protocol
IP	Routing information protocol
Novell IPX	Routing information protocol
Vines IP	Routing table protocol (original) or sequenced routing table protocol (newer and improved, since it sends only a short message indicating that nothing has changed, if nothing has changed)

In RIP, paths are rated by *hop counts* (from 0 to 15); a hop count of 16 means that the node is unreachable. The protocol therefore imposes a network limitation of a maximum of 15 routers between any two hosts.

Other weaknesses include the following:

- Factors other than hop count, such as link speed and delay, are (usually) not included in the calculation to find the "best path" between two hosts.
- Each router's table is broadcasted every (for example) 10 (Apple's RTMP) to 60 (Novell's NetWare's RIP) seconds, whether there are changes from the last broadcast or not (this wastes precious WAN bandwidth).

A new and improved (!) method with many advantages (of course) is called *link-state*. The TCP/IP implementation of this is called OSPF.

The TCP/IP implementation of RIP is UDP-broadcast-based and uses the *well-known port* 520 (so the recipient knows to expect RIP information in the packet).

Novell's RIP includes a field to indicate the speed of each link so that routers can find the fastest path.

Also called *Distance-Vector* and *Bellman-Ford*.

See *IGRP*, *Link-state*, *TCP*, and *TTL* (*Time-to-Live*).

RIPscrip
Remote Imaging Protocol Script Language

A method of providing a graphical user interface for bulletin board systems.

The protocol supports 16-color, 640 × 350 pixel resolution graphical environments, including mouse and on-screen clickable button support, fonts, icons, and graphical primitives (such as elliptical arcs, pie slices, and bezier curves).

Uses 7-bit ASCII (rather than requiring 8-bit transparency), so the communications are compatible with X.25 networks and all computing platforms (that is, it never uses reserved ASCII characters, such as the X-ON or *data link escape* character as part of its protocol).

Is usually supported by newer bulletin board systems.

Callers' communication software must support the protocol and graphics to take advantage of the interface. A royalty-free freeware program (RIPterm) is available. It provides features such as pull-down menus, file transfer using the popular PC protocols, dialing directory, keystroke macros, and support for COM1 through COM4.

A separate program (RIPaint) is used to develop the graphical screens and mouse-clickable menus for the user interface.

Developed by TeleGrafix Communications, Inc.

See *BBS* and *GUI*.

RISC
Reduced Instruction-Set Computer

A central processing unit technology that is supposed to provide faster and lower-cost processing than the other way of doing things: *Complex Instruction-Set Computing* (CISC, which is used by Intel PCs, IBM mainframes, and most other computing platforms).

The technology was pioneered by IBM in the 1970s and resulted in a processor architecture called POWER *(Performance Optimized With Enhanced RISC)*, which was initially implemented in the first IBM RS/6000 (RISC System/6000) workstation (introduced in February 1990) and eventually formed the basis for the Apple/IBM/Motorola PowerPC processor.

The idea is that by simplifying the logic needed to implement a processor (by making it capable of executing only very simple instructions and addressing modes), the processor can be smaller, less expensive, and faster—and maybe use less power too. By using a smarter compiler, the processor can still handle any task required (by efficiently combining simple instructions at compile time).

Major requirements for the success of RISC processors include the following:

- A high-quality, efficient compiler and development environment.
- Getting important existing application programs recompiled (for the processor's *native* mode). Often RISC processors have an *emulation* mode that enables them to run code compiled for other non-RISC processors (such as the Motorola 68000)—that is, the 68000 code is *binary portable* to the RISC processor's emulation mode. This capability is intended to get past the "chicken-and-egg" problem of why would I buy a processor for which there are no application programs, and why would I develop application programs for a processor that doesn't have an installed base?

   However, the emulation mode usually runs more slowly than (the competing) existing processors (in their native CISC mode), so compiling programs to produce efficient and native RISC processor code is required. This creates a tough problem. If the emulation mode runs software too slow, it is useless, and no one uses it. If the emulation is fast enough, no one converts their software, so there is no incentive to recompile the software, and the new processor is simply another way to run the software, so the new processor does not get accepted or get native software written for it. Just ask IBM about their OS/2 operating system and its support for Windows software (hint: you don't find many popular programs that run natively under OS/2).

Ideally, all RISC processor instructions (for example, adding two registers) execute in one clock cycle. In actual practice, some instructions (such as multiplication and division) require additional clock cycles. Depending on the implementation, other instructions (such as shifts and register loads from memory) may require more than one clock cycle—this makes the distinction between RISC and CISC somewhat gray.

Other popular RISC-based processors include DEC's Alpha, HP's PA-RISC, SGI's MIPS, and Sun's SPARC.

See *88open*, *Alpha AXP*, *PA-RISC*, *P7*, *PowerPC*, *Portability*, *SPARC*, and *SPEC*.

RJ-45
Registered Jack 45

See *Connector*.

RJE
Remote Job Entry

IBM's batch-oriented (as opposed to interactive) computing capability.

Uses the 3770 and 3780 family of peripheral equipment and protocols. Jobs can be submitted and monitored, and print output and files can be retrieved. Runs on SNA/SDLC but is otherwise completely incompatible with 3270 protocols and equipment (which are interactive-oriented).

See *3270* and *LU 1*.

RLE
Run Length Encoding

A type of data compression that looks for repeated bytes (such as many sequential ASCII space characters) and represents this in a shorter sequence.

For example, RLE could encode 5 space characters (which would be 20 20 20 20 20 in hexadecimal) as 05 20.

LZW is another type of data compression.

See *Data Compression*, *LZW*, *MNP*, and *V.42bis*.

rlogin

Berkeley UNIX's remote terminal facility, which provides the capability to log in to a machine that is LAN- or WAN-connected to the local one (the one on which you are typing).

The remote machine must be running the rlogin *daemon* (which is called rlogind). Similar to telnet, except that rlogin uses your username from your current session on your local machine (so you don't need to re-type it).

See *telnet* and *UNIX*.

RMON
Remote Network Monitoring MIB

A way of monitoring the loading and performance of remote LAN segments.

An SNMP MIB (described in RFC 1271 for the Ethernet implementation) that specifies the types of information listed in the following table.

RMON MIB Group	Holds Information on
Statistics	Network performance: number of packets, bytes, errors (by type), broadcasts, multicasts, collisions, bandwidth utilization, and the packet size distribution.
History	Automatic time interval (by default at 30-second and 30-minute intervals—though many change this to 30 seconds and 5 minutes) recording of statistical performance data (from the above statistics group) for trend and repeated symptom tracking. This should facilitate proactive network planning (what a concept).
Alarms	Generated when preset rising or falling thresholds (absolute or delta) are exceeded (for any statistic maintained by the agent). Alarms can trigger other actions through the events group.
Hosts Table	Automatically updated list of all nodes (by MAC address) on the network and statistics related to them (such as frames and bytes sent and received, broadcasts and multicasts sent, and errors).
Hosts Top *n* Table	A sorted list of nodes (selected from the Hosts Table group), with the highest specified parameters (for example, highest number of errors or highest usage)—possibly by protocol.
Matrix	Traffic and number of errors between pairs of nodes (by MAC address), for example, frames and bytes exchanged. This group requires more resources to implement than most others, so not all products include this important group.
Filters	Specifies which frames are to be captured by the packet capture group (for example, by protocol or source or destination address).
Events	Records (and time-stamps) specific network errors and user-defined events as log entries and can send alerts (SNMP traps) when thresholds are exceeded, or trigger other actions.

(table continued on next page)

RMON MIB Group	Holds Information on
Packet Capture	Captures entire frames for later forwarding to, and decoding by, software running on the management station. Capture can be of full frames or only specified number of bytes of each frame, started when a trigger condition is met, specified to wrap around or halt when capture memory fills. Captured data are uploaded to a management station on request, after the capture has completed (RMON does not provide real-time capture and display). This group requires more resources to implement than most others, so not all products include this important group.
Token Ring only	Statistics on Token Ring specific parameters, such as error frames, beaconing, source routing details, ring order, and active monitor selection.

Vendors can implement any subset of these groups, and claim RMON MIB compatibility. It is important to verify which groups a product supports (hopefully all). However, if a vendor implements a group, then all features of that group must be implemented. Also, implementation of some groups requires that other groups be implemented (for example, the packet capture group requires the filter group to be implemented as well).

RMON information may be gathered by:

- Dedicated hardware devices (sometimes called *probes* or *pods*) or PCs running special software
- Software built in to data communications equipment, such as routers, bridges, switches, or Ethernet concentrators (this built-in software is sometimes called an *embedded agent*)
- Software built in to file servers (also an embedded agent)

RMON probes are configured to run tests by entering tasks into a *control table* (from a *management station*). Each task is a row of the table and specifies the type of data, frequency of collection, and other details of the task. Each task produces its own results, which can be retrieved by the management station. Standardization of the method of entering, monitoring, and deleting these tasks is not as advanced as are the details of the data collection itself.

Also, the complexity of the actions may differ between products. For example, some products may be able to show the Hosts Top *n* group only after a utilization threshold has been exceeded.

Since SNMP generally works only with TCP/IP, users would need to support TCP/IP to get this information back to an SNMP management station—even if they don't otherwise use (and route) TCP/IP.

See *MIB*, *RMON II*, and *SNMP*.

RMON II
Remote Network Monitoring MIB, Version 2

An enhancement to RMON that generally involves higher-level (than OSI layers 1 and 2) protocol information, such as:

- Examining router ARP caches to determine the original source of packets (not just that they came from a specific router)
- What applications (telnet, WWW, etc.) are being used by (for example) examining the port number in TCP and UDP packets
- What protocols are being used (by examining the frame header information)
- Mapping network connectivity by requesting *hop table* information from routers

See *RMON*.

Rockwell International

A really big company that, in addition to big military-type stuff, makes most of the modem ICs in the world.

They have a WWW site at *http://www.nb.rockwell.com/*.

See *Fax* and *Modem*.

Rockwell Protocol Interface   See **RPI.**

ROFL
Rolling on the Floor, Laughing

A common email abbreviation indicating that something is very funny (unlike this definition).

root

The UNIX account used by the system administrator. Once logged in to it, you can read or write to any directory and file.

See *su*, *TCP*, and *UNIX*.

Routing Information Protocol   See **RIP.**

Routing Table Maintenance Protocol   See **RTMP.**

RPC
Remote Procedure Call

A method of program-to-program communications, usually for implementing cross-platform distributed computing.

Generically, RPC is an inter-process communication API whose strength is communication between different computing platforms, using multiple protocol stacks simultaneously. Most often used with TCP/IP, in which there are (unfortunately) two incompatible standard RPC implementations:

- OSF's DCE
- Sun's ONC+ (probably the more widely implemented of the two)

To an application program, RPCs are local procedure calls that happen to start processes on remote machines. Communication is *synchronous* (sometimes called *blocking*), in that the requester must wait for a response before continuing.

An alternative to this concept is called *messaging*.

See *API*, *DCE*, *Messaging*, *ONC*, *OSF*, and *Sun*.

RPI
Rockwell Protocol Interface

A method of reducing the cost of modems by having the PC's CPU handle the error correction (V.42) and data compression (V.42*bis*), rather than a modem's own processor.

Rockwell International (who make almost all the modem and fax machine modem ICs) make low-cost versions of their modem ICs used anywhere by anyone that support this interface.

The assumption is that people seldom actually use their PCs for multitasking, so the CPU has time to handle these extra tasks while doing data communications.

The argument goes like this: Most file transfer protocols have their own error correction, so the modem's V.42 is redundant. And while RPI's software-based data compression may be slower than that implemented in a modem, most file transfers (which is possibly the most common application that requires high throughput) are of precompressed files (for example, using `pkzip`, etc.), so V.42*bis* "on-the-fly" data compression is not used anyway.

Communication software (or the operating system) must support RPI to get the benefit of error correction or data compression on RPI modems (which do not do any error correction or data compression themselves). Without RPI software, RPI modems behave like standard modems that have no error correction or data compression.

A modem with built-in error correction and data compression is a stand-alone box with known capability (that's a good thing). RPI introduces dependencies (never a good thing), so that your computer's data communications capabilities are dependent on many factors. For example:

- What if the PC's processor is not fast enough to support this extra work?
- What if several communication software packages, or operating systems, are used with the modem—and not all support RPI?
- What if the modem is being used with something other than a PC, for which there is no RPI communication software available?
- What if the data traffic is not precompressed? That is, while it is true that most files on bulletin board systems and the on-line services (such as CompuServe) are precompressed, dial-up data communications requirements are rapidly changing. For example, now that "surfing the Internet" is becoming very popular, downloading uncompressed (but highly compressible) files (such as WWW pages and USENET news) is much more common (and never fast enough).

The idea is that you buy an RPI modem if these concerns are of no concern to you. Otherwise, spend the extra money and get a modem with built-in error correction and data compression.

See *Modem*, *MNP*, *PC*, *Rockwell International*, *V.42*, and *V.42bis*.

RS-232
Recommended Standard 232

See *EIA/TIA-232*.

RSA
Rivest, Shamir, Adleman Public Key Encryption

A patented *public key* (also called *dual-key* or *asymmetric*) *data encryption* scheme that can provide both encryption and *authentication*.

Uses a pair of keys: the public key and the *private* or *secret key*.

When one key (either one) is used to encrypt a message, the only way to decrypt it is by using the other key of the pair. Each participant in secure exchanges has his or her own pair of public and private keys. The private key is kept secret, and the public key is distributed to anyone who wants it.

- When a recipient's public key is used to encrypt the message, then the message is unreadable to everyone but the holder of the secret key. Therefore the message content is kept secret.
- When a sender uses his or her secret key to encrypt the message, then anyone (with a copy of the sender's public key) can decrypt the message, with the assurance that only the holder of the secret key could have encrypted it. Therefore the message has been authenticated.

Combining these methods provides both authentication (analogous to someone's written signature) and encryption. (Now what else could you ask for?)

The technique was developed at Stanford University in 1977, but is named after three Massachusetts Institute of Technology professors (Ronald L. Rivest, Adi Shamir, and Leonard M. Adleman), who made it a useful system and started a company (RSA Data Security, Inc., though only Rivest is still with the company) to license the technology and sell software toolkits for application developers so that they can add these capabilities to their software.

RSA maintains a WWW server at *http://www.rsa.com/*.

See *Authentication*, *DES*, *Encryption*, *PGP*, and *S-HTTP*.

RSVP
Resource Reservation Protocol

A standard for reserving resources required in each network (there could be many networking technologies involved) along an end-to-end path so that a (likely multimedia) application receives the quality of service required.

See *Multimedia*, *QOS*, and *Prioritization*.

RTFM
Read the F_ _ _ _ _ _ Manual

Commonly expressed by technical support personnel (*almost* inaudibly) when the information that a user seeks is already in the manual (which surprises users, since they think that manuals never have the information needed—at least, not so you can find it without reading the whole thing, word by word).

Nonetheless, users usually think that only wimps (need to) read manuals.

If I may expand: It used to be that real programmers used assembler language (you know, LOAD this memory location, MOVE that register—tough, brain-busting work). Most people now concede that it is rarely necessary to use assembler, so the only way to distinguish yourself is by doing your job without reading the manual. Perhaps someday people will write more complete manuals, and users will take (or have) the time to read the manual. Then again, who would need consultants if everyone read (or had the time to read) the manual?

See *FAQ*.

RTMP
Routing Table Maintenance Protocol

Apple's older (but still widely used) distance-vector–based routing protocol. The link-state replacement is AURP (excuse me).

See *AURP*, *Link-state*, and *RIP*.

Run Length Encoding   See **RLE.**

SAA
Systems Application Architecture

An application-layer effort (that is, the APIs) to enable a program to run, and communicate with others, on all of IBM's platforms.

It is a guideline for uniform languages, file structures, and processes. Builds on LU 6.2 and is therefore peer-to-peer (and not *terminal-emulation*) oriented.

See *API*, *Client/Server*, *HLLAPI*, *LU 6.2*, and *SNA*.

Santa Cruz Operation   See **SCO.**

SAP
Service Advertising Protocol

Novell NetWare's *multicast* (that is, a *broadcast* to a specific group of workstations—in this case, those running the IPX protocol) oriented protocol for making file, print, communication, and other servers' capabilities, LAN address, and network number known to workstations.

Runs on top of IPX. Periodic *SAP information broadcasts* are automatically generated by servers (usually every 60 seconds).

A *SAP service query* can be sent by a workstation any time it wishes to learn of available servers—without waiting for up to 60 seconds for the next periodic SAP information broadcast. For example, when the NetX shell is loaded, a SAP service query is sent. Servers then immediately reply with a *SAP service response* frame, which contains the same information as the periodic SAP information broadcast.

If a *preferred server* has not been set in the Net.cfg file, or specified on the command-line, then login is attempted to the first responding server.

See *IPX*, *NLSP*, *Novell*, and *RIP*.

Satellite

A complicated electronic and mechanical wonder hundreds or thousands of miles up in space, put there by some rocket or space shuttle, often to provide communications services.

Communications may use satellites because satellites have a *line-of-sight* (that is, direct—no trees, buildings, mountains, or horizon in the way) view of large geographic areas, owing to their height (no, the satellites are not tall, they are just really high up in the sky). This is important, since the microwave frequencies that are used won't bounce off objects—the transmitter and receiver must be able to "see" each other.

Satellites have some number of *transponders*, each of which receives a signal, amplifies it, and retransmits it (typically at 8.5 to 60 watts—though the new direct broadcast satellites use up to 120 watts so that very small receiving antennas can be used) on a different (so that the satellite does not transmit to its own receiver) frequency.

Transponders typically have a bandwidth of 36 to 72 MHz each (though newer satellites have up to 108-MHz transponder bandwidths).

For comparison, an NTSC standard analog television video (with audio) signal requires 24 to 36 MHz of transponder bandwidth, so each transponder typically carries one, two, or three television signals (two for a 54-MHz transponder, three for a 72-MHz transponder). Video signal digitization and compression schemes allow up to eight television signals to share the bandwidth required by a single uncompressed video signal. However, there is no single standard compression scheme, and this is preventing wider adoption of compression.

Renting satellite time (for example, for a company's nationwide one-way satellite broadcast to its employees) costs about $1,000 per hour. This is for a standard analog, uncompressed video signal.

The bandwidth required by a single television signal can carry about 960 telephone conversations.

Television Receive Only (TVRO) is a very common use of satellite dish antennas (your standard back yard installation, for example).

Traditionally, communication satellites have been placed in a *geostationary* orbit called the "*Clarke Belt*" or "*Clarke Orbit*"—named after Arthur C. Clarke, who thought of geostationary communications satellites back in 1945 (and also wrote the screenplay of *2001: A Space Odyssey* in 1968—and also over 70 books). The Clarke Orbit is where the gravitational force of the earth (which pulls down) exactly counters the centrifugal force (which pulls out), because of the satellite's rotating around the earth (it does this at the same speed at which the earth rotates).

The Clarke Belt is 22,225 miles (more precisely, 35,767.0 km, ± 0.6 km) above the equator. Satellites are typically placed about 2° apart (about 1,500 km at that height) to prevent signals to and from the adjacent satellites from interfering with each other (satellites using different frequency bands, typically C and K_u, can be much closer together). Also, this separation eliminates any chance of the satellites bumping into each other. (Satellites actually drift slightly and need short bursts from their thruster rockets to keep them in the right place. The amount of rocket propellant is often what limits a satellite's life—usually about 10 years.)

Geosynchronous satellites must orbit the earth at a great height (for the physics to work out so that the satellite can "float" at exactly the same location, so the ground-based satellite antennas don't need to move to track the satellite). Also, the speed of light (in a vacuum) is 2.9979250×10^8 m/s (± 100 m/s), which is about 186,282 miles per second.

In air, light slows down a bit (to about 99.97% of this). And radio waves travel at the speed of light (since they are the same thing: electromagnetic waves).

Therefore, to travel from the earth to a geosynchronous satellite, a signal has to go 22,225 miles, at 186,227 miles per second—which takes 120 ms. While this delay does not matter for a television broadcast (though that does mean that you are not getting your CNN news *exactly* as it happens), the round-trip delay for a satellite-based data communications circuit will be four times that (up and down again to get from one end of the satellite-based data communication circuit to the other, up and down to get back), which is almost ½ second (479 ms to be more precise).

For protocols with a window size of 1 (which cannot send a second frame until the first is acknowledged), this means that only one frame of data can be sent every 479 ms (just over two frames per second), regardless of the actual data's bit rate. In contrast, the width of North America is only about 5,500 miles. The round-trip delay would be only about 91 ms (even assuming that the signal would travel in fiber-optic cable, which propagates signals at "only" 65% of the speed of light). Humans cannot perceive delays of under about 100 to 200 ms.

Therefore, switching to a satellite-based data communications circuit can reduce network throughput, even if the bit-note is the same.

A ground-based satellite antenna is usually a large (2.1 to 3.6 m for C-band users, 1 to 1.8 m for K_u-band users, 4.5 to 10 m at the central site), parabolic-shaped dish which gathers lots of signal from the satellite and aims it all at the dish's receiver, usually located at the parabola's focus. The dish points exactly at the satellite from which it is receiving (you can't see it, but that satellite is certainly exactly where its receiving antenna is aimed).

Since there are (only) 360° in a full circle, a 2° separation allows for 180 geosynchronous communications satellites (of which each must be somewhat above the area to which it is to provide communications—this area is called the satellite's *footprint*). Space may be infinite and the final frontier, but when it comes to geosynchronous satellites, there is room up there for only about 180 of them! (Actually, since many satellites do use different frequency bands, there are currently slightly more than 220 geosynchronous satellites in orbit.) Also, if you want to broadcast to North America, getting a satellite position above some ocean won't help you—that is, satellite slots over North America are extremely valuable and completely sold out.

Two frequency bands are commonly used for satellites carrying video (television signals):

- The C-band has been used for many years, requires a larger receiving antenna, and receivers are often only able to receive C-band signals (especially for older receivers).
- The use of K_u-band frequencies for satellites is newer, and requires more careful aiming of the satellite antenna. K_u-band receivers (that is, most new ones) can usually also receive C-band.

The table below shows the actual frequencies used. The *uplink* is from the source of the signal, up to the satellite. The *downlink* is from the satellite, down to all of the receiving satellite dish antennas on the earth.

| | Frequency Band | | | |
| | C | | K_u | |
	Lower (GHz)	Upper (GHz)	Lower (GHz)	Upper (GHz)
Defined frequency range for entire band	4	8	12	18
Defined frequency range for satellite use	3.40	6.425	10.95	14.5
Typical North American satellite uplink frequency	5.945	6.405	14.04	14.44
Typical North American satellite down-link frequency	3.72	4.18	11.7	12.1

The type, designation, and location of the geosynchronous satellites above North America are listed in the table below (for reference, the *Continental U.S.* (CONUS) extends from about 65° to 125° of longitude, west of Greenwich, England). The table also shows the number and bandwidth of the transponders. As shown, many satellites (especially the newer ones) have both C-band and K_u-band capability.

Satellite Name	Desig-nation	Loca-tion[a]	Transponders			
			C-band		K$_u$-band	
			No.	Band-width (MHz)	No.	Band-width (MHz)
GE Americom Satcom SpaceNet 2	S2	69.0	6	72	6	72
			12	36		
Comsat SBS 2	SBS2	71.0			10	86
Hughes Communications Galaxy 6	G6	74.0	24	36		
Comsat SBS 3	SBS3	74.0			10	42
Hughes Communications SBS 4	SBS4	77.0			10	42
GE Americom	K2	81.0			16	54
AT&T Telstar 302	T2	85.0	24	36		
GE Americom (Primestar DBS)	K1	85.0			16	
GE Americom Satcom SpaceNet 3R[b]	S3	87.0	12	36	6	72
			6	72		
Hughes Communications Galaxy 7	G7	91.0	24	36	24	108
GE Americom GStar 3	GST3	93.0			16	108
Hughes Communications Galaxy 3	G3	93.5	24	36		
Hughes Communications SBS 6	SBS6	95.0			19	42
AT&T Telstar 401	T401	97.0	24		16	54
Hughes Communications Galaxy 4	G4	99.0	24	36	24	54
GE American Satcom 4	S4	101.0	12	36	6	72
			6	72		
Hughes Communiations DirecTV	DBS2	100.8			16	
Hughes Communications DirecTV	DBS1	101.3			16	
GE Americom GStar 1	GST1	103.0			16	54
GE Americom GStar 4	GST4	105.0			16	54
Telesat Canada Anik E2	E2	107.3	24	36	16	54
Solidaridad 1	SD1	109.2	12	36	16	54
			6	72		
Telesat Canada Anik E1	E1	111.0	24	36	16	54
Solidaridad 2	SD2	113.0	12	36	16	54
			6	72		
Telesat Canada Anik C3	C3	114.9			16	54

(table continued on next page)

Satellite Name	Desig-nation	Loca-tion[a]	Transponders			
			C-band		K$_u$-band	
			No.	Band-width (MHz)	No.	Band-width (MHz)
Morelos 2	M2	116.8	12	36	4	108
			6	72		
AT&T Telstar 303	T3	123.0	24	36		
Hughes Communications SBS	SBS5	123.0			10	42
					4	108
Hughes Communications Galaxy 5	G5	125.0	24	36		
GE Americom GStar 2	GST2	125.0			16	54
GE Americom Satcom	C3	131.0	24	36		
Hughes Communications Galaxy 1R[b]	G1	133.0	24	36		
GE Americom Satcom	C4	135.0	24	36		
GE Americom Satcom	C1	137.0	24	36		
GE Americom Satcom (Aurora)	C5	139.0	24	36		

[a] Degrees West longitude

[b] The "R" designation means Replacement—usually because the original one didn't make it into orbit and start working successfully.

Many new communication satellite systems use (or are being designed for) lower orbits—*Low Earth Orbit* (LEO) and *Medium Earth Orbit* (MEO)—because almost all geosynchronous orbit slots are filled (and all of the ones over North America are taken). Alos, using lower-orbiting (closer to the earth) satellites permits lower-power transmitters and smaller antennas to be used. This is important for mobile communications—nobody wants to carry a 10-foot satellite dish in their pocket (mind you, think of the prestige—wouldn't I be the most important person in the restaurant?).

By switching between satellites (similar to how cellular telephones hand-off between cell sites), a receiver can provide continuous communication service.

Satellites are sometimes (with respect and affection) called *birds*.

Some excellent satellite information is available from Robert Smathers' WWW Satellite Page at *http://www.nmia.com/~roberts/roberts.html* (especially his South Scanner Satellite Services Chart). The satellite TV FAQ is at *http://www.cis.ohio-state.edu/ hypertext/faq/usenet/Satellite-TV/faq/faq.html*. Less information can be found at *http://www.xmission.com/~keycom/KC_terms.html*. TeleSat Canada has a WWW home page at *http://www.telesat.ca,* and INTELSAT has one at *http://www.intelsat.int:8080/*.

See *AMPS*, *CATV*, *Composite Video Signal*, *GPS*, *NTSC*, *Teleglobe, Inc.*, *Video*, and *VSAT*.

SBD
Smart Battery Data

Part of an effort initiated by Duracell and Intel to define a method to monitor a rechargeable battery pack (see SMBus for the other part).

A specialized IC (which is part of the battery pack) monitors the batteries' voltage, current, and temperature, and interfaces to the SMBus to report information such as the battery pack's:

- Type, model number, manufacturer, and characteristics
- Discharge rate, and the predicted remaining capacity (so you know how much longer you have)
- Almost-discharged alarm (so that the PC can gracefully shut down before the battery is exhausted)
- Temperature and voltage (required by the battery charger so that it can provide fast charging while ensuring the batteries are not damaged)

See *Batteries* and *SMBus*.

Scalable Architecture

A computer system or data communications network design (some would say *architecture*) in which an increase in processing power or capacity (for example, adding processors to an MPP computer or increasing the speed or number of data communications circuits) is transparent to users and their applications.

Upgrading a nonscalable architecture often requires a *"fork-lift upgrade."* The entire system is replaced, usually at high cost, great disruption, and embarrassment (that the system you installed only a short while ago is now good for nothing).

See *MPP*.

Scalable Font

Another name for an outline font.

See *Bitmap Font* and *Outline Font*.

Scalable Processor Architecture   See **SPARC**.

Scale

The standard musical scale is based on an *equally tempered* (also called a *12-tone chromatic*) *scale*. In this scale, an *octave* consists of 12 equally spaced frequencies, each note being $2^{1/12}$ (which is called the twelfth root of 2, which is roughly 1.059463) from the previous note, as shown in the following table for the A440 musical scale. Therefore, the twelfth note is double the frequency of the first note.

Musical Note	Frequency		Koday Equivalent
	Equation	Hz	
A	440	440.00	do
A#	$440 \times 2^{1/12}$	466.16	
B	$440 \times 2^{2/12}$	493.88	re
C	$440 \times 2^{3/12}$	523.25	
C#	$440 \times 2^{4/12}$	554.37	mi
D	$440 \times 2^{5/12}$	587.33	fa
D#	$440 \times 2^{6/12}$	622.25	
E	$440 \times 2^{7/12}$	659.26	sol
F	$440 \times 2^{8/12}$	698.46	
F#	$440 \times 2^{9/12}$	739.99	la
G	$440 \times 2^{10/12}$	783.99	
G#	$440 \times 2^{11/12}$	830.61	ti
A2	$440 \times 2^{12/12}$	880.00	do

As shown, your standard "do re mi" scale (as in the movie *The Sound of Music*) is eight notes from the 12, and this is called the *diatonic scale*.

See *MIDI*.

SCAM
SCSI Configuration Automatically

Provides *Plug and Play* support for SCSI devices.

Automatically assigns I/O addresses, interrupts, and the like, and should load the correct driver for the devices on the SCSI bus. Also provides automatic termination of the SCSI bus and assigning of SCSI *device IDs* (so each device gets a unique ID).

See *PnP* and *SCSI*.

SCO
Santa Cruz Operation

A company that makes a popular UNIX-like operating system that runs on PCs. Their GUI-based, OSF/1-compliant, *Open Desktop UNIX* (ODT) will run on several platforms and will run DOS applications in an emulation mode.

Make sure you pronounce "cruz" as "cruise" (like on a ship); otherwise, you'll feel as silly as I did when I asked for a *La Jolla burger* (what a tourist!) on my first business trip to San Diego (say "hoya," not "jawla").

SCO has a WWW server at (where else, but) *http://www.sco.com/*.

See *COSE*, *iBCS*, *ODT*, and *UNIX*.

Screened Twisted Pair   See **ScTP**.

SCSI
Small Computer System Interface

A method of linking disk drives (and more) to a PC (or Macintosh, or workstation, etc.).

A parallel bus (8 bits wide, now sometimes called SCSI-1 to differentiate it from the subsequent SCSI-2 and SCSI-3) for linking mass storage devices (primarily disk and tape drives) to a computer.

Based on the *selector channel* IBM designed for the IBM System/360 computers, which was later (in 1981) adapted by Shugart Associates and called the *Shugart Associates Systems Interface* (SASI). In 1982, ANSI began work on what is now called SCSI, with the first version of the SCSI standard released in 1986.

Originally supported only hard disk drives but now includes functions for other peripherals, such as CD-ROM drives, scanners, high-speed printers, and Group 4 fax machines.

The connector used is as follows:

- For Macintosh computers, a DB-25 25-pin connector
- For PCs, an RJ-21 TelCo (also called Amp or Centronics) style 50-pin connector, usually used for older SCSI-1 devices, or an HD (high-density) type, usually used for SCSI-2 devices

Up to eight devices (including the controller in the computer) can be on the bus.

Typical maximum sustained transfer rates for a SCSI-connected disk drive is usually 1.5 to 2.5 Mbytes/s (because of the disk drive's rotational speed and seek time limitations).

Predecessor disk drive interface specifications (such as ST506 and ESDI) were bit-serial (only 1 data bit was transferred at a time) and supported only data transfer and hard-wired disk drive control. For example, a specific signal line (wire) stepped the disk drive's read/write head, another wire indicated the step direction, another indicated read or write operation, and another carried the data—in the format needed by the disk drive, such as MFM (*Modified Frequency Modulation*) or RLL (*Run Length Limited*). Therefore the controller used was very dependent on the type of disk drive being controlled.

SCSI handles higher-level commands, such as asking what types of devices are on the bus (`Inquiry`) and `Read` or `Write` a block of data. That is, in addition to specifying the physical characteristics of the bus (connector type, voltages used, etc.), the standard for each type of peripheral (hard disk, CD-ROM, etc.) includes a specification for the supported Commands (usually about 12 for each peripheral) and expected responses. SCSI commands can be either *standard* or *vendor-specific*.

For SCSI-1 the standard commands are grouped into six *device types*, as shown in the following table.

Device Type	Name	Typical Function
1	Write/read random access (hard disk)	Logical block address, length of block to be written
2	Sequential access (tape drive)	Read next record
3	Printer	Page layout control
4	Processor	Simple send and receive
5	WORM (recordable CD-ROM)	Large size, removable
6	Read-only random access	Logical block address, length of block to be read

Having more than one software driver (for example, a disk driver and a tape backup driver) using the same adapter (that is, there is both a disk and a tape drive on the bus) requires software such as Adaptec's ASPI to be installed. The adapter and all drivers using the adapter must be configured for the same type of such sharing software.

Each peripheral (device on the bus) is manually assigned a *SCSI ID* (usually by setting jumpers or a switch on the device), which is a number from 0 through 7. The number of devices supported per bus is limited by the width of the data bus (since each device identifies itself when contending for control of the bus by controlling its corresponding bit on the data bus). Therefore the optional 16-bit-wide SCSI-2 and SCSI-3 bus support up to 16 devices per bus.

SCSI supports up to eight *logical units* per peripheral (that is, they all share the same SCSI ID), but this is rarely used.

The SCSI adapter in the host PC is usually assigned the highest SCSI ID (ID number 7) because the highest number wins a *bus arbitration* (when more than one device attempts to gain control of the bus for a transfer) and it is best to have the host able to control the bus when it needs to.

In fact, ID 7 has the highest priority even for SCSI buses that are wider than 8 bits—since the IDs 0 though 7 are defined to have higher priority than 8 through 15 (this ensures that 8-bit and wider devices can be on the same bus).

SCSI peripherals are usually assigned IDs starting at zero, though slower devices (such as tape and CD-ROM drives) should get higher IDs so that the faster devices (hard disks) can't hog the bus.

Initiators send commands, and *targets* respond. Usually, the host adapter (the SCSI controller) is the initiator ("get me some data, please"), and the peripherals are targets. For some commands, this is reversed—for example, when a CD-ROM has been changed or a tape drive has finished rewinding.

Disks read and write data according to *logical block addresses*; the host has no knowledge of the disk's physical geometry, such as number of surfaces, cylinders, or sectors. A hard disk SCSI command (`Read Capacity`) enables a host adapter to query a disk for its capacity (expressed as a number of logical blocks) and *block size* (512 bytes per block, for example).

SCSI supports more than one host adapter per bus. For example, two computers can be connected to the same SCSI bus (each with its own adapter), and both can therefore control the same peripheral, but this is rarely done.

SCSI data transfers can be either of the following:

- *Asynchronous*: There is a `Request` and `Acknowledge` control line handshake for each transferred byte to ensure that the data are not sent too fast. Data transfer is typically at about 2 Mbytes/s.
- *Synchronous*: The sender is allowed to send at a preset data rate, such as 3.33, 4, or 5 Mbytes/s. By far the most common rate is 5 Mbytes/s (for SCSI-1 devices).

Synchronous transfer is faster, especially on longer buses. To use synchronous data transfers, both the initiator and the target peripheral (no need for all peripherals on a bus to support it, though) must support synchronous transfers (at the same speed).

Nondata transfers (commands, status responses, etc.) use asynchronous mode, though the data portion of a response (for example, the `Inquiry` command, which requests an ASCII string identifying the peripheral—this response is often displayed on a PC's monitor when the SCSI drivers are loaded) can use synchronous (which may explain why some misconfigured SCSI devices can identify themselves but can't read or write data).

Each of the two ends of a SCSI bus must be *terminated* (that is, have *resistors* connected to each signal line). All other devices on the SCSI bus (even if it is the host adapter) must have their termination resistors disconnected or removed. The termination resistors:

- May be switched electronically (by running a configuration program supplied with the SCSI adapter)
- May be *Single In-line Package* (SIP—one row of pins) or *Dual In-line Package* (DIP—two rows of pins) resistor networks. Some important points concerning these resistors follow:
  - The resistor packages typically have 8, 10, or 16 pins, and plug into sockets.
  - A dot or indent at one end or corner of the package identifies pin 1, which *must* be plugged in to pin 1 of the socket (usually identified by a dot on the printed circuit board or a square solder pad).
  - Note that there are different pin-outs and values for these resistor networks. Make sure you record the socket and orientation before removing them (and tape them inside the case so that they don't get lost). Before using resistors from one device in another, verify that the resistance values and pin-out match.

SCSI buses can use either *single-ended* or *differential* electrical signals. Since these use different pin-outs for the connectors, all devices on a bus (including the termination resistors and the cables) *must* be the same type.

Buses for PCs usually use single-ended electrical signals (negative-logic, open-collector 7438 TTL drivers) and are limited to 6 meters total length (because of the poor noise immunity of single-ended buses).

There are two types of single-ended termination resistors:

- *Passive termination* is a 220-Ω pull-up resistor to a 4.25 to 5.25-V supply (called the *termination power*) and a 330-Ω resistor to ground, for each signal line.
- *Active termination* has a *voltage regulator* that provides a 2.85-V output (using power from the termination power supply) and a 110-Ω resistor from each signal line to this 2.85-V source.

Although these two types of terminations are electrically the same (the latter is the *Thévenin equivalent* of the former), the active termination (which is typically a larger, connector-like device) is recommended (because of its better noise immunity).

A bus can mix these types of termination (one at each end) or have both terminations the same type.

SCSI buses for minicomputers and UNIX workstations usually use the higher-cost *differential* electrical interface, which:

- Uses balanced RS-485 voltages rather than unbalanced TTL voltages. While this costs more to implement (two wires, and therefore two electrical drivers, are required for each signal), the bus can be up to 25 meters in length (and longer if lower transfer rates and good quality cables are used).
- Uses passive termination—again, one at each end of the bus. In this case, the termination is a 330 Ω pull up resistor (to the termination power) for the "−" wire of each signal, and a 220 Ω resistor to ground for the "+" wire of each signal.

The two wires of the signal pair are then tied together with a 150-Ω resistor.

For good noise immunity, external SCSI cables (those running outside of a PC's enclosure) not only must use twisted pairs, but also should be built in three concentric layers:

- The center has three pairs: Request, Acknowledge, and Ground.
- The next layer (the control signals) has the pairs twisted in the opposite direction (as compared to the other layers) to reduce the capacitive coupling between layers.
- The third (outside) layer (the data and *parity* wires) has its pairs twisted in the opposite direction (compared to the middle layer).

Putting the control signals in the middle layer ensures that the data and Request/Acknowledge signals do not interfere with each other.

The individual wires should not use PVC insulation, since PVC has electrical characteristics that are too temperature-dependent and has too high a capacitance (though the overall cable jacket can be PVC). These requirements show why SCSI cables are so expensive, made differently for single-ended and differential use (since their pin-outs are different), and are a bad place to save money (by buying no-name cheapo cables, which may not follow these rules).

SCAM provides automatic *Plug and Play* configuration (and other features) for SCSI devices.

A draft of the SCSI-1 specification is at *ftp://ftp.cs.tulane.edu/pub/scsi/area07/*.* (see the file files.BBS there for a description).

See *ASPI, Bus, DB-25, Disk Drive, FAT, Fax, IDE, Parity, PnP, SCAM, SCSI-2, TTL, TWAIN,* and *Winchester.*

SCSI-1
Small Computer System Interface-1

The first version of SCSI, often referred to simply as SCSI.

See *SCSI*.

SCSI-2
Small Computer System Interface-2

An enhancement to the SCSI-1 specification that provides more of the following:

Compatibility—the SCSI-1 specification left much room for (incompatible) inter-pretation by vendors, so (for example) specific disk drivers would work only with specific SCSI controllers

Types of devices supported, as the specification defines the command sets for devices other than disk drives, such as tape drives, CD-ROM drives, and so on.

Speed—faster transfer rates (of up to 10 Mtransfers/s). *Fast SCSI* is a subset of this specification and supports transfer rates of up to 10 Mbytes/s—up from SCSI-1's 5 Mbytes/s (over an 8-bit-wide bus).

A wider bus option (16- and 32-bit-wide buses—called *wide SCSI*) requires two cables, called the *A* (original-8 bit) and *B* (provides the additional 8 bits for the 16-bit-wide bus) *cables*. Since two cables are expensive and messy, most vendors support the 16-bit-wide option using only the 68-pin *P-cable* defined for SCSI-3 (which provides a 16-bit-wide bus using a single cable and connector). The origi-nal 8-bit-wide SCSI bus is therefore sometimes called *narrow SCSI*.

The bus has an *odd parity bit* for every 8 data bits (so 16-bit-wide SCSI has 2 parity bits). Parity was optional for SCSI-1 (therefore, some older devices require it to be disabled) but is mandatory for SCSI-2.

A *fast-wide SCSI* bus supports data transfer at up to 40 Mbytes/s, though maximum sustained actual transfer rates from a single disk drive are typically 4 Mbytes/s or slower, owing to the speed of the disk drive itself.

The *disconnect* and *reconnect* commands enable a peripheral to work on a command (for example a disk drive Seek) while the bus is freed up (the host adapter releases its connection to the peripheral) so the host adapter can communicate with other devices on the bus (connect to them, and issue commands or read data). There-fore, a SCSI bus can have some disk drives seeking while the adapter is transferring data to or from another drive. As for other performance-enhancing options (such as synchronous data transfer support), this must be supported by both the initiator and the target.

Queuing enables a host to give a peripheral many commands, and the peripheral may reorder the commands to optimize performance, for example, choosing the next request that provides the best overall throughput, not necessarily the one that it received first. There are many disk drive algorithms that require this (for example, the *elevator algorithm* requires the disk to serve only queued requests that do not require the read/write head to reverse direction until the end of the disk is reached). This optional feature must be supported by both the host adapter and the peripheral.

Reliability—Active termination (with termination power provided by the host adapter) is recommended for single-ended buses. This provides less line noise and less signal attenuation.

Connectors for the 8- and 16-bit-wide buses are a smaller (than SCSI-1's) connector—0.050" pitch, 50-pin Micro-D type (two such cables and connectors are specified for 16-bit transfers). For the 32-bit-wide bus, a 68-pin P-type connector is specified. The connectors use springy clip locks, as for SCSI-1.

To allow both SCSI-1 and SCSI-2 devices to reside on the same SCSI bus at the same time, SCSI-2 controllers support different transfer speeds to each SCSI device on the bus.

The following table summarizes peak data transfer rates for different disk drive interfaces.

Available	Disk Interface	Theoretical Peak Transfer Rate (Mbytes/s)
1980	Floppy diskette (single density)	0.08
1981	ST-506[a] (interleaved[b] 2:1)	0.3
	ST-506 (MFM, non-interleaved)	0.63
	ST-506 (RLL)	0.94
	ESDI (10 MHz)	1.25
	ESDI (20 MHz)	2.5
	IDE (on an 8-bit ISA bus)	4
1990	IDE (on a 16-bit ISA bus)	8
1986	SCSI-1 (asynchronous)	2
1990	SCSI-1 (synchronous)	5
1993	SCSI-2 fast	10
	SCSI-2 16-bit-wide	10

(table continued on next page)

Available	Disk Interface	Theoretical Peak Transfer Rate (Mbytes/s)
	SCSI–2 fast and 16–bit–wide	20
	SCSI–2 32–bit–wide	20
	SCSI–2 Fast and 32–bit–wide	40

[a] The ST-506 disk interface was developed by Seagate Technology for their Winchester disk drives. See *Winchester*.

[b] Interleaving (which is no longer used) places sequential sectors of data in every second (for 2:1 interleaving) sector on the disk to give the host computer enough time (while the next sector goes by the disk's read/write head) to process the sector just read.

Note that the above rates are burst rates (while the data are actually being transferred on the bus). The actual throughput will be much slower, owing to disk drive seek times, SCSI bus protocol overhead, computer bus contention, CPU processing times, and other factors.

SCSI-2 and SCSI-3 devices must start in 8-bit (not wide) mode, 5 Mtransfers/s (not fast) mode, and in asynchronous (not synchronous) mode to ensure that initial communications will work. Then negotiations between the initiator and the target are supposed to work out the maximum mutual capabilities (though this does not always work, and they may need to be set manually).

SCSI-2 defines an additional five device types, as shown in the following table.

Device Type	Name	Typical Function
6	CD-ROM	Replaces the read-only random access defined in SCSI-1
7	Scanner	A printer in reverse
8	Magneto optical	
9	Medium changer (also called a jukebox; for example, can select one of many CDs loaded into a cassette or magazine)	Controls selection of medium
10	Communication	

A draft of the SCSI-2 specification is in the directory *ftp://ftp.cs.tulane.edu/ pub/scsi/area08/*.*. See the file index for a description of the directory's contents.

See *IDE, Parity, SCSI, SCSI-3,* and *Winchester*.

SCSI-3
Small Computer System Interface-3

An enhancement to SCSI-2 that supports:

- Up to 32 devices per SCSI bus
- 16-bit transfers on a single cable (called the *P-cable*, which is a 68-pin Micro-D connector with 2-56 or 4-40 screw locks)
- A serial option (*serial SCSI*, using a six-pin connector, supporting many types of media including fiber and twisted pair, and distances greater than 1 km)
- Data integrity improvements

A subset of SCSI-3, called *fast-20*, supports up to 20 Mtransfers/s (providing 20 Mbytes/s transfers over the original 8-bit-wide "narrow" bus and 40 Mbytes/s transfers over the 16-bit-wide P-cable). Single-ended fast-20 devices have an optional *active negation* feature that actively drives selected signals high (rather than waiting for the termination's pull-up resistors to do it).

Fast-20 controllers will be able to talk different rates to each device on the SCSI bus, enabling newer (and faster) devices to reside on the same bus as older (slower) devices.

Cable distances will likely be 3 m total for single-ended SCSI buses (this is less than SCSI-2's 6 m—owing to the greater transfer rate) and 25 m for differential busses (which is the same as for SCSI-2).

SCSI-3 requires active termination.

While SCSI-2 was compatible with, and has largely replaced, SCSI-1, SCSI-3 will likely be different enough (and more expensive) that it will not replace SCSI-2.

See *SCSI-2*.

SCSI Configuration Automatically   See **SCAM.**

ScTP
Screened Twisted Pair

Twisted pair cable with some characteristics better than Category 5 UTP; therefore some people used to refer to it as Category 6 (but there is no official Category 6 UTP).

Has four twisted pairs (as UTP does) but has a foil shield (unlike UTP).

Used in Europe (some say more for political than technical reasons). Unlikely to become a standard in North America.

See *Cable* and *UTP*.

SD
Super Density

The current name for the *digital video disk* format promoted by Toshiba and Time-Warner.

A double-sided, CD-ROM-like (but incompatible), play-only disk that is intended to store full-length movies and computer games. The capabilities are:

- 5 Gbytes stored per side. Two 0.6-mm-thick disks are bonded back-to-back for a 10-Gbyte total capacity. The 10 Gbytes provides 180 to 270 minutes (total) of compressed audio (including at least three different language tracks) and video.
- A "parental lockout" feature so that playback skips past violent or risqué scenes.

Developed by Toshiba, Matsushita (maker of the Panasonic, Technics, and Quasar brands), Hitachi, Pioneer, and Time-Warner. Supported by Denon, Hitachi, JVC, Mitsubishi, Samsung, Thomson (maker of the RCA brand), and Zenith, with content from movie producers Warner Brothers, MCA, MGM/UA, Toshiba/EMI, Turner Home Entertainment, and WEA.

A typical two-hour movie requires 3.5 Gbytes. The additional 1.5 Gbytes of capacity could be used for interactive applications, advertising, or another movie. The audio includes five Dolby Digital surround-sound channels plus a subwoofer channel (low frequencies are very nondirectional, so only one such channel—and speaker—is needed). Multiple language soundtracks and subtitles can be stored as well.

Was to compete with Sony and Philips' Video-CD (which was intended more for the computer market, and sacrificed capacity for compatibility with conventional CD-ROMs), but the two groups (under great industry pressure) merged their two efforts in late 1995.

See *CD-ROM* (*Video CD*) and *DVD*.

SDH
Synchronous Digital Hierarchy

The SONet-like, really high-speed transmission standard used outside of North America.

SDH has some additional features, such as improved *operation and maintenance* (OAM) capabilities. Uses multiples of 155.52 Mbits/s, so SDH's STM-1 rate corresponds to SONet's OC-3 rate.

Of the 155.52 Mbits/s bit rate of STM-1, 5.72 Mbits/s (3.7%) is SDH framing overhead, leaving 149.8 Mbits/s for user data.

Standardized by the ITU

See *E1*, *SONet*, and *STM*.

SDK
Software Development Kit

The software (typically APIs, utilities, and documentation) that an application programmer needs to create programs using a particular platform (hardware, operating system, and/or protocol).

See *API*.

SDLC
Synchronous Data Link Control

IBM's name for *High-level Data Link Control* (HDLC).

A bit-oriented, link-layer protocol usually used by SNA on synchronous data links.

Unlike HDLC, IBM usually uses SDLC in a *polling* mode (a *front end processor* continually asks whether the peripherals have any data to send).

IBM's predecessor protocol is BISYNC.

See *BISYNC*, *DLC*, *DLSw*, *Encapsulation*, *FEP*, *HDLC*, *IBM*, *Prioritization*, *SNA*, and *Synchronous*.

SECAM
Séquentiel Couleur Avec Mémoire

The analog color television broadcasting standard that is used in Eastern Europe and Russia.

There are many different implementations, with names like SECAM-B (which requires 7 MHz per channel) and SECAM-L (which requires 8 MHz per channel—and, one hopes, can produce a better picture).

See *HDTV*, *NTSC*, and *PAL*.

Secure Hypertext Transfer Protocol   See **S-HTTP.**

Secure Sockets Layer   See **SSL.**

Semiconductor Chip Protection Act   See **Integrated Circuit Topography Act.**

Sequenced Packet Exchange   See **SPX.**

Serial Line Internet Protocol   See **SLIP.**

Serial Storage Architecture   See **SSA.**

Server Message Block   See **SMB.**

Service Advertising Protocol   See **SAP.**

SESAME
Secure European System for Applications in a Multivendor Environment

A European Computer Manufacturers Association (ECMA) security specification that is similar to, but more comprehensive than, Kerberos.

Definitely one of the nicer (and more descriptive) acronyms you'll see anywhere.

See *Authentication* and *Kerberos.*

SGML
Standard Generalized Markup Language

An open standard (ISO 8879) for describing the structure and content of a document.

A nonproprietary, ASCII (so the document is portable across operating systems and hardware platforms) document format.

It facilitates referencing external data, which simplifies maintenance (since information can then be stored once, in a central database, rather than being duplicated).

SGML documents have three parts:

- The *Declaration* is a header file that contains system-specific information that is needed to enable the document to be used and modified by the target system (for example, that ASCII is used and which characters from that character set may be used).
- The *Document Type Definition* (DTD) or *Style Sheet* is a hierarchical tree-structured definition for the document's *elements* (or *style specifications*). Elements are assigned *attributes*, which (for example) can customize which paragraphs are displayed for different uses of the document.

  The DTD specifies the order allowed for the elements (title, heading, paragraph, etc.). *Tags* (which are delimited with angle brackets) assign *element names* (main title, title, paragraph, etc.) to the content of the document, for example,

  ```
  <MONTH>January</MONTH>
  ```

  The DTD also specifies the type and use of non–SGML *external entities*, such as graphics (and, using an SGML extension called *Hypermedia/Time-based Structuring Language*—HyTime—other objects such as video and audio), that are referenced and not embedded in the *compound document.*

- The *Document Instance* is the actual text (with tags) of the document, in the sequence allowed by the DTD (SGML editors include *validating parsers* to ensure this).

A *transformer* then takes the SGML document instance as input and produces formatted output ("*publication*"). This output is called the *Format Output Specification Instance* (FOSI) and is used (finally) for viewing or printing the document (it includes indents, fonts, and character sizes). SGML does not include or specify a method of producing formatted output.

SGML includes *hypertext* capabilities to enable a reader to easily view a glossary or section reference, or even run a program to accept input to fill in a form in the document.

HTML is sort of a subset.

See *HTML* and *WWW*.

Shadowed BIOS

Typically, EPROM (*Erasable, Programmable, Read-Only Memory*) has a much slower access time than RAM (*Random Access Memory*). Therefore BIOS code that is executed out of EPROM executes relatively slowly (*wait states* are inserted to delay a few clock cycles until the EPROM can provide the next byte of code).

Many PCs copy the BIOS code from EPROM to RAM ("shadowing") and re-map that RAM to be at the same location as the original BIOS. The BIOS code then executes faster, without any changes made to it.

See *BIOS*, *PC*, and *RAM*.

Shared Memory

A method of transferring data from a PC to a LAN or video adapter (for example).

For LAN adapters, usually, 8 to 32 kbytes of memory on the LAN adapter is mapped to a location in the PC's upper memory area (typically in the $C000_{16}$, $D000_{16}$, or $E000_{16}$ page).

For video adapters, the $A000_{16}$ and $B000_{16}$ pages are reserved for this memory mapping (which is why PCs are limited to 640 kbytes of conventional memory—the 64 kbytes of the $A000_{16}$ page starts at 640 kbytes).

A memory-mapped LAN adapter's memory is usually dual-ported. This method causes less interruption (delay while waiting for memory access) to the PC, since (for example) the memory is written (with data received from the LAN) while the PC is doing other things. A problem is that less upper memory is then available for loading device drivers, and other software, high. Western Digital (now SMC) LAN adapters use this technique.

See *DMA*, *IRQ*, *PC*, *RAM*, and *PnP*.

Shielded Twisted Pair   See **STP.**

Shortest Path First   See **SPF.**

S-HTTP
Secure Hypertext Transfer Protocol

A method that is used to support the encryption and decryption of specific WWW documents sent over the Internet (so that people can't watch what you are doing).

Uses RSA public-key encryption. A main use is expected to be for commerce (payments).

An alternative method is SSL, which encrypts all traffic for specific TCP/IP ports.

Supported by America Online, CompuServe, IBM, Netscape, Prodigy, SPRY (at *http://www.spry.com,* and now owned by CompuServe), and Spyglass.

Designed by Allan Schiffman, then at EIT (which is now working with Terisa Systems).

See *Encryption*, *RSA*, *Socket Number*, *SSL*, *TCP*, *Terisa Systems, Inc.*, and *WWW.*

SI
Le Système International d'Unités (The International System of Units)

The international agreement on metrification and other standards to facilitate trade between countries (and get rid of ridiculous units of measure).

See *Paper* and *Winchester.*

Simple Mail Transfer Protocol   See **SMTP.**

Simple Management Protocol   See **SMP.**

Simple Multicast Routing Protocol   See **SMRP.**

Simple Network Management Protocol   See **SNMP and SNMP2.**

Simple Network Paging Protocol   See **SNPP.**

Simplex

Communication that goes one way only. Examples are:

- Radio and television broadcasts
- Sending data to printers (though many newer printers have bidirectional communications to report status and problems)
- Stock trade and other financial data feeds

See *1284*, *Half-Duplex*, and *Full-duplex*.

Simultaneous Peripheral Operation on Line   See **SPOOL.**

Simultaneous Voice and Data   See **SVD.**

Single Large Expensive Disk   See **SLED.**

SIT
Special Information Tone

A series of standardized tones preceding recorded messages used by telephone companies to inform callers that a call could not go through and why.

The specific tones (for example, that you hear after dialing a 1–800 call that cannot be reached from the caller's area) that are used identify the problem so that automated calling equipment can determine what the problem is (and avoid clogging up the telephone network with guaranteed-fruitless retries).

See *800*, *DTMF*, and *POTS*.

Six-σ Quality
Six Sigma Quality

A specification of the number of parts that can be outside of specification (see *NFG*).

A concept that was popularized by Motorola (beginning in 1987) for defining the (acceptable—and very low) number of electronic components that can have characteristics outside of the components' specifications (that is, that are defective).

If a histogram showing the deviation of the actual measured characteristics of individual components compared to their target specifications is made, then a curve such as the one shown in the accompanying graph will be constructed.

This shows that many components are very close to specification and fewer components deviate farther from specification. For many physical processes, the shape

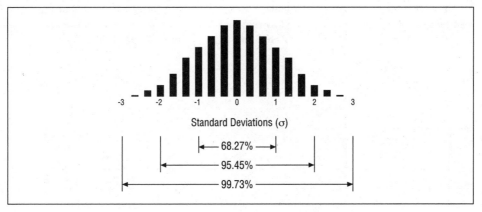

Six-σ Quality—1

of this curve is close to a *normal curve* (because the variation of the components' characteristics follows a *normal distribution*), which is defined by the equation

$$y = \frac{1}{\sqrt{2\pi}}\, e^{-\frac{\left(\frac{x-\mu}{\sigma}\right)^2}{2}}$$

where *y* is the height (number of components), μ (the Greek letter *mu*) is the mean, σ (the Greek letter *sigma*) is the *standard deviation*, and *x* is the particular component's measured characteristics.

As shown in the graph, and integrated numerically (using the integral below—in this example, for six standard deviations)

$$\int_{-6}^{6} \frac{1}{\sqrt{2\pi}}\, e^{-\frac{\left(\frac{x-\mu}{\sigma}\right)^2}{2}}\, dx$$

for such normal curves, 68.27% of all components will have characteristics within one standard deviation of the mean, 95.45% will have characteristics within two standard deviations of the mean, and so on.

This means that (100% − 95.45% =) 4.55% of the components will have characteristics that are more than two standard deviations from the target specifications. Fortunately, fewer and fewer components have specifications even farther from the target, as shown in the following table.

For This Many Standard Deviations from the Target	This Percentage of Components Are Good	Which Leaves This Many Components Defective (per Million[a])
1	68.27	158,650
2	95.45	22,750
3	99.73	1,350
4	99.99366	31.7
4.5	99.99932	3.4
5	99.9999426	0.287
6	99.99999976	0.0012

[a] Actually, there will be twice this number—to include *both* the components that are more than (for example) +6σ greater than *and* those that are less than -6σ less than the target specification.

While the Motorola manufacturing targets are that $\pm6\sigma$ of the components will be within the mean, they allow for the process mean to shift from the target specification by up to 1.5σ. Therefore fewer than 3.4 per million (4.5σ) will be outside of specification.

See *ISO 900x*.

SLED
Single Large Expensive Disk

The opposite of the RAID concept (though in practice, RAID also uses expensive disk drives).

The idea is to use a single, fast disk drive for a storage subsystem when fast access time is a priority, rather than a complicated array of disk drives. (RAID systems often have a relatively slow access time, though they may have a higher reliability.)

See *Disk Drive* and *RAID*.

SLIP
Serial Line Internet Protocol

A protocol for carrying IP over an asynchronous serial communications line (for example, a 9,600-bits/s dial-up or leased line).

In general, PPP is preferable to SLIP, since SLIP:

- Does not include a protocol identifier field (so it can be used only with IP)
- Has no initial negotiation to ensure interoperability
- Does not support error detection or correction
- Supports only asynchronous data communication (which is typically 20% less efficient than synchronous data communication because of the need for start and stop bits in asynchronous data communication)

SLIP is defined in RFC 1055.

See *Asynchronous*, *CSLIP*, *IP*, and *PPP*.

Small Computer System Interface   See **SCSI, SCSI-2, and SCSI-3.**

Small Form Factor Committee

A group that was initially formed to standardize the location of the mounting screw holes in PC disk drives.

The group's function has now expanded to include specifying data transfer rates and timings for new IDE-type disk drive interfaces, such as E-IDE and Fast ATA.

For example, it is no coincidence that the new data transfer rates (such as the *mode 3 PIO* rate of 11.1 Mbytes/s) are faster than IDE's main competitor, SCSI-2 (which supports a transfer rate of 10 Mbytes/s transfers for the 8-bit-wide implementation—currently the most widely installed).

See *E-IDE*, *Fast ATA*, *IDE*, and *SCSI-2*.

Smart Battery Data   See **SBD.**

SMB
Server Message Block

The application-layer protocol used by Microsoft's *LAN Manager* and *Windows for Workgroups* (WFW) products. Runs over NetBEUI.

See *NetBEUI*.

SMBus
System Management Bus

A two-wire bus to enable more intelligent handling of rechargeable batteries in portable equipment such as laptop PCs.

The bus carries clock, data, and instructions between a PC, the battery charger, and the battery pack. Other peripherals could also be attached to the bus (for example, so that they can receive commands to power down in an orderly way before the battery runs down).

The bus is based on the I^2C bus developed by Philips and Signetics.

Vendors using SMBus would be required to pay royalties (which may turn out to be a substantial deterrent to SMBus being widely accepted).

Proposed by Duracell and Intel and supported by:

• Benchmarq Microelectronics and Microchip Technology (they make the ICs)

- Phoenix Technologies and SystemSoft (they make PC BIOSes)
- Canon (they make battery-operated devices that would benefit from this technology)

Benchmarq Microelectronics, Inc., has a WWW server at *http://www.benchmarq.com*.

See *ACCESS.bus*, *Batteries*, *SBD*, and *USB*.

SMDS
Switched Multimegabit Data Service

A carrier-oriented (the specification was written by Bellcore), cell-relay-based, connectionless, WAN-oriented (no distance limitations) data service (that is, it is a completely specified commercial implementation, including usage-based billing, not just a data switching or formatting scheme, such as ATM or frame relay).

All implementations should therefore be interoperable (avoiding the problems that ISDN encountered).

Much more limited than B-ISDN. For example, it does not have an isochronous channel for voice and video (this is a major limitation).

Access is through DS0, T1, T3, or SONet (though currently, most often at T1 or T3). Because of cell relay's large protocol overhead, a T1 provides only 1.17 Mbits/s service (the remaining 374 kbits/s are network overhead), and a T3 provides only 34 Mbits/s. The access speeds supported are listed in the following table.

Access Class	Access Speed (Mbits/s)	Same Speed as
1	4	Token Ring
2	10	Ethernet
3	16	Token Ring
4	25	ATM
5	44.736	T3

Higher access speeds (based on SONet) will likely be defined in the future. More features (such as usage-based billing and network management) are defined than for ATM.

Uses telephone-type 10-digit DNs (*Directory Numbers*—CCITT's E.164 defines these) and charging (per-call or per-byte and dependent on call duration and distance).

User data (up to 9,188 bytes) are first *encapsulated* in an SMDS packet, which has a 36-byte header plus a 4-byte trailer, so CUGs (*Closed User Groups*) and other features can be provided. Data are then segmented into the 48-byte (plus 5 bytes of overhead) cells—though only 44 bytes per cell are available for payload data.

Based on IEEE 802.6 (for example, SMDS uses DQDB, though there is no contention for the bus, since the only other station is at the carrier's central office).

Might be superseded by ATM (though ATM was initially expected to be used only inside a B-ISDN network switch) for high-speed use, and frame relay for lower-speed use.

Can use ATM (AAL 3/4) for its switching.

Concerns are the following:

- Unknown latency (causing possible protocol time-outs, though intra–LATA delays are specified to be kept to less than 20 ms)
- Unsuitable for many digitized voice and video services (again, because of the unknown latency)
- The difficulty of trouble-shooting connectionless services
- Fair allocation of bandwidth

While offered commercially (for example, there is both carrier and router support), little development has occurred recently, and the technology is unlikely to be popular.

Of course, that viewpoint might not be shared by the SMDS Interest Group, who have a WWW server at *http://www.sbexpos.com/sbexpos/associations/smds/home.html.*

See *ATM (Asynchronous Transfer Mode), Bellcore, B-ISDN, Carrier, Connectionless, DN, DQDB, DS-0, E.164, Encapsulation, T1, T3, SONet,* and *WAN.*

SMP
Simple Management Protocol

Another name for SNMP2.

See *SNMP2.*

SMP
Symmetric Multiprocessing

Using more than one CPU to handle data processing (to speed things up), where any processor can handle any task (so the processors are considered symmetric).

Requires support from the operating system (such as DEC's VMS or Windows NT), the computer hardware (such as having an EISA or PCI bus to support multiple processors), and possibly the CPUs (which would simplify the other support required).

See *EISA, MPP, PCI, Pentium,* and *Scalable Architecture.*

SMR
Specialized Mobile Radio

A two-way radio technology used for dispatching of trucks, taxi cabs, emergency service vehicles, and couriers and by the construction industry. Individual radios can be addressed, so only the selected radio(s) will be part of a particular conversation.

See *ESMR*.

SMRP
Simple Multicast Routing Protocol

A protocol that was developed to support conferencing.

An Apple Computer AppleTalk routing protocol that sends only a single copy of multicast traffic to a router, which then splits it and sends it out to all (and only those) downstream ports that need a copy of the traffic.

Competes with several other TCP/IP-based multicast routing protocols.

See *Apple*, *IP Multicast*, and *QTC*.

SMTP
Simple Mail Transfer Protocol

The protocol used in TCP/IP networks for transferring electronic mail messages between end user computers and *mail servers*.

Popular freeware SMTP mail programs for user workstations are `Elm` and `Pine`.

Since mail messages cannot have control characters in them, binary files must first be converted into ASCII often using `uuencode` (usually a separate program; the corresponding program at the other end is then `uudecode`, which converts the file back to binary) or MIME.

SMTP is used only when both the mail sender and receiver are ready at the same time. If (for example) the destination PC is not connected (it dials in periodically to an ISP), then a *post office* must be used to temporarily store the mail. A post office protocol (such as IMAP or POP) must then be used to retrieve the mail.

See *IMAP*, *ISP*, *MIME*, and *POP*.

SNA
Systems Network Architecture

IBM's proprietary data communication protocols.

- Original SNA (introduced in 1974) is now sometimes called *Subarea SNA*. Was *Mainframe-centric*, since all communications were directly from your dumb 3270-type terminal to a mainframe (running *Advanced Communication Facilities/Virtual Telecommunications Access Method*—ACF/VTAM).

- APPN is the "new SNA" (but you can't call it that for long, because what do you call the thing after the "new SNA"?). APPN, or new SNA, is therefore sometimes called second-generation SNA. It supports *peer-to-peer* communications (for example, between AS/400 midrange computers and/or workstations without the involvement of mainframes) initiated by either party.

See *3270, APPC, APPN, DLC, FEP, LU 6.2, Mainframe, SDLC, SAA,* and *VTAM.*

SNAP
Subnetwork Access Protocol

A frame format often used for TCP/IP and Apple's EtherTalk on 802.3 ("Ethernet") LANs.

See *802.3.*

SNMP
Simple Network Management Protocol

A query/command/response protocol to examine and change configuration parameters and counters of LAN- and WAN-connected repeaters, bridges, routers, and other devices.

Agents (software running in the monitored/controlled equipment) communicate with *management stations.* Agents store variables as counters, or variables in two-dimensional or simpler tables.

The SNMP protocol supports only the following functions:

- Get (a specified variable's current value from an agent)
- GetNext (get the next variable's value)
- Set (a variable)
- Trap (the agent sends a message when a threshold is exceeded)

All variables are defined by MIBs (*Management Information Bases*), though most equipment has manufacturer-specific extensions. These extensions are described by using a subset of a language called *Abstract Syntax Notation One* (ASN.1), which is described in the *Structure of Management Information* (SMI—see RFCs 1155 and 1212). An *MIB compiler* is then used to integrate the extensions into the management station's SNMP software.

Uses TCP/IP's UDP connectionless transport. (IPX, AppleTalk, and OSI transports have been defined but are seldom used or implemented.) IBM is working on an SNA implementation.

Very little security is defined. All communicating agents are assigned a *community string* (sort of a weak password), which is not encrypted when it is sent over the network. By default, the read-access community string is `Public`, and the write-access community string is `Private`. These default passwords are a security problem because many installations do not change them.

A recent extension S-SNMP (*Secure SNMP*) adds security features such as user authentication and data encryption (DES) but adds significant network overhead.

The major UNIX-based management stations (in decreasing order of number of installations and third-party applications available) are:

- Hewlett-Packard's *Open View Network Node Manager*, running on an HP Apollo (running HP-UX), Sun (running SunOS), or Microsoft Windows platform
- Sun's *SunNet Manager*, running on a Sun SPARCstation (used to be the most popular)
- IBM's *Netview/6000* (which is based on HP's Openview), running on an IBM RS/6000 workstation (running AIX), Sun, or Microsoft Windows platform

Standardized in RFC 1157.

See *DMI*, *DTMF* (*Desktop Management Taskforce*), *MIB*, *RMON*, *SNMP2*, and *UDP*.

SNMP2 *(sometimes called SMP)*
Simple Network Management Protocol 2

A proposed enhancement to SNMP and Secure SNMP to support larger and faster networks (for example, 64-bit counters are supported) with more complex reporting while causing less network traffic (more than one variable can be retrieved per query, for example).

SNMP2 can run over AppleTalk, IPX, and OSI transport layer software, in addition to TCP/IP.

Other enhancements include:

- Agents can be *locked*, so only one management station can configure it at a time
- Better error reporting is supported
- A single station can be both a manager and an agent, allowing for hierarchical management
- Proxy agents are supported, so one TCP/IP management station can report on many non-TCP/IP agents
- DES encryption is used for passwords passed over the network, and there are no default passwords

Also called *Simple Management Protocol* (SMP).

See *DES*, *SNMP*, and *TCP/IP*.

SNPP
Simple Network Paging Protocol

A TCP/IP-based protocol to send alphanumeric messages to a *gateway computer* connected to a paging system.

Messages can be up to 900 characters in length.

Support is included for transmitting pagers so that confirmation that the recipient received the page can be sent to the original sender.

See *TCP/IP*.

Sockets

A nonstandardized software interface (API) between a user application program and a TCP/IP protocol stack.

Initially developed for the BSD version of UNIX. The programming interface is somewhat like that of a file and has the following functions:

- accept (an incoming connection)
- bind (an address to an outbound call)
- initiate (a connection)
- listen (for an incoming connection)
- receive (a message from a socket)
- send (a message to a socket)
- socket (create one)
- close, read, and write, too

See *API*, *BSD UNIX*, *TCP*, *UNIX*, and *WinSock*.

Socket Number

In TCP/IP, the socket number is the concatenation of the sender's (or receiver's) IP address and *port numbers* (the service being used). The pair of these (the sender's and receiver's socket numbers) uniquely specifies the connection in the entire internet.

See *internet*, *TCP*, and *TCP/IP*.

Software Development Kit   See **SDK.**

Solaris

Usually considered to be Sun's newer Operating System, but Sun would say Solaris 1.*x* is SunOS 4.1.*x* (which has been around for a long time), and Solaris 2.*x* is Sun's newer and SVR4–based operating system.

The Intel platform version of Solaris runs on the 80386 (and up) processors and uses parts of Interactive Systems' *Interactive UNIX*, which is derived from a *Big Endian* version of SVR3.2. Sun liked Interactive UNIX so much, they bought the company, and Sun still enhances and sells Interactive UNIX as a separate product (currently Version 4.2).

A current version of Solaris is 2.4, and it is available for both SPARC and Intel platforms. All important features are implemented consistently on these two platforms.

See *Big Endian*, *iBCS*, *Intel*, *ONC*, *Sun*, *SunOS*, *SVR4*, and *UNIX*.

Somerset

The company formed by the IBM-Motorola joint venture to develop the PowerPC processor. Named after the place where King Arthur's knights put aside their swords to join the Round Table (which was round so no one was at the head of the table).

See *PowerPC*.

SONet
Synchronous Optical Network

A synchronous data framing and transmission scheme for (usually single-mode) fiber-optic cable. Based on multiples of a base rate of 51.84 Mbits/s. This base rate (called OC-1) can carry 672 DS-0s, or 28 T1s, or 21 E1s, or 7 T2s, or 7 digitized television channels (typical for submarine fiber-optic cables), or 1 T3, or combinations of these. It has additional capacity for an *order-wire* (a digitized-voice intercom for technicians to use), error detection, and framing and bit-rate matching.

The 51.84 Mbits/s comes from the basic frame of 810 bytes (nine rows of 90 columns of bytes each), which is sent 8,000 times per second.

Speeds up to 9.6 Gbits/s (OC-192) are currently standardized. An equivalent scheme for copper media (called STS-1) has identical rates, formats, and features.

SONet can be used to carry ATM traffic as well as any other type of traffic (for example, it can be a "faster point-to-point T1").

T1 and T3 are asynchronous, so it is difficult to drop and insert channels, since the entire T1 or T3 needs to be demultiplexed. Since SONet bit rates are all integer multiples of the OC-1 rate, dropping and inserting channels are facilitated.

Another advantage of SONet is that it can be implemented as a *dual ring* for redundancy (traffic travels around the backup ring to temporarily bypass the problem—the reconfiguration to using the backup ring causes less than a 50-ms disruption to the traffic).

Similar to SDH, which is used outside of North America (though SDH is based on multiples of 155.52 Mbits/s).

Common ATM and SDH bit rates currently used are shown in the table below.

SONet		SDH	Data Rate (Mbits/s)	Number of Digitized Voice or 64,000-bits/s Data Circuits
Optical Fiber	Copper			
OC–1	STS–1		51.84	672
OC–3	STS–3	STM–1	155.52	2,016
		STM–2	311.04	4,032
OC–12	STS–12	STM–4	622.08	8,064
OC–48	STS–48	STM–16	2,488.32	32,256

Standardized in ANSI T1.105.

See *ATM (Asynchronous Transfer Mode)*, *Carrier*, *E1*, *SDH*, *STM*, *STS*, *T1*, *T2*, and *T3*.

Source Route Bridging   See **SRB.**

SPARC
Scalable Processor Architecture

Sun's RISC-based processor family used in their workstations.

In an effort to make the processor less proprietary and more widely supported, Sun formed an industry group (including Amdahl, Cypress, Fujitsu, LSI Logic, and Texas Instruments) in which each vendor can design its own implementation of the chip. (This has not turned out to be a popular thing to do.)

See *RISC*, *SPEC*, and *Sun*.

SPEC
Standard Performance Evaluation Corporation

A nonprofit organization formed to "establish, maintain and endorse a standardized set of relevant benchmarks that can be applied to the newest generation of high-performance computers." The goal is to enable the speed of different computer processors and system designs to be compared. Since the benchmark *source code* is available, it can be compiled and run on machines with different architectures.

The most frequently quoted SPEC benchmarks are:

- *SPECint92*, which measures integer arithmetic performance, expressed as the geometric mean of the time required to run six integer-math-intensive application programs
- *SPECfp92*, which measures floating point math performance and is expressed as the geometric mean of the time required to run 14 floating-point math-intensive application programs.

Both results are expressed as the *SPECratio*—that is, relative to the time required to run the same benchmarks on a DEC VAX-11/780 minicomputer.

Also, while both benchmarks are very CPU-intensive (so operating system overhead and disk access time are not significant factors), the results are also dependent on:

- The size (and implementation) of the computer system's *Level 2 cache* (which may be different for different models of computer systems, even those based on the same CPU)
- The optimizations or efficiency of code generated by the computer system's compiler, since the benchmarks are distributed as C or Fortran source code

Therefore, because of a faster cache, more effective compiler optimizations selected, or a compiler that produces faster code, the same CPU, operated at the same clock frequency, will often be reported with different SPEC ratings—often by 10% or more.

Recent benchmark results often include *baseline* values as well. These are the same benchmark tests but with the requirement that the compilers not be optimized differently for each application program in the benchmark (that is, the same compiler optimizations must be selected for all benchmark tests). The intent is to provide results that are closer to what actual users would see, rather than best-case results.

There are other SPEC benchmark tests:

- *SPECrate_int92* and *SPECrate_fp92* are the same benchmark tests, but multiple copies (the benchmark results will quote how many) are simultaneously run (using a multitasking operating system). The number of times the benchmark tests can be completed in a week (yes, a *week*) is expressed as the ratio to the number that a DEC VAX-11/780 could complete in a week. The test attempts to show the multiuser characteristics of a computer—again, reflecting more real-world results, since some computers share their CPU time among many users.

- Tests for frequently used (at least by software developers) UNIX commands
- Tests of NFS performance

The previous *SPECint89* and *SPECfp89* benchmarks were replaced, since they:

- Ran too quickly (making small timing errors more significant)
- Had a total of only 10 application programs (it was thought that they did not include a wide enough range of types of computations)
- Had some portions that could be optimized to the point of becoming meaningless

SPEC membership is composed of over 33 organizations in the computer industry, including semiconductor manufacturers, system manufacturers, and academic institutions. SPEC can be contacted at *spec-ncga@cup.portal.com*.

A copy of the SPEC FAQ is at *http://performance.netlib.org/performance/ html/specFAQ.html* (that WWW server has lots of other interesting computer performance–related information too).

More SPEC results (than are shown in the table below) are available by ftp from *ftp.cdf.toronto.edu* in `/pub/spectable` (or try using your WWW browser specifying a URL of *ftp://ftp.cdf.toronto.edu/pub/spectable*).

Processor (L2 Instruction and Data Cache Size in kbytes)	Speed (MHz)	SPECint92	SPECfp92
DEC Alpha AXP 21066	233	94	110
DEC Alpha AXP 21164	300	330	500
HP PA-RISC 7100 (64/64)	50	37.1	71.8
HP PA-RISC 7100 (256/256)	99	109.1	167.9
	125	132.8	195.7
HP PA-RISC 7100LC	64	66.6	96.5
	80	83.5	120.9
	100	100.1	137.0
HP PA-RISC 7150	99	109	168
	125	136	201
HP PA-RISC 7200		250[a]	
Intel 486SX	33	14.9	[b]
Intel 486DX2	25/50	30.1	13.9
Intel 486DX2	33/66	39.6	18.8

(table continued on next page)

Processor (L2 Instruction and Data Cache Size in kbytes)	Speed (MHz)	SPECint92	SPECfp92
Intel DX4	100	51.4	26.6
Intel Pentium (256)	60	70.4	55.1
	66	78.0	63.6
Intel Pentium (512)	25/75	89.1	68.5
	60/90	106.5	81.4
Intel Pentium (1,024)		110.1	84.4
Intel Pentium (512)	66/100	118.1	89.9
Intel Pentium (1,024)		121.9	93.2
Intel Pentium (512)	60/120	133.7	99.5
Intel Pentium (1,024)		140.0	103.9
Intel Pentium	133	150[a]	
	180	200[a]	
Intel P6	66.5/133	200[a]	
	166	250	
	231	350	
Motorola PowerPC 601	80	85	105
Motorola PowerPC 601v	100	105	125
	120	125	150
Motorola PowerPC 602	66	40	[b]
	80	40	[b]
Motorola PowerPC 603	66	60	70
	80	75	85
Motorola PowerPC 603e	100	120	105
	133	160	140
Motorola PowerPC 604	100	160	165
	150	225	250
Motorola PowerPC 620	133	225	300
	200	330	410
Sun microSPARC	50	26.4	21.0
Sun microSPARC-II	60	47.5	40.3
	85	65.3	53.1
	110	78.6	65.3

(table continued on next page)

Processor (L2 Instruction and Data Cache Size in kbytes)	Speed (MHz)	SPECint92	SPECfp92
Sun SuperSPARC	50	76.9	81.8
	60	98.2	107.2
Sun hyperSPARC	75	125.8	121.2
	125	131.2	153.0

ᵃ Estimated.

ᵇ Has no floating-point unit.

See *Alpha AXP*, *Cache*, *iComp*, *Intel*, *MIPS*, *NFS*, *PA-RISC*, *PC*, *PowerPC*, *SPARC*, *Superscalar*, and *TPS*.

Special Information Tone   See **SIT.**

Specialized Mobile Radio   See **SMR.**

Speedo

A font technology from Bitstream, Inc. Font file functions are shown in the following table.

Font Filename Extension	Function	Comments
*.SPD	Scalable font	Can be used in Windows using Bitstream's Facelift font-rasterizing software
*.BCO	Bitmapped (non-scalable) fonts	
*.CSD		
*.TDF		

Bitstream has a WWW server at *http://www.bistream.com.*

Competes with PostScript and TrueType.

See *Bitmap Font*, *Font*, *Outline Font*, *PostScript Page Description Language*, and *True-Type*.

SPF
Shortest Path First

The routing algorithm used in OSI.

Each node determines its immediate connectivity and broadcasts this information to all other nodes, which then build their own topological map of the entire network so that they can determine the best routes independently.

Better than distance-vector (the most common current method) for larger networks, since SPF finds alternate routes faster and is more secure, and the entire network learns of connectivity changes faster (that is, it *converges* faster).

See *Link-state*, *OSI*, and *RIP*.

Spoofing

A technique often used to get a network device (which was not designed to work over a WAN) to work over a slower or larger network than originally intended.

Usually involves *local polling* and *acknowledgments* (also called *local termination*) in which (for example) a fake acknowledgment to polls is created by the local device and the polls are recreated at the remote device so that the polls don't load the WAN and the acknowledgments arrive fast enough.

May involve eliminating broadcasts (such as NetWare SAPs or IP RIPs) over WANs by recreating them at the far end of the link, and only commands to start or stop the periodic broadcasts are sent over the WAN.

See *DLC*, *DLSw*, *LLC2*, and *RIP*.

SPOOL
Simultaneous Peripheral Operation On Line

Another one of those acronyms that may have been made up after the term was already in use—like ping.

Often used to mean that something (such as a print job) is *queued* (temporarily stored in a disk file so that many users can share a resource "simultaneously") until the peripheral (often a printer) is available (finished printing the previous job or finally has been powered on or has more paper loaded).

In the old mainframe days (before large disks were popular—that is, inexpensive), this spooling was to a reel of ½-inch-wide magnetic tape. Since this is a spool of tape, perhaps that is the original source of the name.

See *Ping*.

Spread Spectrum Technology   See **SST**.

SPX
Sequenced Packet Exchange

An optional (and used by only a few applications, such as print servers and RConsole) Novell NetWare protocol layered on their IPX that supports connection-oriented data transfer and window sizes larger than 1.

See *IPX* and *NCP*.

SQL
Structured Query Language

An English-like (as long as you talk like a programmer), ASCII text, standardized language that is used to define and manipulate data in a *database server*.

The format of the requests is standardized, but the APIs that are used to generate the queries are not part of the SQL standard. Also, most database vendors provide desirable nonstandard SQL extensions (making SQL implementations less portable still).

The four main data manipulation statements are:

- `Select` (retrieve data)
- `Delete`
- `Update`
- `Insert`

Data are stored in two-dimensional *tables* (each *database record* being a *row* in the table). Tables can be *joined* (according to their *keys*) on the fly, as needed to service queries.

A typical query could be the following:

`Select` *Temperature, Pressure* `From` *Table_3* `Where` *Temperature < 160*

SQL database suppliers usually provide an API that provides application programmers with the interface they need to submit these queries to a database (which is usually elsewhere on a LAN or WAN). For example, two of the industry-leading SQL database software suppliers are Oracle Corporation and Sybase, Inc., which have Pro*C and OpenClient, respectively.

An *atomic* (smallest useful) sequence of data manipulations (terminated by a `commit` statement) is called a *transaction*.

A good SQL implementation will automatically *roll back* an uncompleted transaction (a less-good implementation may require the application program to check a *transaction log* at start-up and reverse the first steps of uncompleted transactions).

Application programs usually make use of SQL database servers utilizing *embedded SQL*, in which a high-level language (such as C or FORTRAN) is used to generate the SQL statements.

Call it "sequel" (not "s, q, l") if you want any respect from programmers.

Initially developed by IBM Research in the 1970s. First standardized as NIST FIPs 127 in 1987, then as ANSI X3.135 in 1989.

Oracle Corporation and Sybase, Inc., have WWW servers at *http://www.oracle.com* and *http://www.sybase.com*, respectively.

See *API*, *Client/Server*, *DBA*, *ODBC*, *LAN*, *OLTP*, *Portability*, *SQL2*, *WAN*, and *XBase*.

SQL2
Structured Query Language 2

A new version of SQL that, among other changes, provides enhanced error reporting and troubleshooting support, as well as new data types, such as `bit`. To reduce SQL's problematic nonportability due to proprietary vendor extensions, it includes three defined levels of conformance: *entry* (similar to the current SQL), *intermediate*, and *full*.

See *SQL*.

SRB
Source Route Bridging

The type of bridging that is used in Token Ring networks. The sender determines the best route to the destination. This usually is done by first broadcasting (along all possible paths) a request for the destination to respond (this is called a route discovery frame). The path taken by the fastest round-trip response is the path that is used for subsequent communication (even if that path later becomes slower than others, because of network loading, for example).

See *Remote Bridge* and *Token Ring*.

SSA
Serial Storage Architecture

A proposed high-end solution for connecting fault-tolerant disks.

See *RAID*.

SSL
Secure Sockets Layer

An open standard proposed by Netscape Communications for providing secure (encrypted and authenticated) WWW (and other applications, such as mail, ftp, and telnet) service over the Internet.

Uses RSA *public-key encryption* for specific TCP/IP ports. Intended for handling commerce (payments).

An alternative method is Secure-HTTP (S-HTTP), which is used to encrypt specific WWW documents (rather than the entire session).

See *Authentication, Encryption, RSA, S-HTTP, TCP, Terisa Systems, Inc.*, and *WWW*.

SST
Spread Spectrum Technology

A form of digital radio communications that trades off speed for improved reliability (immunity to noise and interference).

Originally developed by the military, since it can be made to be very resistant to jamming, which is the enemy transmitting at high power on your frequency to disrupt your radio communications.

The *frequency hopping* method continuously changes the frequency of the carrier signal (about every 10 bit-times), in a pattern known to both the sender and the receiver. The pattern can be dynamically changed to avoid detected noisy frequencies. Most important, by using different frequency hopping patterns (*hopping sequences*), several pairs of conversations can simultaneously use the same bandwidth (range of frequencies over which the frequency hops).

For frequency hopping, the U.S. FCC requires the following:

- The signal bandwidth (while dwelling at one frequency) is limited to 500 kHz (at 900 MHz) and 1 MHz (at 2.4 GHz).
- Transmitters cannot transmit at a given frequency more than 400 ms every 20 seconds (at 900 MHz) or every 30 seconds (at 2.4 GHz). Typical systems hop every 100 ms.
- The frequency hop pattern must include at least 50 frequencies (at 900 MHz) or 75 frequencies (2.4 GHz).

The other spread spectrum method is *direct sequence*. This method is:

- Usually more expensive to implement, and requires more power for a given level of performance
- More commonly implemented
- More resistant to the *multipath interference* which is common indoors (that is, the received signal interferes with itself, as it bounces off many surfaces between sender and receiver)

Direct sequence changes each one-bit to be transmitted into a many-bit pattern (and each zero-bit to the inverse of that pattern), which is known to the receiver. The bit pattern (called the *spreading code*) may repeat every bit-time, or (more commonly) may be much longer. For example, the CDMA cellular telephone standard uses a pseudo-random sequence $2^{41}-1$ bits long. CDMA also uses:

- A *chip rate* (the rate that the spreading code, which in this case amounts to a pseudo-random bit pattern exclusive-ored with the data) of at least 10 (as required by the FCC), and up to 1,000 times the data rate. This limits the data rate to 2 Mbits/s (when using the 900-MHz band) or 8 Mbits/s (when using the 2.4-GHz band). The faster the chip rate, the wider the bandwidth used by the transmitter, making it more immune to interference at specific frequencies, but resulting in a lower data rate.
- Only a portion of the available bandwidth per conversation, so that more than one conversation can occur simultaneously.

Spread spectrum uses a maximum transmitted signal power of up to 250 mW in either of the following frequency bands:

- *Industrial, Scientific, and Medical* (ISM) frequency band (902 to 928 MHz). This band is usually not available (or requires a license) for spread spectrum use outside of Canada, the U.S., and Mexico
- 2.4000 to 2.4835 GHz (an 83.5-MHz bandwidth) frequency band. An advantage of this band is that products do not require licensing in Canada, the U.S., or Mexico, and usually not anywhere else either. Also, the IEEE 802.11-compliant products that use this frequency band should be interoperable. Some disadvantages of this frequency band are that the signals do not propagate as far, and users may encounter interference from microwave ovens (which operate at 2.450 GHz).

The IEEE 802.11 standard:

- May limit the frequency hopping method to the 2.4-GHz band
- Specifies that frequency hopping systems have a data rate of between 1 and 2 Mbits/s and a chip rate of 11

Typical actual user data throughput for both methods is about 200 kbits/s.

See *802.11*, *CDMA*, and *PCCA*.

Stac

A company that is big on data compression.

It maintains a WWW server at *http://www.stac.com*.

See *CCP*, *Data Compression*, and *LZS*.

Standard Generalized Markup Language   See **SGML.**

Standard Performance Evaluation Corporation   See **SPEC.**

Standard Wireless At Command Set   See **SWATS.**

Standards

Many organizations produce standards with different mandates, authorities, and emphases. The following table lists some of these.

Group	Produces	Emphasis	Standard Designations	
			Format	Example
ANSI	American national standards	Standardization of existing industry standards. Coordinates U.S. voluntary standards system.		X3.135, X3.T9
ITU-T	Recommendations	International communications	letter.numbers	X.25, H.320
CSA	National standards of Canada (after they are approved by the Standards Council of Canada)	Health, safety, building and construction, and the environment	Canada/CSA-standard-date	Can/CSA-Z234.1-89
EIA	Recommended standards	Electrical and electronics	RS-numbers-version or EIA-numbers-version	RS-232-C, EIA-485
IEEE	Standards	Development of new standards	IEEE-numbers.number	IEEE-802.3
ISO	International standards	Promoting international trade	ISO numbers	ISO 7498
TIA	Recommended standards	Telecommunications	TIA-numbers-version or EIA/TIA-numbers-version	EIA/TIA-568

Standards may specify *patented* technologies, in which case standards-setting organizations (such as the IEEE) require companies owning such patents to file a *letter of intent* showing that they will license the technology for a reasonable fee. The fee is negotiated and paid directly between the patent owner and the manufacturer.

Companies owning patents that are specified in standards may be obligated to collect such royalties; otherwise, the patent could be declared invalid (since the company is not enforcing it). The royalty may be included as part of the cost of purchasing a crucial IC needed to implement the technology, and the IC manufacturer would pay the royalty (or could be the owner of the patent).

Obtaining standards documents is often the best way to verify details of a technology. While Internet-related standards (for example, all of the RFCs) are available at no cost over the Internet, most standards-setting organizations fund much of their work from standards sales.

Sources of standards are listed in the following table.

Standards Organization	Phone Number
ANSI	212-642-4900 (ANSI can also supply ISO standards)
EIA, ISO, ITU-T (CCITT), and TIA	1-800-854-7179 or 303-792-2181—for Global Engineering Documents, which supplies these (and many more, such as ANSI's) standards under royalty agreement with the standards organizations. Standards ordered through Global usually cost more, but arrive faster than if ordered directly from the standards organizations (then again, some standards organizations won't even deal directly with you).
CSA	416-747-4044
IEEE	1-800-678-4333 or 908-981-0060

Also, many standards are available from Micromedia Limited. They are at the site *http://www.mmltd.com*.

All-encompassing references to on-line standards documents are at the site *http://www.cmpcmm.cc.com/cc/standards.html*.

An equally fantastic reference to standards organizations is at the site *http://hsdWWW.res.utc.com/std/gateway/orgindex.html*.

Some telecommunications references are at *http://ippsweb.ipps.lsa.umich.edu/telecom/telecom-info.html,* and there are still more at *http://www.rpi.edu/Internet/Guides/decemj/icmc/organizations-standards.html*.

Pacific Bell has some brief technical information and excellent cost information at *http://www.pacbell.com/Products/fastrak.htm*. Of course, the costs are applicable only for Pacific Bell's serving area, but a rough idea of relative costs is always an important thing to know when comparing alternatives.

See *Carrier, Compatible, Compliant, de facto Standard, de jure Standard, IEEE, ISO, ITU, ITU-T, Patent, RBOC, RFC, TIA (Telecommunications Industry Association),* and *TSB.*

Stentor

An alliance of the nine major Canadian telephone companies:

- Bell Canada (Ontario and Québec)
- BC Tel
- AGT Limited (which was called Alberta Government Telephones before it was bought by Telus Corporation)
- Manitoba Telephone Systems
- SaskTel
- Maritime Telephone and Telegraph
- New Brunswick Tel
- Island Tel
- Newfoundland Tel

Stentor's purpose is to deliver national and international telecommunications solutions (since individual telephone companies are regional). Consists of several parts:

- *Stentor Canadian Network Management* is the current name for Telecom Canada (which was previously called Trans Canada Telephone Systems). It is an unincorporated association of carriers, and is responsible for managing and monitoring the phone companies' interprovincial networks and their connections to the U.S. and Mexico. It is also responsible for handling the division of revenue among the members—which include the above nine telephone companies plus Telesat Canada (a full member) and Québec Tel (an associate member).
- *Stentor Resource Centre, Inc.* provides product and service development functions for the nine telephone companies. It has these groups: Marketing and Development, Engineering and Research, and Signature Strategic Management.
- *Stentor Telecom Policy, Inc.* is the government relations advisory arm, providing national lobbying functions.

Stentor maintains a WWW server at *http://www.stentor.ca.*

See *Carrier* and *Telephone Companies*.

STM
Synchronous Transport Module

SDH's 155.52 Mbits/s speed units. STM-4 is therefore 622.08 Mbits/s.

See *SONet* and *SDH*.

STP
Shielded Twisted Pair

150-ohm characteristic impedance, two pair, each pair individually foil shielded (with another overall braid shield), data communications cable. Specified by the *IBM cabling system*. Often used for Token Ring.

Now that IBM does not scare users into thinking that STP is required to provide reliable data communications, it is not very popular for new installations because of its:

- Higher cost for cable and connectors (much more complex than those for UTP)
- Larger size of cable and connectors (compared to UTP)
- Longer installation time for connectors (compared to UTP)
- Additional problems of *ground loops*, where the ground voltage at each end of a cable run is different, causing current to flow in the cable's shield, which creates a magnetic field, which in turn induces current (noise) into the same cable that the shield was supposed to protect!

Also, while some may say that STP cable provides a higher-quality signal, STP cable runs are still limited to 100 m runs (same as for UTP) by EIA 568 (the *Commercial Building Telecommunications Wiring Standard*). Also, STP is limited to use for data communications for IBM computers and Token Ring communications—that is, there is no standard for STP for ISDN, Ethernet, and analog telephone (but there is for UTP).

STP cabling uses an IBM *universal data connector* (for wall plates and hubs) or a DB-9 connector (for the back of PCs, since the IBM universal data connector is too wide).

See *Cable*, *Connector*, *Token Ring*, and *UTP*.

Structured Query Language   See **SQL and SQL2.**

STS
Synchronous Transport Signal

The standard for SONet data transmission over copper (usually coaxial) cables. The rates correspond to the SONet OC-*x* rates (so STS Level 1 is the same speed and bit format as OC-1, etc.).

See *SONet*.

su

A UNIX command (su) that enables someone knowing the root account password to log in as if he or she were another user. Once this person is logged in as the superuser, the command-line prompt changes from "%" to "#".

See *root* and *UNIX*.

Subnet Bit Mask

To facilitate intra-network routing, a single IP network can be divided into many *subnets* by using some of the MS bits of the *host* address portion of the IP address as a subnet ID.

For example, Network `129.5.0.0` has 16 bits assigned as the network ID (specifically `129.5`, in dotted decimal, which is `10000001.00000101` in binary) as it is a *Class B* address (the first number is between 128 and 192).

This leaves the lower 16 bits as the host address.

Using a *Subnet Bit Mask* of `255.255.255.0` (which in binary is `11111111.11111111.11111111.00000000`), specifies that the upper 24 bits (those that are set to a 1) are the network plus subnet address—that is, the 16 bits that we already expected *plus* the upper 8 bits of the host address. Therefore the network `129.5.0.0` (in this example) would consist of up to 254 subnets (`129.5.1.0` through `129.5.254.0`) of up to 254 hosts each.

This is useful for subdividing networks, for example, to reduce the number of stations that must receive broadcasts.

See *MS* and *IP Address*.

Subnetwork Access Protocol   See **SNAP**.

Subrate

A data communications access line that runs at less than the DS-0 (56,000-bits/s) data rate. Usually, several subrate lines can be multiplexed into a DS-0.

See *DS-0*, *T1*, and *WAN*.

Sun

Multibillion-dollar (annual sales) maker of UNIX workstations and software (second fastest company to reach $1 billion in annual sales—Compaq Computer Corporation was the fastest—so far!). Scott McNealy is a co-founder, and is now chairman and CEO.

Sun's workstations have had several generations of hardware:

- The initial workstations (Sun 1 and Sun 2 product lines) used Motorola 68000 processors
- The next products used Intel processors (Sun 386i product line)
- The Sun 4 product line used a custom LSI (Large Scale Integration) processor
- The first SPARC-based product was the SPARCstation 1

Subsequently, there have been many other products, such as X terminals, really fast workstations, and multiprocessor-based devices that are intended as multiuser database servers and the like.

Sun has a WWW server at *http://www.sun.com.*

See *COSE, Motorola, SPARC, SunConnect, SunOS, Solaris, OPENLOOK, Operating System, OSF, UNIX,* and *X Terminal.*

SunConnect

A subsidiary of Sun that has a *port* (a version that runs on a different platform) of Novell's NetWare. SunNet Manager (SNMP support) is also a product.

See *Portability, SNMP,* and *Sun.*

SunOS
Sun Operating System

Sun's older UNIX–like operating system, based on BSD UNIX.

Sometimes called Solaris 1.*x*, where the *x* corresponds to SunOS version 4.1.*x*.

See *Solaris, Sun,* and *UNIX.*

Super Density   See **SD.**

SuperATM
Super Adobe Type Manager

A new version of ATM that uses one of Adobe's two *multiple master* fonts to generate characters for fonts that are not otherwise available to the destination printer (or other display device).

See *ATM (Adobe Type Manager)* and *Multiple Master.*

Superscalar

A processor (such as Intel's Pentium or NexGen's Nx586) that can execute more than one instruction per clock cycle by using more than one *instruction execution unit* (sounds rather serious to me).

The execution units may not be identical; for example, only one of the Pentium's two execution units (or *pipelines*) can execute floating-point instructions.

All of this makes comparing the clock speed (to determine processing power) of different processors meaningless. The following table shows how superscalar recent processors are.

Processor Family	Average Clock Cycles per Instruction (≥1 Is Not Superscalar)[a]	Instructions per Clock Cycle (>1 Is Superscalar)
DEC Alpha AXP 21164	0.25	4
Motorola PowerPC 601	0.33	3
Intel P6	0.33	3[b]
Intel Pentium	0.50	2[c]
Intel 486	1.95	0.51
Intel 80386	4.90	0.20
Intel 80286	4.90	0.20
Intel 8086	12.00	0.08

[a] For clock–doubled processors (such as the 486DX2), this is relative to the internal (faster) clock.
[b] Intel calls this Superscalar Level 3.
[c] Intel calls this Superscalar Level 2.

See *Alpha AXP, iComp, Intel, Pentium, PC, PowerPC,* and *SPEC.*

SVD
Simultaneous Voice and Data

Supporting (though for some methods, only somewhat) simultaneous dial-up voice and data communications between two parties. Usually refers to *single-line SVD*, which uses the same dial–up telephone line for voice (a normal interactive telephone conversation) and data (for example, sending a file or fax, using *electronic whiteboard* software) at the same time.

Several *classes* of support for simultaneous voice and data have been (informally) defined, as shown in the following table.

Class	Support for Voice and Data
0	*Out-of-band SVD.* Two separate circuits are established, one for voice and the other for data (for example, a 2B+D ISDN interface offers this).
1	One circuit is established, and the users somehow agree on when to switch between voice mode and data mode. This can be done currently, with standard fax machines (for example).

(table continued on next page)

Class	Support for Voice and Data
2	*Alternating* or *switched SVD*. One circuit is established, and the equipment determines when to switch between voice mode and data mode—voice waits for the current data use of the line (sending a file or a fax) to complete, so this is not suited to continuous streams of data (such as digitized video conferencing) or large file transfers. Radish Communications Systems' VoiceView equipment uses this method, which is built in to Windows 95 and licensed to Rockwell (for implementation in their modem ICs), Boca Research, and others.
3	One circuit is established, and voice and data can be carried simultaneously (either by splitting the analog bandwidth or, more commonly, by digitizing the voice and multiplexing it in with the data, by packetizing each). Typically, the data are transferred more slowly while the talking occurs (voice gets priority). MultiTech System's *Supervisory Protocol* (MSP, which supports its *Talk AnyTime* feature) and AT&T Paradyne's VoiceSpan both use the latter method.

Class 3 is preferable to Class 2 but costs more to implement (voice digitizing is required).

Digital SVD sends voice and low-rate video on top of data (promoted by Intel).

Sometimes called *voice/data integration*.

The future of this technology will likely be ISDN-oriented.

See *EIA/TIA-232*, *ISDN*, *Modem*, *MP-MLQ*, *PCM*, *Rockwell International*, and *WAN*.

SVID
System Five Interface Definition

A *de facto* standard established by *UNIX Systems Laboratories* describing the functions application programmers can expect at the programming level.

A predecessor of POSIX. Originated features such as interprocess communication.

A copy of issue 4 of SVID is at *ftp://ftp.usl.com/unix-standards/svid/issue4/*.

See *de facto Standard*, *Operating System*, *POSIX OSE*, *UNIX*, and *USL*.

SVR4
UNIX System Five Release 4

The version of UNIX that *UNIX System Laboratories* supports (or did, when it was still around).

Intel, Sun, and ACE (ha!) use it. It attempts to unify several of the major variants of UNIX, including AT&T UNIX System V, University of California at Berkeley BSD 2.0, and Sun SunOS.

Generally considered to be the mainstream of UNIX implementations.

See *ACE*, *BSD UNIX*, *SunOS*, *UNIX*, and *USL*.

SVVS
System Five Verification Suite

A POSIX-conformance test suite.

See *POSIX OSE*.

SWATS
Standard Wireless AT Command Set

An extension to the *AT command set* to support wireless modems, such as those used with standard AMPS analog cellular telephones.

See *AMPS*, *AT Command Set*, and *PCCA*.

Swedish Confederation of Professional Employees   See **TCO**.

Switched 56

A full-duplex, wide area, digital data communications service offering 56-kbits/s service on a dial-up basis.

Tariffs are usually the same as for voice calls: local calls are free (if local voice telephone calls in your area are free); long-distance calls are at standard per-minute voice long-distance rates.

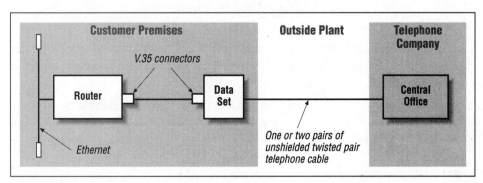

Switched 56—1

A *data set* provides the conversion between the telephone company's one or two pairs of wires (to the central office) and the customer's digital equipment (such as a router or video conferencing CODEC), as shown in the accompanying figure. The interface between the customer equipment and the data set is usually V.35.

Three *service types* are defined in EIA/TIA-596 according to the number of cable pairs (two wires are twisted together to make a pair) to the central office and the method of signaling the telephone number dialed. These service types are described in the following table.

Service Type	Characteristics	Comments
I	Four-wire	Developed and used by AT&T. Connects to something called a USDC in an AT&T 4ESS or 5ESS central office switch. 18,000-foot 26-gauge cable distance maximum.
II	Two-wire with in-band signaling	Call setup uses DTMF tones. Developed and used by AT&T. Also used by GTE. Not popular. 13,100-foot 26-gauge cable-distance maximum.
III	Two-wire with out-of-band signaling	Developed and used by Northern Telecom in its Data-path equipment. Licensed to many DSU manufacturers. Most popular technology. Supports switched 64-kbits/s clear channel service (in addition to an 8 kbits/s full-duplex channel used for call setup and signaling). Maximum cable distance to central office is 4.3 km (14,100 feet) on 26-gauge cable and 5.5 km (18,000 feet) on 22- or 24-gauge cable (repeaters can extend this). Usually limited to 56 kbits/s by central office equipment. Speeds of 9,600 bits/s and lower send each byte of data more than once (since the link between DSUs still runs at 64,000 bits/s). This provides *forward error correction* (using the redundant information, many errors can be corrected without retransmissions).

Note that for the cable distances given in the above table, it is assumed that the cable is *nonloaded* (also called *metallic*) cable. That is, the cable is simply a pair of copper wires with:

- No *loading coils*—these are *inductors*, and improve the voice frequency response (this is called *conditioning* the circuit, but is only beneficial for voice frequencies)
- No *amplifiers* (which are used to boost the signal, but only work for signals up to 3,000 Hz)
- No digitizing (such as going through a T1 circuit)

The two-wire service types use *Time Compression Multiplexing* (TCM, or "Ping-Pong"), in which a faster *half-duplex* communication speed (144 kbits/s for Type II and 160 kbits/s for Type III) is used, rapidly switching the direction, providing the appearance of *full-duplex* service.

DSUs of the same service type must be used at both ends of the cable. Since carriers use DS-0 channels to carry this traffic over their network, different types of DSUs can be used at each end of a data communications circuit. For example, the

DSU at the customer side in City A must be compatible with the DSU used in the telephone company central office in City A. However, in City B, at the other end of the circuit, the pair of DSUs can be a different service type.

There are several ways to specify the number to be dialed, as shown in the following table.

Method	Works by	Commonly Used by
Manual dial	Manually dialing the number, using a keypad on the unit	People's fingers
RS-366	A separate connector is used to send the number to be dialed to the DSU	Video conferencing CODECs
V.25*bis*	In-band signaling over the synchronous link to the DSU	Bridges and routers
Hayes AT	In-band signaling, asynchronous data communications (either DSU subsequently handles asynchronous traffic or it switches to synchronous mode once a connection is established)	PCs

Competes with the following:

- ISDN, which supports neato features, such as Caller ID and faster call setup times, as well as higher speed—64,000 bits/s per B channel (and basic rate ISDN has two B channels, which can often combined to provide 128,000-bits/s connections)
- Digital 800, which is just beginning to be offered (bad) and supports connections between different carriers (good)

See *AT Command Set*, *B8ZS*, *Bonding*, *CODEC*, *Digital 800*, *DS-0*, *DSU*, *Full-duplex*, *Half-Duplex*, *In-Band*, *ISDN*, *Out-of-band*, *V.25bis*, *V.35*, and *WAN*.

Switched LAN

A local area network in which, rather than all users sharing the media, a central switch routes traffic between only those ports that require it. Each port may be connected to a single computer (a heavily loaded file server, for example) or a concentrator which may share that port's bandwidth among many users.

The first products were for Ethernet LANs and from Kalpana (which has since been bought by Cisco Systems). Now there are many suppliers—and Token Ring switches as well.

In contrast, traditional Ethernet often uses a *shared media* concentrator.

Kalpana has a WWW server at *http://www.kalpana.com/kalpana.*

See *Cisco Systems*, *Ethernet*, and *Token Ring*.

Switched Multimegabit Data Service   See **SMDS.**

Symmetric Multiprocessing   See **SMP.**

Synchronous

When referring to data communications, the characters or bytes of data are sent with no gaps between them. That is, they are synchronized in that there is a defined timing between them (that is, exactly no time at all between them). This is possible when all the data (a full frame) have already been prepared and stored—ready for sending.

The frame of data is prefaced by synchronization information: two or more sync characters for BISYNC and one or more flag characters for HDLC.

Once synchronization is achieved, one of the following methods is used so that the receiver can stay "locked on" to the transmitter's exact bit rate:

- A separate *clock* signal is made available (usually by the modem or DSU, on its EIA-232 or V.35 side)
- *Encoding* (such as *NRZI*, *Manchester*, or *Differential Manchester*) is used to combine both the clock and data into a single signal (usually by the modem or DSU, on its WAN side)

Synchronous data links usually use a protocol (such as BISYNC or HDLC) that provides error detection, error correction (usually through retransmission), and flow control.

See *Asynchronous*, *Baud*, *BISYNC*, *DSU*, *EIA/TIA-232*, *Encoding*, *HDLC*, *Modem*, *Parity*, *SDLC*, and *WAN*.

Synchronous Data Link Control   See **SDLC.**

Synchronous Digital Hierarchy   See **SDH.**

Synchronous Optical Network   See **SONet.**

Synchronous Transport Module   See **STM.**

Synchronous Transport Signal   See **STS.**

System 7

Apple's Macintosh operating system (called Macintosh System Software, Version 7.*x*, or simply Macintosh OS 7.*x*). Supports file sharing (*shared folders*) without a dedicated file server (any user can make their files shared—*published*).

See *Operating System* and *TrueType*.

System Five Interface Definition   See **SVID**.

System Five Verification Suite   See **SVVS**.

System Management Bus   See **SMBus**.

Systems Application Architecture   See **SAA**.

Système International d'Unités (International System of Units)   See **SI**.

Systems Network Architecture   See **SNA**.

T
Tesla

The metric (SI) unit for *magnetic flux density*, used (for example) to measure the *Electromagnetic Field* (EMF) radiation from computer video monitors. For comparison, the earth's magnetic field has a strength of about 50 μT.

Named after Nikola Tesla, who did a lot with electrical generators and transformers.

See *EMF*, *MPR II*, *SI*, and *TCO*.

T1
Digital Transmission Rate 1

A point-to-point digital communications circuit that carries 24 64,000-bits/s (though sometimes only 56,000 bits/s are accessible to end users) *channels*, each of which may be used for data or digitized voice.

The bits on the T1 circuit are sent as *frames*, and each T1 frame of data is 24 *timeslots* (or channels—one from each user) of 8 bits each. That is, there are (24 channels × 8 bits/s per channel =) 192 bits of data per frame.

The frames are sent 8,000 times per second, for an aggregate payload data rate of (192 × 8,000 =) 1,536,000 bits/s. A *framing bit* is required for synchronization (so that the other end can determine which bit is the beginning of each frame). This produces a total of 193 bits per frame, so the actual T1 bit rate is 8,000 bits/s more than this: 1.544 Mbits/s.

The user data rate will be 1.536 Mbits/s (64,000 × 24), if *clear channel* 64,000-bits/s DS-0 channels are supported (so the only overhead is the framing bit). If clear channel DS-0s are not supported (that is, each channel only supports 56,000 bits/s of user data), then the user data rate is 1.344 Mbits/s (56,000 × 24).

The framing bit cycles through a pattern, and by looking for that pattern, the receiver can be sure that it has found the framing bit, and synchronization has been achieved.

T1 was first implemented in the 1960s to improve the signal-to-noise ratio of multiplexed links—as compared to the analog *frequency division multiplexing* that was then being used. The type of framing (called "D1") that was first used (a framing bit pattern of 01010101 . . .) was too easily confused by repetitive digitized audio, such as the 1,000-Hz test tones that telephone companies commonly used (1,004-Hz test tones were adopted because of this problem).

Framing evolved to D4 and then to ANSI's *Extended Superframe* (ESF). These are immune to the 1,000-Hz problem and also provide features such as *line supervision* and error detection.

Line supervision involves signaling whether the telephones at each end of the link are on-hook (hung up) or off-hook. (Also, dial-pulse dialing is basically hanging up and going off-hook 10 times per second.)

Since this signaling on the *local loop* (the pair of wires from a central office to a customer's site) uses D.C. current (for example, greater current flows when the phone is off-hook, and some trunks reverse polarity to indicate certain functions), a different method of providing line supervision is required for voice conversations digitized and sent over a T1 link. (The digitizing process represents only frequencies from about 300 to 3,300 Hz and ignores D.C.)

For voice circuits carried by T1 links, line supervision is often carried by using *bit-robbing* (also called *bit-stealing*). Every sixth and twelfth frame, the speech is digitized into only 7 bits rather than 8 bits. The eighth bits are called the A bits and B bits, depending on which frame in the 12- or 24-frame D4 or ESF framing sequence it is in. Combinations of these indicate on-hook, off-hook, and other supervisory information.

Instead of the intrusive and limited bit-robbing method, newer T1 circuits use the *Common Channel Signaling standard number 7*. This is a protocol running over a separate packet-switching network, which carries line supervision and other information—such as the phone number of the caller (so phone companies can offer Caller ID and other advanced services and charge lots of money for them).

The actual T1 line usually consists of two (often shielded) twisted pairs of copper conductors, which cannot have any *bridge taps* (that is, T connections).

The *Line Build-Out* (LBO, which provides selectable attenuation) of the *Line Interface Unit* (LIU) of a T1 transmitter (for example, in a CSU) can usually be configured for *short-haul lines* (up to 655 feet), typically within a building, and *long-haul lines* (up to 6,000 feet), typically between buildings.

At greater distances than these a *T1 repeater* is required to boost the signal. Along rural roads, you will often see the weatherproof enclosures housing these—they are usually painted white or bare stainless steel (to reflect the heat from the sun) cylinders, about 30 cm in diameter and 50 cm high, mounted at waist height on telephone poles or short posts. They are typically installed every 6,000 feet (1.83 km)—something to check for next time you are cruising in the country. To allow for cabling within buildings, repeaters are usually installed within 3,000 feet of central offices and customer sites.

A *Digital Access and Cross-connect System* (DACS) can split out and recombine DS-0 channels into different T1 circuits. To ensure that the bits from each original T1 are running at exactly the same rate, a central (and super-duper accurate) 1.544-MHz frequency standard is maintained in Hillsboro, Missouri (which is apparently near the geographic center of the U.S.), to minimize the phase difference of the signal throughout the U.S.

T1 circuits can be either of the following:

- *Wet*, which means that the central office provides 60-mA or 140-mA *span power* on the same pairs of wires that carry the data—to provide power to the CSUs or repeaters (this ensures that even if there is a local power failure at a customer site, the CSU will still provide valid ones density data). Such a *constant current* type of power supply is used to accommodate the very long cable distances. (The power supply automatically adjusts its output voltage to maintain this current—regardless of the cable length or number of repeaters—within design limits, of course.)
- *Dry*, which has no span power. T1 equipment outside the C.O. is powered by local power.

Current T1 circuits to customers are typically dry, and modern central office equipment doesn't get that upset if it does not receive valid ones density data (apparently, with not enough ones, central office alarms used to go off, and T1 repeaters could start oscillating and interfere with other circuits).

The term "T1" is usually used interchangeably with "DS-1," though strictly speaking T1 refers to the medium (the bit rate and the copper transmission system described above) and DS-1 refers to the bit format and framing.

T1 is also called *T-carrier*, or simply *carrier*.

The similar European service is sometimes called E1.

See *ADSL*, *B8ZS*, *CSU*, *DS-0*, *DS-1*, *DSU*, *E1*, *ESF*, *HDSL*, *PCM*, *POTS*, *PRI*, *SONet*, *Subrate*, *T3*, and *WAN*.

T1C

A communications circuit that supports two T1s. The actual bit rate is 3.152 Mbits/s.

Rarely implemented.

See *T1* and *T3*.

T.120

ITU-T's series of standards for multivendor, multipoint document conferencing (sharing an editable, on-line document, in real time) between several users.

Dial-up, asynchronous communication is initially supported, with other types of WAN connections to be supported in the future. Included capabilities are:

- Binary file transfer
- Shared "whiteboards"
- Multipoint communications

Additional information is at *http://www.csn.net/imtc/t120.html.*

See *Multicast* and *PCS (Personal Conferencing Specification).*

T2
Digital Transmission Rate 2

A communications circuit that supports four T1s.

The actual bit rate is 6.312 Mbits/s.

Rarely implemented.

See *T1* and *T3*.

T3
Digital Transmission Rate 3

A communications circuit that supports 28 T1s, which is a total of 672 DS-0 channels. Each DS-0 carries 64,000 bits/s of data (which could also be a digitized voice conversation).

The actual bit rate is 44.736 Mbits/s.

The physical interface is as follows:

- Within buildings: usually two coaxial cables (one for receive, the other for transmit), each with a BNC connector. For RG-59B/U coaxial cable, the length can be can be up to 250 feet. Other types of coaxial cables support lengths up to 450 feet or longer.

- Outside: usually fiber-optic cable (two strands—one for receive, the other for transmit).

Like T1, the term "T3" is usually used interchangeably with "DS-3," though strictly speaking:

- T3 refers to the medium (the copper transmission system described above)
- DS-3 refers to the bit format

T3 circuits are very popular among those that can afford them (and need them), such as telephone companies (though SONet is becoming much more popular).

See *Coax*, *DS-0*, *DS-3*, *HSSI*, *PCM*, *SONet*, *T1*, and *WAN*.

T4

A communications circuit that supports six T3s (which is a total of 168 T1s, which is 4,032 DS-0s).

The actual bit rate is 274.176 Mbits/s.

Rarely implemented.

See *T1* and *T3*.

Tagged Image File Format   See **TIFF.**

Taligent

The operating system software company formed from the Apple-IBM alliance to create an *object-oriented* (everything is supposed to be object-oriented these days) operating system. It is based on Apple's work on a portable operating system with the codename *Pink*.

Like Kaleida, it seems to have gone into vaporware heaven (where software does what is was dreamt to do). Then again, it may just be too early to be so harsh—people are writing books on Taligent.

See *Apple-IBM Alliance* and *Pink*.

TAPI
Telephony Application Programming Interface

Microsoft's and Intel's method of integrating telephone services and computers so that your computer can control your telephone.

The API supports functions such as:

- Controlling a telephone from a computer (dialing the telephone, transferring calls, etc.)
- Receiving caller ID information into a computer (so that a customer's name or account information can be displayed before the call is answered)

A *desktop-centric* method (not a surprise, considering who developed the interface), in which a desktop PC (or Macintosh, or whatever) is directly connected to the telephone on the desktop. TAPI includes the specification for the physical link between a telephone (not the telephone's PBX) and its controlling computer (typically the telephone user's PC). The PC does not need to be LAN-connected.

Emphasizes *first-party control*, in that once a call is transferred away, it is out of the original answerer's control (just like when you transfer a call—once someone else gets the call and you hang up, you don't know what they do with the call).

Competes with TSAPI, though TSAPI is not desktop-centric.

Stardust Technologies has an ftp server at *ftp://ftp.stardust.com/pub/tapi/* with lots of TAPI information.

See *CTI*, *TSAPI*, and *WinSock*.

TAXI
Transparent Asynchronous Transmitter/Receiver Interface

A 100-Mbits/s ATM interface.

See *ATM* (*Asynchronous Transfer Mode*).

Tcl/Tk
Tool Command Language/Tool Kit

This programming system for building graphical user interfaces and systems controlled from them has become very popular over the last few years. It was initially developed for (and is most popular under) UNIX, but implementations for Windows are available, and implementations for Macintosh are in development.

Tcl (pronounced "tickle") is an interpreted (that is, not compiled) command language (also called a scripting language). It is:

- A programming environment
- A method of controlling and extending application programs; includes generic programming facilities such as variables, loops, and procedures
- Extensible (using the C language, end-users can add new features to the core library functions)
- Easy to learn, powerful, and has many sophisticated functions

Tcl code is called a *script*.

Tk is an X11 (X Window System) toolkit based on Tcl, providing a "graphical scripting language." It is a C language extension of Tcl, and it can be used for easily creating Motif-like graphical user interfaces under the X Window System, often without writing C code. In contrast, writing in C (which is much more difficult) is required to use the X Window System through other interfaces (most frequently Motif).

Together with an extension called WISH (Windowing Shell), Tcl/Tk can be used for facilitating application development by providing features such as:

• Linking applications and running subprocesses
• Hypertext and hypergraphics

Developed by John Ousterhout, beginning in 1988. He has since been hired by Sun and continues his work there.

Some WWW information is available at *http://cuiwww.unige.ch/eao/www/TclTk.html* and *http://www.sunlabs.com/research/tcl*.

See *GUI*, *Motif*, *Perl*, *Sun*, *X*, and *UNIX*.

TCO
Swedish Confederation of Professional Employees

A standard for the allowable strength of *Electromagnetic Field* (EMF) emissions from computer monitors.

It requires lower levels of emissions than the *MPR II* standard allows.

For ELF (*Extra Low Frequencies*), less than 0.2 μT (millionths of a tesla) 50 cm around the monitor and 30 cm in front of it are allowed.

For VLF (*Very Low Frequencies*) the same levels as for MPR II are allowed.

See *ELF*, *EMF*, *MPR II*, *T*, and *VLF*.

TCP
Transmission Control Protocol

UNIX's *connection-oriented* layer 4 (also called *transport*) protocol, which provides an error-free connection between two cooperating programs, which are typically on different computers.

That is, a connection must be established (using the `connect` and `accept` functions) before communication begins. This is similar to a telephone call—you can't just pick up the phone and start talking (well, you can, but you would be talking to a dial-tone—which some would consider a waste of time).

A TCP-based communication between programs is often called a *stream service* (or even a *reliable stream service*), in that the receiving program is guaranteed to receive all the data, with nothing corrupted, and no duplicates, and nothing lost, and in the same sequence as sent. The data will be received as a stream of bytes—the actual packaging (the number and boundaries of packets of data) of the bytes received may be different from how it was sent.

Expanding on that last sentence: if a sending process sends a packet with 100 bytes of data, it may be received as a 100-byte packet or as a 75-byte packet followed by a 25-byte packet. (I could go on for some time with more examples, but we'll just leave it at that.)

In any case, the receiving program does not see the packet boundaries; it simply asks (its TCP stack) for a specified number of bytes from the input queue, and up to that number of bytes is given to the receiving program, regardless of whether those bytes happen to span more than one incoming packet or not. The application protocol must therefore have a protocol for identifying the boundaries of the data structures exchanged (since the TCP protocol does not provide this service).

TCP uses a 16-bit *port number* to identify which process on the destination machine should handle the packet. Port numbers below 512 (by convention, port numbers are always in decimal) are officially assigned (in RFCs) and are therefore called "well-known ports." Ports under 1024 can be used only by processes owned by the root user.

As shown in the following table, some of these use only UDP, some only TCP, and some can use either.

Service	Port	Protocol
ping echo	7	UDP
ping echo	7	TCP
FTP data	20	TCP
FTP control	21	TCP
telnet	23	TCP
SMTP	25	TCP
DNS	53	UDP
DNS	53	TCP
TFTP	69	UDP
finger	79	TCP
http	80	TCP
pop-2	109	TCP

(table continued on next page)

Service	Port	Protocol
pop-3	110	TCP
SNMP	161	UDP
route	520	UDP
UUCP	540	TCP

A full list (for a specific UNIX computer) is in the file /etc/services (unless the computer is using NIS; then the file is ignored, and the information is obtained over the network).

The nomenclature for specifying a connection to a specific host and port is 199.12.1.1, 23 (or sometimes 199.12.1.1 23 or 199.12.1.1:23).

To establish such a connection, a source process requests a connection to the destination machine, specifying the destination port number for the desired service. The *source* port number is any number greater than 255 and will be used by the destination machine to identify where to return the responses. Only the root user can provide services on ports below 1024.

User Datagram Protocol (UDP) is the corresponding *connectionless* layer 4 TCP/IP protocol.

See *Connection-oriented, Connectionless, DNS (Domain Name System), Finger, ftp, HTTP, Home Page, NIS, Ping, POP, RFC, root, Socket Number, Sockets, TCP/IP, telnet, tftp, UDP, uucp,* and *WinSock*.

TCP/IP
Transmission Control Protocol/Internet Protocol

A very popular data communications protocol, since it is available for most operating systems and hardware platforms—so these computers (UNIX workstations; PCs running MS-DOS, Windows, or OS/2; Apple Macintoshes, IBM Mainframes; DEC Minicomputers; etc.) can all communicate.

A protocol *suite* (or *stack*, since it involves more than one protocol) endorsed by the U.S. Department of Defense in 1978 as a data communications standard and was specified as the required protocol on Arpanet and Milnet by the U.S. Office of the Secretary of Defense in 1983.

Usually refers to the applications that are commonly run on TCP/IP as well, such as ftp, SMTP, telnet, DNS, RPC, rexec, and tftp. The protocols are well suited to providing communications between dissimilar computer systems.

Network congestion control is usually by discarding packets. Does not support fair sharing of bandwidth by applications nor congestion control by *class of service*.

While TCP/IP comes built in to most versions of the UNIX operating system, it is usually purchased as separate software for DOS and other older operating systems. Some popular packages are listed in the following table.

Software	Company	WWW server
PCTCP	ftp Software, Inc.	*http://www.ftp.com*
PC-NFS	Sun Microsystems, Inc.	*http://www.sun.com*
PathWay Access	The Wollongong Group, Inc.	*http://www.twg.com*
Reflection	Walker Richer & Quinn	*http://www.wrq.com*

TCP/IP was first standardized in U.S. Department of Defense MIL STD 1777 and MIL STD 1778.

See *ARP, ARPAnet, Bootp, DNS* (*Domain Name System*)*, Finger, IP, netstat, Operating System, OSI, Ping, QOS, rlogin, SMTP, SNMP, TCP, telnet, tftp, UDP, UNIX, VJ,* and *WinSock.*

TDMA   IS-54
Time Division Multiple Access

One of several cellular telephone schemes that improve on AMPS (standard cellular telephone service) to provide more capacity.

With significant *base station* changes, it uses a standard AMPS 30-kHz frequency pair (one 30-kHz channel for receive, the other for transmit). For standard AMPS, this is one full-duplex conversation, but for TDMA, it provides a 48,600-bits/s (24,300 bits/s per direction) data stream of 40-ms frames, which is shared among the users on a *round-robin* basis (each gets a turn, in a fixed sequence).

Current implementations digitize speech at 8,000 bits/s, providing up to three conversations (or 8,000-bits/s data channels) where only one was supported before (since $3 \times 8,000$ bits/s is all that fits into 24,300 bits/s).

It therefore triples (actually more than that—a factor of 3.4, because of the advantages of *trunking*) the number of simultaneous conversations supported by a given number of AMPS frequency pairs.

Future "*half-rate*" speech digitizers (4,000 bits/s per direction) will enable six conversations to be carried in one AMPS 30-kHz frequency pair, providing a capacity increase of 7.2 times (720%), assuming that the voice is intelligible—there are already many complaints about the current 8,000-bits/s voice quality.

TDMA is currently widely installed (typically a few channels per base station site) but not widely accepted, because of:

- Poor voice quality
- No new features (for example, it had been expected that Caller ID would be offered)
- Insufficient testing (there was no large-scale test as AMPS had)
- The potential for greater efficiency (that is, capacity improvements) of other schemes, such as CDMA (still in development) and GSM (currently not used in North America). Sometimes this is called the FUD (*fear, uncertainty, and doubt*) factor.

Defined in IS-54.

Also called *North American Digital Cellular* (NADC) and *Digital AMPS* (or D-AMPS or AMPS-D).

See *AMPS*, *CDMA*, *FUD*, and *GSM*.

Technical Service Bulletin   See **TSB**.

Telecommunications Industry Association   See **TIA**.

Teleglobe, Inc.

The carrier that has a legal monopoly of providing overseas satellite communications services for Canada.

They have a WWW server at *http://www.teleglobe.ca*.

See *Carrier*, *Satellite*, and *Telesat Canada*.

Telephone Companies

The three main telephone companies in Canada are listed in the following table.

Phone Company	Associated with
Stentor	Uses MCI's billing software, Intelligent Networking (permitting Stentor and U.S. MCI customers to establish virtual networks), and frame relay technology.
Unitel	20% owned by AT&T.
Sprint Canada	25% owned by Sprint (U.S.). Owned by, and was called, Call-Net Enterprises before this purchase.

See *Carrier*, *POTS*, and *Stentor*.

Telephony Application Programming Interface   See **TAPI.**

Telephony Services Application Programming Interface   See **TSAPI.**

Telesat Canada

The carrier that has a legal monopoly of providing satellite communication services within Canada.

They have a WWW server at *http://www.telesat.ca.*

See *Carrier, Satellite,* and *Teleglobe, Inc..*

telnet

Terminal emulation with communications to the host over a network (rather than through an EIA-232 connection).

That is, typing `telnet servername` connects you to the host `servername`. Your session then continues as if your terminal (likely actually a PC running a data communications program that makes your PC emulate a terminal) was directly connected to the remote host. You are prompted for a username and a password.

See *EIA/TIA-232, rlogin, TCP,* and *tn3270.*

Telnet 3270   See **tn3270.**

Teradata

A company that makes large SQL-based database servers. Bought by NCR, which was then bought by AT&T.

See *AT&T* and *SQL.*

Terisa Systems, Inc.

A joint venture, formed in 1994, of Enterprise Integration Technologies (EIT), which developed S-HTTP, and RSA Data Security, Inc. (which is big on encryption).

With some (equal) investments by America Online, CompuServe, Netscape (which developed the competing SSL), and IBM/Prodigy (IBM's on-line service), it is working to combine the S-HTTP and SSL methods of providing secure (*authenticated* and *encrypted*) transactions over the Internet.

Terisa Systems maintains a WWW server at *http://www.terisa.com.* It has good technical information on S-HTTP and SSL.

See *Authentication, Encryption, RSA, S-HTTP, SSL,* and *WWW.*

tftp
Trivial File Transfer Protocol

A simple file transfer protocol (a simplified version of ftp) that is often used to boot diskless workstations and other network devices (such as routers) over a network (typically a LAN).

Has no password security. Can be turned off by commenting-out the loading of the tftp server process (or "daemon"—`tftpd`) in the file `/etc/inetd.conf`.

See *Bootp*, *ftp*, and *TCP*.

Thread

One execution of software by one user's process or task.

Modern multiuser (which means that it requires some level of security) and multitasking (which means that it can do more than one thing at a time) operating systems support multiple threads, which would allow many activities to execute (almost) simultaneously (for example, searches on many remote databases all launched by one task).

Three Letter Acronyms   See **TLA.**

TIA
Telecommunications Industry Association

A group that grew out of the Electronic Industries Association (EIA) and produces telecommunications-related standards. (I guess there are many electronic industries but only one telecommunications industry—hey, I don't make up these acronyms, I just try to write them all down.)

See *EIA*, *Standards*, and *TSB*.

TIA
Thanks In Advance

A common email abbreviation.

TIC
Token Ring Interface Coupler

A Token Ring LAN adapter (especially the one in an IBM FEP).

The *printed circuit board* in a computer that connects the computer to the LAN cabling.

See *Cable*, *FEP*, *IBM*, *LAN*, *NIC*, and *Token Ring*.

Tick

Microsoft's DOS operating system sets a PC's hardware timer to interrupt about every 55 ms (slightly more than 18 times per second). This is therefore the finest resolution available through DOS for timing things.

See *IRQ*, *PC*, and *UTC*.

TIES
Time Independent Escape Sequence

For standard asynchronous dial-up modems, a method of *escaping* from data to command mode (so that the modem will interpret and act on the commands you send it, rather than sending them as data to the remote modem). It does not use the Hayes Microcomputer Products' *Improved Escape Sequence with Guard Time* method and therefore avoids having to pay royalties to Hayes, while remaining compatible with existing communications software.

TIES uses a specific string of characters (usually +++AT), with no requirement for idle time between them and the rest of the data, to cause the modem to escape from data mode to command mode.

The problem with TIES is that the data (or a CRC in it) may contain this escape sequence, so the file transfer will fail.

MultiTech Systems and Maxtech/GVC use TIES—which is simply the Hayes method with the "Guard Time" removed—the AT following the +++ is the AT that precedes almost all AT commands.

Around 1992, when Hayes began enforcing their patent, there was some controversy (initiated by Hayes) about the reliability of TIES (to pressure vendors using TIES to pay royalties, by telling the public that file transfers may fail occasionally).

See *AT Command Set*, *CRC*, and *Modem*.

TIFF
Tagged Image File Format

One of many standard methods of storing digitized graphic images. Many TIFF file formats are defined, including fax Group 3 and Group 4.

See *EPS* and *Fax*.

Time Division Multiple Access   See **TDMA**.

Time Independent Escape Sequence   See **TIES**.

Time Sharing Option   See **TSO.**

Time-stamp

Many UNIX systems maintain the current time and date as a 32-bit value representing the number of seconds since midnight January 1, 1970, *Greenwich Mean Time* (sometimes written as 1970-1-1 00:00:00 GMT), though in 1972, UTC replaced GMT as the time reference.

DOS's FAT also uses a 32-bit value but in a different format and relative to a different time:

- A 16-bit time value of the time since the most recent midnight, with the bits representing hhhhhmmmmmmssssss—as in hours:minutes:seconds (each in binary)
- A 16-bit date offset from January 1, 1980, with the bits representing yyyyyyymmmmddddd—as in year:month:date (each in binary)

The DOS scheme overflows when the year 2108 begins. (I hope DOS files are not used any more by then!)

See *FAT*, *GMT*, and *UTC*.

Time-To-Live   See **TTL.**

Tip and Ring

The name for the two wires on a telephone line, derived from the electrical contacts on old-style telephone plugs (which are similar to ¼-inch headphone plugs). One electrical contact is at the *tip* of the plug, and the other is a *ring* just above it (and there is a *sleeve* above that), as shown in the accompanying figure.

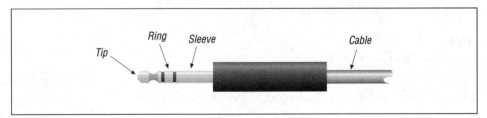

Tip and Ring–1

The following table lists some characteristics of Tip and Ring wiring.

		Wire Name	
		Tip	**Ring**
¼–inch phone jack electrical contact		Tip	Ring
Voltage (D.C. volts)		0	–48
Residential wiring (pair)	1	Green	Red
	2	Black	Yellow
	3	White	Blue
RJ11 pin (pair)	1	3	4
	2	5	2
	3	1	6
Office wiring (pair)	1	White with blue band	Blue with white band
	2	White with orange band	Orange with white band
	3	White with green band	Green with white band
	4	White with brown band	Brown with white band
RJ45 Pin (pair)	1	5	4
	2	3	6
	3	1	2
	4	7	8

See *Cable, Connector, POTS,* and *RJ-45.*

TLA
Three-Letter Acronym

An acronym for the acronyms, showing that there are too many acronyms. (Some people refer to an EFLA—*Extended Four-Letter Acronym,* too.)

Some Internet-accessible acronym look-up servers are at *http://curia.ucc.ie/cgi-bin/ acronym, http://slarti.ucd.ie/inttelec/top_level.html,* and *http://www.ucc.ie/htbin/acronym.*

tn3270
Telnet 3270

A *terminal emulation* (running a program on a computer so that the computer acts like a computer terminal) capability for UNIX workstations and TCP/IP-capable PCs that permits them to access an IBM mainframe as a 3270 terminal.

The IBM mainframe requires TCP/IP and telnet support, often in the form of an IBM 3172 interconnect controller (which is a souped-up IBM PS/2 PC). 3270 data from the terminal emulator are encapsulated in telnet TCP/IP packets.

See *3172*, *3270*, *FEP*, and *telnet*.

Token Ring

A LAN commercialized by IBM and standardized as IEEE 802.5.

Was initially conceived and is patented by Olof S. Söderblom (who gets *lots* of licensing fees—even from IBM) when he was an MIS (*Management Information Systems*) manager for a bank in Sweden (he later moved to Holland).

Token Ring is often described as being best suited to larger frames of data and heavier loading than Ethernet. The maximum frame size is about 4,500 bytes (4-Mbits/s Token Ring) and 17,800 bytes (16-Mbits/s Token Ring); the maximum frame size is actually defined by the amount of time you are allowed to transmit data.

See *ASTRAL*, *Encoding*, *Ethernet*, *LAN*, *LLC2*, *Remote Bridge*, *SRB*, *STP*, and *TIC*.

Token Ring Interface Coupler   See **TIC**.

Tool Command Language/Tool Kit   See **Tcl/Tk**.

Toolkit Without An Interesting Name   See **TWAIN**.

TPC
Transaction Processing Council

A group that defines benchmark tests for transaction-oriented database applications. Results are often measured in *Transactions Per Second* (TPS). The TPC-A benchmark is a debit/credit type that is best for demonstrating commercial I/O type loads and indicates the number of users that could be supported. TPC-B is more of a CPU and disk load test.

See *OLTP* and *TPS*.

TP-PMD
Twisted Pair–Physical Medium Dependent

An unshielded twisted pair medium option for FDDI.

See *FDDI* and *UTP*.

TPS
Transactions Per Second

A common unit when measuring the performance of transaction-oriented systems.

See *MIPS*, *SPEC*, *SQL*, and *TPC*.

Trade Secret

A (usually not recommended) alternative to a *patent* (patents require full disclosure of the information—which is unpalatable to some) to protect inventions (including those that are not protectable by patents) or business information from competition.

There is no *registration* (that is, you don't have to file any forms with some government office). It is simply up to the owner of the information or invention to actively keep the information or process from the public—for example, by having everyone who is exposed to the secret sign a *nondisclosure agreement* (acknowledging that the information is a *trade secret*).

If you are trying to sue someone who (allegedly) blabbed your secret, you would have to show a court that the person had access to your secret and that you took every reasonable precaution to keep your secret secret.

If the invention or information is discovered independently or by analyzing publicly available (including by accident from the owner) information, then the trade secret protection and status are lost (people can no longer be bound to keep what they know a secret).

Such independent discoverers can use or publish the information, and even file a patent application—potentially preventing the original trade secret user from using their own invention.

Trade secret protection is therefore a silly idea for things that can be *reverse-engineered* (figured out by analyzing it). Manufacturing processes and other procedures that cannot be surmised from the finished (and sold) product are well suited to trade secret protection.

See *Intellectual Property Protection* and *Patent*.

Trademark

A trademark is a word, symbol, or a combination of these that is used to distinguish the products or services of one person or company from those of another.

Trademark legislation is a form of *intellectual property protection* that protects:

- Slogans
- Names of products (including names for computer programs and games)
- Distinctive packages
- Unique product shapes

Restrictions generally involve not being able to trademark words that:

- Would be deceptive (the name claims that a product is from a certain country or city, and it is not, or that a product has certain features that it does not actually have)
- Would restrict others from fair business (for example, the name claims product features that all other products would also have)
- Are common descriptive words or names in other languages
- Are similar to, or would commonly be confused with, another company's (or institution's, government agency's, etc.) name or trademark

Registering provides legal title to the trademark (which can then be *assigned* to others, as can any other property).

Under *common law*, a trademark that is used for a certain length of time (an unregistered trademark) establishes ownership for *most* purposes (an exception is that precious metals shipped between countries require a *registered trademark*), but registration is highly recommended in all cases. For example, common law trademark rights protect you only in the geographic area where the trademark is used. Also, someone who registers your unregistered trademark may be able to force you to stop using "yours"—and just think of the legal costs of arguing common law use (lawyers love that sort of thing).

Products using the trademark must be on the market before registration can occur (so that the trademark becomes *associated* with the product), though the *trademark application* can be filed before this (based on *proposed use*).

There are three types of trademarks:

- *Ordinary marks* are words or symbols that distinguish the products or services of a specific person or company
- *Certification marks* are owned by a standards setter and show that the products or services that are *licensed* and using that certification mark meet a defined standard.
- *Distinguishing guise*, which provides protection for a product or package with a unique shape

There is no requirement to *mark* the use of the trademark, but these can be used:

- "™" indicates that the item is a registered or unregistered trademark
- "®" indicates that the item is a registered trademark

As for *copyrights* and *patents*, it is up to the owner of a trademark to find cases of *infringement* (this includes both uses of the trademark and of similar trademarks that might cause confusion) and to obtain an injunction. It is also the responsibility of the owner of a trademark to ensure that the trademark is used correctly (that is, to ensure that the term does not become part of normal conversation to refer to other similar products or services—from competitors).

Trademark protection is lost if it is not used (that is, products using it must be available on the market).

In Canada, trademarks are administered by the *Trademarks Office*, which is part of the CIPO. Registration provides 15 years of protection, which can be renewed at 15-year intervals, and requires filling out an application form and submitting a fee.

In the U.S., trademarks are registered with the U.S. Patent and Trademark Office (*http://www.uspto.gov*). The U.S. Patent Court adjudicates disputes (such as whether a term can be trademarked).

The Cornell Law School has a WWW page on U.S. trademark law at *http://www.law.cornell.edu/topics/trademark.html*.

See *CIPO* and *Intellectual Property Protection*.

Transaction Processing Council   See **TPC**.

Transactions Per Second   See **TPS**.

Transistor-Transistor Logic   See **TTL**.

Transmission Control Protocol   See **TCP and TCP/IP**.

Transparent Asynchronous Transmitter/Receiver Interface   See **TAXI**.

Trivial File Transfer Protocol   See **tftp**.

TrueType

Apple and Microsoft's *scalable* (or *outline*) font format.

Included with Windows 3.1 and Apple's System 7, enabling the same fonts to be used for both display and printing, so the printed output matches that displayed.

Windows TrueType fonts are not resolution-independent, so a change in printer resolution may produce different pagination, because of rounding errors.

Supports *hinting* (see *Outline Font*) and competes with *PostScript*—though PostScript is a general-purpose *page description language* and TrueType is more flexible but is limited to font scaling and hinting.

On a PC, the actual font files are in the `c:\windows\system` directory. Windows font files such as `VGA*.FON` and `EGA*.FON` are screen fonts (nonscalable fonts that provide optimal screen display for each video resolution). The following table shows the font filename extensions used by TrueType fonts.

Font Filename Extension	Function	Comments
`*.FOT`	Font header file	Required to provide font support under Windows
`*.TTF`	Font information file	
`*.TT`	Temporary file	Can likely be deleted

Installed TrueType fonts will be identified with "`(TrueType)`" and an extension of `*.FOT`, in the `[fonts]` section of the `c:\windows\win.ini` file.

See *Speedo*, *Outline Font*, *PostScript Page Description Language*, and *System 7*.

TSAPI
Telephony Services Application Programming Interface

AT&T's and Novell's method of integrating telephone services and computers.

Emphasizes *third-party* control, in that the call can be tracked as it is transferred, making it more suited to large offices than the somewhat competing TAPI.

Performs *first-party* type control (see TAPI) from the PBX (Private Branch Exchange—the telephone switch), rather than from the telephone. For example, to make a call the PBX rather than the telephone would dial the phone number, and the call would then be transferred to the telephone.

Specifies the physical link between a server (for example a Novell NetWare file server running the *NetWare Telephony Services* NLM) and a PBX (such as an AT&T Definity 3Gi). The link may be an EIA-232 connection or ISDN link (requiring ISDN boards and software support for both the file server and PBX).

Functions supported include:

- Placing outgoing calls
- Answering, transferring, and conferencing incoming calls
- Viewing the status of a current call (such as Caller ID, ringing, or on-hold)

See *CTI*, *EIA/TIA-232*, *ISDN*, *NLM*, *PBX*, and *TAPI*.

TSB
Technical Service Bulletin

A document from the EIA or TIA which is a "compilation of engineering data or information useful to the technical community, and represents approaches to good engineering practices." Often these are later included in updated versions of related standards.

See *EIA*, *EIA/TIA TSB-37a*, *Standards*, and *TIA* (*Telecommunications Industry Association*).

TSO
Time Sharing Option

An IBM mainframe user interface providing an editor and program driver that are well-suited to software development. Runs under MVS. An alternative is CICS.

See *CICS*, *Mainframe*, and *MVS*.

TTL
Time-To-Live

An 8-bit field in an IP packet header that is set to the maximum number of routers a message could pass through to reach a destination (typically 15).

The field is decremented by each router that handles the packet. If it is decremented to zero, that router discards the packet and should send an ICMP *TTL exceeded* message back to the sender. This capability ensures that packets cannot get stuck in a loop (therefore creating significant network loading) because of a network problem such as (possibly temporarily) incorrect routing tables.

See *ICMP*, *IP*, and *RIP*.

TTL
Transistor-Transistor Logic

An old *logic family* (method of making basic binary logic circuits, such as and, Exclusive-or, and nand) that uses a 5-volt D.C. power supply and represents the two binary states as follows:

- Anything from 0 to 0.8 V D.C. is considered OFF or a binary 0
- Anything from 2.0 to 5 V is ON or a binary 1 (voltages between 0.8 and 2.0 V are allowed only while quickly going from one state to the other)

Rarely used now (too slow and too high in power consumption), but the voltage levels have become an industry standard. For example, PC parallel printer ports and *single-ended* SCSI use TTL voltages.

There are many logic families newer than the original TTL. These feature lower power consumption, faster propagation times, and other advantages, and are typically TTL-compatible.

See *de facto Standard*, *Parallel Port*, and *SCSI*.

Tunneling   See **Encapsulation.**

TWAIN
Toolkit Without An Interesting Name

A standard software interface for the imaging data from *raster image*–generating devices (for example, from document scanners, video frame grabbers, and digital cameras, which produce horizontal scans digitizing the intensity and possibly the color of the image) so that they can be input into graphics application software.

Requires a SCSI interface on both the computer and the digitizing device and is platform–independent (Macintosh and PCs) and operating system–independent (Macintosh and Windows, later OS/2 and UNIX).

Each device manufacturer must provide a TWAIN-compliant driver (and SCSI interface) with their hardware. The application software (that supports TWAIN) can then receive the data. Before this, applications software had to supply drivers for each digitizing device it supported.

Developed by Aldus, Caere, Kodak, Hewlett-Packard, and Logitech.

See *SCSI*.

Twisted Pair–Physical Medium Dependent   See **TP-PMD.**

Typeface Family

A font family, such as Times or Helvetica. Each family often consists of variations, such as the following:

• Different weight strokes: **Helvetica bold**
• Character width: Helvetica narrow
• Slant: *Helvetica italic* or ***oblique*** (which is simply slanted, not a modified font)

See *Bitmap Font*, *Font*, and *Outline Font*.

UA
User Agent

The software that interacts with a *message transfer agent* to retrieve, display, and send X.400 messages on behalf of a user.

See *MTA* and *X.400*.

UART
Universal Asynchronous Receiver Transmitter

The *Integrated Circuit* (IC) that handles the data communications for a computer.

It converts the parallel data (so called because they are stored, retrieved, and transferred 8 or more bits at a time) in a PC (for example) to serial *asynchronous data communications* (in which data are sent and received 1 bit at a time) for transmission over a data link, such as an EIA-232 cable or modem connection. It is always less expensive (and usually simpler) to send data 1 bit at a time, especially on links that are longer than a few meters.

Also, a UART converts received serial data to parallel for further processing by the receiving computer.

Other UART functions include the following:

- Adding start and stop bits to the transmitted data so that the receiver's UART can synchronize with the sender (that is, so that it can know where the bit edges are and which bit is the first bit of data)
- Generating a hardware interrupt when a character is received and when the UART is ready for another character to send
- Controlling and reading the status of the modem signals (RTS, CTS, etc.)

Early PCs used the 8250 (or the equivalent 16450) UART. Current PCs use the 16550A (or an equivalent), which has built-in hardware buffering.

If the UART also supports *synchronous data communications*, then it is sometimes called a *Universal Synchronous/Asynchronous Receiver Transmitter* (USART); other times, it is simply called a UART. The USART would then be able to support BISYNC and HDLC and provides features such as:

- *Sync* or *flag character* detection and generation
- Zero-bit stuffing
- CRC generation and checking

See *16550A*, *Asynchronous*, *BISYNC*, *CRC*, *EIA/TIA-232*, *ESP HDLC*, *IRQ*, *Modem*, *Out-of-band*, *Parity*, and *Synchronous*.

UDP
User Datagram Protocol

A connectionless transport protocol that runs on top of TCP/IP's IP.

Provides an unreliable *datagram* service. That is, packets may be duplicated, lost, or received in a different order than the one in which they were sent.

The receiving program requests a number of bytes (up to the number in the received packet). If less that the full packet is read, then the remainder is discarded, and the next read is from the next packet. That is, the boundaries of the original packet are preserved (which is different than for TCP). The application program must handle error correction.

Best suited for small, independent requests, such as requesting a MIB value from an SNMP agent, in which first setting up a connection would take more time than sending the data. Less efficient than TCP, since the full address must be sent with each packet.

Used by DNS, NFS, ping, RIP, RPCs, SMTP, SNMP, and tftp (the /etc/services file on a UNIX computer has a complete list for that computer).

See *Connectionless*, *DNS (Domain Name System)*, *NFS*, *Ping*, *RIP*, *RPC*, *SMTP*, *SNMP*, *TCP*, *TCP/IP*, *tftp*, and *WinSock*.

UI
UNIX International

A now defunct consortium of over 200 vendors and users (including AT&T, Sun, NCR, and SCO) that promoted UNIX System V systems.

They promoted something called UI-ATLAS—a "comprehensive architecture for the development, operation and management of distributed multivendor applications in mixed computing environments." It was to compete with OSF's DME. But like so many other efforts, you don't hear much about this one any more.

See *DME*, *OSF*, *UNIX*, and *X/Open*.

UNI
User-to-Network Interface

The specification for the interface between a user's equipment (a router with an ATM interface, for example) and an ATM network (likely a SONet OC-3, or slower link, to an ATM switch).

See *ATM* (*Asynchronous Transfer Mode*), *DXI*, and *SONet*.

Unicode

A character coding scheme designed to be an extension to ASCII.

By using 16 bits for each character (rather than ASCII's 7), virtually every character of every language, as well as many symbols (such as "•"), can be represented in an internationally standard way, and the current complexity of incompatible *extended character sets* and *code pages* should be eliminated.

The first 128 codes of Unicode correspond to standard ASCII.

See *ASCII*, *Baud*, and *EBCDIC*.

Unified System Display Architecture   See **USDA.**

Uniform Resource Locator   See **URL.**

UniForum

A nonprofit trade association dedicated to the promotion of the UNIX operating system and other efforts that are important to the acceptance of UNIX—such as POSIX.

Formally though, their mission statement is much more broad and does not even mention UNIX: "UniForum is a vendor independent, not-for-profit professional association that helps individuals and their organizations increase their information system's effectiveness through the use of open systems, based on shared industry standards. Central to UniForum's mission is the delivery of high quality educational programs, trade shows and conferences, publications, on-line services, and peer group interactions."

Formerly /usr/group.

They have a WWW server at *http://www.uniforum.org/.*

See *POSIX OSE* and *UNIX*.

Univel

A Novell subsidiary that used to produce UnixWare (which they bought from USL). In 1995 Novell sold UnixWare to SCO.

UnixWare integrates USL's UNIX System V Release 4.2 with Novell NetWare client software. Competes with other Intel platform UNIXes, such as Sunsoft's Interactive UNIX, SCO UNIX System V, Xenix, and Open Desktop.

See *COSE*, *Novell*, *SCO*, *UNIX*, and *USL*.

Universal Asynchronous Receiver Transmitter   See **UART**.

Universal Serial Bus   See **USB**.

Universal Time Coordinated   See **UTC**.

UNIX
Uniplexed Information and Computing System

A usually non-real-time (for example, most implementations don't support task preemption) operating system, now written in the C language. Popular because it is available for so many hardware platforms and because it is well documented (but cryptic), with much source code available. Also popular because it is widely used at universities, so graduates are comfortable with it.

The initial development was by Ken Thompson and Dennis M. Ritchie, two programmers for AT&T. UNIX was developed starting in 1969 on a DEC PDP-7 minicomputer and ran a game called *Space Travel*. *UNIX Version 1* was completed in 1971. It ran on a DEC PDP-11/20, was written in assembler, was documented in "*Edition 1*" of the manual (so this version of UNIX was sometimes referred to as Edition 1), and was used as a text processing tool for the preparation of patents.

While the SVR4.2 (System five, release 4.2) family versions are currently the most popular implementation, much development work was done by the University of California at Berkeley, which resulted in the BSD (Berkeley Software Distribution) versions (or "flavors") of UNIX. A gross simplification of the many variants is shown in the accompanying figure.

As to the name, the story goes that there was once an effort to make an all-singing, all-dancing operating system. It was to do everything and was called *Multiplexed Information and Computing System*—that is, "Multics." Although Multics was used on a small percentage of Honeywell mainframe computers in the late 1970s and early 1980s (the larger percentage used GCOS—General Comprehensive Operating System), the effort mostly failed.

So the Multics developers tried something simpler (the "opposite") and therefore called it *Uniplexed Information and Computing System*—that is, "Unics." This was later written UNIX, as it is today.

UNIX System Laboratories (USL) is responsible for the ongoing development of the original AT&T UNIX. USL was bought from AT&T by Novell in early 1993.

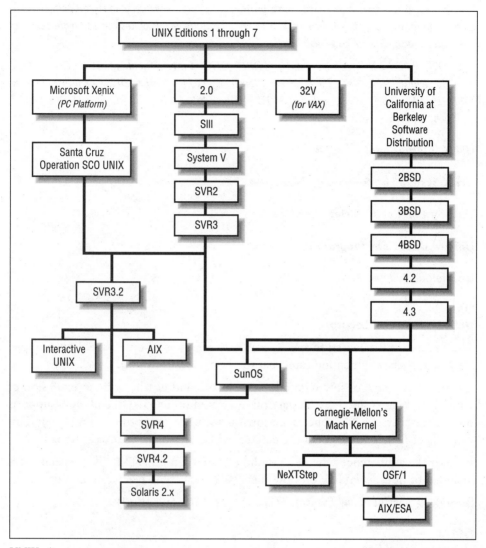

UNIX-1

In late 1993, Novell gave the rights to the UNIX name to the X/Open Company Ltd. (which licenses it to others to use).

The UNIX and Advanced Computing Systems Professional and Technical Association has a WWW server at *http://www.usenix.org/,* and Michigan State University maintains some WWW pointers at *http://clunix.msu.edu.*

Some UNIX manuals are available at *http://www.cis.ohio-state.edu/hypertext/ man_pages.html/*. Some history of UNIX is at *http://www.cis.ohio-state.edu/hypertext/faq/ usenet/unix-faq/faq/part6/faq-doc-2.html*.

See *AIX, A/UX, BSD UNIX, CDE, COSE, DEC, Finger, Gopher, iBCS, IRC, Mach, MOTD, Motif, NIS, NFS, NeXTStep, Novell, ODT, OPENLOOK, Operating System, OSF, POSIX OSE, SCO, Solaris, SVID, SVR4, UI, UniForum, Univel, USL, WABI, X/Open, X, Xenix,* and *XPG*.

UNIX International   See **UI**.

UNIX System Five Release 4   See **SVR4**.

Unix System Laboratories   See **USL**.

Unix to Unix Copy Program   See **uucp**.

Unshielded Twisted Pair   See **UTP**.

URL
Uniform Resource Locator

The "address" that is used to specify a WWW server and home page. For example, *http://www.ieee.org/*, which indicates that the host's address is `www.ieee.org`.

Often, a filename (possibly with a long path to it and usually with an extension of `.html`, or `.htm`—since the files are often created on DOS PCs, and DOS supports only three-character filename extensions) is included (after the trailing "/"). This would specify a file other than the default, which is usually `Welcome.html`.

It can make a difference whether a trailing "/" (when no HTML file is specified) is included or not, depending on how the WWW server has been configured.

See *DNS (Domain Name System), Home Page, HTML,* and *WWW*.

USB
Universal Serial Bus

A 12-Mbits/s, daisy-chain, *serial bus* proposed by Intel to connect up to 63 peripherals (such as a backup tape drive, CD-ROM drive, digital telephone, joystick, keyboard, mouse, printer, and digitized audio devices) to a PC. A major motivation is that all these peripherals would require only a single port on the PC. This would be a dramatic cost savings over the current situation, in which a PC needs separate ports (electronics and connectors) for each of these devices.

Also intended to replace the use of EIA-232 for modem connections (EIA-232 isn't fast enough, and a PC often does not have enough serial ports), and also to support CTI.

Supports:

- Multiple isochronous data streams (so is well suited to multimedia)
- Multiple data streams (for traffic that is not delay-sensitive)
- Hot-plugging of devices (they can be plugged in and activated without rebooting the PC)

Uses two-pair cable and a four-pin connector. Cabling will likely go to connectors on the PC (for digital phone, modem, and printer), monitor (for microphone and speaker), and/or keyboard (for pointing devices).

Promoted by Compaq, DEC, IBM, Intel (which will provide USB support built in to PCI support ICs—this pretty much guarantees that USB will be widely accepted), Microsoft, NEC, and Northern Telecom.

For lower-speed applications, would compete with ACCESS.bus. For higher-speed requirements, would compete with 1394.

See *1394*, *ACCESS.bus*, *Bus*, *CTI*, *DDC*, *EIA/TIA-232*, *Isochronous*, *PCI*, and *PnP*.

USDA
Unified System Display Architecture

A proposed method of sharing 64-bit-wide memory between that needed for a PC's main memory (which is used for programs, data, and disk caching) and video display memory. The intent is to both enhance performance and avoid wasting memory not needed for a particular display resolution.

For example, a 1,024 × 768 pixel display using 256 colors requires 768 kbytes of RAM. If the video board has 2 Mbytes of RAM (more of which would be needed for higher resolutions or more colors), then 1,280 kbytes would be wasted. USDA would permit this otherwise-wasted memory to be used for other PC requirements (nice, big caches, etc.).

Has nothing whatsoever to do with the U.S. Department of Agriculture.

See *Cache*, *PC*, and *VESA*.

Usenet

One of the main things people read and contribute to on the Internet. Equivalent to a worldwide BBS (*Bulletin Board System*) with over 10,000 forums, and many new ones every day.

Updates are distributed constantly, or downloaded overnight to *news servers* (typically located at ISPs or large companies).

Usually, new newsgroups are formed when approved by a vote. (There are rules for this procedure; for example, the proposed new group and the votes for and against it may need to be posted in and below the `news.announce` and `news.groups` Usenet newsgroups.)

Since useful FAQs are often posted to newsgroups but scroll off (as the newsgroups servers need the disk space), they are archived on Usenet FAQ servers such as *http://www.cis.ohio-state.edu/hypertext/faq/usenet/faq-List.html*.

Usenet was created by Tom Truscott, Steve Bellovin, and Jim Ellis in 1979 as an experiment to create a method to post and read news messages and notices—initially primarily UNIX bug reports.

See *BBS*, *Bugs*, *FAQ*, *Internet*, *ISP*, *UNIX*, and *uucp*.

User Agent   See **UA**.

User Datagram Protocol   See **UDP**.

USL
UNIX System Laboratories

The previous owners of the UNIX name and source code.

USL (along with the UNIX name and the UNIX software development rights) was bought by Novell from AT&T and renamed *Summit UNIX System Group* (the company is in Summit, New Jersey). The X/Open Company now owns the UNIX name.

There is still an ftp server at *ftp://ftp.usl.com* with some useful information.

See *AT&T*, *COSE*, *Novell*, *UNIX*, and *X/Open*.

UTC
Universal Time Coordinated

UTC is the SI replacement for *Greenwich Mean Time* (GMT). GMT is (was) defined as the time in Greenwich, England (actually, at a lovely old observatory there), and used to be the basis for timekeeping.

In 1972, *International Atomic Time* (IAT) was adopted, as part of the SI metric stuff.

An example of IAT is that rather than the year being defined in terms of the earth's rotation around the sun (or was that the other way around?), the year is now defined as 31,558,150 seconds (or less, if you define a year according to the phases of the moon or by vernal equinoxes). In any case, a second is defined as 9,192,631,770 oscillations of the Cesium 133 atom. That is, the stars have been replaced by an oscillator.

UNIX computers maintain their time-of-day clocks as a 32-bit counter of the number of seconds since midnight January 1, 1970, UTC. The counter will overflow after 136 years (around February 4 in the year 2106)—I just can't wait to see the havoc). The same 32-bit counter method is used by YModem's file date-stamp.

On some computer systems, "Time 0" is defined as midnight January 6, 1980, UTC. Many time-of-day clocks count the number of microseconds since this time. There are about 3×10^{13} μs per year, so a 64-bit counter ($2^{64} \approx 2 \times 10^{19}$) can count about 600,000 years (maybe that one I won't see wrap-around).

See *Daylight Savings Time*, *GMT*, *Satellite*, *SI*, *PC*, *Time-stamp*, *YModem*, and *UNIX*.

User-to-Network Interface   See **UNI**.

UTP
Unshielded Twisted Pair

A popular type of cable for LANs and other in-building voice and data communications applications.

It turns out that there are advantages to the following:

- Using two wires, rather than one for each signal. This permits *differential signaling* to be used, which is more immune to the effects of external electrical noise.
- Twisting each pair. This keeps the wires of a signal's pair as close together as possible, and periodically exposes the opposite side of the pair to the noise. Both of these factors help to cancel out the effects of outside interference. Also, each pair has a different *twist pitch* (so the pairs also appear twisted to each other), and the pairs are each moved somewhat randomly relative to the other pairs in the cable jacket. Both of these help to reduce cross-talk between the pairs.
- Not using cable *shielding* (a foil or braided metallic covering). While this can increase the effects of outside interference, not using shielding reduces the cost, size, and installation time of the cable and connectors and eliminates the possibility of *ground loops* (which is current flowing in the shield because of the ground voltage at each end of the cable not being exactly the same—and this current inducing interference into the cable that was supposed to be better protected through the use of the shield).

Unshielded twisted pair implements all of these.

While any cable with twisted pairs of conductors and no shield could be referred to as unshielded twisted pair, the term "UTP" usually refers to unshielded twisted pair cable as specified in the EIA/TIA-568 *Commercial Building Telecommunications Wiring Standard*. This standard specifies the electrical and physical requirements for

UTP, STP, coaxial cables, and optical fiber cables. For UTP, the requirements include:

- Four individually twisted pairs per cable
- Each pair has a *characteristic impedance* of 100 Ω ± 15% (when measured at frequencies of 1 to 16 MHz)
- 24 gauge (0.5106-mm-diameter) or optionally 22 gauge (0.6438 mm diameter) copper conductors are used

Additionally, EIA/TIA-568 specifies the color coding, cable diameter, and other electrical characteristics, such as the maximum:

- *Cross-talk* (how much a signal in one pair interferes with the signal in another pair—through *capacitive*, *inductive*, and other types of coupling). Since this is measured as how many *decibels* (dB) quieter the induced signal is than the original interfering signal, larger numbers are better.
- *Attenuation* (the most a signal can get quieter for a given length of cable, measured at several specific key frequencies). Since this is measured as dB of attenuation, smaller numbers are better.

An important feature of UTP is that it can be used for Ethernet, Token Ring, FDDI, ATM, EIA-232, ISDN, analog telephone (POTS), and other types of communication. This enables the same type of cable (and connectors) to be used for an entire building—unlike STP.

EIA/TIA-568 (and the subsequent TSB-36) defines five *categories*, as shown in the following table. These are used to quantify the quality of the cable (for example, only Categories 3, 4, and 5 are considered "datagrade UTP").

Category	Characteristics specified up to (MHz)	Use
1	None	Alarm systems and other noncritical applications.
2	None	Voice, EIA-232, and other low speed data.
3	16	10BASE-T Ethernet, 4-Mbits/s Token Ring, 100BASE-T4, 100VG-AnyLAN, basic rate ISDN. Generally the minimum standard for new installations.
4	20	16-Mbits/s Token Ring. Not widely used.
5	100	TP-PMD, SONet, OC-3 (ATM), 100BASE-TX. The most popular for new data installations.

Underwriter's Laboratory defines a *level* system, which has minor differences from EIA/TIA-568's category system. For example, UL requires the characteristics to be measured at various temperatures. However, generally (for example), UL Level V (Roman numerals are used) is the same as EIA's Category 5, and cables are usually marked with both EIA and UL designations.

Typically (for example, Token Ring and 10BASE-T Ethernet), only two of the four pairs of wires per cable are used (one pair for the receive data, one for the transmit data). The additional two pairs per cable would then be available so that the cable could be used for other types of data communications. For example, ISDN sometimes requires the third and possibly fourth pair to provide power to the networked devices; 100BASE-T4 and 100VG-AnyLAN can split the data among all four pairs to reduce the bit rate on each pair so that a lower-quality cable (Category 3) can be used instead of Category 5, which would normally be required for 100-Mbits/s data communications (this is supposed to reduce costs); and some sites use the extra pairs for other signals, such as a second 10BASE-T connection or a telephone line or for future uses.

A Category 5 cable installation requires more than just Category 5 cable. For example, installation practices (such as not untwisting a pair more than ½ inch when terminating it onto a connector) must be met. All components (such as data jacks, cross-patch panels, and patch cables) must be certified for Category 5 installations and to work together to make a Category 5 installation (this usually restricts an installation to components from a single vendor).

It is anticipated that many sites that spent extra money to install Category 5 cable will be disappointed when they learn (likely the hard way) that they still can't carry (for example) 100BASE-TX Fast Ethernet because either the installation practices were not adequate or some components were not Category 5 compliant.

Rather than (or perhaps in addition to) ensuring that all components and the installation practices meet the Category 5 requirements, some say that an end-to-end *certification test* should be used.

EIA/TIA's TSB 67 (Technical Systems Bulletin) sets out some definitions for such hand-held Category 5 cable *certification testers*, which (so far) defines two levels:

- *Level I* testers are accurate to 4 dB and are not accurate enough for certification
- *Level II* testers are accurate to 2 dB and are suitable for Category 5 certification

See *100BASE-TX*, *100VG-AnyLAN*, *10BASE-T*, *ATM (Asynchronous Transfer Mode)*, *Cable*, *Connector*, *EIA/TIA-232*, *Ethernet*, *FDDI*, *ISDN*, *POTS*, *SCSI*, *ScTP*, *STP*, and *TSB*.

uucp
Unix-to-Unix Copy Program

Simple, automatic file transfers between UNIX machines (originally using auto-dial modem connections).

Initially developed as a low-cost way to support email. The Internet's Usenet was initially supported by an extension of this capability.

See *AT Command Set, Internet, Modem,* and *Usenet.*

V.8

A method used by V.34 modems to negotiate connection features and options.

Using V.21 modem modulation (which is 300 bits/s FSK—the same as the initial negotiation done by Group III fax machines), the calling modem sends its *calling menu* (a message containing a list of the features it supports). The answering modem replies with a *joint menu*, which is a list of the features it supports in common with the calling modem.

Previous modem negotiations (for example, that used by V.32 modems) used tones. This method became too slow and inflexible for the large number of options that V.34 needs to negotiate.

See *Fax*, *Modem*, *V.21*, and *V.34*.

V.17

A modem modulation standard that provides *simplex* 14,400-bits/s data transfer over a standard one-pair (that is, two-wire) POTS dial-up telephone line.

Has a *fallback* (used when the line is too noisy) speed of 12,000 bits/s. In addition, most V.17 modems can do V.29 modulation, so fallback speeds of 9,600 and 7,200 bits/s are also supported.

The most popular use of V.17 modulation is for Group III facsimile communications—especially for fax boards and data/fax modems (as most Group III fax *machines* are still V.29 only).

V.17 uses a type of modulation called *Trellis Code Modulation* (TCM).

See *Fax*, *POTS*, *Simplex*, and *V.29*.

V.21

A modem modulation standard that provides full-duplex, asynchronous, data transfer at any speed from 0 to 300 bits/s (though usually at 300 bits/s) over a standard one-pair, dial-up telephone line.

Currently used by fax machines and also by V.34 modems during their negotiations. Was also used (a long time ago) in Europe (as Bell 103 was in North America) for everyday dial-up terminal to computer data communications (though the faster recent standards, such as V.32*bis* and V.34, have made V.21 all but obsolete for this application).

Similar to (in that they both use *frequency shift keying* modulation), but incompatible with, Bell 103 (they use different frequencies); that is, they are homologous. (Now there's a word you don't get to use often.)

See *Asynchronous*, *Bell 103*, *Fax*, *Full-duplex*, *Modem*, *V.8*, and *V.34*.

V.22

A modem modulation standard that provides full-duplex, 1,200-bits/s data transfer over a standard one-pair, dial-up telephone line. Handles synchronous or asynchronous data. (Data transfer between modems is synchronous, but the modems have a built-in converter, so DTEs can use asynchronous data communications).

Is an older method, which was used mostly in Europe (and the similar technology but slightly different Bell 212A was used here). Most V.22 modems can be configured to either manually or automatically work with Bell 212A.

See *Asynchronous*, *Bell 212A*, *DTE*, *Modem*, and *Synchronous*.

V.22*bis*

A modem modulation standard providing full-duplex, 2,400-bits/s data transfer over a standard one-pair, dial-up telephone line. In a manner similar to that of V.22 modems, both *asynchronous data communications* and *synchronous data communications* are supported.

See *Asynchronous*, *Modem*, *Synchronous*, and *V.22*.

V.25*bis*

A serial, in-band (that is, the commands are sent on the same wires as are used to carry data) command language for auto-dialing modems and data sets (so the DTE can specify the phone number the modem should dial).

The standard is specified for three types of serial links:

- Character-oriented (BISYNC) synchronous
- Bit-oriented (SDLC) synchronous (for example, for CSU/DSUs, such as those for switched 56 service), in which case it uses NRZI (*Non-Return to Zero, Inverted*) encoding
- Asynchronous (for standard asynchronous modems)

However, V.25*bis* is usually used only for synchronous data communications, as the *AT command set* is usually used on asynchronous links.

Common uses include enabling computer or communications equipment to request that a particular number be dialed for a Group IV fax machine, synchronous auto-dialing modem, or switched 56 backup data link.

RS-366 is a rarely used out-of-band (that is, a separate connector to signal the dialing information) alternative.

See *Asynchronous, AT Command Set, BISYNC, CSU, DSU, EIA/TIA-232, DTE, Encoding, Fax, In-Band, Modem, Out-of-band, SDLC, Switched 56*, and *Synchronous*.

V.27ter

A full-duplex (on four-wire leased lines) or half-duplex (on two-wire dial-up lines) synchronous 4,800- and 2,400-bits/s modem modulation standard.

Currently used mostly for lower-speed (4,800 and 2,400 bits/s) Group III facsimile communications. (V.29 and V.17 are higher-speed modulation methods.)

Typically, V.27*ter* is used only to reduce the cost of the fax's modem or because the communication line for that call was too noisy to support higher-speed communications. Uses a type of modulation called *Differential Phase Shift Keying* (DPSK).

See *Fax, Synchronous*, and *V.29*.

V.29

A full-duplex (on four-wire leased lines) or half-duplex (on two-wire dial-up lines) synchronous 9,600- and 7,200-bits/s modem modulation standard.

The two-wire, 9,600-bits/s version is used for standard Group III facsimile machines—which fall back to 7,200 (and to 4,800 and 2,400 bits/s, using V.27*ter*)—if the communication line cannot handle 9,600 bits/s (for example, because the line is too noisy or is being digitized at less than 64,000 bits/s).

Uses a type of modulation called *Quadrature Amplitude Modulation* (QAM).

See *Fax, Full-duplex, Half-Duplex, Modem, PCM, V.17*, and *V.27ter*.

V.32

A modem modulation standard providing full–duplex, 9,600–bits/s data transfer over a standard one-pair, dial–up telephone line.

Asynchronous (through the use of a built-in asynchronous-to-synchronous converter) and synchronous data communications are supported.

However, to save money, some modems (low-end) do not provide synchronous user-data support, which at first glance seems strange, since the modem uses synchronous data communications to the remote modem and requires (and has) extra circuitry to handle asynchronous data communications. One would expect that it would be easy to provide synchronous user-data support (by simply bypassing the asynchronous converter). The bottom line is that it costs more money to support synchronous user-data, since it requires extra signals—the clocking—on the EIA-232 interface. And very few users require it, especially in the home-PC market, in which saving money is more important than seldom-used features.

Also, *internal modems* (the modem is a card in the PC rather than an external box) usually do not support synchronous data communications. This is because the built-in COM port required by internal modems uses a standard PC UART, and these UARTs do not support synchronous data communications.

The above discussion concerning synchronous data communications support applies to all modems from Bell 212A through to V.34.

A fallback speed of 4,800 bits/s is included in the V.32 standard.

See *Asynchronous, EIA/TIA-232, Modem, Synchronous, UART, V.42,* and *V.42bis.*

V.32*bis*

A modem modulation standard providing full–duplex, 14,400 bits/s data transfer over a standard one-pair, dial–up telephone line.

Synchronous and asynchronous data communications are supported. Fallback speeds of 12,000, 9,600, 7,200, and 4,800 bits/s are included in the standard.

Modulation handshaking can take up to 8 seconds, and subsequent V.42 and V.42*bis* handshaking can require an additional 10 to 20 seconds.

See *Modem, V.32, V.42,* and *V.42bis.*

V.34

A modem modulation standard providing full–duplex, 28,800–bits/s data transfer over a standard one-pair, dial–up telephone line.

Synchronous and asynchronous data communications are supported. A handshaking method based on V.8 provides faster (under 5 seconds) call setup negotiation than V.32*bis,* V.FC, or V.*terbo.*

Other enhancements over V.32*bis* (and its predecessors) include the following:

- *Line Probing* (choosing a *carrier frequency* between 2,400 and 3,429 Hz) at call setup time. The choice is based on detected line impairments and which frequencies the line best carries—perhaps because of telephone company digitizing. Previous modem modulation methods specify only a single carrier frequency. V.34 modems are supposed to perform line probing continuously after a connection is established, to adjust to changing line conditions. A good implementation will make these adjustments quickly.

- *Precoding*—the receiving modem tells the transmitting modem about detected line distortion (for example, because of PCM digitization of the analog phone line) so that the transmitting modem can precompensate for these deficiencies in the communications channel (for example, by boosting the frequencies that are attenuated more than the others).

- *Retrain/Entrain* during a data call to adjust the transmitting modem's precoding, receiving modem's *equalization* (compensating for the communication line's deficiencies), or the data transmission rate (faster and slower) as required because of changing line conditions. Data transfer is suspended during the few seconds that this occurs.

- A half-duplex version (which could, for example, be used in Group III fax machines).

- Smaller fallback (due to noisy lines) data transmission speed increments (or should that be decrements?) of 2,400 bits/s (many previous modems have 4,800-bits/s increments). A total of 12 speeds (from 2,400 to 28,800 bits/s) are therefore available.

The modulation scheme maps up to 9 data bits to each *symbol* (baud) sent over the telephone line. Therefore, a bit rate (data bits into the modem's EIA-232 connector) of 28,800 bits/s results in a baud rate of 3,200 (9-bit) symbols per second out the analog phone line (since $3,200 \times 9 = 28,800$ bits/s).

Implementation options are listed in the following table.

Feature	Provides
Asymmetrical Transmission Rates	Sending and receiving data rates can be different so that they can each be as high as the communication circuit supports.
Auxiliary Channel	Supports a 200-bits/s in-band data channel for diagnostics, line quality monitoring, and modem configuration.

(table continued on next page)

Feature	Provides
Baud Rate	The standard baud rates are 2,400, 3,000, and 3,200 symbols per second. Optional rates of 2,743 and 2,800 baud may be the highest that work for links that use ADPCM (for example, satellite data links usually can't handle the 3,000-baud rate). This provides a higher data rate than if the 2,400-baud rate was used. An optional baud rate (implemented by Motorola) of 3,429 9-bit symbols per second results in a data rate of 33,600 bits/s.
Nonlinear Encoding	Allows better operation over PCM-digitized analog communication circuits by using amplitudes that are less sensitive to *quantization* noise.
Precoding	Reduces high-frequency noise and reduces inter-symbol interference—important for noisier analog communication circuits.
Trellis Coding	Modems must be able to transmit using 16-, 32-, *and* 64-state codes. Modems only need to be able to receive using any one (though optionally two or all three) of these Trellis codes. Higher-state codes provide better operation on noisier communication circuits—ideally, avoiding the need to drop to a lower baud rate. Trellis coding specifies which *points* of a *constellation* are allowed next, given the current point (which is the combination of *phase* and *amplitude* defining the symbol). Therefore the circuit will be more immune to noise.

Note that vendors can call the modem a "V.34 modem" if it implements none, any, or all of these options. Also options will be used only if both modems in a session support the option.

Other implementation options (which are entirely up to the vendor and not part of any standard) include the following:

- How the modem's software (sometimes called *firmware*, because it is more like hardware that is built in to the modem) is upgraded (Flash ROM with downloading from a bulletin board system is best; plugging in a new EPROM is next best)
- Configuration by the front panel, a management system, or remotely (in addition to *AT Commands*)
- *Distinctive ringing* detection
- *Caller ID* detection

Other differences between V.34 modems include the quality of the data compression algorithm (not that errors will occur, but that the data will not be compressed as much as possible) and the processing power available (if it is inadequate, transmission may slow significantly if data are sent full-duplex).

See the discussion about synchronous data communications support in the entry for *V.32*, as this applies to all modems from Bell 212A through V.32.

During its lengthy standards development process, V.34 was called "V.*fast*" (since it was expected to be the modem modulation standard that provided the fastest possible data rate over standard POTS analog telephone lines).

See *ADPCM, AT Command Set, Baud, BBS, EIA/TIA-232, In-Band, Modem, PCM, POTS, V.8, V.32, V.34bis, V.42, V.42bis, V.FC,* and *V.terbo.*

V.34*bis*

A modem modulation standard (still under development) providing full-duplex, 32,000- (or maybe 33,600-) bits/s data transfer over a standard one-pair, dial-up telephone line.

Rather than being called a separate standard (V.34*bis*), this may end up being an enhancement to V.34 (and just another speed option within the V.34 standard).

See *Modem* and *V.34.*

V.35

An obsolete 48,000-bits/s group modem. The device is no longer used, but the *interface* (voltages, connector type, pin-out, etc.) specified is frequently used to interconnect other high-speed devices (for example, a router to a DSU).

V.35 is the most popular interface (in North America) for serial data at speeds greater than EIA-232's official maximum of 20,000 bits/s. Specifically, V.35 is typically used for 56,000-bits/s to 1.544-Mbits/s (T1) data communications.

The connector is a squarish block about 5 cm high × 2 cm wide × 4 cm deep that has two large knurled retaining thumbscrews (to keep the connector from unplugging). The connector can accommodate 34 pins, but several are usually not used.

V.35 is usually used only for carrying *synchronous* data. High-speed asynchronous data are not very common. The most common application for higher-speed asynchronous data communications is from a PC to a V.34 modem, and EIA-232 is typically used here (the cables are short enough that it usually works, even though using EIA-232 at this speed is outside of the EIA-232 specification).

V.35 competes with these other (incompatible) high-speed serial interfaces:

• EIA-449, which uses a DB-37 connector and an optional DB-9 as well. It is used in Europe and by the military.

- EIA-530, which uses a DB-25 connector and is being implemented (but slowly—people just don't seem to order it when it is offered as an interface option, because the rest of their equipment is V.35).

There are other proposed methods for handling high-speed data from PCs, for example, USB and IEEE-1394.

See *1394*, *DCE*, *DTE*, *DSU*, *EIA/TIA-232*, *Synchronous*, *Switched 56*, *T1*, *USB*, and *WAN*.

V.42

A standard for *error detection and error correction* (through retransmission) that is often implemented in modems.

V.42 actually specifies two error correction protocols: LAPM and MNP Level 4. MNP 4 is usually used only as a fallback (when the remote modem does not support LAPM).

See *CRC*, *HDLC*, *LAPM*, *MNP*, *Modem*, and *RPI*.

V.42*bis*

A *data compression* capability that is often implemented in modems. (Both communicating modems must support V.42*bis* for it to be used—this is detected and negotiated at the beginning of a dial-up modem connection.)

The data compression algorithm:

- Can compress data by more than an 8:1 ratio (though this high compression ratio would occur only for extremely redundant data, such as 10,000 consecutive "A"s in the data stream). The compression ratio is more often quoted as 4:1, to represent more real-world data, but is actually about 2.5:1 if you (and I mean you, not your modem supplier) actually measure it.
- Requires V.42 (so that the link is known to be error-free).
- Usually works with asynchronous data only (because of the necessity for flow control if the data are not compressible enough to match the DTE speed used with the modem throughput).

As a fallback, modems usually also support the older MNP *Level 5*, which has a maximum compression ratio of 2:1 and can actually increase the transfer time of files that are already compressed. Therefore, V.42*bis* is preferred.

Uses a variation (developed by British Telecom) of the *Lempel-Ziv* data compression method, which is called BTLZ (not to be confused with a bacon-lettuce-tomato sandwich, which is quite a different thing—though a BLT may require compression if there is too much lettuce).

A *dictionary* (512 to 2,048 bytes in length) of frequently occurring strings of (usually up to six) characters is constructed by the transmitting modem and sent to the receiving modem. The transmitter then uses shorter bit patterns to represent the most-common *strings* (or *sequences*) of characters.

The length of the dictionary and the speed at which data compression occurs are determined by the transmitting modem's design (and therefore designers). For example, while the V.42*bis* standard documents the compression algorithm by using the C language, a good implementation will re-code this for efficiency and speed. Therefore, different (and compatible) V.42*bis* modems can have significantly different compression ratios (for the same data!) and throughput (expressed in bits/s transferred) rates.

Note that the serial port speeds of the PCs (or whatever is sending the data) at both ends of the link should be set to at least four times (which is the maximum compression ratio) the modem data-pump speed (the bit rate at which the modems are actually sending data); otherwise, you don't get the full (or any) benefit of data compression.

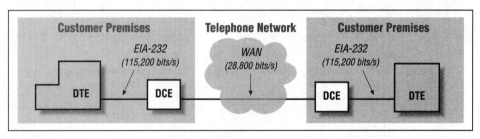

V.42bis−1

For example, PCs using V.34 modems (with V.42*bis* data compression) should have their serial ports set to 4 × 28,800 bits/s = 115,200 bits/s, as shown in the accompanying figure. Not all PCs support this speed.

Also, the PC's communication software used must be configured to enable *flow control* (either x-on/x-off or RTS/CTS—whatever matches the modem's configuration). Flow control is required so that the PC does not send data too fast when the data are not very compressible. Also, flow control is required to stop the data from the PC while the modem retransmits during error correction.

Finally, only very short EIA-232 cables (since EIA-232 is supposed to work only at speeds up to 20,000 bits/s) should be used, and the serial port UARTs should be 16550s (at both ends).

See *16550A, Asynchronous, Data Compression, EIA/TIA-232, In-Band, LZW, MNP, Out-of-band, RPI*, and *V.42*.

V.54

The ITU-T standard that describes where *loopbacks* (referred to as *L1*, *L2*, *L3*, and *L4*) should be supported for troubleshooting.

The standard does not specify how to enable the loopbacks or whether they can be enabled *remotely* (that is, from the other end of the link). Therefore each device that supports V.54 should specify which loopbacks it supports and how to enable them. (You will need to dig through the manual to figure this out—usually an *AT command* or a front-panel button-push sequence.)

The accompanying figure shows an example of the loopback locations for the classic DTE (terminal) to DCE (modem) to DCE (remote modem) to DTE (host) connection.

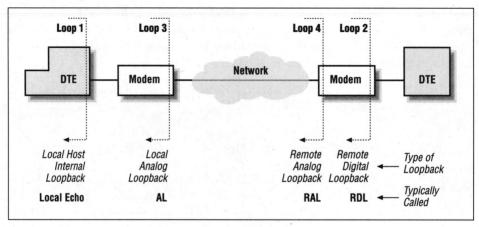

V.54–1

By first testing a single component (by enabling *Loop 1*), that part of the network can be tested. If the terminal is shown to be working, then removing Loop 1 and enabling *Loop 3* will test more of the network.

Loop 3 is called a *local analog loopback*, since the local device (to where the tests are initiated) takes the digital data from the local DTE, converts it to analog (suitable for transmission over the network), redirects it back to the DCE's input from the network, and converts the signal back to digital. The loopback occurs at and exercises the analog portion of the DCE.

Similarly (for example), Loop 2 is called *remote digital loopback*, since that is where the loopback occurs.

This standard troubleshooting technique (start by testing a small, isolated component and then add more components of the system—one at a time) is continued until the problem is identified.

See *AT Command Set*, *DCE*, *DTE*, *EIA/TIA-232*, *Modem*, *RTFM*, and *WAN*.

V.56*bis*
V.56*bis* Intercontinental Network Model

A standard describing many typical analog communication circuit impairments (delays, attenuations, and other distortions).

The purpose is to characterize a wide range of real-world less-than-perfect data communication circuits (short, long, noisy, satellite, digitized, etc.) so that modems can be designed to work well on them. Modem evaluations (and the benchmark test results that are published in magazines) often use these types of lines in their throughput and connection-success comparisons.

Builds on the EIA/TIA TSB-37a.

See *EIA/TIA-232*, *EIA/TIA TSB-37a*, *TSB*, *Modem*, *PCM*, *Satellite*, and *TSB*.

V.120

A standard for *encapsulating* asynchronous data communications traffic into ISDN data streams (which are synchronous). This enables two devices (typically PCs) to communicate over an ISDN connection, using their standard asynchronous-only COM ports (an external V.120 adapter is then used) or an internal board that plugs into the PC's bus (the board then includes the COM port and V.120 adapter functionality).

This data communications alternative to modems and analog telephone lines is expected to become quite popular, since ISDN has a much faster call setup time (about 2 seconds compared to at least 20 seconds) and a faster data transmission rate (64,000 or 128,000 bits/s compared to 28,800 bits/s).

See *Asynchronous*, *Encapsulation*, *ISDN*, *Modem*, *Synchronous*, and *UART*.

V.fast

The name that was used for V.34 before it was approved as a standard.

See *Modem* and *V.34*.

V.FC
V.Fast Class

A modem modulation scheme (promoted by Rockwell International) that is based on an early, not yet standardized version of V.34.

Transmits data at the same speeds as V.34, but a significant difference is that V.FC has a less powerful handshaking method (V.FC does not use the V.8 scheme).

Now made obsolete by V.34.

See *Modem*, *Rockwell International*, *V.8*, and *V.34*.

V.terbo

A nonstandard enhancement to V.32*bis* (promoted by AT&T Microelectronics).

Transmits data at up to 19,200 bits/s (with fallback speeds down to 4,800 bits/s, in decrements of 2,400 bits/s).

Now made obsolete by V.34.

See *AT&T*, *Modem*, and *V.34*.

Van Jacobsen   See **VJ**.

Vendor Independent Messaging   See **VIM**.

Very Long Instruction Word   See **VLIW**.

Very Low Frequency   See **VLF**.

Very Small Aperture Terminals   See **VSAT**.

VESA
Video Electronics Standards Association

The group that developed the *VESA local bus* standard (also called *VL-bus* or *VLB*), as well as many other standards concerning PCs and their video displays.

VESA recommends that a monitor have at least a 75-Hz (though 72 Hz is acceptable) *vertical refresh* rate (also called the *vertical scan* rate—the number of times per second that the screen is rewritten) at all resolutions from 640 × 480 to 1,280 × 1,024 (horizontal × vertical pixels).

VESA is developing the standard to provide *Plug and Play* support for monitors (which is called the *display data channel* standard).

See *DDC*, *DPMS*, *Local Bus*, *PnP*, *RAMDAC*, *USDA*, *Video*, and *VL-Bus*.

VESA Local Bus   See **VL-Bus**.

VGA
Video Graphics Array

A graphics standard for PCs that provides a resolution of 640 × 480 (that is, 480 rows of 640 pixels per row).

See *Pixel* and *VESA*.

VHS
Video Home System

The recording and playback method used by standard home VCRs (*Video Cassette Recorders*).

Competed with Sony's *Beta* format, and VHS won (largely for marketing and timing reasons, though Beta is better technically and as a result is still very popular for professional recording).

See *NTSC*.

Video

A standard broadcast (and CATV) video signal uses 6 MHz of bandwidth to carry 29.97 frames per second of color picture and sound information.

Several *studio-quality* (also called *broadcast-* or *production-quality*) digitization schemes are available, as shown in the following table.

System	Data rate at 10 bits per sample (Mbits/s)
SMPTE 240 M (HDTV at 1,150 horizontal lines of resolution)	1,485
CCIR 601 (525 horizontal pixels or lines of resolution)	270
NTSC (composite signal)	143.2

CCIR 601 has 525 lines (total), 483 lines active (visible), and 720 horizontal pixels per line.

Note that even for the same video format and without using data compression, the digitized video data rate will depend on the number of samples per horizontal scan line, usually 400 to 720 (for production-quality NTSC video), and the number of bits per sample (typically 8 or 10).

A 640 × 480 pixel, full-color (24-bit), full-motion (30 frames per second), video signal requires about 27 Mbytes/s (before compression).

PC–quality video often uses one of the standards listed in the following table.

Standard	Horizontal	Vertical
NTSC	352	240
PAL	352	288

Several compression schemes are available, as shown in the following table.

Feature	JPEG	MPEG-1	MPEG-2	Px64
Full–color, still images	✓			
Full–color, motion video	✓	✓	✓	✓
Broadcast quality	✓		✓	
Resolution (pixels)	65,536 × 65,536	352 × 240	1,920 × 1,152 1,440 × 1,152 720 × 486 352 × 288	
Compres-sion ratio	5:1 to 80:1	Up to 200:1	Up to 100:1	100:1 to 2,000:1
Compressed data rate (Mbits/s)	10 to 48	1.544	4 to 80	0.064 to 2
Optimized for	Interlaced or noninterlaced	Noninter-laced	Interlaced	Noninterlaced

✓ = Suitable for

Current broadcasting typically uses the MPEG-2 720 × 486 resolution and has a compressed data rate of 15 Mbits/s.

The Px64 scheme is a video-conferencing standard that is specified in the H.261 standard.

Different video formats have different *frame rates*, as listed in the following table.

Standard	Frame Rate (frames/second)	Comments
Film	24	Standard movies—but each frame is projected twice (resulting in a 48-Hz flicker rate), so the flicker is not noticeable
PAL	25	*Phase Alternate Line*, the method used in Europe
NTSC	29.97	Standard broadcast and cable TV
Desktop video	30	Such as that produced from MPEG-1 and .avi files

A common production-quality 35 mm movie film digitizing process uses 2,664 lines of 3,656 pixels each, using 36 bits of color information for each pixel (12 bits per primary color).

See *CATV, CCIR, Color, Composite Video Signal, JPEG, H.261, H.320, HDTV, Lossy Data Compression, MPEG, NTSC, PAL, PCS (Personal Conferencing Specification), PRI, RAMDAC,* and *VESA.*

Video Electronics Standards Association   See **VESA.**

Video Graphics Array   See **VGA.**

Video Home System   See **VHS.**

Video Random Access Memory   See **VRAM.**

VIM
Vendor Independent Messaging

An effort sponsored by Novell, WordPerfect (which was bought by Novell, then by Corel), IBM, Lotus (which is now owned by IBM), Apple, and Borland to provide application-level APIs for all popular computing platforms, to send and receive messages between application programs.

Used mostly by Lotus 1-2-3 and cc:Mail, and OS/2 messaging.

Competes with MAPI and XAPIA's CMC.

See *API, CMC, MAPI,* and *XAPIA.*

Virtual LAN   See **VLAN.**

Virtual Loadable Module   See **VLM.**

Virtual Machine   See **VM.**

Virtual Memory System   See **VMS.**

Virtual Reality Modeling Language   See **VRML.**

Virtual Telecommunications Access Method   See **VTAM.**

VJ
Van Jacobsen

Someone who did lots of work on the TCP protocol and has been immortalized by having his TCP header compression method named after him. This method does not compress the data in TCP packets, nor any part of UDP packets.

Same as *CSLIP*.

See *TCP/IP*.

VLAN
Virtual LAN

A switched LAN technology (which can be implemented using ATM) that uses an *administrative console* (using a drag-and-drop type GUI) to determine which traffic gets forwarded on which ports.

The requirement is that it is important to keep users grouped according to some plan (for example, by job function or company department) for the following reasons:

- *Administrative*: for example, the computers on a single IP subnet must usually be kept together (typically on one floor of a building) so that they all connect (through a *concentrator*) to one port of a router—but typical company reorganizations usually result in people being moved all over a building, which would require new IP addresses to be assigned.
- *Network loading*: LAN protocols typically use broadcasts for many functions, and these cause substantial network load.
- *Security*: LAN troubleshooting and management tools can trap information that is intended for other users.

The idea is that since user locations physically move frequently (reorganizations, project changes, etc.), rather than trying to keep up with these *moves, adds, and changes* using patch panels, how about putting all the traffic on a high-speed backbone and using ATM (and other switching technologies) to forward traffic for each *group* only on those switch ports that have at least one member of that group?

Switch ports may have individual users, or hubs (also called *concentrators*) with many users.

See *802.10* and *ATM*.

VL-Bus
VESA Local Bus

A 16- or 32-bit wide bus that was introduced in 1992 and can be used to connect a PC's motherboard to video, SCSI-2, LAN, or other adapters (though the original intent was, and most available adapters are, video adapters) at the processor's full speed.

Was very popular for 486-based PCs but rarely implemented on Pentium-based PCs. PCI is typically used for Pentium-based PCs.

Peak theoretical throughput is 130 Mbytes/s, but a more typical rate is 66 Mbytes/s (which is two bus cycles on a 33-MHz bus per 32-bit word transfer). A *burst mode* of one address cycle followed by four data cycles results in 105 Mbytes/s on a 33-MHz bus.

Can be implemented as a chip-level bus implemented on a motherboard (no connectors) or by using an MCA-style connector (112 pins) in-line with an ISA connector, so the slot can be used for either an ISA or VL-Bus card; if used for VL-Bus, then the card uses the ISA bus for power, interrupts, DMA, and I/O.

Up to three cards can reside on the bus (though most PCs require only one or two cards), which is basically a 486 processor's local system bus (and the bus runs at the same speed as the processor).

Runs at 16 to 33 MHz (higher speeds would require wait states or fewer devices on the bus).

Two types of *programmed I/O* transfers are supported: a single block of 512 bytes, or multiple blocks of 512 bytes (this requires an enhanced BIOS and device driver support).

Some limitations of the version 1.0 standard are that 3.3-volt devices are not supported, it does not support *Plug and Play* automatic configuration, burst mode is not supported, and while it supports *bus mastering*, the CPU cannot run concurrently with bus-mastering peripherals.

Version 2.0 of the specification supports:

- A 64-bit bus (this requires an additional in-line connector)
- 50-MHz operation (resulting in a peak speed of 320 Mbytes/s)
- *Plug and Play*

However, VL-Bus 2.0 will likely never be widely implemented, owing to PCI.

A compatibility testing effort should result in "VESA-compatible" stickers on products. (Currently, there is no compatibility testing or assurance.)

Competes with PCI, though PCI won for Pentium-based PCs—since PCI is less 486-specific and already has Plug and Play support.

See *Bus*, *Local Bus*, *MCA*, *PCI*, *PIO*, *PnP*, and *VESA*

VLB
VESA Local Bus

Another name for VL-Bus.

See *VL-Bus*.

VLF
Very Low Frequency

Frequencies from more than 300 Hz (300 cycles per second) up to (and including) 30,000 Hz (30 kHz).

See *ELF*, *EMF*, and *MPR II*.

VLIW
Very Long Instruction Word

A proposed new technology (for example, being worked on through an alliance between Hewlett-Packard and Intel) for increasing the processing capacity of CPUs.

Many instructions, which can all be executed at the same time (as determined by the compiler), are presented to the processor simultaneously as a 128-bit (or wider) input from memory.

The P7 from Intel might use this technology.

See *HP*, *Intel*, and *P7*.

VLM
Virtual Loadable Module

Novell's newer workstation shells (the software that redirects disk drive and other local resource calls to networked devices).

Supports:

- Running the shell software out of extended memory (to leave the 640 kbytes of conventional memory available for application programs)
- More customization of features supported (you need only to load those functions required, to reduce memory usage)

- Features needed for NetWare 4.*x* (for example, support for NetWare Directory Services)

The VLMs replace (for example) the NetX TSRs.

See *NDS* and *Novell*.

VM
Virtual Machine

IBM's most recent mainframe operating system (which is many years old).

Suited to more casual and interactive use than MVS. Partitions a machine into multiple *virtual machines*, each running native VM or MVS (VM's predecessor) applications.

See *CMS*, *Mainframe*, and *MVS*.

VMS
Virtual Memory System

DEC's minicomputer operating system that initially ran only on DEC's VAX (*Virtual Address Extension*) CPUs. The newer portable version (*OpenVMS*) runs on other platforms, such as DEC's Alpha processor.

See *Alpha AXP*, *DEC*, *OpenVMS*, and *Operating System*.

Voice/Data Integration   See **SVD.**

VRAM
Video Random Access Memory

Memory optimized for use on video adapters.

It is *dual-ported*, in that there are two ports. The PC can write into the memory (to change what will be displayed), while the video adapter continuously reads the memory (to refresh the monitor's display).

Usually needed only when the display has high resolution (more than $1,024 \times 768$ pixels), more than 65,536 colors, and a high refresh rate (more than 70 Hz).

See *RAM* and *VESA*.

VRML
Virtual Reality Modeling Language

A possible future extension of HTML to support simulation and modeling.

See *HTML*.

VSAT
Very Small Aperture Terminals

Satellite stations with up to 256-kbits/s data communication links and small (0.75 to 2.4 m) ground-based satellite dish antennas.

Networks are run by *service providers*, which (typically) lease large blocks of capacity from satellite owners and provide a *point-to-multipoint* architecture to the end users.

A *backhaul* connection (usually a terrestrial link) links the user's main data center to the service provider. The service provider (which has a really big satellite dish) then uses the satellite to broadcast to the user's many remote sites (often hundreds).

In addition to the small satellite dish antennas, the remote sites each have "magic boxes" that:

- Provide users with a standard interface, such as SDLC or X.25 (for example)
- Ensure that users cannot adversely affect other users and get only the capacity they have arranged for
- Provide network diagnostics and control functions for the service provider

Using *time division multiple access*, permits many such groups of users to share the same satellite capacity (each gets a coordinated slice of communications time).

See *Satellite* and *SDLC*.

VTAM
Virtual Telecommunications Access Method

IBM's communications method for linking user applications running under any of their mainframe operating systems (VM and MVS, for example) to user terminals and printers (such as the 3270 series). Supports SNA (OSI layers 3, 4, and 5) and SDLC (layer 2).

See *3270*, *DLC*, *Mainframe*, *PU 5*, *SDLC*, and *SNA*.

WABI
Windows Applications Binary Interface

Sun Microsystems' SunSelect operating unit's software that converts documented Microsoft Windows function calls to X Window System calls—so that Windows programs can run on Sun and other RISC-based UNIX computers.

Included with Sun's Solaris operating system and licensed by SunSelect to other UNIX vendors (including HP and IBM).

Sounds like a great idea, but you don't hear much about this anymore (perhaps because non-Windows calls and instructions are interpreted, which provides very slow performance).

See *Sun*, *UNIX*, and *X*.

WAIS
Wide Area Information Service

A method for searching for information on the Internet. The process involves three components:

- An *indexer*, that generates seven indices from the indexed documents; for example, an index of the words in the documents, an index of the words in the document abstracts (which are called "headlines"), and an index of the file names. A link to this index is established from the central servers.
- Servers store the documents and indices and are referenced from gopher menus or WWW links in HTML documents.
- Client software runs on user PCs or is accessed by WWW or gopher browsers.

See *Gopher*, *HTML*, *Internet*, and *WWW*.

WAN
Wide Area Network

A data communications network that spans any distance and is usually provided by a public carrier. You get access to the two ends of a circuit; the carrier does everything in between—which is typically drawn as a "grey cloud," since you don't know (or usually care) how the carrier implements it. In contrast, a LAN typically has a diameter (the maximum distance between any two stations) limited to less than a few kilometers and is entirely owned by the user.

WAN options are shown in the accompanying figure. Stentor Canada's marketing names for the services are shown in *italics*.

See *ATM (Asynchronous Transfer Mode)*, *Carrier*, *CSU*, *DCS*, *DDS*, *DSU*, *Dataroute*, *Digital 800*, *EIA/TIA-232*, *Frame Relay*, *FT1*, *HDLC*, *Inverse Multiplexer ISDN*, *LAN*, *MAN*, *Modem*, *POTS*, *Satellite*, *SONet*, *Stentor*, *Switched 56*, *T1*, *T3*, and *V.35*.

Wide Area Information Service   See **WAIS.**

Wideband ISDN

Primary rate 23B+D ISDN service on a T1 (1.544 Mbits/s) speed line. Or the equivalent service on an E1 line (if you are in Europe).

Some would say that there is no wideband ISDN and this primary rate ISDN is part of narrowband ISDN.

See *B-ISDN*, *E1*, *ISDN*, *Narrowband ISDN*, *T1*, and *WAN*.

Winchester

In the late 1970s, IBM developed a disk drive read/write head technology that was initially used in its Winchester disk drives and has since become the standard for all hard disk drives. In fact, for several years in the early 1980s, all hard disk drives were called Winchester drives.

The technology uses very lightweight read/write heads that "fly" just above (less than the thickness of a piece of paper) the disk surface (the air moves at almost the disk surface's speed so close to it—about 100 km/h). The entire disk assembly is *sealed* to ensure that no dirt particles can get between the read/write head and the disk surface—a common cause of *disk head crashes*, which is when the read/write head touches the spinning disk surface, scraping off the magnetic stuff where all the bits live.

The next question is why IBM called their initial disk drive a Winchester. The story goes that this initial drive had two 30 Mbyte sides, or sections, or platters (one might have been removable, as was common then), and this "30-30" reminded someone of the famous Winchester 30-30 repeating, lever-action rifle.

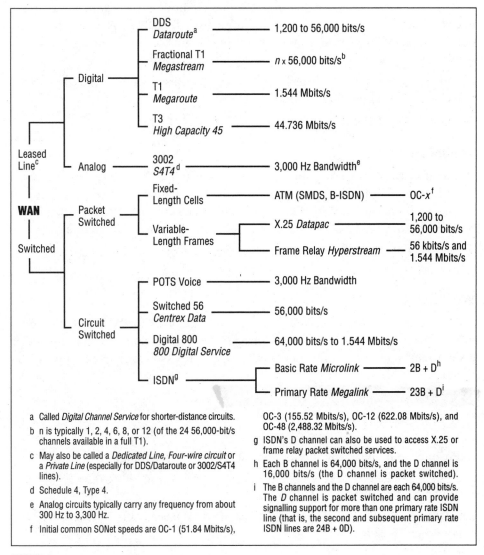

WAN–1

The rifle's "30-30" refers to the type of *cartridge* (which is the assembly of a lead bullet, its brass case, and the black powder inside) for which the rifle was *chambered* (the same type of rifle can be built to accept different sizes of cartridges). The 30-30 cartridge uses a .30 caliber bullet (that is, the diameter of the bullet itself is 0.30 inch), and 30 *grains* of black powder (there are 7,000 grains to a pound— these pre-metric units of weight are so quaint).

The cartridge was designed for the Winchester model 1894, which was introduced a long time ago, in the year—you guessed it—1894. (It seems they were not very imaginative in their product naming then and were confident that they would not introduce more than one new product per year!)

For its time, this was a high-tech rifle. It was the first to use a smokeless round (cartridge), and this required a nickel-steel barrel.

See *Disk Drive*, *IDE*, *SCSI*, and *SI*.

Windows 3.0

Released in May 1990. Was the first popular version of Windows, since it had a good-looking user interface (previous versions were criticized as having colors that looked as though they were selected by computer nerds—I wonder why), computer hardware was finally powerful enough, and good development and debugging tools were available.

See *Operating System*, *Windows 95*, and *Windows NT*.

Windows 95

The successor to Microsoft's Windows 3.1 and Windows for Workgroups. Code-named (for marketing purposes) "Chicago" during development (though other code names were selected for other countries where "Chicago" doesn't mean anything).

Does not run over DOS, but is bootable itself. Offers:

- A 32-bit memory space
- Long filenames
- Preemptive multitasking (but not symmetric multiprocessing)
- Multithreading and memory protection (as OS/2 and Windows NT do already)
- Support for *Plug and Play*

See *DLL*, *FUD*, *PC 95*, *Operating System*, *PnP*, *Windows 3.0*, *Windows NT*, and *Winx Windows APIs*.

Windows Applications Binary Interface   See **WABI**.

Windows Open Services Architecture   See **WOSA**.

Windows NT
Windows New Technology

This effort initially was to produce OS/2 3.0, but when IBM and Microsoft separated their development efforts, Microsoft renamed it to this (possibly because the development is being led by Dave Cutler, who had a lot to do with DEC's VMS, and the next letters after *v*, *m*, and *s* are *w*, *n*, and *t*).

Runs on other platforms (such as DEC's Alpha AXP). Will not replace Windows 3.*x* and Windows 95 but is a higher-end product requiring a more powerful platform (a PC requires at least 8 Mbytes of RAM).

Has peer-to-peer networking built in. Is single-user but multitasking. Add-on products provide it with POSIX 1003.1 and NFS. Apparently has 4 to 5 million lines of code and required 200 software developers years to develop.

See *Alpha AXP, Cairo, CDE, DEC, NFS, Operating System, POSIX OSE, VMS,* and *Winx Windows APIs.*

WinISDN
Windows ISDN APIs

A set of 18 APIs developed by NetManage, PSI, and ISDN*tek to enable Windows applications to communicate over ISDN lines, using synchronous PPP (which is more efficient than asynchronous PPP, which is used over dial-up modem lines).

See *ISDN, Modem, PPP,* and *SLIP.*

WinSock
Windows Sockets

The standard APIs (often called the *socket interface*) between Microsoft Windows (3.1, 95, and NT) application software and TCP/IP protocol software (often called a protocol stack).

WinSock enables any vendor's WinSock-compliant application to work over any vendors' WinSock protocol stack. WinSock version 1.1 was released in January 1993.

WinSock is based on the *Berkeley Sockets* APIs (version 4.3), which was developed for TCP/IP communications on UNIX-based computers. Changes required to these BSD sockets APIs for WinSock include the following:

- Unlike Microsoft Windows 3.1, UNIX does *preemptive multitasking* (that is, a task can be waiting for data to be sent, and other tasks will still run). Since Windows 3.1 supports only *cooperative multitasking* (one task with nothing to do but wait for input must periodically call the operating system, which will then give CPU time to the other tasks), *blocking* (also called *synchronous*) calls (which don't return until the function, such as a read, completes) therefore cannot be used under Windows 3.1.

  WinSock therefore includes *asynchronous* functions that return immediately (and other functions that are used to check the status of the pending asynchronous function).

- There is no support for UNIX-style interprocess communication on the same computer.

WinSock development work is done by the WinSock Group (which was formed in the fall of 1991 and included Microsoft from the start). Much of the original development work was done by Martin Hall, now of Stardust Technologies, Inc., which is an "independent testing, research, and consultancy organization providing services, facilities and tools to developers and users of WinSock software." The goal is to "provide an independent center of high quality information, services, and facilities dedicated to promoting the development of fast, high-quality, interoperable communications software for Microsoft Windows." Their offices include the *WinSock Interoperability Laboratories*, where testing is done.

WinSock Version 2 adds support for:

- Protocol stacks in addition to TCP/IP (such as Novell's IPX, DEC's DECnet, and OSI protocols)
- Media other than LANs (for example, wireless)
- A wide range of WANs (such as ISDN, frame relay, and ATM)

Many of these new capabilities require specifying *quality of service* required, and Version 2 supports this.

Specification and development of the standard is done by the *WinSock 2 Forum*. New features include API functions to reply to the application program whether the link is currently available (for example, a wireless link may currently be out of range of the home office network), whether modem battery power available, time delay (that is, the *latency*) of the link (which may affect how the use of the link is optimized), and wireless signal strength and base station identification.

WinSock version 2 protocol stacks will be binary-compatible with applications written for WinSock version 1.1.

A very popular public-domain version of WinSock is *Trumpet WinSock*, which is often provided free by *Internet service providers* (along with other public-domain and shareware software such as Eudora Mail and Netscape). Trumpet WinSock was written by Peter Tattam (*peter@psychnet.psychol.utas.edu.au*) in Hobart, Tasmania (Australia). The ftp site is *ftp.utas.edu.au*, and the files are in /PC/trumpet/ wintrump/*.

Stardust Technologies has a WWW server (with lots of WinSock information) at *http://www.stardust.com*.

See *API, BSD UNIX, ISP, Netscape, PCCA, QOS, Sockets, TAPI, UNIX*, and *WOSA*.

Winx Windows APIs

Microsoft has defined several *Application Program Interfaces* between application programs and the different versions of Windows. These are listed in the following table in increasing order of capability.

API	Use
Win16	The API used for Windows 3.1.
Win32s	A 32-bit version of Win16 that has virtually none of the enhancements of Win32 (so this API is a *subset* of Win32, hence the "s" in Win32s). Mostly handled by a DLL that converts the 32-bit application calls to 16-bit calls supported by Windows 3.1. Only runs on 80386 or better. Intended for (likely math-based) applications that need 32-bit code but need to run on Windows 3.1.
Win32c	The API used by Windows 95 that is almost as extensive as Win32 (so this API is supposed to be *compatible* with Win32, hence the "c" in Win32c).
Win32	The 32-bit API used for Windows NT. Mostly a superset of Win16.

See *API*, *Windows 3.0*, *Windows 95*, and *Windows NT*.

WORM
Write Once, Read Mostly (or Many)

A storage device that can be written to by an end user—but only once (it is non-erasable, but sometimes it can be written to incrementally until it is full). Examples include nonerasable optical and CD-R storage media (often used for archival backup).

See *CD-ROM*.

WOSA
Windows Open Services Architecture

Microsoft's framework (and APIs) for providing services (such as receiving real-time stock market data or supporting retail banking transactions) for Windows applications.

WOSA includes WinSock (which replaces NetBEUI as Microsoft's preferred communications API) and Microsoft's ODBC.

See *API*, *ODBC*, *WinSock*, and *Winx Windows APIs*.

WWW
World Wide Web

The network of *servers* on the Internet, each of which has one or more *home pages*, which provide information and hypertext links to other documents on that and (usually) other servers.

Developed in 1989 by Tim Berners-Lee at the *European Laboratory for Particle Physics*, which is usually called "CERN" as it was previously called *Conseil Européen pour la Recherche Nucléaire*. (It is near Geneva, Switzerland, and many people speak

French there.) It was first implemented on a NeXT Workstation and was originally intended as a method of making graphical images available on the Internet.

Servers communicate with *clients* by using the *Hypertext Transfer Protocol* (HTTP). A secure version (S-HTTP) is currently under development.

WWW server addresses (*Uniform Resource Locators* or URLs) are typically of the form *http://www.orgname.com,* where `orgname.com` is the DNS name of the organization running the server.

Sources for WWW server software can be found by snooping around, starting at *http://www.w3.org*, for example, or *http://emwac.ed.ac.uk/html/internet_toolchest/top.html.*

Popular software packages used to access WWW sites include the following:

- Lynx (though rapidly declining in popularity, since it does not support graphics and sound)
- The National Center for Supercomputing Applications at the University of Illinois'   Windows   Mosaic (*http://www.ncsa.uiuc.edu/SDG/Software/Mosaic/NCSAMosaicHome.html)*,   which   was released in 1993. This package's ease of use is what made the Web quickly become extremely popular. A commercial version, Enhanced Mosaic from Spyglass, Inc., features additional security and speed.
- Navisoft (*http://www.navisoft.com*)
- Netscape Communications Corporation's *Netscape Navigator*, from *ftp.mcom.com* (using ftp) or *http://home.mcom.com/home/welcome.html* or *http://www.netscape.com*. It is available for Macintosh, X Window System, and Microsoft Windows environments and is free for academic use and as shareware for commercial use. Because of a better implementation (more integrated handling of graphics, for example), many people now prefer Netscape to Mosaic.

While "Web browsing" is usually done with a specialized software package, users with Internet access that does not support WWW or that do not have the necessary software can still get the text of WWW pages, along with a list of the links to other WWW pages, by emailing to *listproc@www0.cern.ch*. The subject does not matter. The text of the message can be up to 10 lines of WWW pages to retrieve (they are returned in a few minutes by email to the sender).

For example, if the text is WWW *http://www.zdnet.com/~pcmag/special/web100/ top100f.htm,* then by return email you will receive *PC* Magazine's list of the 100 WWW home pages the staff believes are the most interesting, useful, and fun. If the text on a line is just WWW, then a help message is returned.

The operation of a WWW server is determined by a configuration file (also called a rule file), by default `/etc/httpd.conf`.

For WWW servers, the document `Welcome.html` is returned when no document is specified (though this can be changed to any other filename, usinf the `Welcome` directive) . This `Welcome` file is located in a directory pointed to in the configuration file (using the `ServerRoot` directive).

By default, a trailing "/" is not required in the URL. If one is not in the URL, then the server software adds one, and the default document name (typically `Welcome.html`) is appended to this (to construct the full URL for the document to be returned). This behavior can be changed by setting the `AlwaysWelcome` directive to `Off`. This permits URLs that do not specify a document (and specify only a directory—perhaps the `ServerRoot` directory that is used when no directory is specified) to be used to retrieve a directory listing rather than the Welcome document (so now you—and I—know why only sometimes a trailing "/" is required).

By default, the *well known port* 80 is used for HTTP, but the WWW server's configuration file can specify another port to be used (with the `Port` directive). Optionally, this default port can be specified in the URL (for example, *http://ds1.internic.net:80/rfc/rfc-index.txt),*. If a nonstandard port is required (sometimes 8000, 8001, or 8080 is used instead, since ports less than 1024 can have only services provided by the root user), then it must be specified in the URL (unless the WWW server does a redirect to the correct port).

The tilde character is often used in subdirectory names (e.g., `/~pcmag`), since it marks a *user-supported directory*. This is a subdirectory (specified with the `UserDir` directive, typically set to `www`) below each user's actual directory on the WWW server that is *exported* (made available to the calling public) where users (with accounts on the WWW server) can maintain their own HTML pages.

In January 1995, CERN handed over its development of the WWW to the *World Wide Web Consortium* ("W3" or "W3C"), which "promotes the Web by producing specifications and reference software, and is funded by industrial members but its products are freely available to all."

The Consortium is run by MIT (the *Massachusetts Institute of Technology*) in Cambridge, Massachusetts, with INRIA (*Institut National de Recherche en Informatique et en Automatique*—which is France's National Computing Research Institute) acting as European host, in collaboration with CERN.

The W3C maintains a WWW server at *http://www.w3.org* (which replaces *http://info.cern.ch* as the main source of WWW information). The W3 server has:

- Specifications for HTML and HTTP
- Lists of WWW servers by country and city (see *http://www.w3.org/hypertext/DataSources/www/servers.html*)
- The status of new developments
- Lots of other useful WWW information

A FAQ is at *http://sunsite.unc.edu/boutell/faq*.

Companies that produce server software include O'Reilly & Associates (*http://www.ora.com/*), Silicon Graphics (*http://www.sgi.com*), and Sun Microsystems (*http://www.sun.com*).

See *CGI, DNS* (*Domain Name System*), *Home Page, HTML, HTTP, NeXTStep, S-HTTP, SSL, TCP, URL, WAIS*, and *YAHOO*.

WXModem

The XModem file transfer protocol with a *window size* of 4 (that is, up to 4 frames of data can be outstanding before the sender must stop sending and wait for an ack).

Improves throughput on communication links with longer delays.

See *XModem* and *YModem*.

X
X Window System

A very popular standard for the low-level functions required to support graphical user interfaces in the UNIX environment.

A *de facto* standard, initially developed by the Massachusetts Institute of Technology, for sending graphics primitives to a display server. This display server can be either a dedicated X terminal or a more general-purpose computer, such as a workstation or PC (with the necessary software). The X Window System was preceded by a system called "W," perhaps as in "Window" (and since "X" is the next letter in the alphabet, maybe that's where the name came from).

The X Window System usually uses TCP and sockets for communications. The standard is maintained by the *X Consortium* at MIT.

The functions (or *user interface library*) that are available to the host computer (which is the *client* and runs the application software) are defined by and referred to as *Xlib* (a series of C language APIs). However, the exact program interface (APIs) to generate the Xlib commands is not specified.

The communication over a network is specified as the *X-wire protocol*.

X11R6 is the name of a recent version of the standard (X11, release 6).

The higher-level toolkit for generating menus, scroll bars, push buttons, and other basic elements of a GUI is called *Widgets*.

Any user interface (that is, the look and action of push-buttons, the menu scheme, and so on) can be built by using the Xlib and the Widget functions.

A *style guide* specifies how the application should react to the user's manipulation of Widgets and therefore describes the look and feel of the GUI. The *window manager* controls the interface elements in accordance with a set of rules that specify the allowable sizes and positions of Windows and Widgets. The most common user interface is *Motif*.

See *CDE*, *Client/Server*, *de facto Standard*, *GUI*, *LBX*, *Motif*, *OPENLOOK*, *OSF*, *Tcl/Tk*, *TCP*, *WABI*, and *X Terminal*.

X-10
X-10 Powerhouse

A patented (by X-10, Inc.) method for sending control signals (ON, OFF, Dim, etc.) through 110-V A.C. wiring, typically to modules into which are plugged the appliances and lights to be controlled.

While there are many weaknesses to the system (poor error detection and correction, limited command set and address range, etc.), there are too many proposed new methods, so manufacturers are not building in this capability to new appliances and electronic equipment.

Some information is at *http://www.hometeam.com/*.

X.25

A packet–switched WAN.

That is, rather than having dedicated bandwidth (such as a circuit-switched or leased line, which you pay for by time, regardless of how much data you send), your packets of data go onto a high-speed shared connection (just as your driveway eventually leads to a highway). You pay only for the bits you send.

Charging is typically by the *packet* (usually up to 128 or 256 bytes of data per packet), *segment* (which are billing units of up to 64 bytes of data in a packet), or *character* (byte of data).

Different networks have different charging methods (which makes it very difficult to compare rates—you need to know your packet-size distribution).

A connection-oriented protocol, in that you need to establish a connection before exchanging data—analogous to a telephone call.

See *Connection-oriented*, *EDI*, *NPSI*, *QLLC*, *WAN*, *X.400*, and *ZModem*.

X.400

The OSI messaging (electronic mail—and some day more) standard.

The connections between MTAs (*Message Transfer Agents*) and service providers (each of which is an *administrative domain*) are usually X.25. A hierarchical addressing scheme is used, with at least the field names listed in the following table.

X.400 Address Field Name	Meaning	Comments
C	Country	Such as USA
ADMD or A	Administrative Domain	The internationally registered service provider, to which a private organization connects for X.400 mail service
PRMD or P	Private Domain	The name of the MTA to which the service provider forwards mail
O	Organization	Periods (".") can be used in fields to give the appearance of additional levels of hierarchy. These fields are optional.
OU	Organization Unit	
D or DDA	Domain-Defined Attribute	A user identifier for a user on a non-X.400 mail system. For example, an Internet address or a CompuServe ID. This field is optional.
PN	Personal Name	Could be MShnier, but is usually divided into S (Surname), G (Given Name), and I (Middle Initial) fields

Unfortunately, the use of optional fields (and whether they are optional for a specific installation) is determined by the *private mail domain's* X.400 mail administrator (that is, the guy who sets up your company's X.400 software). Therefore you can never guess or figure out someone's X.400 mail address. They have to tell it to you (or put it on their business cards, or maybe the X.500 directory service will help some day).

X.400 messages cannot be routed through intermediate X.400 service providers, so there must be direct connections between them (X.25 or a leased line).

There are about 12 U.S. service providers, including ATTMail, CompuServe, GEIS, IBM, MCI, and Sprint (Telemail).

Sample X.400 addresses are

```
C:USA,A:Telemail,P:Internet,"RFC-822":<72567.3304(a)CompuServe.com>
```

and

```
(C:USA, A:Telemail, O:LearnTree, FN:Mitchell, SN:Shnier)
```

Not a very user-friendly thing (especially compared to Internet mail addresses).

A site with X.400 messaging capability uses a *message transfer agent* (software on a computer) to send and receive messages from a service provider. *User agents* run on user computers to assist with composing, viewing, sending, and retrieving messages to and from a message transfer agent.

See *DNS*, *MTA*, *OSI*, *SMTP*, *UA*, *X.25*, and *X.500*.

X.400 Application Program Interface Association   See **XAPIA**.

X.500

The *directory services* specification originally intended to be used with X.400 messaging (electronic mail). It is a database system with the following features:

- The database is distributed and hierarchical, so that the database servers can be located near their administrators (for example, each company would maintain their own data on their own database server). The database can be searched without users having to know where the retrieved data is stored.
- The database servers can be implemented on different platforms.
- The database can be customized to store most any type of information about any type of object. For example, users' email addresses and PGP encryption keys or descriptions of the applications and printers available on file servers could be stored.

A simple use would be to respond to queries ("find me all the people with first name Mitchell who work for Integrated Intelligence's Toronto office"), likely posed with a clicky-mousey kind of user interface. Other capabilities include:

- The ability to search on different fields
- Storing what type of computer a mail message recipient has so that the correct file format will be automatically used (or generated) when sending a file as an attachment to a mail message
- Storing public keys for secure mail messaging

Improvements of the 1993 version of the specification over the original version (1988) include:

- *Replication* (storing multiple copies of the information for improved response time, capacity, and availability—and specified in X.525)
- *Certificate Management* (a security feature that tracks which users have access to which resources—and specified in X.509)
- Additional TCP/IP support functions

X.500 defines two *agents* (implemented in software):

- *Directory Service Agent* (DSA), which is the part that resides in an X.500 server, which communicates with clients and other X.500 directory servers (through their DSAs)

- *Directory User Agent* (DUA), which is the part that resides in a client and communicates with DSAs to get directory information for the client

As shown in the figure, the data communication uses these OSI-based protocols:

- *Directory Access Protocol* (DAP)—used by the client (through its DUA) to request and obtain directory information from a DSA
- *Directory Service Protocol* (DSP)—used by the X.500 server (through its DSA) to communicate with other servers
- *Directory Information Shadowing Protocol* (DISP)—used to replicate the data between servers

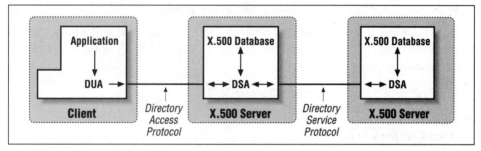

X.500—1

Since most clients will not have an OSI protocol stack, the IETF has defined the Lightweight Directory Access Protocol (LDAP), which uses TCP/IP rather than OSI. Since OSI-based communication is currently required for the DSP, X.500 database servers will require an OSI protocol stack.

The IETF has also defined how certain types of information are to be stored, to facilitate interoperability between X.500 servers. For example, RFC 1274 defines how to store and reference telephone numbers.

Directory entries are identified by a *Distinguished Name* (DN), which is a concatenation of the *values* for (for example) these *attributes* (which are standardized for X.400 electronic-mail use). Some examples are shown in the following table.

Attribute		Typical Value
Abbreviation	**Name**	
CN	Common Name	Mitchell Shnier
OU	Organizational Unit	Engineering
O	Organization	Integrated Intelligence
ST	State/Province	On
C	Country	Canada

A single distinguished name can match to more than one value for a specific attribute (for example, Mitchell Shnier and M. Shnier).

Access Control Lists (ACLs) determine who can access which entries and which fields of those entries. For example, only the engineering department can see the workstation type attribute values, and outside users can see only the sales department's telephone extensions.

Predecessor directory services have been proprietary, or unique to specific platforms (such as Novell's NetWare MHS and Directory Services, or Banyan's Intelligent Messaging Architecture and StreetTalk)—a big problem when an organization has multiple platforms, as information might need to be entered multiple times or might not be available from certain platforms.

Implementations will likely always support TCP/IP, since the OSI protocols that were initially expected to be used for X.500 are not widely accepted (now there's a big understatement).

See *Encryption*, *NDS*, *OSI*, *TCP/IP*, *PGP*, and *X.400*.

X/Open
X/Open Company Ltd.

A not-for-profit consortium of end users and open system vendors (originally mostly European) that specifies user requirements for open systems and selects the standards and most suitable options to achieve interoperability. The goal is to increase the number of open applications that are available.

OSF is, and UI was, a member. Produces the XPG and provides a certification service. Conforming products receive a stylized "*X*" brand.

X/Open was formed in 1988 and is also the owner of the UNIX name. It controls the licensing of the name. For example, vendors using the name must comply with X/Open's "SPEC 1170," which describes the common API which all UNIXes must support.

See *CDE*, *OSF*, *UI*, *USL*, *UNIX*, and *XPG*.

X/Open Portability Guide   See **XPG**.

X-stone

A graphics performance benchmark.

See *SPEC*.

X Server

An *X Window System* display server—that is, an X terminal (since the X terminal is doing the actual processing and therefore displaying of the commands). The client typically executes on a computer elsewhere on the network, using the X server (that is, X terminal) for the display functions (just as the database server would be used for the database functions).

See *X Terminal*.

X Terminal

A graphics terminal (usually with an integrated Ethernet interface) that is an *X Window System* display server. Has a keyboard and mouse. The monitor may be color or monochrome.

See *X*.

X Windows

An incorrect name for *The X Window System*.

See *X*.

XAPIA
X.400 Application Program Interface Association

A standards-setting organization that has published an interface specification for X.400 systems. Lotus, Microsoft, and Novell are members. They are also working on the *Common Mail Calls* (CMC) API.

See *CMC*, *MAPI*, *VIM*, and *X.400*.

XBase

Database systems and application environments derived from Ashton-Tate's (now owned by Borland) dBase systems.

See *SQL*.

Xenix

Microsoft's UNIX-like operating system for the Intel platform, first released in 1979.

See *UNIX*.

Xerox Network System   See **XNS**.

XGA
Extended Graphics Adapter

IBM's improvement on its 8514/a (a superset). Never widely accepted.

See *8514/a* and *VGA*.

XModem

The original XModem file transfer protocol. Uses a PC's COM port to transfer files to another PC (usually through modems).

It has many limitations and weaknesses (but was state-of-the-art in its day—there was no other way to transfer files error-free between two microcomputers using their serial ports):

- The size of transferred files must be a multiple of 128 bytes (the program was first written for the CP/M operating system, and this was the disk *sector size*), so sent files may be longer than the original files.
- Frames are always (only) 128 bytes in length (larger frames would improve the efficiency of file transfers).
- Since data are sent exactly as they appear in the file being sent (they are not encoded), a transparent 8-bit (that is, any 8-bit value must be carried) communications channel is required. This can be provided by a direct dial-up modem connection between PCs, but is a problem for many operating systems and networks (such as X.25). These often have the restriction that they can only carry 7-bit data, or that they reserve certain *control* characters (such as Carriage Return or DLE—*Data Link Escape*) for their own use, or for software flow control (which requires use of the x-on and x-off ASCII control characters—11_{16} and 13_{16}). Even PCs need flow control, so they should be configured for hardware flow control (or a very slow data rate).
- It does not transfer the file's name or any other file attributes.
- The *window size* is limited to 1—that is, a second frame cannot be sent until the first is acknowledged (this significantly reduces throughput on high-speed and long-delay data links, as the sender must stop sending until the ack arrives).
- Recovery of synchronization is difficult, since the data and the checksum characters could be the same as the beginning of frame character (which is soh).
- The ack response is a single character and is not covered by an error check, so a *spurious* (generated by line noise) ack could be generated by noise on a poor communications link.
- The checksum is only 8 bits, which does not provide very robust detection (1 in 256 errored frames will not be detected, as it will have the same checksum as an uncorrupted frame).

Was originally developed, and the Intel 8080 *source code* was placed in the public domain, by a nice guy named Ward Christensen. The first implementation was in his `Modem` program, which was developed for CP/M (*Control Program for Microcomputers*, which was popular in the late 1970s and early 1980s) computers. An improved version (`Modem2`) was released in August 1977. The program permitted two computers running the program to transfer binary or text files through their serial ports (and typically, through modems), with a simple error check.

Others added features (to the program and protocol) and incremented the program's name until `Modem7` was released (it could handle transferring more than one file at a time and was able to run unattended and have the dialing-in computer control the file transfers).

The XModem protocol uses an 8-bit sequence counter (to check for lost frames), which is repeated (as the one's complement, in which each bit is inverted) so that a corrupted (and lost) frame or a 7-bit data channel will be detected reliably and immediately.

File transfers can be aborted by typing an ASCII can (`Control-X`) twice. (YModem and ZModem require `Control-X` to by typed more times.)

Sometimes called *XModem-Checksum* to differentiate it from a subsequent version (called XModem-CRC) that used a more reliable form of error detection.

Subsequent improvements (XModem-CRC, WXModem, XModem-K, YModem, YModem-G, ZModem, and ZModem-90) address the shortcomings described above.

See *Checksum, Disk Formatting, In-Band, Kermit, Out-of-band, XModem-CRC, WXModem, XModem-K, YModem, YModem-G, ZModem,* and *ZModem-90*.

XModem-CRC

XModem with better (and unfortunately more CPU-intensive) error detection. (But who cares? CPUs are powerful-enough to handle this now.)

It uses the standard 16-bit CCITT CRC, rather than an 8-bit checksum (which is simply an `Exclusive-or` of the data).

XModem-CRC programs can detect and work with programs that support only XModem-Checksum (by using the 8-bit checksum for that file transfer).

See *CRC, XModem,* and *YModem*.

XModem-K

XModem with support for 1,024-byte frames (file transfers can use any mix of the 128 or 1,024 byte frames).

The larger frame size improves the protocol efficiency, though on noisy lines, efficiency will be worse than with XModem, since more data must be retransmitted—and there is a greater chance of errors in each frame.

See *XModem* and *YModem*.

XModem-1K-G   See **YModem-G.**

XNS
Xerox Network System

A LAN protocol developed a long time ago by Xerox Corporation. Has (only) a 576-byte maximum packet size.

Is also the basis for Novell's, 3Com's, and Ungermann-Bass's (OSI) layers 3 and 4 LAN protocol, which explains why those protocols (IPX, NetBEUI, etc.) also (at least initially) had a small maximum packet size.

See *IPX* and *NetBEUI*.

XPG
X/Open Portability Guide

A guide (for example XPG4, which would be the fourth edition) produced by the *X/Open Company Ltd.* that specifies the standards to be used to ensure cross-platform, vendor-independent interoperability and compatibility. It specifies the requirements of systems, such as the commands, interfaces, utilities, and languages.

See *X/Open*.

YAHOO
Yet Another Hierarchical Officious Oracle

A WWW index created in April 1994 by two Stanford University Ph.D. candidates.

See *http://www.sun.com/cgi-bin/show?950523/yahoostory.html* for an interview with them.

See *WWW*.

YModem

A very popular file transfer protocol in the PC environment.

XModem-K with the addition of an initial frame that specifies the file's name, length, and date (so the file name gets transferred automatically), and support for sending more than one file in a session (often called a *batch* capability), by using wildcards in the filename (for example *.doc).

Like XModem-K, YModem supports both 128- and 1,024-byte frames and checksum or CRC error detection. Also, many YModem implementations will work with XModem at the other end of the link.

Still has a *window size* of 1, resulting in poor throughput.

Called YModem either because it succeeded XModem or because it is based on YAM (Yet Another Modem), which was written by Chuck Forsberg.

Sometimes called *YModem-batch* to emphasize that more than one file can be sent during a file transfer session, by using a wildcard character in the filenames specified (for example, *.tmp would result in sending all files with a filename extension of tmp).

See *Kermit*, *UTC*, *XModem*, *XModem-K*, and *YModem-G*.

YModem-G

YModem with CRC error detection, but acknowledgments are only expected for the initial file information (name, length, and date) frame and after the entire file has been transferred successfully.

That is, there is no error correction (only error detection), so an error-free data link must be used. Modems with V.42 or MNP Level 4 error correction or an X.25 network provide this—but these were rare when YModem-G was released (early 1980s). The transfer is aborted if errors are detected.

See *YModem* and *ZModem*.

YP
Yellow Pages

The previous name for NIS.

See *NIS*.

YUV
Luminance (Y), Chrominance (UV)

A method of representing color information.

See *Color*.

ZModem

A very popular file transfer protocol in the PC environment.

Whereas YModem was a slight improvement on XModem, ZModem is a dramatically different protocol from YModem. Enhancements include the following:

- Character encoding (usually only for 7 to 10 of the ASCII control characters), so that control characters, such as the x-on (11_{16}), x-off (13_{16}) and Carriage Return ($0D_{16}$) characters are sent as other characters that X.25 networks can carry—specifically, for these examples, can Q (18_{16} 51_{16}), can S (18_{16} 53_{16}) and can M (18_{16} $4D_{16}$) are sent.
- Support for both 16-bit and 32-bit CRCs.
- Acknowledgments are covered by error detection, so there is little chance of a *spurious* ack, and are sent only when the sender requests them—of benefit, since some error correcting modems work faster if they don't need to process data in both directions (that is, the data plus acknowledgments) at once.
- Data are sent as a constant stream, with CRCs (covering all the data since the previous CRC) sent at least every 1,024 bytes. If the sender wants an ack, then this request is included in the CRC frame, to which the receiver replies with the file position (a count of the bytes that have been successfully received so far, where byte 0 is the start of the file). This capability of having more than one unacknowledged frame of data outstanding is often called *sliding windows*. This improves file transfer throughput—especially on networks with long round-trip delays.
- If the receiver detects an error, whether it was requested to ack or not, the receiver requests the sender to back up to the last successfully received file position for error recovery.
- An initial negotiation to confirm that both sides are capable of the normal full-duplex (or *streaming*) file transfer, in which acks are sent during the file transfer, as requested by the sender.

If both sides cannot support this, then a half-duplex (or *segmented streaming*, where the window size is set to 1) mode is used, and only one frame (of a negotiated size, called the *burst-length*) is sent, with a pause until the mandatory acknowledgment is received by the sender.

- *Crash Recovery*—restarting aborted file transfers (for example, because the communication line became noisy and the modem abruptly hung up) where they left off (once the connection is reestablished). This is a really nice feature when someone elsewhere in the house picks up the phone to make a call when you have almost completed a multimegabyte download.
- Commands to:
  - Determine how much available disk space the destination computer has—a good thing to check before sending a large file.
  - Specify what the receiver should do with a file if it already has one with the same name. For example, replace it always, or only if the sender's file is newer or longer or has different contents, or append it to the existing one. Determining whether the contents of the files are different is done by comparing the 32 bit CRCs for each of the files.
  - Request that a (usually user-typed) command be sent to the remote computer's ZModem program or its operating system's command interpreter.
- Data compression, using LZW, though this is seldom implemented (since the algorithm is patented).

Developed by Chuck Forsberg under contract with the operator of a large U.S. X.25 packet-switched network (GTE Telenet, now called SprintNet). X.25 networks typically have low error rates but long time delays (500 ms and longer) and a few reserved characters, so it was in Telenet's interest to have a PC (and other platform) file transfer protocol widely available that would work well with their network. It was therefore part of the contract that the protocol details and source code would be placed in the public domain.

See *Full-duplex*, *Half-Duplex*, *Kermit*, *LZW*, *X.25*, *YModem*, and *ZModem-90*.

ZModem-90

A proprietary enhanced ZModem (developed by Chuck Forsberg's company, Omen Technology) that supports additional features, such as:

- Operation over 7-bit data channels
- Data encryption
- *Run-length encoding* data compression, which is good for files with bytes that are repeated (contiguously) many times

See *RLE* and *ZModem*.

ABOUT THE AUTHOR

Mitchell has been interested in computers since 1974, when he spent the nights and weekends of his final year of high school designing and building a 16-bit programmable computer for a science fair project, the MJS-18 (his age at the time). This experience, followed by the designing and building of several more generations of computers, gave Mitchell an appreciation for hardware, data communications, and the difficulty of getting clear explanations of how things work.

Mitchell received his B.A.Sc. in Electrical Engineering from the University of Toronto. He is a professional engineer, a member of the International Brotherhood of Magicians, and a Beaver leader (where you learn that just like on LANs, the key is sharing, sharing, sharing).

After having worked for a few large- and medium-sized companies at summer jobs and after graduating, Mitchell decided to work for a really small company, and has been an independent data communications consultant for over eight years. He specializes in network analysis and design and implementation, as well as presenting computer courses in Europe and throughout North America.

He also built a nice cedar fence and deck, and frequently notices that he is not as young as he used to be.

COLOPHON

Edie Freedman designed the cover of this book. The graphic is adapted from a copper engraving explaining "Electricity" that Edie found in a London print shop. The engraving, by A. Bell, was originally published in 1797. The cover layout was produced using Quark XPress 3.3 and Adobe Photoshop 3.0 software, in Adobe Copperplate font.

Nancy Priest designed the interior layout. Text was prepared in SGML using the DocBook 2.1 DTD. The print version of this book was created by translating the SGML source into a set of gtroff macros using a filter developed at O'Reilly & Associates by Norman Walsh. Steve Talbott designed and wrote the underlying macro set on the basis of the GNU gtroff -gs macros; Lenny Muellner adapted them to SGML and implemented the book design. The GNU groff text formatter version 1.09 was used to generate PostScript output. The fonts used are Monotype Bembo and Gill Sans.

The illustrations that appear in the book were created in Macromedia Freehand 5.0 by Chris Reilley.

Inside the Windows 95 Registry

By Ron Petrusha
1st Edition Summer 1996
594 pages, Includes diskette, ISBN 1-56592-170-4

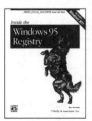

What Windows 95 developers have been looking for! An in-depth examination of the Windows 95 registry, the new central "storage facility" for settings that replaces most of the old SYSTEM.INI and WIN.INI settings found in Windows 3.x.

This book covers remote registry access, differences between the Win95 and NT registries, and registry backup. You'll also find a thorough examination of the role that the registry plays in OLE, coverage of undocumented registry services, and more. Petrusha shows programmers how to access the Win95 registry from Win32, Win16, and DOS programs, in C and Visual Basic. VxD sample code is also included.

The book includes a diskette with registry tools such as REGSPY, a program that shows exactly how Windows applications, libraries, and drivers use settings in the registry.

The Whole Internet for Windows 95

By Ed Krol & Paula Ferguson
1st Edition October 1995
650 pages, ISBN 1-56592-155-0

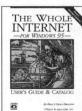

The best book on the Internet. . . now updated for Windows 95! *The Whole Internet for Windows 95* is the most comprehensive introduction to the Internet available today. For Windows users who in the past have struggled to take full advantage of the Internet's powerful utilities, Windows 95's built-in Internet support is a cause for celebration. And when you get online with Windows 95, this new edition of *The Whole Internet* will guide you every step of the way.

This book shows you how to use Microsoft Internet Explorer (the World Wide Web multimedia browser) and Microsoft Exchange (an email program). It also covers Netscape Navigator, the most popular Web browser on the market, and shows you how to use Usenet readers, file transfer tools, and database searching software.

But it does much more. You'll also want to take advantage of alternative popular free software programs that are downloadable from the Net. This book shows you where to find them and how to use them to save you time and money.

Dictionary of PC Hardware and Data Communications Terms

By Mitchell Shnier
1st Edition April 1996
532 pages, ISBN 1-56592-158-5

The *Dictionary of PC Hardware and Data Communications Terms* covers terms in two of the most volatile and interesting areas of computer development: personal computers and networks. It provides up-to-date information about everything from a common item like "batteries" to an obscure font technology called "Speedo."

The book's strength is that it is comprehensive. The author has combed the Internet and other online services to find the latest and most vexing acronyms and terms. Each entry has three sections: a listing of the acronym, an expansion of the acronym, and a full definition.

In a way, it's inaccurate to call this a dictionary because it provides long and useful descriptions of the complex terms in these two computer areas. For example, the description of PGP (Pretty Good Privacy), a popular data encryption protocol, covers three and one-half pages. The entry for PowerPC contains a table listing the clock speed, number of transistors, width in bits, cache in kilobytes, and pins of each PowerPC processor currently in use.

The author has carefully cross-referenced the terms as well (to other sections of the book, and to ftp and web sites on the Internet).

O'Reilly's new *Dictionary of PC Hardware and Data Communications Terms* is now freely available on the World Wide Web. Web content providers can link to definitions in the online version of this book to find authoritative, complete, and current information.

The terms are updated frequently, to provide immediate access to new definitions. By linking your documents to these terms over the World Wide Web, you can avoid having to update your own documents' definitions. See http://www.ora.com/reference/dictionary/ for details.

Network Administration

Getting Connected: The Internet at 56K and up

By Kevin Dowd
1st Edition June 1996
424 pages, ISBN 1-56592-154-2

A complete guide for businesses, schools, and other organizations who want to connect their computers to the Internet. This book covers everything you need to know to make informed decisions, from helping you figure out which services you really need to providing down-to-earth explanations of telecommunication options, such as frame relay, ISDN, and leased lines. Once you're online, it shows you how to set up basic Internet services, such as a World Wide Web server. Tackles issues for the PC, Macintosh, and UNIX platforms.

DNS and BIND

By Paul Albitz & Cricket Liu
1st Edition October 1992
412 pages, ISBN 1-56592-010-4

DNS and BIND contains all you need to know about the Internet's Domain Name System (DNS) and the Berkeley Internet Name Domain (BIND), its UNIX implementation. The Domain Name System is the Internet's "phone book"; it's a database that tracks important information (in particular, names and addresses) for every computer on the Internet. If you're a system administrator, this book will show you how to set up and maintain the DNS software on your network.

TCP/IP Network Administration

By Craig Hunt
1st Edition August 1992
502 pages, ISBN 0-937175-82-X

A complete guide to setting up and running a TCP/IP network for practicing system administrators. *TCP/IP Network Administration* covers setting up your network, configuring important network applications including sendmail, and issues in troubleshooting and security. It covers both BSD and System V TCP/IP implementations.

Networking Personal Computers with TCP/IP

By Craig Hunt
1st Edition July 1995
408 pages, ISBN 1-56592-123-2

This book offers practical information as well as detailed instructions for attaching PCs to a TCP/IP network and its UNIX servers. It discusses the challenges you'll face and offers general advice on how to deal with them, provides basic TCP/IP configuration information for some of the popular PC operating systems, covers advanced configuration topics and configuration of specific applications such as email, and includes a chapter on NetWare, the most popular PC LAN system software.

sendmail

By Bryan Costales, with Eric Allman & Neil Rickert
1st Edition November 1993
830 pages, ISBN 1-56592-056-2

Although *sendmail* is used on almost every UNIX system, it's one of the last great uncharted territories—and most difficult utilities to learn—in UNIX system administration. This book provides a complete sendmail tutorial, plus extensive reference material. It covers the BSD, UIUC IDA, and V8 versions of sendmail.

Using & Managing UUCP

By Ed Ravin, Tim O'Reilly, Dale Dougherty & Grace Todino
1st Edition Fall 1996
350 pages (est.), ISBN 1-56592-153-4

Using and Managing UUCP describes, in one volume, this popular communications and file transfer program. UUCP is very attractive to computer users with limited resources, a small machine, and a dial-up connection. This book covers Taylor UUCP, the latest versions of HoneyDanBer UUCP, and the specific implementation details of UUCP versions shipped by major UNIX vendors.

For information: **800-998-9938**, 707-829-0515; **info@ora.com; http://www.ora.com/**
To order: **800-889-8969** (credit card orders only); **order@ora.com**

Security

Practical UNIX & Internet Security, 2nd Edition

By Simson Garfinkel & Gene Spafford
2nd Edition April 1996
1004 pages, ISBN 1-56592-148-8

This second edition of the classic *Practical UNIX Security* is a complete rewrite of the original book. It's packed with twice the pages and offers even more practical information for UNIX users and administrators. In it you'll find coverage of features of many types of UNIX systems, including SunOS, Solaris, BSDI, AIX, HP-UX, Digital UNIX, Linux, and others.

Contents include UNIX and security basics, system administrator tasks, network security, and appendixes containing checklists and helpful summaries.

Building Internet Firewalls

By D. Brent Chapman & Elizabeth D. Zwicky
1st Edition September 1995
546 pages, ISBN 1-56592-124-0

More than a million systems are now connected to the Internet, and something like 15 million people in 100 countries on all seven continents use Internet services. More than 100 million email messages are exchanged each day, along with countless files, documents, and audio and video images. Although businesses are rushing headlong to get connected to the Internet, the security risks have never been greater.

Some of these risks have been around since the early days of networking—password attacks (guessing them or cracking them via password dictionaries and cracking programs), denial of service, and exploiting known security holes. Some risks are newer and even more dangerous—packet sniffers, IP (Internet Protocol) forgery, and various types of hijacking. Firewalls are a very effective way to protect your system from these Internet security threats.

Building Internet Firewalls is a practical guide to building firewalls on the Internet. If your site is connected to the Internet, or if you're considering getting connected, you need this book. It describes a variety of firewall approaches and architectures and discusses how you can build packet filtering and proxying solutions at your site. It also contains a full discussion of how to configure Internet services (e.g., FTP, SMTP, Telnet) to work with a firewall, as well as a complete list of resources, including the location of many publicly available firewall construction tools.

PGP: Pretty Good Privacy

By Simson Garfinkel
1st Edition January 1995
430 pages, ISBN 1-56592-098-8

PGP is a freely available encryption program that protects the privacy of files and electronic mail. It uses powerful public key cryptography and works on virtually every platform. This book is both a readable technical user's guide and a fascinating behind-the-scenes look at cryptography and privacy. It describes how to use PGP and provides background on cryptography, *PGP*'s history, battles over public key cryptography patents and U.S. government export restrictions, and public debates about privacy and free speech.

Computer Crime

By David Icove, Karl Seger & William VonStorch
(Consulting Editor Eugene H. Spafford)
1st Edition August 1995
462 pages, ISBN 1-56592-086-4

This book is for anyone who needs to know what today's computer crimes look like, how to prevent them, and how to detect, investigate, and prosecute them if they do occur. It contains basic computer security information as well as guidelines for investigators, law enforcement, and system administrators. It includes computer-related statutes and laws, a resource summary, detailed papers on computer crime, and a sample search warrant.

Computer Security Basics

By Deborah Russell & G.T. Gangemi, Sr.
1st Edition July 1991
464 pages, ISBN 0-937175-71-4

Computer Security Basics provides a broad introduction to the many areas of computer security and a detailed description of current security standards. This handbook uses simple terms to describe complicated concepts like trusted systems, encryption, and mandatory access control, and it contains a thorough, readable introduction to the "Orange Book."

Stay in touch with O'REILLY™

Visit Our Award-Winning World Wide Web Site

http://www.ora.com/

VOTED

"Top 100 Sites on the Web" —*PC Magazine*
"Top 5% Websites" —*Point Communications*
"3-Star site" —*The McKinley Group*

Our Web site contains a library of comprehensive product information (including book excerpts and tables of contents), downloadable software, background articles, interviews with technology leaders, links to relevant sites, book cover art, and more. File us in your Bookmarks or Hotlist!

Join Our Two Email Mailing Lists

LIST #1   NEW PRODUCT RELEASES: To receive automatic email with brief descriptions of all new O'Reilly products as they are released, send email to: listproc@online.ora.com and put the following information in the first line of your message (NOT in the Subject: field, which is ignored): **subscribe ora-news "Your Name" of "Your Organization"** (for example: **subscribe ora-news Kris Webber of Fine Enterprises)**

List #2   O'REILLY EVENTS: If you'd also like us to send information about trade show events, special promotions, and other O'Reilly events, send email to: **listproc@online.ora.com** and put the following information in the first line of your message (NOT in the Subject: field, which is ignored): **subscribe ora-events "Your Name" of "Your Organization"**

Visit Our Gopher Site

- Connect your Gopher to **gopher.ora.com**, or
- Point your Web browser to **gopher://gopher.ora.com/**, or
- telnet to **gopher.ora.com** (login: **gopher**)

Get Example Files from Our Books Via FTP

There are two ways to access an archive of example files from our books:

REGULAR FTP — ftp to: **ftp.ora.com** (login: **anonymous**—use your email address as the password) or point your Web browser to: **ftp://ftp.ora.com/**

FTPMAIL — Send an email message to: **ftpmail@online.ora.com** (write "help" in the message body)

Contact Us Via Email

order@ora.com — To place a book or software order online. Good for North American and international customers.

subscriptions@ora.com — To place an order for any of our newsletters or periodicals.

software@ora.com — For general questions and product information about our software.
- Check out O'Reilly Software Online at **http://software.ora.com/** for software and technical support information.
- Registered O'Reilly software users send your questions to **website-support@ora.com**

books@ora.com — General questions about any of our books.

cs@ora.com — For answers to problems regarding your order or our products.

booktech@ora.com — For book content technical questions or corrections.

proposals@ora.com — To submit new book or software proposals to our editors and product managers.

international@ora.com — For information about our international distributors or translation queries.
- For a list of our distributors outside of North America check out: **http://www.ora.com/www/order/country.html**

O'REILLY™

101 Morris Street, Sebastopol, CA 95472 USA
TEL 707-829-0515 or 800-998-9938 (6 A.M. to 5 P.M. PST)
FAX 707-829-0104

Listing of Titles from O'REILLY™

INTERNET PROGRAMMING

CGI Programming on the
World Wide Web
Designing for the Web
Exploring Java
HTML: The Definitive Guide
Web Client Programming with Perl
Learning Perl
Programming Perl, 2nd.Edition
(Fall '96)
JavaScript: The Definitive Guide, Beta
Edition (Summer '96)
Webmaster in a Nutshell
The World Wide Web Journal

USING THE INTERNET

Smileys
The Whole Internet User's Guide
and Catalog
The Whole Internet for Windows 95
What You Need to Know:
Using Email Effectively
Marketing on the Internet (Fall 96)
What You Need to Know: Bandits on the
Information Superhighway

JAVA SERIES

Exploring Java
Java in a Nutshell
Java Language Reference
(Fall '96 est.)
Java Virtual Machine

WINDOWS

Inside the Windows '95 Registry

SOFTWARE

WebSite™ 1.1
WebSite Professional™
WebBoard™
PolyForm™

SONGLINE GUIDES

NetLearning
NetSuccess for Realtors
NetActivism (Fall '96)

SYSTEM ADMINISTRATION

Building Internet Firewalls
Computer Crime:
A Crimefighter's Handbook
Computer Security Basics
DNS and BIND
Essential System Administration,
2nd ed.
Getting Connected:
The Internet at 56K and Up
Linux Network Administrator's Guide
Managing Internet Information Services
Managing Usenet (Fall '96)
Managing NFS and NIS
Networking Personal Computers
with TCP/IP
Practical UNIX & Internet Security
PGP: Pretty Good Privacy
sendmail
System Performance Tuning
TCP/IP Network Administration
termcap & terminfo
Using & Managing UUCP (Fall '96)
Volume 8: X Window System
Administrator's Guide

UNIX

Exploring Expect
Learning GNU Emacs, 2nd Edition
(Fall '96 est.)
Learning the bash Shell
Learning the Korn Shell
Learning the UNIX Operating System
Learning the vi Editor
Linux in a Nutshell (Fall '96 est.)
Making TeX Work
Linux Multimedia Guide (Fall '96)
Running Linux, 2nd Edition
Running Linux Companion
CD-ROM, 2nd Edition
SCO UNIX in a Nutshell
sed & awk
Unix in a Nutshell: System V Edition
UNIX Power Tools
UNIX Systems Programming
Using csh and tsch
What You Need to Know:
When You Can't Find Your
UNIX System Administrator

PROGRAMMING

Applying RCS and SCCS
C++: The Core Language
Checking C Programs with lint
DCE Security Programming
Distributing Applications Across
DCE and Windows NT
Encyclopedia of Graphics File
Formats, 2nd ed.
Guide to Writing DCE Applications
lex & yacc
Managing Projects with make
ORACLE Performance Tuning
ORACLE PL/SQL Programming
Porting UNIX Software
POSIX Programmer's Guide
POSIX.4: Programming for
the Real World
Power Programming with RPC
Practical C Programming
Practical C++ Programming
Programming Python (Fall '96)
Programming with curses
Programming with GNU Software
(Fall '96 est.)
Pthreads Programming
(Fall '96)
Software Portability with imake
Understanding DCE
Understanding Japanese Information
Processing
UNIX Systems Programming for SVR4

BERKELEY 4.4 SOFTWARE DISTRIBUTION

4.4BSD System Manager's Manual
4.4BSD User's Reference Manual
4.4BSD User's Supplementary Docs.
4.4BSD Programmer's Reference Man.
4.4BSD Programmer's Supp. Docs.

X PROGRAMMING
THE X WINDOW SYSTEM

Volume 0: X Protocol Reference Manual
Volume 1: Xlib Programming Manual
Volume 2: Xlib Reference Manual
Volume. 3M: X Window System
User's Guide, Motif Ed.
Volume. 4: X Toolkit Intrinsics
Programming Manual
Volume 4M: X Toolkit Intrinsics
Programming Manual, Motif Ed.
Volume 5: X Toolkit Intrinsics
Reference Manual
Volume 6A: Motif Programming Man.
Volume 6B: Motif Reference Manual
Volume 6C: Motif Tools
Volume 8 : X Window System
Administrator's Guide
Programmer's Supplement for Release 6
X User Tools (with CD-ROM)
The X Window System in a Nutshell

HEALTH, CAREER, & BUSINESS

Building a Successful Software Business
The Computer User's Survival Guide
Dictionary of Computer Terms
The Future Does Not Compute
Love Your Job!
Publishing with CD-ROM

TRAVEL

Travelers' Tales: Brazil (Summer '96 est.)
Travelers' Tales: Food (Summer '96)
Travelers' Tales: France
Travelers' Tales: Hong Kong
Travelers' Tales: India
Travelers' Tales: Mexico
Travelers' Tales: San Francisco
Travelers' Tales: Spain
Travelers' Tales: Thailand
Travelers' Tales: A Woman's World

TO ORDER: **800-889-8969** (CREDIT CARD ORDERS ONLY); **order@ora.com; http://www.ora.com/**

OUR PRODUCTS ARE AVAILABLE AT A BOOKSTORE OR SOFTWARE STORE NEAR YOU.

International Distributors

Customers outside North America can now order O'Reilly & Associates books through the following distributors. They offer our international customers faster order processing, more bookstores, increased representation at tradeshows worldwide, and the high-quality, responsive service our customers have come to expect.

EUROPE, MIDDLE EAST AND NORTHERN AFRICA (except Germany, Switzerland, and Austria)

INQUIRIES
International Thomson Publishing Europe
Berkshire House
168-173 High Holborn
London WC1V 7AA, United Kingdom
Telephone: 44-171-497-1422
Fax: 44-171-497-1426
Email: **itpint@itps.co.uk**

ORDERS
International Thomson Publishing Services, Ltd.
Cheriton House, North Way
Andover, Hampshire SP10 5BE,
United Kingdom
Telephone: 44-264-342-832 (UK orders)
Telephone: 44-264-342-806 (outside UK)
Fax: 44-264-364418 (UK orders)
Fax: 44-264-342761 (outside UK)
UK & Eire orders: **itpuk@itps.co.uk**
International orders: **itpint@itps.co.uk**

GERMANY, SWITZERLAND, AND AUSTRIA

International Thomson Publishing GmbH
O'Reilly International Thomson Verlag
Königswinterer Straße 418
53227 Bonn, Germany
Telephone: 49-228-97024 0
Fax: 49-228-441342
Email: **anfragen@arade.ora.de**

AUSTRALIA

WoodsLane Pty. Ltd.
7/5 Vuko Place, Warriewood NSW 2102
P.O. Box 935, Mona Vale NSW 2103
Australia
Telephone: 61-2-9970-5111
Fax: 61-2-9970-5002
Email: **woods@tmx.mhs.oz.au**

NEW ZEALAND

WoodsLane New Zealand Ltd.
21 Cooks Street (P.O. Box 575)
Wanganui, New Zealand
Telephone: 64-6-347-6543
Fax: 64-6-345-4840
Email: **info@woodslane.com.au**

ASIA (except Japan & India)

INQUIRIES
International Thomson Publishing Asia
60 Albert Street #15-01
Albert Complex
Singapore 189969
Telephone: 65-336-6411
Fax: 65-336-7411

ORDERS
Telephone: 65-336-6411
Fax: 65-334-1617

JAPAN

O'Reilly Japan, Inc.
Kiyoshige Building 2F
12-Banchi, Sanei-cho
Shinjuku-ku
Tokyo 160 Japan
Telephone: 8-3-3356-5227
Fax: 81-3-3356-5261
Email: **kenji@ora.com**

INDIA

Computer Bookshop (India) PVT. LTD.
190 Dr. D.N. Road, Fort
Bombay 400 001
India
Telephone: 91-22-207-0989
Fax: 91-22-262-3551
Email: **cbsbom@giasbm01.vsnl.net.in**

THE AMERICAS

O'Reilly & Associates, Inc.
101 Morris Street
Sebastopol, CA 95472 U.S.A.
Telephone: 707-829-0515
Telephone: 800-998-9938 (U.S. & Canada)
Fax: 707-829-0104
Email: **order@ora.com**

SOUTHERN AFRICA

International Thomson Publishing Southern Africa
Building 18, Constantia Park
240 Old Pretoria Road
P.O. Box 2459
Halfway House, 1685 South Africa
Telephone: 27-11-805-4819
Fax: 27-11-805-3648

O'REILLY™